CRITIQUE
OF
PURE REASON

CRITIQUE
OF
PURE REASON

Translated by
J. M. D. Meiklejohn

IMMANUEL
KANT

GREAT BOOKS IN PHILOSOPHY

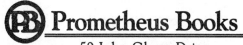 **Prometheus Books**

59 John Glenn Drive
Amherst, NewYork 14228-2197

Published 1990 by Prometheus Books
59 John Glenn Drive, Amherst, New York 14228-2197.
716-691-0133. FAX: 716-691-0137.

Library of Congress Catalog Number: 89-64203
ISBN 0-87975-596-2

Printed in the United States of America on acid-free paper.

Titles on Metaphysics and Epistemology in Prometheus's Great Books in Philosophy Series

See the back of this volume for a complete list of titles in Prometheus's Great Books in Philosophy and Great Minds series.

IMMANUEL KANT, born in Königsberg, East Prussia (in what is now Kaliningrad, Russia), on April 22, 1724, was reared by parents who were members of the Lutheran sect known as Pietists. Though his upbringing was religious, Kant did not find himself subjected to a dogmatic or doctrinaire home environment.

After completing his early education in the Collegium Fridericianum, he entered the University of Königsberg in 1740 at the age of sixteen. Though it was originally thought that he would make the ministry his life's pursuit, Kant took the minimum number of required courses in theology and then dedicated himself to philosophy, mathematics, and physical science. During the years between 1746 and 1755 he worked as a private tutor in an effort to support himself through graduate work after the death of his parents left him without financial assistance. Receiving his doctorate in 1755, he taught at the University of Königsberg for fifteen years until 1770 when he was finally promoted to Professor of Logic and Metaphysics. Kant held this position until his death on February 12, 1804.

Among Kant's most important philosophical works are: the *Critique of Pure Reason* (1781), *Prolegomena to Any Future Metaphysics* (1783), *Idea for a Universal History* (1784), *Fundamental Principles of the Metaphysic of Morals* (1785), *Metaphysical Foundations of Natural Science* (1786), *Critique of Practical Reason* (1787), *Critique of Judgment* (1790), *Religion within the Limits of Reason Alone* (1793), *Perpetual Peace* (1795), *Metaphysics of Ethics* (1797), and *Anthropology from a Pragmatic Point of View* (1798).

CONTENTS

INTRODUCTION

CONTENTS

TRANSCENDENTAL DOCTRINE OF ELEMENTS

Part First: Transcendental Aesthetic

Part Second: Transcendental Logic

First Division

CONTENTS

INTRODUCTION

I.—Of the Difference Between Pure and Empirical Knowledge

THAT all our knowledge begins with experience there can be no doubt. For how is it possible that the faculty of cognition should be awakened into exercise otherwise than by means of objects which affect our senses, and partly of themselves produce representations, partly rouse our powers of understanding into activity, to compare, to connect, or to separate these, and so to convert the raw material of our sensuous impressions into a knowledge of objects, which is called experience? In respect of time, therefore, no knowledge of ours is antecedent to experience, but begins with it.

But, though all our knowledge begins with experience, it by no means follows that all arises out of experience. For, on the contrary, it is quite possible that our empirical knowledge is a compound of that which we receive through impressions, and that which the faculty of cognition supplies from itself (sensuous impressions giving merely the *occasion*), an addition which we cannot distinguish from the original element given by sense, till long practice has made us attentive to, and skilful in separating it. It is, therefore, a question which requires close investigation, and is not to be answered at first sight—whether there exists a knowledge altogether independent of experience, and even of all sensuous impressions? Knowledge of this kind is called *à priori*, in contradistinction to empirical knowledge, which has its sources *à posteriori*, that is, in experience.

But the expression, " *à priori*," is not as yet definite enough adequately to indicate the whole meaning of the question above started. For, in speaking of knowledge which has its sources in experience, we are wont to say, that this or that may be known *à priori*, because we do not derive this knowledge immediately from experience, but from a general rule, which, however, we have itself borrowed from experience. Thus, if a man undermined his house, we say, " he might know *à priori* that it would have fallen "; that is, he needed not to have waited for the experience that it did actually fall. But still, *à priori*, he could not know even this much. For, that bodies are heavy, and, consequently, that they fall when their supports are taken away, must have been known to him previously, by means of experience.

By the term " knowledge *à priori*," therefore, we shall in the sequel understand, not such as is independent of this or that kind of experience, but such as is absolutely so of *all* experience. Opposed to this is empirical knowledge, or that which is possible only *à posteriori*, that is, through experience. Knowledge *à priori* is either pure or impure. Pure knowledge *à priori* is that with which no empirical element is mixed up. For example, the proposition, " Every change has a cause," is a proposition *à priori*, but impure, because change is a conception which can only be derived from experience.

II.—THE HUMAN INTELLECT, EVEN IN AN UNPHILOSOPHICAL STATE, IS IN POSSESSION OF CERTAIN COGNITIONS *à PRIORI*

The question now is as to a *criterion*, by which we may securely distinguish a pure from an empirical cognition. Experience no doubt teaches us that this or that object is constituted in such and such a manner, but not that it could not possibly exist otherwise. Now, in the first place, if we have a proposition which contains the idea of necessity in its very conception, it is a judgment *à priori;* if, moreover, it is not derived from any other proposition, unless from one equally involving the idea of necessity, it is absolutely *à priori*. Secondly, an empirical judgment never exhibits strict and absolute, but only assumed and comparative universality (by induction); therefore, the most we can say is—so far as we have hitherto observed, there is no exception to this or that rule. If, on the other hand, a judgment carries with it strict and absolute universality, that is, admits of no possible exception, it is not derived from experience, but is valid absolutely à *priori*.

Empirical universality is, therefore, only an arbitrary extension of validity, from that which may be predicated of a proposition valid in most cases, to that which is asserted of a proposition which holds good in all; as, for example, in the affirmation, " all bodies are heavy." When, on the contrary, strict universality characterizes a judgment, it necessarily indicates another peculiar source of knowledge, namely, a faculty of cognition à *priori*. Necessity and strict universality, therefore, are infallible tests for distinguishing pure from empirical knowledge, and are inseparably connected with each other. But as in the use of these criteria the empirical limitation is sometimes more easily detected than the contingency of the judgment, or the unlimited universality which we attach to a judgment is often a more convincing proof than its necessity, it may be advisable to use the criteria separately, each being by itself infallible.

Now, that in the sphere of human cognition, we have judgments which are necessary, and in the strictest sense universal, consequently pure à *priori*, it will be an easy matter to show. If we desire an example from the sciences, we need only take any proposition in mathematics. If we cast our eyes upon the commonest operations of the understanding, the proposition, " every change must have a cause," will amply serve our purpose. In the latter case, indeed, the conception of a cause so plainly involves the conception of a necessity of connection with an effect, and of a strict universality of the law, that the very notion of a cause would entirely disappear, were we to derive it, like Hume, from a frequent association of what happens with that which precedes, and the habit thence originating of connecting representations—the necessity inherent in the judgment being therefore merely subjective. Besides, without seeking for such examples of principles existing à *priori* in cognition, we might easily show that such principles are the indispensable basis of the possibility of experience itself, and consequently prove their existence à *priori*. For whence could our experience itself acquire certainty, if all the rules on which it depends were themselves empirical, and consequently fortuitous? No one, therefore, can admit the validity of the use of such rules as first principles. But, for the present, we may content ourselves with having established the fact, that we do possess and exercise a faculty of pure *à priori* cognition; and, secondly, with having pointed out the proper tests of such cognition, namely, universality and necessity.

Not only in judgments, however, but even in conceptions, is an *à priori* origin manifest. For example, if we take away by degrees from our conceptions of a body all that can be referred to mere sensuous experience—color, hardness or softness, weight, even impenetrability—the body will then vanish; but the space which it occupied still remains, and this it is utterly impossible to annihilate in thought. Again, if we take away, in like manner, from our empirical conception of any object, corporeal or incorporeal, all properties which mere experience has taught us to connect with it, still we cannot think away those through which we cogitate it as substance, or adhering to substance, although our conception of substance is more determined than that of an object. Compelled, therefore, by that necessity with which the conception of substance forces itself upon us, we must confess that it has its seat in our faculty of cognition *à priori*.

III.—Philosophy Stands in Need of a Science which Shall Determine the Possibility, Principles, and Extent of Human Knowledge *à Priori*

Of far more importance than all that has been above said, is the consideration that certain of our cognitions rise completely above the sphere of all possible experience, and by means of conceptions, to which there exists in the whole extent of experience no corresponding object, seem to extend the range of our judgments beyond its bounds. And just in this transcendental or supersensible sphere, where experience affords us neither instruction nor guidance, lie the investigations of *Reason*, which, on account of their importance, we consider far preferable to, and as having a far more elevated aim than, all that the understanding can achieve within the sphere of sensuous phenomena. So high a value do we set upon these investigations, that even at the risk of error, we persist in following them out, and permit neither doubt nor disregard nor indifference to restrain us from the pursuit. These unavoidable problems of mere pure reason are God, Freedom (of will) and Immortality. The science which, with all its preliminaries, has for its especial object the solution of these problems is named metaphysics—a science which is at the very outset dogmatical, that is, it confidently takes upon itself the execution of this task without any previous investigation of the ability or inability of reason for such an understanding.

Now the safe ground of experience being thus abandoned, it seems nevertheless natural that we should hesitate to erect a building with the cognitions we possess, without knowing whence they come, and on the strength of principles, the origin of which is undiscovered. Instead of thus trying to build without a foundation, it is rather to be expected that we should long ago have put the question, how the understanding can arrive at these à priori cognitions, and what is the extent, validity, and worth which they may possess? We say, this is natural enough, meaning by the word natural that which is consistent with a just and reasonable way of thinking; but if we understand by the term, that which usually happens, nothing indeed could be more natural and more comprehensible than that this investigation should be left long unattempted. For one part of our pure knowledge, the science of mathematics, has been long firmly established, and thus leads us to form flattering expectations with regard to others, though these may be of quite a different nature. Besides, when we get beyond the bounds of experience, we are of course safe from opposition in that quarter; and the charm of widening the range of our knowledge is so great, that unless we are brought to a standstill by some evident contradiction, we hurry on undoubtingly in our course. This, however, may be avoided, if we are sufficiently cautious in the construction of our fictions, which are not the less fictions on that account.

Mathematical science affords us a brilliant example, how far, independently of all experience, we may carry our à priori knowledge. It is true that the mathematician occupies himself with objects and cognitions only in so far as they can be represented by means of intuition. But this circumstance is easily overlooked, because the said intuition can itself be given à priori, and therefore is hardly to be distinguished from a mere pure conception. Deceived by such a proof of the power of reason, we can perceive no limits to the extension of our knowledge. The light dove cleaving in free flight the thin air, whose resistance it feels, might imagine that her movements would be far more free and rapid in airless space. Just in the same way did Plato, abandoning the world of sense because of the narrow limits it sets to the understanding, venture upon the wings of ideas beyond it, into the void space of pure intellect. He did not reflect that he made no real progress by all his efforts; for he met with no resistance which might serve him for a support, as it were, whereon to rest, and on which he might apply his powers, in order to let the intellect acquire momentum for its progress. It is, indeed, the common fate of human reason in speculation, to finish the imposing edifice of thought as rapidly as possible, and then for the first time to begin to examine whether the foundation is a solid one or no. Arrived at this point, all sorts of excuses are sought after, in order to console us for its want of stability, or rather indeed, to enable us to dispense altogether with so late and dangerous an investigation. But what frees us during the process of building from all apprehension or suspicion, and flatters us into the belief of its solidity, is this. A great part, perhaps the greatest part, of the business of our reason consists in the analyzation of the conceptions which we already possess of objects. By this means we gain a multitude of cognitions, which, although really nothing more than elucidations or explanations of that which (though in a confused manner) was already thought in our conceptions, are, at least in respect of their form, prized as new introspections; while, so far as regards their matter or content, we have really made no addition to our conceptions, but only disinvolved them. But as this process does furnish real à priori knowledge, which has a sure progress and useful results, reason, deceived by this, slips in, without being itself aware of it, assertions of a quite different kind; in which, to given conceptions it adds others, à priori indeed, but entirely foreign to them, without our knowing how it arrives at these, and, indeed, without such a question ever suggesting itself. I shall therefore at once proceed to examine the difference between these two modes of knowledge.

IV.—OF THE DIFFERENCE BETWEEN ANALYTICAL AND SYNTHETICAL JUDGMENTS

In all judgments wherein the relation of a subject to the predicate is cogitated (I mention affirmative judgments only here; the application to negative will be very easy), this relation is possible in two different ways. Either the predicate B belongs to the subject A, as somewhat which is contained (though covertly) in the conception A; or the predicate B lies completely out of the conception A, although it stands in connection with it. In the first instance, I term the judgment analytical, in the second, synthetical. Analytical judgments (affirmative) are therefore those in which the connection of the predicate with the subject is cogitated through identity; those in which this connection is cogitated without identity, are called synthetical judgments. The former may be called *explicative*, the latter *augmentative* * judgments; because the former add in the predicate nothing to the conception of the subject, but only analyze it into its constituent conceptions, which were thought already in the subject, although in a confused manner; the latter add to our conceptions of the subject a predicate which was not contained in it, and which no analysis could ever have discovered therein. For example, when I say, " all bodies are extended," this is an analytical judgment. For I need not go beyond the conception of *body* in order to find extension connected with it, but merely analyze the conception, that is, become conscious of the manifold properties which I think in that conception, in order to discover this predicate in it: it is therefore an analytical judgment. On the other hand, when I say, " all bodies are heavy," the predicate is something totally different from that which I think in the mere conception of a body. But the addition of such a predicate therefore, it becomes a synthetical judgment.

Judgments of experience, as such, are always synthetical. For it would be absurd to think of grounding an analytical judgment on experience, because in forming such a judgment, I need not go out of the sphere of my conceptions, and therefore recourse to the testimony of experience is quite unnecessary. That " bodies are extended " is not an empirical judg-

* That is, judgments which really add to, and do not merely analyze or explain the conceptions which make up the sum of our knowledge.

ment, but a proposition which stands firm *à priori*. For before addressing myself to experience, I already have in my conception all the requisite conditions for the judgment, and I have only to extract the predicate from the conception, according to the principle of contradiction, and thereby at the same time become conscious of the necessity of the judgment, a necessity which I could never learn from experience. On the other hand, though at first I do not at all include the predicate of weight in my conception of body in general, that conception still indicates an object of experience, a part of the totality of experience, to which I can still add other parts; and this I do when I recognize by observation that bodies are heavy. I can cognize beforehand by analysis the conception of body through the characteristics of extension, impenetrability, shape, etc., all which are cogitated in this conception. But now I extend my knowledge, and looking back on experience from which I had derived this conception of body, I find weight at all times connected with the above characteristics, and therefore I synthetically add to my conceptions this as a predicate, and say, " All bodies are heavy." Thus it is experience upon which rests the possibility of the synthesis of the predicate of weight with the conception of body, because both conceptions, although the one is not contained in the other, still belong to one another (only contingently, however), as parts of a whole, namely, of experience, which is itself a synthesis of intuitions.

But to synthetical judgments *à priori*, such aid is entirely wanting. If I go out of and beyond the conception A, in order to recognize another B as connected with it, what foundation have I to rest on, whereby to render the synthesis possible? I have here no longer the advantage of looking out in the sphere of experience for what I want. Let us take, for example, the proposition, " Everything that happens has a cause." In the conception of *something that happens*, I indeed think of an existence which a certain time antecedes, and from this I can derive analytical judgments. But the conception of a cause lies quite out of the above conception, and indicates something entirely different from " that which happens," and is consequently not contained in that conception. How then am I able to assert concerning the general conception—" that which happens "—something entirely different from that conception, and to recognize the conception of cause although not contained in it, yet as belonging to it, and even necessarily? What is here the unknown $= X$, upon which the understanding rests when it believes it has found, out of the conception A a foreign predicate B, which it nevertheless considers to be connected with it? It cannot be experience, because the principle adduced annexes the two representations, cause and effect, to the representation existence, not only with universality, which experience cannot give, but also with the expression of necessity, therefore completely *à priori* and from pure conceptions. Upon such synthetical, that is augmentative propositions depends the whole aim of our speculative knowledge *à priori;* for although analytical judgments are indeed highly important and necessary, they are so only to arrive at that clearness of conceptions which is requisite for a sure and extended synthesis, and this alone is a real acquisition.

V.—IN ALL THEORETICAL SCIENCES OF REASON, SYNTHETICAL JUDGMENTS *à PRIORI* ARE CONTAINED AS PRINCIPLES

1. Mathematical judgments are always synthetical. Hitherto this fact, though incontestably true and very important in its consequences, seems to have escaped the analysts of the human mind, nay, to be in complete opposition to all their conjectures. For as it was found that mathematical conclusions all proceed according to the principle of contradiction (which the nature of every apodictic certainty requires), people became persuaded that the fundamental principles of the science also were recognized and admitted in the same way. But the notion is fallacious; for although a synthetical proposition can certainly be discerned by means of the principle of contradiction, this is possible only when another synthetical proposition precedes, from which the latter is deduced, but never of itself.

Before all, be it observed, that proper mathematical propositions are always judgments *à priori*, and not empirical, because they carry along with them the conception of necessity, which cannot be given by experience. If this be demurred to, it matters not; I shall then limit my assertion to *pure* mathematics, the very conception of which implies that it consists of knowledge altogether non-empirical and *à priori*.

We might, indeed, at first suppose that the proposition $7 + 5$

$= 12$, is a merely analytical proposition, following (according to the principle of contradiction), from the conception of the sum of seven and five. But if we regard it more narrowly, we find that our conception of the sum of seven and five contains nothing more than the uniting of both sums into one, whereby it cannot at all be cogitated what this single number is which embraces both. The conception of twelve is by no means obtained by merely cogitating the union of seven and five; and we may analyze our conception of such a possible sum as long as we will, still we shall never discover in it the notion of twelve. We must go beyond these conceptions, and have recourse to an intuition which corresponds to one of the two— our five fingers, for example, or like Segner in his " Arithmetic," five points, and so by degrees, add the units contained in the five given in the intuition, to the conception of seven. For I first take the number 7, and, for the conception of 5 calling in the aid of the fingers of my hand as objects of intuition, I add the units, which I before took together to make up the number 5, gradually now by means of the material image my hand, to the number 7, and by this process, I at length see the number 12 arise. That 7 should be added to 5, I have certainly cogitated in my conception of a sum $= 7 + 5$, but not that this sum was equal to 12. Arithmetical propositions are therefore always synthetical, of which we may become more clearly convinced by trying large numbers. For it will thus become quite evident, that, turn and twist our conceptions as we may, it is impossible, without having recourse to intuition, to arrive at the sum total or product by means of the mere analysis of our conceptions. Just as little is any principle of pure geometry analytical. " A straight line between two points is the shortest," is a synthetical proposition. For my conception of *straight*, contains no notion of *quantity*, but is merely *qualitative*. The conception of the *shortest* is therefore wholly an addition, and by no analysis can it be extracted from our conception of a straight line. Intuition must therefore here lend its aid, by means of which and thus only, our synthesis is possible.

Some few principles preposited by geometricians are, indeed, really analytical, and depend on the principle of contradiction. They serve, however, like identical propositions, as links in the chain of method, not as principles—for example, $a = a$, the whole is equal to itself, or $(a + b) > a$, the whole is greater than its part. And yet even these principles themselves, though they derive their validity from pure conceptions, are only admitted in mathematics because they can be presented in intuition. What causes us here commonly to believe that the predicate of such apodictic judgments is already contained in our conception, and that the judgment is therefore analytical, is merely the equivocal nature of the expression. We must join in thought a certain predicate to a given conception, and this necessity cleaves already to the conception. But the question is, not what we must join in thought to the given conception, but what we really think therein, though only obscurely, and then it becomes manifest, that the predicate pertains to these conceptions, necessarily indeed, yet not as thought in the conception itself, but by virtue of an intuition, which must be added to the conception.

2. The science of Natural Philosophy (Physics) contains in itself synthetical judgments *à priori*, as principles. I shall adduce two propositions. For instance, the proposition, " In all changes of the material world, the quantity of matter remains unchanged "; or, that, " in all communication of motion, action and reaction must always be equal." In both of these, not only is the necessity, and therefore their origin, *à priori* clear, but also that they are synthetical propositions. For in the conception of matter, I do not cogitate its permanency, but merely its presence in space, which it fills. I therefore really go out of and beyond the conception of matter, in order to think on to it something *à priori*, which I did not think in it. The proposition is therefore not analytical, but synthetical, and nevertheless conceived *à priori;* and so it is with regard to the other propositions of the pure part of natural philosophy.

3. As to Metaphysics, even if we look upon it merely as an attempted science, yet, from the nature of human reason, an indispensable one, we find that it must contain synthetical propositions *à priori.* It is not merely the duty of metaphysics to dissect, and thereby analytically to illustrate, the conceptions which we form *à priori* of things; but we seek to widen the range of our *à priori* knowledge. For this purpose, we must avail ourselves of such principles as add something to the original conception—something not identical with, nor con-

tained in it, and by means of synthetical judgments *à priori*, leave far behind us the limits of experience; for example, in the proposition, " the world must have a beginning," and such like. Thus metaphysics, according to the proper aim of the science, consists merely of synthetical propositions *à priori*.

VI.—The Universal Problem of Pure Reason

It is extremely advantageous to be able to bring a number of investigations under the formula of a single problem. For in this manner, we not only facilitate our own labor, inasmuch as we define it clearly to ourselves, but also render it more easy for others to decide whether we have done justice to our undertaking. The proper problem of pure reason, then, is contained in the question, " How are synthetical judgments *à priori* possible ? "

That metaphysical science has hitherto remained in so vacillating a state of uncertainty and contradiction is only to be attributed to the fact that this great problem, and perhaps even the difference between analytical and synthetical judgments, did not sooner suggest itself to philosophers. Upon the solution of this problem, or upon sufficient proof of the impossibility of synthetical knowledge *à priori*, depends the existence or downfall of the science of metaphysics. Among philosophers David Hume came the nearest of all to this problem; yet it never acquired in his mind sufficient precision, nor did he regard the question in its universality. On the contrary, he stopped short at the synthetical proposition of the connection of an effect with its cause (*principium causalitatis*), insisting that such proposition *à priori* was impossible. According to his conclusions, then, all that we term metaphysical science is a mere delusion, arising from the fancied insight of reason into that which is in truth borrowed from experience, and to which habit has given the appearance of necessity. Against this assertion, destructive to all pure philosophy, he would have been guarded, had he had our problem before his eyes in its universality. For he would then have perceived that, according to his own argument, there likewise could not be any pure mathematical science, which assuredly cannot exist without synthetical propositions *à priori*—an absurdity from which his good understanding must have saved him.

In the solution of the above problem is at the same time comprehended the possibility of the use of pure reason in the foundation and construction of all sciences which contain theoretical knowledge *à priori* of objects, that is to say, the answer to the following questions:

How is pure mathematical science possible?

How is pure natural science possible?

Respecting these sciences, as they do certainly exist, it may with propriety be asked, *how* they are possible?—for that they must be possible, is shown by the fact of their really existing.* But as to metaphysics, the miserable progress it has hitherto made, and the fact that of no one system yet brought forward, as far as regard its true aim, can it be said that this science really exists leaves anyone at liberty to doubt with reason the very possibility of its existence.

Yet, in a certain sense, this kind of knowledge must unquestionably be looked upon as *given;* in other words, metaphysics must be considered as really existing, if not as a science, nevertheless as a natural disposition of the human mind (*metaphysica naturalis*). For human reason, without any instigations imputable to the mere vanity of great knowledge, unceasingly progresses, urged on by its own feeling of need, towards such questions as cannot be answered by any empirical application of reason, or principles derived therefrom; and so there has ever really existed in every man some system of metaphysics. It will always exist, so soon as reason awakes to the exercise of its power of speculation. And now the question arises— How is metaphysics, as a natural disposition, possible? In other words, how, from the nature of universal human reason, do those questions arise which pure reason proposes to itself, and which it is impelled by its own feeling of need to answer as well as it can?

But as in all the attempts hitherto made to answer the questions which reason is prompted by its very nature to propose to itself, for example, whether the world had a beginning, or has existed from eternity, it has always met with unavoidable

---

* As to the existence of pure natural science, or physics, perhaps many may still express doubts. But we have only to look at the different propositions which are commonly treated of at the commencement of proper (empirical) physical science—those, for example, relating to the permanence of the same quantity of matter, the *vis inertiæ*, the equality of action and reaction, etc.— to be soon convinced that they form a science of pure physics (*physica pura*, or *rationalis*), which well deserves to be separately exposed as a special science, in its whole extent, whether that be great or confined.

contradictions, we must not rest satisfied with the mere natural disposition of the mind to metaphysics, that is, with the existence of the faculty of pure reason, whence, indeed, some sort of metaphysical system always arises; but it must be possible to arrive at certainty in regard to the question whether we know or do not know the things of which metaphysics treats. We must be able to arrive at a decision on the subjects of its questions, or on the ability or inability of reason to form any judgment respecting them; and therefore either to extend with confidence the bounds of our pure reason, or to set strictly defined and safe limits to its action. This last question, which arises out of the above universal problem, would properly run thus: How is metaphysics possible as a science?

Thus, the critique of reason leads at last, naturally and necessarily, to science; and, on the other hand, the dogmatical use of reason without criticism leads to groundless assertions, against which others equally specious can always be set, thus ending unavoidably in scepticism.

Besides, this science, cannot be of great and formidable prolixity, because it has not to do with objects of reason, the variety of which is inexhaustible, but merely with reason herself and her problems; problems which arise out of her own bosom, and are not proposed to her by the nature of outward things, but by her own nature. And when once reason has previously become able completely to understand her own power in regard to objects which she meets with in experience, it will be easy to determine securely the extent and limits of her attempted application to objects beyond the confines of experience.

We may and must, therefore, regard the attempts hitherto made to establish metaphysical science dogmatically as nonexistent. For what of analysis, that is, mere dissection of conceptions, is contained in one or other, is not the aim of, but only a preparation for metaphysics proper, which has for its object the extension, by means of synthesis, of our *à priori* knowledge. And for this purpose, mere analysis is of course useless, because it only shows what is contained in these conceptions, but not how we arrive, *à priori*, at them; and this it is her duty to show, in order to be able afterwards to determine their valid use in regard to all objects of experience, to all knowledge in general. But little self-denial, indeed, is needed to give up these pretensions, seeing that the undeniable and, in the dogmatic mode of procedure, inevitable contradictions of Reason with herself have long since ruined the reputation of every system of metaphysics that has appeared up to this time. It will require more firmness to remain undeterred by difficulty from within, and opposition from without, from endeavoring, by a method quite opposed to all those hitherto followed, to further the growth and fruitfulness of a science indispensable to human reason—a science from which every branch it has borne may be cut away, but whose roots remain indestructible.

VII.—Idea and Division of a Particular Science, Under the Name of a Critique of Pure Reason

From all that has been said, there results the idea of a particular science, which may be called the *Critique of Pure Reason*. For reason is the faculty which furnishes us with the principles of knowledge *à priori*. Hence, pure reason is the faculty which contains the principles of cognizing anything absolutely *à priori*. An Organon of pure reason would be a compendium of those principles according to which alone all pure cognitions *à priori* can be obtained. The completely extended application of such an organon would afford us a system of pure reason. As this, however, is demanding a great deal, and it is yet doubtful whether any extension of our knowledge be here possible, or if so, in what cases; we can regard a science of the mere criticism of pure reason, its sources and limits, as the *propædeutic* to a system of pure reason. Such a science must not be called a Doctrine, but only a Critique of Pure Reason; and its use, in regard to speculation, would be only negative, not to enlarge the bounds of, but to purify our reason, and to shield it against error—which alone is no little gain. I apply the term *transcendental* to all knowledge which is not so much occupied with objects as with the mode of our cognition of these objects, so far as this mode of cognition is possible *à priori*. A system of such conceptions would be called *Transcendental Philosophy*. But this, again, is still beyond the bounds of our present essay. For as such a science must contain a complete exposition not only of our synthetical *à priori*, but of our analytical *à priori* knowledge, it is of too wide a range for our present purpose, because we do not require to carry our analysis any farther than is necessary to understand, in their full extent, the principles of synthesis *à priori,* with which alone we have to do. This investigation, which we cannot properly call a doctrine, but only a transcendental critique, because it aims not at the enlargement, but at the correction and guidance of our knowledge, and is to serve as a touchstone of the worth or worthlessness of all knowledge *à priori,* is the sole object of our present essay. Such a critique is consequently, as far as possible, a preparation for an organon; and if this new organon should be found to fail, at least for a canon of pure reason, according to which the complete system of the philosophy of pure reason, whether it extend or limit the bounds of that reason, might one day be set forth both analytically and synthetically. For that this is possible, nay, that such a system is not of so great extent as to preclude the hope of its ever being completed, is evident. For we have not here to do with the nature of outward objects, which is infinite, but solely with the mind, which judges of the nature of objects, and, again, with the mind only in respect of its cognition *à priori.* And the object of our investigations, as it is not to be sought without, but altogether within ourselves, cannot remain concealed, and in all probability is limited enough to be completely surveyed and fairly estimated, according to its worth or worthlessness. Still less let the reader here expect a critique of books and systems of pure reason; our present object is exclusively a critique of the faculty of pure reason itself. Only when we make this critique our foundation do we possess a pure touchstone for estimating the philosophical value of ancient and modern writings on this subject; and without this criterion, the incompetent historian or judge decides upon and corrects the groundless assertions of others with his own, which have themselves just as little foundation.

Transcendental philosophy is the idea of a science, for which the Critique of Pure Reason must sketch the whole plan architectonically, that is, from principles, with a full guarantee for the validity and stability of all the parts which enter into the building. It is the system of all the principles of pure reason. If this Critique itself does not assume the title of transcendental philosophy, it is only because, to be a complete system, it ought to contain a full analysis of all human knowledge *à priori.*

Our critique must, indeed, lay before us a complete enumeration of all the radical conceptions which constitute the said pure knowledge. But from the complete analysis of these conceptions themselves, as also from a complete investigation of those derived from them, it abstains with reason; partly because it would be deviating from the end in view to occupy itself with this analysis, since this process is not attended with the difficulty and insecurity to be found in the synthesis, to which our critique is entirely devoted, and partly because it would be inconsistent with the unity of our plan to burden this essay with the vindication of the completeness of such an analysis and deduction, with which, after all, we have at present nothing to do. This completeness of the analysis of these radical conceptions, as well as of the deduction from the conceptions *à priori* which may be given by the analysis, we can, however, easily attain, provided only that we are in possession of all these radical conceptions, which are to serve as principles of the synthesis, and that in respect of this main purpose nothing is wanting.

To the Critique of Pure Reason, therefore, belongs all that constitutes transcendental philosophy; and it is the complete idea of transcendental philosophy, but still not the science itself; because it only proceeds so far with the analysis as is necessary to the power of judging completely of our synthetical knowledge *à priori*.

The principal thing we must attend to, in the division of the parts of a science like this, is   that no conceptions must enter it which contain aught empirical; in other words, that the knowledge *à priori* must be completely pure. Hence, although the highest principles and fundamental conceptions of morality are certainly cognitions *à priori*, yet they do not belong to transcendental philosophy; because, though they certainly do not lay the conceptions of pain, pleasure, desires, inclinations, etc. (which are all of empirical origin), at the foundation of its precepts, yet still into the conception of duty—as an obstacle to be overcome, or as an incitement which should not be made into a motive—these empirical conceptions must necessarily enter, in the construction of a system of pure morality. Transcendental philosophy is consequently a philosophy of the pure and merely speculative reason. For all that is practical, so far as it contains motives, relates to feelings, and these belong to empirical sources of cognition.

If we wish to divide this science from the universal point of view of a science in general, it ought to comprehend, first, a *Doctrine of the Elements,* and, secondly, a *Doctrine of the Method* of pure reason. Each of these main divisions will have its subdivisions, the separate reasons for which we cannot here particularize. Only so much seems necessary, by way of introduction or premonition, that there are two sources of human knowledge (which probably spring from a common, but to us unknown root), namely, sense and understanding. By the former, objects are *given* to us; by the latter, *thought.* So far as the faculty of sense may contain representations *à priori,* which form the conditions under which objects are given, in so far it belongs to transcendental philosophy. The transcendental doctrine of sense must form the first part of our science of elements, because the conditions under which alone the objects of human knowledge are given must precede those under which they are thought.

TRANSCENDENTAL DOCTRINE

OF

ELEMENTS

PART FIRST

TRANSCENDENTAL ÆSTHETIC

INTRODUCTORY

IN whatsoever mode, or by whatsoever means, our knowledge may relate to objects, it is at least quite clear, that the only manner in which it immediately relates to them, is by means of an intuition. To this as the indispensable groundwork, all thought points. But an intuition can take place only in so far as the object is given to us. This, again, is only possible, to man at least, on condition that the object affect the mind in a certain manner. The capacity for receiving representations (receptivity) through the mode in which we are affected by objects, is called *sensibility*. By means of sensibility, therefore, objects are given to us, and it alone furnishes us with intuitions; by the understanding they are *thought,* and from it arise conceptions. But all thought must directly, or indirectly, by means of certain signs, relate ultimately to intuitions; consequently, with us, to sensibility, because in no other way can an object be given to us.

The effect of an object upon the faculty of representation, so far as we are affected by the said object, is sensation. That sort of intuition which relates to an object by means of sensation is called an empirical intuition. The undetermined object of an empirical intuition, is call *phenomenon.* That which in the phenomenon corresponds to the sensation I term its *matter;* but that which effects that the content of the phenomenon can be arranged under certain relations I call its *form.* But that in which our sensations are merely arranged, and by which they are susceptible of assuming a certain form, cannot be itself sensation. It is, then, the matter of all phenomena that is given to us à *posteriori;* the form must lie ready à *priori* for them in the mind, and consequently can be regarded separately from all sensation.

I call all representations *pure*, in the transcendental meaning of the word, wherein nothing is met with that belongs to sensation. And accordingly we find existing in the mind, *à priori*, the pure form of sensuous intuitions in general, in which all the manifold content of the phenomenal world is arranged and viewed under certain relations. This pure form of sensibility I shall call pure intuition. Thus, if I take away from our representation of a body, all that the understanding thinks as belonging to it, as substance, force, divisibility, etc., and also whatever belongs to sensation, as impenetrability, hardness, color, etc.; yet there is still something left us from this empirical intuition, namely, extension and shape. These belong to pure intuition, which exists *à priori* in the mind, as a mere form of sensibility, and without any real object of the senses or any sensation.

The science of all the principles of sensibility *à priori*, I call Transcendental Æsthetic.* There must, then, be such a science, forming the first part of the transcendental doctrine of elements, in contradistinction to that part which contains the principles of pure thought, and which is called transcendental logic.

In the science of transcendental æsthetic accordingly, we shall first isolate sensibility or the sensuous faculty, by separating from it all that is annexed to its perceptions by the conceptions of understanding, so that nothing be left but empirical intuition. In the next place we shall take away from this intuition all that belongs to sensation, so that nothing may remain but pure intuition, and the mere form of phenomena, which is all that the sensibility can afford *à priori*. From this investigation it will be found that there are two pure

---

* The Germans are the only people who at present use this word to indicate what others call the critique of taste. At the foundation of this term lies the disappointed hope, which the eminent analyst, Baumgarten, conceived, of subjecting the criticism of the beautiful to principles of reason, and so of elevating its rules into a science. But his endeavors were vain. For the said rules or criteria are, in respect to their chief sources, merely empirical, consequently never can serve as determinate laws *à priori*, by which our judgment in matters of taste is to be directed. It is rather our judgment which forms the proper test as to the correctness of the principles. On this account it is advisable to give up the use of the term as designating the critique of taste, and to apply it solely to that doctrine, which is true science—the science of the laws of sensibility—and thus come nearer to the language and the sense of the ancients in their well-known division of the objects of cognition into αἰσθητα και νοητα, or to share it with speculative philosophy, and employ it partly in a transcendental, partly in a psychological signification.

forms of sensuous intuition, as principles of knowledge *à priori*, namely, space and time. To the consideration of these we shall now proceed.

Section I.—Of Space

Metaphysical Exposition of this Conception

By means of the external sense (a property of the mind), we represent to ourselves objects as without us, and these all in space. Therein alone are their shape, dimensions, and relations to each other determined or determinable. The internal sense, by means of which the mind contemplates itself or its internal state, gives, indeed, no intuition of the soul as an object; yet there is nevertheless a determinate form, under which alone the contemplation of our internal state is possible, so that all which relates to the inward determinations of the mind is represented in relations of time. Of time we cannot have any external intuition, any more than we can have an internal intuition of space. What then are time and space? Are they real existences? Or, are they merely relations or determinations of things, such, however, as would equally belong to these things in themselves, though they should never become objects of intuition; or, are they such as belong only to the form of intuition, and consequently to the subjective constitution of the mind, without which these predicates of time and space could not be attached to any object? In order to become informed on these points, we shall first give an exposition of the conception of space. By exposition, I mean the clear, though not detailed, representation of that which belongs to a conception; and an exposition is metaphysical, when it contains that which represents the conception as given *à priori*.

1. Space is not a conception which has been derived from outward experiences. For, in order that certain sensations may relate to something without me (that is, to something which occupies a different part of space from that in which I am); in like manner, in order that I may represent them not merely as without of and near to each other, but also in separate places, the representation of space must already exist as a foundation. Consequently, the representation of space cannot be borrowed from the relations of external phenomena through

experience; but, on the contrary, this external experience is itself only possible through the said antecedent representation.

2. Space then is a necessary representation *à priori*, which serves for the foundation of all external intuitions. We never can imagine or make a representation to ourselves of the non-existence of space, though we may easily enough think that no objects are found in it. It must, therefore, be considered as the condition of the possibility of phenomena, and by no means as a determination dependent on them, and is a representation *à priori*, which necessarily supplies the basis for external phenomena.

3. Space is no discursive or, as we say, general conception of the relations of things, but a pure intuition. For in the first place, we can only represent to ourselves one space, and when we talk of divers spaces, we mean only parts of one and the same space. Moreover these parts cannot antecede this one all-embracing space, as the component parts from which the aggregate can be made up, but can be cogitated only as existing in it. Space is essentially one, and multiplicity in it, consequently the general notion of spaces, of this or that space, depends solely upon limitations. Hence it follows that an *à priori* intuition (which is not empirical) lies at the root of all our conceptions of space. Thus, moreover, the principles of geometry—for example, that " in a triangle, two sides together are greater than the third," are never deduced from general conceptions of line and triangle, but from intuition, and this *à priori* with apodictic certainty.

4. Space is represented as an infinite given quantity. Now every conception must indeed be considered as a representation which is contained in an infinite multitude of different possible representations, which, therefore, comprises these under itself; but no conception, as such, can be so conceived, as if it contained within itself an infinite multitude of representations. Nevertheless, space is so conceived of, for all parts of space are equally capable of being produced to infinity. Consequently, the original representation of space is an intuition *à priori*, and not a conception.

Transcendental exposition of the conception of Space

By a transcendental exposition, I mean the explanation of a conception, as a principle, whence can be discerned the possibility of other synthetical à *priori* cognitions. For this purpose, it is requisite, firstly, that such cognitions do really flow from the given conception; and, secondly, that the said cognitions are only possible under the presupposition of a given mode of explaining this conception.

Geometry is a science which determines the properties of space synthetically, and yet à *priori*. What, then, must be our representation of space, in order that such a cognition of it may be possible? It must be originally intuition, for from a mere conception, no propositions can be deduced which go out beyond the conception,* and yet this happens in geometry. (Introd. V.) But this intuition must be found in the mind à *priori*, that is, before any perception of objects, consequently, must be pure, not empirical, intuition. For geometrical principles are always apodictic, that is, united with the consciousness of their necessity, as, " Space has only three dimensions." But propositions of this kind cannot be empirical judgments, nor conclusions from them. (Introd. II.) Now, how can an external intuition anterior to objects themselves, and in which our conception of objects can be determined à *priori*, exist in the human mind? Obviously not otherwise than in so far as it has its seat in the subject only, as the *formal* capacity of the subject's being affected by objects, and thereby of obtaining immediate representation, that is, intuition; consequently, only as the *form of the external sense* in general.

Thus it is only by means of our explanation that the possibility of geometry, as a synthetical science à *priori*, becomes comprehensible. Every mode of explanation which does not show us this possibility, although in appearance it may be similar to ours, can with the utmost certainty be distinguished from it by these marks.

Conclusions from the foregoing conceptions

1. Space does not represent any property of objects as things in themselves, nor does it represent them in their relations to

---

* That is, the analysis of a conception only gives you what is contained in it, and does not add to your knowledge of the object of which you have a conception, but merely evolves it.—J. M. D. M.

each other; in other words, space does not represent to us any
determination of objects such as attaches to the objects themselves, and would remain, even though all subjective conditions
of the intuition were abstracted. For neither absolute nor relative determinations of objects can be intuited prior to the existence of the things to which they belong, and therefore not
à priori.

2. Space is nothing else than the form of all phenomena of
the external sense, that is, the subjective condition of the sensibility, under which alone external intuition is possible. Now,
because the receptivity or capacity of the subject to be affected
by objects necessarily antecedes all intuitions of these objects,
it is easily understood how the form of all phenomena can be
given in the mind previous to all actual perceptions, therefore
à priori, and how it, as a pure intuition, in which all objects
must be determined, can contain principles of the relations of
these objects prior to all experience.

It is therefore from the human point of view only that we
can speak of space, extended objects, etc. If we depart from
the subjective condition, under which alone we can obtain external intuition, or, in other words, by means of which we are
affected by objects, the representation of space has no meaning
whatsoever. This predicate (of space) is only applicable to
things in so far as they appear to us, that is, are objects of
sensibility. The constant form of this receptivity, which we
call sensibility, is a necessary condition of all relations in which
objects can be intuited as existing without us, and when abstraction of these objects is made, is a pure intuition, to which
we give the name of space. It is clear that we cannot make the
special conditions of sensibility into conditions of the possibility
of things, but only of the possibility of their existence as far
as they are phenomena. And so we may correctly say that
space contains all which can appear to us externally, but not
all things considered as things in themselves, be they intuited
or not, or by whatsoever subject one will. As to the intuitions
of other thinking beings, we cannot judge whether they are
or are not bound by the same conditions which limit our own
intuition, and which for us are universally valid. If we join
the limitation of a judgment to the conception of the subject,
then the judgment will possess unconditioned validity. For
example, the proposition, " All objects are beside each other in

space," is valid only under the limitation that these things are taken as objects of our sensuous intuition. But if I join the condition to the conception, and say, " all things, as external phenomena, are beside each other in space," then the rule is valid universally, and without any limitation. Our expositions, consequently, teach the *reality* (*i.e.* the objective validity) of space in regard of all which can be presented to us externally as objects, and at the same time also the *ideality* of space in regard to objects when they are considered by means of reason as things in themselves, that is, without reference to the constitution of our sensibility. We maintain, therefore, the *empirical reality* of space in regard to all possible external experience, although we must admit its *transcendental ideality;* in other words, that it is nothing, so soon as we withdraw the condition upon which the possibility of all experience depends, and look upon space as something that belongs to things in themselves.

But, with the exception of space, there is no representation, subjective and referring to something external to us, which could be called objective *à priori*. For there are no other subjective representations from which we can deduce synthetical propositions *à priori*, as we can from the intuition of space. Therefore, to speak accurately, no ideality whatever belongs to these, although they agree in this respect with the representation of space, that they belong merely to the subjective nature of the mode of sensuous perception; such a mode, for example, as that of sight, of hearing, and of feeling, by means of the sensations of color, sound, and heat, but which, because they are only sensations, and not intuitions, do not of themselves give us the cognition of any object, least of all, an *à priori* cognition. My purpose, in the above remark, is merely this: to guard anyone against illustrating the asserted ideality of space by examples quite insufficient, for example, by color, taste, etc.; for these must be contemplated not as properties of things, but only as changes in the subject, changes which may be different in different men. For in such a case, that which is originally a mere phenomenon, a rose, for example, is taken by the empirical understanding for a thing in itself, though to every different eye, in respect of its color, it may appear different. On the contrary, the transcendental conception of phenomena in space is a critical admonition, that, in general, nothing which is intuited in space is a thing in itself, and that space is not a form which belongs as a property to things; but that objects are quite unknown to us in themselves, and what we call outward objects, are nothing else but mere representations of our sensibility, whose form is space, but whose real correlate, the thing in itself, is not known by means of these representations, nor ever can be, but respecting which, in experience, no inquiry is ever made.

Section II.—Of Time

Metaphysical exposition of this conception

1. Time is not an empirical conception. For neither coexistence nor succession would be perceived by us, if the representation of time did not exist as a foundation *à priori*. Without this presupposition we could not represent to ourselves that things exist together at one and the same time, or at different times, that is, contemporaneously, or in succession.

2. Time is a necessary representation, lying at the foundation of all our intuitions. With regard to phenomena in general, we cannot think away time from them, and represent them to ourselves as out of and unconnected with time, but we can quite well represent to ourselves time void of phenomena. Time is therefore given *à priori*. In it alone is all reality of phenomena possible. These may all be annihilated in thought, but time itself, as the universal condition of their possibility, cannot be so annulled.

3. On this necessity *à priori* is also founded the possibility of apodictic principles of the relations of time, or axioms of time in general, such as, " Time has only one dimension," " Different times are not coexistent but successive " (as different spaces are not successive but coexistent). These principles cannot be derived from experience, for it would give neither strict universality, nor apodictic certainty. We should only be able to say, " so common experience teaches us," but not it must be so. They are valid as rules, through which, in general, experience is possible; and they instruct us respecting experience, and not by means of it.

4. Time is not a discursive or, as it is called, general conception, but a pure form of the sensuous intuition. Different times are merely parts of one and the same time. But the

representation which can only be given by a single object is an intuition. Besides, the proposition that different times cannot be coexistent, could not be derived from a general conception. For this proposition is synthetical, and therefore cannot spring out of conceptions alone. It is therefore contained immediately, in the intuition and representation of time.

5. The infinity of time signifies nothing more than that every determined quantity of time is possible only through limitations of one time lying at the foundation. Consequently, the original representation, time, must be given as unlimited. But as the determinate representation of the parts of time and of every quantity of an object can only be obtained by limitation, the *complete* representation of time must not be furnished by means of conceptions, for these contain only partial representations. Conceptions, on the contrary, must have immediate intuition for their basis.

Transcendental exposition of the conception of time

I may here refer to what is said above, where, for the sake of brevity, I have placed under the head of metaphysical exposition, that which is properly transcendental. Here I shall add that the conception of change, and with it the conception of motion, as change of place, is possible only through and in the representation of time; that if this representation were not an intuition (internal) *à priori*, no conception, of whatever kind, could render comprehensible the possibility of change, in other words, of a conjunction of contradictorily opposed predicates in one and the same object, for example, the presence of a thing in a place and the non-presence of the same thing in the same place. It is only in time, that it is possible to meet with two contradictorily opposed determinations in one thing, that is, after each other.* Thus our conception of time explains the possibility of so much synthetical knowledge *à priori*, as is exhibited in the general doctrine of motion, which is not a little fruitful.

* Kant's meaning is: You cannot affirm and deny the same thing of a subject, except by means of the representation, time. No other idea, intuition, or conception, or whatever other form of thought there be, can mediate the connection of such predicates.—J. M. D. M.

Conclusions from the above conceptions

1. Time is not something which subsists of itself, or which inheres in things as an objective determination, and therefore remains, when abstraction is made of the subjective conditions of the intuition of things. For in the former case, it would be something real, yet without presenting to any power of perception any real object. In the latter case, as an order or determination inherent in things themselves, it could not be antecedent to things, as their condition, nor discerned or intuited by means of synthetical propositions à priori. But all this is quite possible when we regard time as merely the subjective condition under which all our intuitions take place. For in that case, this form of the inward intuition can be represented prior to the objects, and consequently à priori.

2. Time is nothing else than the form of the internal sense, that is, of the intuitions of self and of our internal state. For time cannot be any determination of outward phenomena. It has to do neither with shape nor position; on the contrary, it determines the relation of representations in our internal state. And precisely because this internal intuition presents to us no shape or form, we endeavor to supply this want by analogies, and represent the course of time by a line progressing to infinity, the content of which constitutes a series which is only of one dimension; and we conclude from the properties of this line as to all the properties of time, with this single exception, that the parts of the line are coexistent, while those of time are successive. From this it is clear also that the representation of time is itself an intuition, because all its relations can be expressed in an internal intuition.

3. Time is the formal condition à priori of all phenomena whatsoever. Space, as the pure form of external intuition, is limited as a condition à priori to external phenomena alone. On the other hand, because all representations, whether they have or have not external things for their objects, still in themselves, as determinations of the mind, belong to our internal state; and because this internal state is subject to the formal condition of the internal intuition, that is, to time—time is a condition à priori of all phenomena whatsoever—the *immediate* condition of all internal, and thereby the *mediate* condition of all external phenomena. If I can say à priori, " all outward

phenomena are in space, and determined *à priori* according to the relations of space," I can also, from the principle of the internal sense, affirm universally, " all phenomena in general, that is, all objects of the senses, are in time, and stand necessarily in relations of time."

If we abstract our internal intuition of ourselves, and all external intuitions, possible only by virtue of this internal intuition, and presented to us by our faculty of representation, and consequently take objects as they are in themselves, then time is nothing. It is only of objective validity in regard to phenomena, because these are things which we regard as objects of our senses. It is no longer objective, if we make abstraction of the sensuousness of our intuition, in other words, of that mode of representation which is peculiar to us, and speaks of things in general   Time is therefore merely a subjective condition of our (human) intuition (which is always sensuous, that is, so far as we are affected by objects), and in itself, independently of the mind or subject, is nothing. Nevertheless, in respect of all phenomena, consequently of all things which come within the sphere of our experience, it is necessarily objective. We cannot say, " all things are in time," because in this conception of things in general, we abstract and make no mention of any sort of intuition of things. But this is the proper condition under which time belongs to our representation of objects. If we add the condition to the conception, and say, " all things, as phenomena, that is, objects of sensuous intuition, are in time," then the proposition has its sound objective validity and universality *à priori.*

What we have now set forth teaches, therefore, the empirical reality of time; that is, its objective validity in reference to all objects which can ever be presented to our senses. And as our intuition is always sensuous, no object ever can be presented to us in experience, which does not come under the conditions of time. On the other hand, we deny to time all claim to absolute reality; that is, we deny that it, without having regard to the form of our sensuous intuition, absolutely inheres in things as a condition or property. Such properties as belong to objects as things in themselves, never can be presented to us through the medium of the senses. Herein consists, therefore, the transcendental ideality of time, according to which, if we abstract the subjective conditions of sensuous intuition, it is nothing, and cannot be reckoned as subsisting or inhering in objects as things in themselves, independently of its relation to our intuition. This ideality, like that of space, is not to be proved or illustrated by fallacious analogies with sensations, for this reason—that in such arguments or illustrations, we make the presupposition that the phenomenon, in which such and such predicates inhere, has objective reality, while in this case we can only find such an objective reality as is itself empirical, that is, regards the object as a mere phenomenon. In reference to this subject, see the remark, elsewhere in this work, on Space.

Elucidation

Against this theory, which grants empirical reality to time, but denies to it absolute and transcendental reality, I have heard from intelligent men an objection so unanimously urged, that I conclude that it must naturally present itself to every reader to whom these considerations are novel. It runs thus: " Changes are real " (this the continual change in our own representations demonstrates, even though the existence of all external phenomena, together with their changes, is denied). Now, changes are only possible in time, and therefore time must be something real. But there is no difficulty in answering this. I grant the whole argument. Time, no doubt, is something real, that is, it is the real form of our internal intuition. It therefore has subjective reality, in reference to our internal experience, that is, I have really the representation of time, and of my determinations therein. Time, therefore, is not to be regarded as an object, but as the mode of representation of myself as an object. But if I could intuite myself, or be intuited by another being, without this condition of sensibility, then those very determinations which we now represent to ourselves as changes, would present to us a knowledge in which the representation of time, and consequently of change, would not appear. The empirical reality of time, therefore, remains, as the condition of all our experience. But absolute reality, according to what has been said above, cannot be granted it. Time is nothing but the form of our internal intuition.* If we take away from it the special condition of our

* I can indeed say " my representations follow one another, or are successive "; but this means only that we are conscious of them as in a succession, that is, according to the form of the internal sense. Time, therefore, is not a thing in itself, nor is it any objective determination pertaining to or inherent in things.

sensibility, the conception of time also vanishes; and it inheres not in the objects themselves, but solely in the subject (or mind) which intuites them.

But the reason why this objection is so unanimously brought against our doctrine of time, and that too by disputants who cannot start any intelligible arguments against the doctrine of the ideality of space, is this—they have no hope of demonstrating apodictically the absolute reality of space, because the doctrine of idealism is against them, according to which the reality of external objects is not capable of any strict proof. On the other hand, the reality of the object of our internal sense (that is, myself and my internal state) is clear immediately through consciousness. The former—external objects in space—might be a mere delusion, but the latter—the object of my internal perception—is undeniably real. They do not, however, reflect that both, without question of their reality as representations, belong only to the genus phenomenon, which has always two aspects, the one, the object considered as a thing in itself, without regard to the mode of intuiting it, and the nature of which remains for this very reason problematical, the other, the form of our intuition of the object, which must be sought not in the object as a thing in itself, but in the subject to which it appears—which form of intuition nevertheless belongs really and necessarily to the phenomenal object.

Time and space are, therefore, two sources of knowledge, from which, *à priori*, various synthetical cognitions can be drawn.—Of this we find a striking example in the cognitions of space and its relations, which form the foundation of pure mathematics.—They are the two pure forms of all intuition, and thereby make synthetical propositions *à priori* possible. But these sources of knowledge being merely conditions of our sensibility, do therefore, and as such, strictly determine their own range and purpose, in that they do not and cannot present objects as things in themselves, but are applicable to them solely in so far as they are considered as sensuous phenomena. The sphere of phenomena is the only sphere of their validity, and if we venture out of this, no further objective use can be made of them. For the rest, this formal reality of time and space leaves the validity of our empirical knowledge unshaken; for our certainty in that respect is equally firm, whether these forms necessarily inhere in the things themselves, or only in our intuitions of them. On the other hand, those who maintain the absolute reality of time and space, whether as essentially subsisting, or only inhering, as modifications, in things, must find themselves at utter variance with the principles of experience itself. For, if they decide for the first view, and make space and time into substances, this being the side taken by mathematical natural philosophers, they must admit two self-subsisting nonentities, infinite and eternal, which exist (yet without there being anything real) for the purpose of containing in themselves everything that is real. If they adopt the second view of inherence, which is preferred by some metaphysical natural philosophers, and regard space and time as relations (contiguity in space or succession in time), abstracted from experience, though represented confusedly in this state of separation, they find themselves in that case necessitated to deny the validity of mathematical doctrines *à priori* in reference to real things (for example, in space)—at all events their apodictic certainty. For such certainty cannot be found in an *à posteriori* proposition; and the conceptions *à priori* of space and time are, according to this opinion, mere creations of the imaginations,* having their source really in experience, inasmuch as, out of relations abstracted from experience, imagination has made up something which contains, indeed, general statements of these relations, yet of which no application can be made without the restrictions attached thereto by nature. The former of these parties gains this advantage, that they keep the sphere of phenomena free for mathematical science. On the other hand, these very conditions (space and time) embarrass them greatly, when the understanding endeavors to pass the limits of that sphere. The latter has, indeed, this advantage, that the representations of space and time do not come in their way when they wish to judge of objects, not as phenomena, but merely in their relation to the understanding. Devoid, however, of a true and objectively valid *à priori* intuition, they can neither furnish any basis for the possibility of mathematical cognitions *à priori,* nor bring the propositions of experience into necessary accordance with those of mathematics. In our theory of the true nature of these two original forms of the sensibility, both difficulties are surmounted.

* This word is here used, and will be hereafter always used, in its primitive sense. That meaning of it which denotes a poetical inventive power is a secondary one.—J. M. D. M.

In conclusion, that transcendental Æsthetic cannot contain any more than these two elements—space and time, is sufficiently obvious from the fact that all other conceptions appertaining to sensibility, even that of motion, which unites in itself both elements, presuppose something empirical. Motion, for example, presupposes the perception of something movable. But space considered in itself contains nothing movable, consequently motion must be something which is found in space only through experience—in other words, is an empirical datum. In like manner, transcendental Æsthetic cannot number the conception of change among its data à priori; for time itself does not change, but only something which is in time. To acquire the conception of change, therefore, the perception of some existing object and of the succession of its determinations, in one word, experience, is necessary.

General Remarks on Transcendental Æsthetic

I. In order to prevent any misunderstanding, it will be requisite, in the first place, to recapitulate, as clearly as possible, what our opinion is with respect to the fundamental nature of our sensuous cognition in general. We have intended, then, to say, that all our intuition is nothing but the representation of phenomena; that the things which we intuite, are not in themselves the same as our representations of them in intuition, nor are their relations in themselves so constituted as they appear to us; and that if we take away the subject, or even only the subjective constitution of our senses in general, then not only the nature and relations of objects in space and time, but even space and time themselves disappear; and that these, as phenomena, cannot exist in themselves, but only in us. What may be the nature of objects considered as things in themselves and without reference to the receptivity of our sensibility is quite unknown to us. We know nothing more than our own mode of perceiving them, which is peculiar to us, and which, though not of necessity pertaining to every animated being, is so to the whole human race. With this alone we have to do. Space and time are the pure forms thereof; sensation the matter. The former alone can we recognize à priori, that is, antecedent to all actual perception; and for this reason such cognition is called pure intuition. The latter is that in our cognition which is called cognition à posteriori, that is, empirical intuition. The former appertain absolutely and necessarily to our sensibility, of whatsoever kind our sensations may be; the latter may be of very diversified character. Supposing that we should carry our empirical intuition even to the very highest degree of clearness, we should not thereby advance one step nearer to a knowledge of the constitution of objects as things in themselves. For we could only, at best, arrive at a complete cognition of our own mode of intuition, that is, of our sensibility, and this always under the conditions originally attaching to the subject, namely, the conditions of space and time;—while the question—" What are objects considered as things in themselves?" remains unanswerable even after the most thorough examination of the phenomenal world.

To say, then, that all our sensibility is nothing but the confused representation of things containing exclusively that which belongs to them as things in themselves, and this under an accumulation of characteristic marks and partial representations which we cannot distinguish in consciousness, is a falsification of the conception of sensibility and phenomenization, which renders our whole doctrine thereof empty and useless. The difference between a confused and a clear representation is merely logical and has nothing to do with content. No doubt the conception of *right,* as employed by a sound understanding, contains all that the most subtle investigation could unfold from it, although, in the ordinary practical use of the word, we are not conscious of the manifold representations comprised in the conception. But we cannot for this reason assert that the ordinary conception is a sensuous one, containing a mere phenomenon, for *right* cannot appear as a phenomenon; but the conception of it lies in the understanding, and represents a property (the moral property) of actions, which belongs to them in themselves. On the other hand, the representation in intuition of a body contains nothing which could belong to an object considered as a thing in itself, but merely the phenomenon or appearance of something, and the mode in which we are affected by that appearance; and this receptivity of our faculty of cognition is called sensibility, and remains *toto cœlo* different from the cognition of an object in itself, even though we should examine the content of the phenomenon to the very bottom.

It must be admitted that the Leibnitz-Wolfian philosophy

has assigned an entirely erroneous point of view to all investigations into the nature and origin of our cognitions, inasmuch as it regards the distinction between the sensuous and the intellectual as merely logical, whereas it is plainly transcendental, and concerns not merely the clearness or obscurity, but the content and origin of both. For the faculty of sensibility not only does not present us with an indistinct and confused cognition of objects as things in themselves, but, in fact, gives us no knowledge of these at all. On the contrary, so soon as we abstract in thought our own subjective nature, the object represented, with the properties ascribed to it by sensuous intuition, entirely disappears, because it was only this subjective nature that determined the form of the object as a phenomenon.

In phenomena, we commonly, indeed, distinguish that which essentially belongs to the intuition of them, and is valid for the sensuous faculty of every human being, from that which belongs to the same intuition accidentally, as valid not for the sensuous faculty in general, but for a particular state or organization of this or that sense. Accordingly, we are accustomed to say that the former is a cognition which represents the object itself, while the latter presents only a particular appearance or phenomenon thereof. This distinction, however, is only empirical. If we stop here (as is usual), and do not regard the empirical intuition as itself a mere phenomenon (as we ought to do), in which nothing that can appertain to a thing in itself is to be found, our transcendental distinction is lost, and we believe that we cognize objects as things in themselves, although in the whole range of the sensuous world, investigate the nature of its objects as profoundly as we may, we have to do with nothing but phenomena. Thus, we call the rainbow a mere appearance or phenomenon in a sunny shower, and the rain, the reality or thing in itself; and this is right enough, if we understand the latter conception in a merely physical sense, that is, as that which in universal experience, and under whatever conditions of sensuous perception, is known in intuition to be so and so determined, and not otherwise. But if we consider this empirical datum generally, and inquire, without reference to its accordance with all our senses, whether there can be discovered in it aught which represents an object as a thing in itself (the rain drops of course are not such, for they are, as phenomena, empirical objects), the question of the rela-

tion of the representation to the object is transcendental; and
not only are the rain drops mere phenomena, but even their
circular form, nay, the space itself through which they fall,
is nothing in itself, but both are mere modifications or fundamental dispositions of our sensuous intuition, while the transcendental object remains for us utterly unknown.

The second important concern of our Æsthetic is, that it
do not obtain favor merely as a plausible hypothesis, but possess as undoubted a character of certainty as can be demanded
of any theory which is to serve for an organon. In order fully
to convince the reader of this certainty, we shall select a case
which will serve to make its validity apparent.

Suppose, then, that Space and Time are in themselves objective, and conditions of the possibility of objects as things in
themselves. In the first place, it is evident that both present us
with very many apodictic and synthetic propositions *à priori*,
but especially space—and for this reason we shall prefer it for
investigation at present. As the propositions of geometry are
cognized synthetically *à priori*, and with apodictic certainty,
I inquire—whence do you obtain propositions of this kind, and
on what basis does the understanding rest, in order to arrive
at such absolutely necessary and universally valid truths?

There is no other way than through intuitions or conceptions,
as such; and these are given either *à priori* or *à posteriori*.
The latter, namely, empirical conceptions, together with the
empirical intuition on which they are founded, cannot afford
any synthetical proposition, except such as is itself also empirical, that is, a proposition of experience. But an empirical
proposition cannot possess the qualities of necessity and absolute universality, which, nevertheless, are the characteristics of
all geometrical propositions. As to the first and only means
to arrive at such cognitions, namely, through mere conceptions
or intuitions *à priori*, it is quite clear that from mere conceptions no synthetical cognitions, but only analytical ones, can
be obtained. Take, for example, the proposition, " Two straight
lines cannot inclose a space, and with these alone no figure is
possible," and try to deduce it from the conception of a straight
line, and the number two; or take the proposition, " It is possible to construct a figure with three straight lines," and endeavor, in like manner, to deduce it from the mere conception
of a straight line and the number three. All your endeavors

are in vain, and you find yourself forced to have recourse to intuition, as, in fact, geometry always does. You therefore give yourself an object in intuition. But of what kind is this intuition? Is it a pure *à priori*, or is it an empirical, intuition? If the latter, then neither an universally valid, much less an apodictic proposition can arise from it, for experience never can give us any such proposition. You must therefore give yourself an object *à priori* in intuition, and upon that ground your synthetical proposition. Now if there did not exist within you a faculty of intuition *à priori;* if this subjective condition were not in respect to its form also the universal condition *à priori* under which alone the object of this external intuition is itself possible; if the object (that is, the triangle) were something in itself, without relation to you the subject, how could you affirm that that which lies necessarily in your subjective conditions in order to construct a triangle must also necessarily belong to the triangle in itself? For to your conceptions of three lines, you could not add anything new (that is, the figure), which, therefore, must necessarily be found in the object, because the object is given before your cognition, and not by means of it. If, therefore, Space (and Time also) were not a mere form of your intuition, which contains conditions *à priori*, under which alone things can become external objects for you, and without which subjective conditions the objects are in themselves nothing, you could not construct any synthetical proposition whatsoever regarding external objects. It is therefore not merely possible or probable, but indubitably certain, that Space and Time, as the necessary conditions of all our external and internal experience, are merely subjective conditions of all our intuitions, in relation to which all objects are therefore mere phenomena, and not things in themselves, presented to us in this particular manner. And for this reason, in respect to the form of phenomena, much may be said *à priori*, while of the thing in itself, which may lie at the foundation of these phenomena, it is impossible to say anything.

II. In confirmation of this theory of the ideality of the external as well as internal sense, consequently of all objects of sense, as mere phenomena, we may especially remark, that all in our cognition that belongs to intuition contains nothing more than mere relations. The feelings of pain and pleasure, and the will, which are not cognitions, are excepted. The relations, to-wit, of place in an intuition (extension), change of place (motion), and laws according to which this change is determined (moving forces). That, however, which is present in this or that place, or any operation going on, or result taking place in the things themselves, with the exception of change of place, is not given to us by intuition. Now by means of mere relations, a thing cannot be known in itself; and it may therefore be fairly concluded, that, as through the external sense nothing but mere representations of relations are given us, the said external sense in its representation can contain only the relation of the object to the subject, but not the essential nature of the object as a thing in itself.

The same is the case with the internal intuition, not only because, in the internal intuition, the representation of the external senses constitutes the material with which the mind is occupied; but because time, in which we place, and which itself antecedes the consciousness of, these representations in experience, and which, as the formal condition of the mode according to which objects are placed in the mind, lies at the foundation of them, contains relations of the successive, the coexistent, and of that which always must be coexistent with succession, the permanent. Now that which, as representation, can antecede every exercise of thought (of an object), is intuition; and when it contains nothing but relations, it is the form of the intuition, which, as it presents us with no representation, except in so far as something is placed in the mind, can be nothing else than the mode in which the mind is affected by its own activity, to-wit—its presenting to itself representations, consequently the mode in which the mind is affected by itself; that is, it can be nothing but an internal sense in respect to its form. Everything that is represented through the medium of sense is so far phenomenal; consequently, we must either refuse altogether to admit an internal sense, or the subject, which is the object of that sense, could only be represented by it as phenomenon, and not as it would judge of itself, if its intuition were pure spontaneous activity, that is, were intellectual. The difficulty here lies wholly in the question— How the subject can have an internal intuition of itself? But this difficulty is common to every theory. The consciousness of self (apperception) is the simple representation of the "Ego"; and if by means of that representation alone, all the manifold representations in the subject were spontaneously given, then our internal intuition would be intellectual. This consciousness in man requires an internal perception of the manifold representations which are previously given in the subject; and the manner in which these representations are given in the mind without spontaneity, must, on account of this difference (the want of spontaneity), be called sensibility. If the faculty of self-consciousness is to apprehend what lies in the mind, it must affect that, and can in this way alone produce an intuition of self. But the form of this intuition, which lies in the original constitution of the mind, determines, in the representation of time, the manner in which the manifold representations are to combine themselves in the mind; since the subject intuites itself, not as it would represent itself immediately and spontaneously, but according to the manner in which the mind is internally affected, consequently, as it appears, and not as it is.

III. When we say that the intuition of external objects, and also the self-intuition of the subject, represent both, objects and subject, in space and time, as they affect our senses, that is, as they appear—this is by no means equivalent to asserting that these objects are mere illusory appearances. For when we speak of things as phenomena, the objects, nay, even the properties which we ascribe to them, are looked upon as really given; only that, in so far as this or that property depends upon the mode of intuition of the subject, in the relation of the given object to the subject, the object as phenomenon is to be distinguished from the object as a thing in itself. Thus I do not say that bodies seem or appear to be external to me, or that my soul seems merely to be given in my self-consciousness, although I maintain that the properties of space and time, in conformity to which I set both, as the condition of their existence, abide in my mode of intuition, and not in the objects in themselves. It would be my own fault, if out of that which I should reckon as phenomenon, I made mere illusory appearance.* But this will not happen, because of our principle of

* The predicates of the phenomenon can be affixed to the object itself in relation to our sensuous faculty; for example, the red color or the perfume of the rose. But (illusory) appearance never can be attributed as a predicate to an object, for this very reason, that it attributes to this object in itself that which belongs to it only in relation to our sensuous faculty, or to the subject in general, as, for instance, the two handles which were formerly ascribed to Saturn. That which is never to be found in the object itself, but always in the relation of the object to the subject, and which, moveover, is inseparable

the ideality of all sensuous intuitions. On the contrary, if we ascribe objective reality to these forms of representation, it becomes impossible to avoid changing everything into mere appearance. For if we regard space and time as properties, which must be found in objects as things in themselves, as *sine quibus non* of the possibility of their existence, and reflect on the absurdities in which we then find ourselves involved, inasmuch as we are compelled to admit the existence of two infinite things, which are nevertheless not substances, nor anything really inhering in substances, nay, to admit that they are the necessary conditions of the existence of all things, and moreover, that they must continue to exist, although all existing things were annihilated—we cannot blame the good Berkeley for degrading bodies to mere illusory appearances. Nay, even our own existence, which would in this case depend upon the self-existent reality of such a mere nonentity as time, would necessarily be changed with it into mere appearance—an absurdity which no one has as yet been guilty of.

IV. In natural theology, where we think of an object—God—which never can be an object of intuition to us, and even to himself can never be an object of sensuous intuition, we carefully avoid attributing to his intuition the conditions of space and time—and intuition all his cognition must be, and not thought, which always includes limitation. But with what right can we do this if we make them forms of objects as things in themselves, and such moreover, as would continue to exist as *à priori* conditions of the existence of things, even though the things themselves were annihilated? For as conditions of all existence in general, space and time must be conditions of the existence of the Supreme Being also. But if we do not thus make them objective forms of all things, there is no other way left than to make them subjective forms of our mode of intuition—external and internal; which is called sensuous, because it is not primitive, that is, is not such as gives in itself the existence of the object of the intuition (a mode of intuition which, so far as we can judge, can belong only to the Creator), but is dependent on the existence of the object, is possible,

from our representation of the object, we denominate phenomenon. Thus the predicates of space and time are rightly attributed to objects of the senses as such, and in this there is no illusion. On the contrary, if I ascribe redness to the rose as a thing in itself, or to Saturn his handles, or extension to all external objects, considered as things in themselves, without regarding the determinate relation of these objects to the subject, and without limiting my judgment to that relation—then, and then only, arises illusion.

therefore, only on condition that the representative faculty of the subject is affected by the object.

It is, moreover, not necessary that we should limit the mode of intuition in space and time to the sensuous faculty of man. It may well be, that all finite thinking beings must necessarily in this respect agree with man (though as to this we cannot decide), but sensibility does not on account of this universality cease to be sensibility, for this very reason, that it is a deduced (*intuitus derivativus*), and not an original (*intuitus originarius*), consequently not an intellectual intuition; and this intuition, as such, for reasons above mentioned, seems to belong solely to the Supreme Being, but never to a being dependent, *quoad* its existence, as well as its intuition (which its existence determines and limits relatively to given objects). This latter remark, however, must be taken only as an illustration, and not as any proof of the truth of our æsthetical theory.

Conclusion of the Transcendental Æsthetic

We have now completely before us one part of the solution of the grand general problem of transcendental philosophy, namely, the question—How are synthetical propositions *à priori* possible? That is to say, we have shown that we are in possession of pure *à priori* intuitions, namely, space and time, in which we find, when in a judgment *à priori* we pass out beyond the given conception, something which is not discoverable in that conception, but is certainly found *à priori* in the intuition which corresponds to the conception, and can be united synthetically with it. But the judgments which these pure intuitions enable us to make, never reach farther than to objects of the senses, and are valid only for objects of possible experience.

PART SECOND

TRANSCENDENTAL LOGIC

I.—Of Logic in General

OUR knowledge springs from two main sources in the mind, the first of which is the faculty or power of receiving representations (receptivity for impressions); the second is the power of cognizing by means of these representations (spontaneity in the production of conceptions). Through the first an object is given to us; through the second, it is, in relation to the representation (which is a mere determination of the mind), thought. Intuition and conceptions constitute, therefore, the elements of all our knowledge, so that neither conceptions without an intuition in some way corresponding to them, nor intuition without conceptions, can afford us a cognition. Both are either pure or empirical. They are empirical, when sensation (which presupposes the actual presence of the object) is contained in them; and pure, when no sensation is mixed with the representation. Sensations we may call the matter of sensuous cognition. Pure intuition consequently contains merely the form under which something is intuited, and pure conception only the form of the thought of an object. Only pure intuitions and pure conceptions are possible à priori; the empirical only à posteriori.

We apply the term sensibility to the receptivity of the mind for impressions, in so far as it is in some way affected; and, on the other hand, we call the faculty of spontaneously producing representations, or the spontaneity of cognition, understanding. Our nature is so constituted, that intuition with us never can be other than sensuous, that is, it contains only the mode in which we are affected by objects. On the other hand, the faculty of thinking the object of sensuous intuition, is the understanding. Neither of these faculties has a preference over the other. Without the sensuous faculty no object would be given to us, and without the understanding no object would be thought. Thoughts without content are void; intuitions without conceptions, blind. Hence it is as necessary for the mind to make its conceptions sensuous (that is, to join to them the object in intuition), as to make its intuitions intelligible (that is, to bring them under conceptions). Neither of these faculties can exchange its proper function. Understanding cannot intuite, and the sensuous faculty cannot think. In no other way than from the united operation of both, can knowledge arise. But no one ought, on this account, to overlook the difference of the elements contributed by each; we have rather great reason carefully to separate and distinguish them. We therefore distinguish the science of the laws of sensibility, that is, Æsthetic, from the science of the laws of the understanding, that is, Logic.

Now, logic in its turn may be considered as twofold—namely, as logic of the general [universal], or of the particular use of the understanding. The first contains the absolutely necessary laws of thought, without which no use whatever of the understanding is possible, and gives laws therefore to the understanding, without regard to the difference of objects on which it may be employed. The logic of the particular use of the understanding contains the laws of correct thinking upon a particular class of objects. The former may be called elemental logic—the latter, the organon of this or that particular science. The latter is for the most part employed in the schools, as a propædeutic to the sciences, although, indeed, according to the course of human reason, it is the last thing we arrive at, when the science has been already matured, and needs only the finishing touches towards its correction and completion; for our knowledge of the objects of our attempted science must be tolerably extensive and complete before we can indicate the laws by which a science of these objects can be established.

General logic is again either pure or applied. In the former, we abstract all the empirical conditions under which the understanding is exercised; for example, the influence of the senses, the play of the fantasy or imagination, the laws of the memory, the force of habit, of inclination, etc., consequently also, the sources of prejudice—in a word, we abstract all causes from which particular cognitions arise, because these causes regard the understanding under certain circumstances of its application, and to the knowledge of them experience is required. Pure general logic has to do, therefore, merely with pure *à priori* principles, and is a canon of understanding and reason, but only in respect of the formal part of their use, be the content what it may, empirical or transcendental. General logic is called applied, when it is directed to the laws of the use of the understanding, under the subjective empirical conditions which psychology teaches us. It has therefore empirical principles, although, at the same time, it is in so far general, that it applies to the exercise of the understanding, without regard to the difference of objects. On this account, moreover, it is neither a canon of the understanding in general, nor an organon of a particular science, but merely a cathartic of the human understanding.

In general logic, therefore, that part which constitutes pure logic must be carefully distinguished from that which constitutes applied (though still general) logic. The former alone is properly science, although short and dry, as the methodical exposition of an elemental doctrine of the understanding ought to be. In this, therefore, logicians must always bear in mind two rules:—

1. As general logic, it makes abstraction of all content of the cognition of the understanding, and of the difference of objects, and has to do with nothing but the mere form of thought.

2. As pure logic, it has no empirical principles, and consequently draws nothing (contrary to the common persuasion) from psychology, which therefore has no influence on the canon of the understanding. It is a demonstrated doctrine, and everything in it must be certain completely *à priori.*

What I call applied logic (contrary to the common acceptation of this term, according to which it should contain certain exercises for the scholar, for which pure logic gives the rules), is a representation of the understanding, and of the rules of its necessary employment *in concreto*, that is to say, under the accidental conditions of the subject, which may either hinder or promote this employment, and which are all given only empirically. Thus applied logic treats of attention, its impediments and consequences, of the origin of error, of the state of doubt, hesitation, conviction, etc., and to it is related pure general logic in the same way that pure morality, which contains only the necessary moral laws of a free will, is related to practical ethics, which considers these laws under all the impediments of feelings, inclinations, and passions to which men are more or less subjected, and which never can furnish us with a true and demonstrated science, because it, as well as applied logic, requires empirical and psychological principles.

II.—Of Transcendental Logic

General logic, as we have seen, makes abstraction of all content and cognition, that is, of all relation of cognition to its object, and regards only the logical form in the relation of cognitions to each other, that is, the form of thought in general. But as we have both pure and empirical intuitions (as transcendental æsthetic proves), in like manner a distinction might be drawn between pure and empirical thought (of objects). In this case, there would exist a kind of logic, in which we should not make abstraction of all content of cognition; for that logic which should comprise merely the laws of pure thought (of an object), would of course exclude all those cognitions which were of empirical content. This kind of logic would also examine the origin of our cognitions of objects, so far as that origin cannot be ascribed to the objects themselves; while, on the contrary, general logic has nothing to do with the origin of our cognitions, but contemplates our representations, be they given primitively à priori in ourselves, or be they only of empirical origin, solely according to the laws which the understanding observes in employing them in the process of thought, in relation to each other. Consequently, general logic treats of the form of the understanding only, which can be applied to representations, from whatever source they may have arisen.

And here I shall make a remark, which the reader must bear well in mind in the course of the following considerations, to-wit, that not every cognition à priori, but only those through which we cognize that and how certain representations (intuitions or conceptions) are applied or are possible only à priori; that is to say, the à priori possibility of cognition and the *à priori* use of it are transcendental. Therefore neither is space, nor any *à priori* geometrical determination of space, a transcendental representation, but only the knowledge that such a representation is not of empirical origin, and the possibility of its relating to objects of experience, although itself *à priori,* can be called transcendental. So also, the application of space to objects in general, would be transcendental; but if it be limited to objects of sense, it is empirical. Thus, the distinction of the transcendental and empirical belongs only to the critique of cognitions, and does not concern the relation of these to their object.

Accordingly, in the expectation that there may perhaps be conceptions which relate *à priori* to objects, not as pure or sensuous intuitions, but merely as acts of pure thought (which are therefore conceptions, but neither of empirical nor æsthetical origin)—in this expectation, I say, we form to ourselves, by anticipation, the idea of a science of pure understanding and rational cognition, by means of which we may cogitate objects entirely *à priori.* A science of this kind, which should determine the origin, the extent, and the objective validity of such cognitions, must be called *Transcendental Logic,* because it has not, like general logic, to do with the laws of understanding and reason in relation to empirical as well as pure rational cognitions without distinction, but concerns itself with these only in an *à priori* relation to objects.

III.—Of the Division of General Logic Into Analytic and Dialectic

The old question with which people sought to push logicians into a corner, so that they must either have recourse to pitiful sophisms or confess their ignorance, and consequently the vanity of their whole art, is this—" What is truth? " The definition of the word *truth,* to-wit, " the accordance of the cognition with its object," is presupposed in the question; but we desire to be told, in the answer to it, what is the universal and secure criterion of the truth of every cognition.

To know what questions we may reasonably propose, is in itself a strong evidence of sagacity and intelligence. For if a question be in itself absurd and unsusceptible of a rational answer, it is attended with the danger—not to mention the shame that falls upon the person who proposes it—of seducing the unguarded listener into making absurd answers, and we are presented with the ridiculous spectacle of one (as the ancients said) "milking the he-goat, and the other holding a sieve."

If truth consists in the accordance of a cognition with its object, this object must be, *ipso facto*, distinguished from all others; for a cognition is false if it does not accord with the object to which it relates, although it contains something which may be affirmed of other objects. Now an universal criterion of truth would be that which is valid for all cognitions, without distinction of their objects. But it is evident that since, in the case of such a criterion, we make abstraction of all the content of a cognition (that is, of all relation to its object), and truth relates precisely to this content, it must be utterly absurd to ask for a mark of the truth of this content of cognition; and that, accordingly, a sufficient, and at the same time universal, test of truth cannot possibly be found. As we have already termed the content of a cognition its *matter*, we shall say: "Of the truth of our cognitions in respect of their matter, no universal test can be demanded, because such a demand is self-contradictory."

On the other hand, with regard to our cognition in respect to its mere form (excluding all content), it is equally manifest that logic, in so far as it exhibits the universal and necessary laws of the understanding, must in these very laws present us with criteria of truth. Whatever contradicts these rules is false, because thereby the understanding is made to contradict its own universal laws of thought; that is, to contradict itself. These criteria, however, apply solely to the form of truth, that is, of thought in general, and in so far they are perfectly accurate, yet not sufficient. For although a cognition may be perfectly accurate as to logical form, that is, not self-contradictory, it is notwithstanding quite possible that it may not stand in agreement with its object. Consequently, the merely logical criterion of truth, namely, the accordance of a cognition with the universal and formal laws of understanding and reason, is nothing more than the *conditio sine quâ non*, or negative condition of all truth. Farther than this logic cannot go, and the error which depends not on the form, but on the content of the cognition, it has no test to discover.

General logic, then, resolves the whole formal business of understanding and reason into its elements, and exhibits them as principles of all logical judging of our cognitions. This part of logic may, therefore, be called *Analytic,* and is at least the negative test of truth, because all cognitions must first of all be estimated and tried according to these laws before we proceed to investigate them in respect of their content, in order to discover whether they contain positive truth in regard to their object. Because, however, the mere form of a cognition, accurately as it may accord with logical laws, is insufficient to supply us with material (objective) truth, no one, by means of logic alone, can venture to predicate anything of or decide concerning objects, unless he has obtained, independently of logic, well-grounded information about them, in order afterwards to examine, according to logical laws, into the use and connection, in a cohering whole, of that information, or, what is still better, merely to test it by them. Notwithstanding, there lies so seductive a charm in the possession of a specious art like this—an art which gives to all our cognitions the form of the understanding, although with respect to the content thereof we may be sadly deficient—that general logic, which is merely a canon of judgment, has been employed as an organon for the actual production, or rather for the semblance of production of objective assertions, and has thus been grossly misapplied. Now general logic, in its assumed character of organon, is called *Dialectic.*

Different as are the significations in which the ancients used this term for a science or an art, we may safely infer, from their actual employment of it, that with them it was nothing else than a logic of illusion—a sophistical art for giving ignorance, nay, even intentional sophistries, the coloring of truth, in which the thoroughness of procedure which logic requires was imitated, and their topic employed to cloak the empty pretensions. Now it may be taken as a safe and useful warning, that general logic, considered as an organon, must always be a logic of illusion, that is, be dialectical, for, as it teaches us nothing whatever respecting the content of our cognitions, but merely the formal conditions of their accordance with the understanding, which do not relate to and are quite indifferent in respect of objects, any attempt to employ it as an instrument (organon) in order to extend and enlarge the range of our knowledge must end in mere prating; anyone being able to maintain or oppose, with some appearance of truth, any single assertion whatever.

Such instruction is quite unbecoming the dignity of philosophy. For these reasons we have chosen to denominate this part of logic *Dialectic,* in the sense of a critique of dialectical illusion, and we wish the term to be so understood in this place.

IV.—OF THE DIVISION OF TRANSCENDENTAL LOGIC INTO TRANSCENDENTAL ANALYTIC AND DIALECTIC

In transcendental logic we isolate the understanding (as in transcendental æsthetic the sensibility) and select from our cognition merely that part of thought which has its origin in the understanding alone. The exercise of this pure cognition, however, depends upon this as its condition, that objects to which it may be applied be given to us in intuition, for without intuition, the whole of our cognition is without objects, and is therefore quite void. That part of transcendental logic, then, which of the elements of pure cognition of the understanding, and of the principles without which no object at all can be thought, is transcendental analytic, and at the same time a logic of truth. For no cognition can contradict it, without losing at the same time all content, that is, losing all reference to an object, and therefore all truth. But because we are very easily seduced into employing these pure cognitions and principles of the understanding by themselves, and that even beyond the boundaries of experience, which yet is the only source whence we can obtain matter (objects) on which those pure conceptions may be employed—understanding runs the risk of making, by means of empty sophisms, a material and objective use of the mere formal principles of the pure understanding, and of passing judgments on objects without distinction—objects which are not given to us, nay, perhaps cannot be given to us in any way. Now, as it ought properly to be only a canon for judging of the empirical use of the understanding, this kind of logic is misused when we seek to employ it as an organon of the universal and unlimited exercise of the understanding, and attempt with the pure understanding alone to judge synthetically, affirm, and determine respecting objects in general. In this case the exercise of the pure understanding becomes dialectical. The second part of our transcendental logic must therefore be a critique of dialectical illusion, and this critique we shall term Transcendental Dialectic—not meaning it as an art of producing dogmatically such illusion (an art which is unfortunately too current among the practitioners of metaphysical juggling), but as a critique of understanding and reason in regard to their hyperphysical use. This critique will expose the groundless nature of the pretensions of these two faculties, and invalidate their claims to the discovery and enlargement of our cognitions merely by means of transcendental principles, and show that the proper employment of these faculties is to test the judgments made by the pure understanding, and to guard it from sophistical delusion.

FIRST DIVISION

Transcendental Analytic

Transcendental analytic is the dissection of the whole of our *à priori* knowledge into the elements of the pure cognition of the understanding. In order to effect our purpose, it is necessary, 1st, that the conceptions be pure and not empirical; 2d, that they belong not to intuition and sensibility, but to thought and understanding; 3d, that they be elementary conceptions, and as such, quite different from deduced or compound conceptions; 4th, that our table of these elementary conceptions be complete, and fill up the whole sphere of the pure understanding. Now this completeness of a science cannot be accepted with confidence on the guarantee of a mere estimate of its existence in an aggregate formed only by means of repeated experiments and attempts. The completeness which we require is possible only by means of an idea of the totality of the *à priori* cognition of the understanding, and through the thereby determined division of the conceptions which form the said whole; consequently, only by means of their connection in a system. Pure understanding distinguishes itself not merely from everything empirical, but also completely from all sensibility. It is a unity self-subsistent, self-sufficient, and not to be enlarged by any additions from without. Hence the sum of its cognition constitutes a system to be determined by and comprised under an idea; and the completeness and articulation of this system can at the same time serve as a test of the correctness and genuineness of all the parts of cognition that belong to it. The whole of this part of transcendental logic consists of two books, of which the one contains the conceptions, and the other the principles of pure understanding.

BOOK I

ANALYTIC OF CONCEPTIONS

By the term "Analytic of Conceptions," I do not understand the analysis of these, or the usual process in philosophical investigations of dissecting the conceptions which present themselves, according to their content, and so making them clear; but I mean the hitherto little attempted dissection of the faculty of understanding itself, in order to investigate the possibility of conceptions à priori, by looking for them in the understanding alone, as their birthplace, and analyzing the pure use of this faculty. For this is the proper duty of a transcendental philosophy; what remains is the logical treatment of the conceptions in philosophy in general. We shall therefore follow up the pure conceptions even to their germs and beginnings in the human understanding, in which they lie, until they are developed on occasions presented by experience, and, freed by the same understanding from the empirical conditions attaching to them, are set forth in their unalloyed purity.

CHAPTER I

Of the Transcendental Clue to the Discovery of All Pure Conceptions of the Understanding

When we call into play a faculty of cognition, different conceptions manifest themselves according to the different circumstances, and make known this faculty, and assemble themselves into a more or less extensive collection, according to the time or penetration that has been applied to the consideration of them. Where this process, conducted as it is, mechanically, so to speak, will end, cannot be determined with certainty. Besides, the conceptions which we discover in this haphazard manner present themselves by no means in order and systematic unity, but are at last coupled together only according to resemblances to each other, and arranged in series, according to the quantity of their content, from the simpler to the more complex —series which are anything but systematic, though not altogether without a certain kind of method in their construction.

Transcendental philosophy has the advantage, and moreover the duty, of searching for its conceptions according to a principle; because these conceptions spring pure and unmixed out of the understanding as an absolute unity, and therefore must be connected with each other according to one conception or idea. A connection of this kind, however, furnishes us with a ready prepared rule, by which its proper place may be assigned to every pure conception of the understanding, and the completeness of the system of all be determined *à priori*—both which would otherwise have been dependent on mere choice or chance.

Transcendental Clue to the Discovery of All Pure Conceptions of the Understanding

Section I.—Of the Logical use of the Understanding in general

The understanding was defined above only negatively, as a non-sensuous faculty of cognition. Now, independently of sensibility, we cannot possibly have any intuition; consequently, the understanding is no faculty of intuition. But besides intuition there is no other mode of cognition, except through conceptions; consequently, the cognition of every, at least of every human, understanding is a cognition through conceptions —not intuitive, but discursive. All intuitions, as sensuous, depend on affections; conceptions, therefore, upon functions. By the word function, I understand the unity of the act of arranging diverse representations under one common representation. Conceptions, then, are based on the spontaneity of thought, as sensuous intuitions are on the receptivity of impressions. Now, the understanding cannot make any other use of these conceptions than to judge by means of them. As no representation, except an intuition, relates immediately to its object, a conception never relates immediately to an object, but only to some other representation thereof, be that an intuition or itself a conception. A judgment, therefore, is the mediate cognition of an object, consequently the representation of a representation of it. In every judgment there is a conception which applies to, and is valid for many other conceptions, and which among these comprehends also a given representation, this last being immediately connected with an object. For example, in the judgment—" All bodies are divisible," our conception of *divisible* applies to various other conceptions; among these, however, it is here particularly applied to the conception of body, and this conception of body relates to certain phenomena which occur to us. These objects, therefore, are mediately represented by the conception of divisibility. All judgments, accordingly, are functions of unity in our representations, inasmuch as, instead of an immediate, a higher representation, which comprises this and various others, is used for our cognition of the object, and thereby many possible cognitions are collected into one. But we can reduce all acts of the understanding to judgments, so that *understanding* may be represented as the *faculty of judging*. For it is, according to what has been said above, a faculty of thought. Now thought is cognition by means of conceptions. But conceptions, as predicates of possible judgments, relate to some representation of a yet undetermined object. Thus the conception of *body* indicates something— for example, metal—which can be cognized by means of that conception. It is therefore a conception, for the reason alone that other representations are contained under it, by means of which it can relate to objects. It is therefore the predicate to a possible judgment; for example, " Every metal is a body." All the functions of the understanding therefore can be discovered, when we can completely exhibit the functions of unity in judgments. And that this may be effected very easily, the following section will show.

Section II.—*Of the Logical Function of the Understanding in Judgments*

If we abstract all the content of a judgment, and consider only the intellectual form thereof, we find that the function of thought in a judgment can be brought under four heads, of which each contains three momenta. These may be conveniently represented in the following table:—

I

Quantity of judgments

Universal.
Particular.
Singular.

II   III
Quality   *Relation*
Affirmative.   Categorical.
Negative.   Hypothetical.
Infinite.   Disjunctive.

IV

Modality

Problematical.
Assertorical.
Apodictical.

As this division appears to differ in some, though not essential points, from the usual technic of logicians, the following observations, for the prevention of otherwise possible misunderstanding, will not be without their use.

1. Logicians say, with justice, that in the use of judgments in syllogisms, singular judgments may be treated like universal ones. For, precisely because a singular judgment has no extent at all, its predicate cannot refer to a part of that which is contained in the conception of the subject and be excluded from the rest. The predicate is valid for the whole conception just as if it were a general conception, and had extent, to the whole of which the predicate applied. On the other hand, let us compare a singular with a general judgment, merely as a cognition, in regard to quantity. The singular judgment relates to the general one, as unity to infinity, and is therefore in itself essentially different. Thus, if we estimate a singular judgment *judicium singulare*) not merely according to its intrinsic validity as a judgment, but also as a cognition generally, according to its quantity in comparison with that of other cognitions, it is then entirely different from a general judgment (*judicium com-*

mune), and in a complete table of the momenta of thought deserves a separate place—though, indeed, this would not be necessary in a logic limited to the consideration of the use of judgments in reference to each other.

2. In like manner, in transcendental logic, infinite must be distinguished from affirmative judgments, although in general logic they are rightly enough classed under affirmative. General logic abstracts all content of the predicate (though it be negative), and only considers whether the said predicate be affirmed or denied of the subject. But transcendental logic considers also the worth or content of this logical affirmation— an affirmation by means of a merely negative predicate, and inquires how much the sum total of our cognition gains by this affirmation. For example, if I say of the soul, " It is not mortal "—by this negative judgment I should at least ward off error. Now, by the proposition, " The soul is not mortal," I have, in respect of the logical form, really affirmed, inasmuch as I thereby place the soul in the unlimited sphere of immortal beings. Now, because, of the whole sphere of possible existences, the mortal occupies one part, and the immortal the other, neither more nor less is affirmed by the proposition, than that the soul is one among the infinite multitude of things which remain over, when I take away the whole mortal part. But by this proceeding we accomplish only this much, that the infinite sphere of all possible existences is in so far limited, that the mortal is excluded from it, and the soul is placed in the remaining part of the extent of this sphere. But this part remains, notwithstanding this exception, infinite, and more and more parts may be taken away from the whole sphere, without in the slightest degree thereby augmenting or affirmatively determining our conception of the soul. These judgments, therefore, infinite in respect of their logical extent, are, in respect of the content of their cognition, merely limitative; and are consequently entitled to a place in our transcendental table of all the momenta of thought in judgments, because the function of the understanding exercised by them may perhaps be of importance in the field of its pure *à priori* cognition.

3. All relations of thought in judgments are those (*a*) of the predicate to the subject; (*b*) of the principle to its consequence; (*c*) of the divided cognition and all the members of the division to each other. In the first of these three classes,

we consider only two conceptions; in the second, two judgments; in the third, several judgments in relation to each other.
The hypothetical proposition, "If perfect justice exists, the
obstinately wicked are punished," contains properly the relation
to each other of two propositions, namely, "Perfect justice exists," and "The obstinately wicked are punished." Whether
these propositions are in themselves true, is a question not here
decided. Nothing is cogitated by means of this judgment except a certain consequence. Finally, the disjunctive judgment
contains a relation of two or more propositions to each other—
a relation not of consequence, but of logical opposition, in so
far as the sphere of the one proposition excludes that of the
other. But it contains at the same time a relation of community, in so far as all the propositions taken together fill up the
sphere of the cognition. The disjunctive judgment contains,
therefore, the relation of the parts of the whole sphere of a
cognition, since the sphere of each part is a complemental part
of the sphere of the other, each contributing to form the sum
total of the divided cognition. Take, for example, the proposition, "The world exists either through blind chance, or
through internal necessity, or through an external cause."
Each of these propositions embraces a part of the sphere of
our possible cognition as to the existence of a world; all of
them taken together, the whole sphere. To take the cognition
out of one of these spheres is equivalent to placing it in one
of the others; and, on the other hand, to place it in one sphere
is equivalent to taking it out of the rest. There is, therefore,
in a disjunctive judgment a certain community of cognitions,
which consists in this, that they mutually exclude each other,
yet thereby determine, as a whole, the true cognition, inasmuch
as, taken together, they make up the complete content of a particular given cognition. And this is all that I find necessary,
for the sake of what follows, to remark in this place.

4. The modality of judgments is a quite peculiar function,
with this distinguishing characteristic, that it contributes nothing to the content of a judgment(for besides quantity, quality,
and relation, there is nothing more that constitutes the content
of a judgment), but concerns itself only with the value of the
copula in relation to thought in general. Problematical judgments are those in which the affirmation or negation is accepted
as merely possible (*ad libitum*). In the assertorical, we regard

the proposition as real (true) ; in the apodictical, we look on it as *necessary*.* Thus the two judgments (*antecedens et consequens*), the relation of which constitutes a hypothetical judgment, likewise those (the members of the division) in whose reciprocity the disjunctive consists, are only problematical. In the example above given, the proposition, " There exists perfect justice," is not stated assertorically, but as an *ad libitum* judgment, which someone may choose to adopt, and the consequence alone is assertorical. Hence such judgments may be obviously false, and yet, taken problematically, be conditions of our cognition of the truth. Thus the proposition, " The world exists only by blind chance," is in the disjunctive judgment of problematical import only: that is to say, one may accept it for the moment, and it helps us (like the indication of the wrong road among all the roads that one can take) to find out the true proposition. The problematical proposition is, therefore, that which expresses only logical possibility (which is not objective) ; that is, it expresses a free choice to admit the validity of such a proposition—a merely arbitrary reception of it into the understanding. The assertorical speaks of logical reality or truth ; as, for example, in a hypothetical syllogism, the *antecedens* presents itself in a problematical form in the *major*, in an assertorical form in the *minor*, and it shows that the proposition is in harmony with the laws of the understanding. The apodictical proposition cogitates the assertorical as determined by these very laws of the understanding, consequently as affirming *à priori*, and in this manner it expresses logical necessity. Now because all is here gradually incorporated with the understanding—inasmuch as in the first place we judge problematically; then accept assertorically our judgment as true; lastly, affirm it as inseparably united with the understanding, that is, as necessary and apodictical—we may safely reckon these three functions of modality as so many momenta of thought.

---

* Just as if thought were in the first instance a function of the *understanding;* in the second, of *judgment;* in the third of *reason*. A remark which will be explained in the sequel.

Section III.—Of the pure Conceptions of the Understanding, or Categories

General logic, as has been repeatedly said, makes abstraction of all content of cognition, and expects to receive representations from some other quarter, in order, by means of analysis, to convert them into conceptions. On the contrary, transcendental logic has lying before it the manifold content of *à priori* sensibility, which transcendental æsthetic presents to it in order to give matter to the pure conceptions of the understanding, without which transcendental logic would have no content, and be therefore utterly void. Now space and time contain an infinite diversity of determinations of pure *à priori* intuition, but are nevertheless the condition of the mind's receptivity, under which alone it can obtain representations of objects, and which, consequently, must always affect the conception of these objects. But the spontaneity of thought requires that this diversity be examined after a certain manner, received into the mind, and connected, in order afterwards to form a cognition out of it. This process I call synthesis.

By the word *synthesis,* in its most general signification, I understand the process of joining different representations to each other, and of comprehending their diversity in one cognition. This synthesis is pure when the diversity is not given empirically but *à priori* (as that in space and time). Our representations must be given previously to any analysis of them; and no conceptions can arise, *quoad* their content, analytically. But the synthesis of a diversity (be it given *à priori* or empirically) is the first requisite for the production of a cognition, which in its beginning, indeed, may be crude and confused, and therefore in need of analysis—still, synthesis is that by which alone the elements of our cognitions are collected and united into a certain content, consequently it is the first thing on which we must fix our attention, if we wish to investigate the origin of our knowledge.

Synthesis, generally speaking, is, as we shall afterwards see, the mere operation of the imagination—a blind but indispensable function of the soul, without which we should have no cognition whatever, but of the working of which we are seldom even conscious. But to reduce this synthesis to conceptions is a function of the understanding, by means of which we attain to cognition, in the proper meaning of the term.

Pure synthesis, represented generally, gives us the pure conception of the understanding. But by this pure synthesis, I mean that which rests upon a basis of *à priori* synthetical unity. Thus, our numeration (and this is more observable in large numbers) is a synthesis according to conceptions, because it takes place according to a common basis of unity (for example, the decade). By means of this conception, therefore, the unity in the synthesis of the manifold becomes necessary.

By means of analysis different representations are brought under one conception—an operation of which general logic treats. On the other hand, the duty of transcendental logic is to reduce to conceptions, not representations, but the pure synthesis of representations. The first thing which must be given to us in order to the *à priori* cognition of all objects, is the diversity of the pure intuition; the synthesis of this diversity by means of the imagination is the second; but this gives, as yet, no cognition. The conceptions which give unity to this pure synthesis, and which consist solely in the representation of this necessary synthetical unity, furnish the third requisite for the cognition of an object, and these conceptions are given by the understanding.

The same function which gives unity to the different representations in a judgment, gives also unity to the mere synthesis of different representations in an intuition; and this unity we call the pure conception of the understanding. Thus, the same understanding, and by the same operations, whereby in conceptions, by means of analytical unity, it produced the logical form of a judgment, introduces, by means of the synthetical unity of the manifold in intuition, a transcendental content into its representations, on which account they are called pure conceptions of the understanding, and they apply *à priori* to objects, a result not within the power of general logic.

In this manner, there arise exactly so many pure conceptions of the understanding, applying *à priori* to objects of intuition in general, as there are logical functions in all possible judgments. For there is no other function or faculty existing in the understanding besides those enumerated in that table. These conceptions we shall, with Aristotle, call categories, our purpose being originally identical with his, notwithstanding the great difference in the execution.

TABLE OF THE CATEGORIES.

I.	II
Of Quantity	*Of Quality*
Unity.	Reality.
Plurality.	Negation.
Totality.	Limitation.

III

Of Relation

Of Inherence and Subsistence (substantia et accidens).
Of Causality and Dependence (cause and effect).
Of Community (reciprocity between the agent and patient).

IV

Of Modality

Possibility.—Impossibility.
Existence.—Non-existence.
Necessity.—Contingence.

This, then, is a catalogue of all the originally pure conceptions of the synthesis which the understanding contains *à priori*, and these conceptions alone entitle it to be called a pure understanding; inasmuch as only by them it can render the manifold of intuition conceivable, in other words, think an object of intuition. This division is made systematically from a common principle, namely, the faculty of judgment (which is just the same as the power of thought), and has not arisen rhapsodically from a search at haphazard after pure conceptions, respecting the full number of which we never could be certain, inasmuch as we employ induction alone in our search, without considering that in this way we can never understand wherefore precisely these conceptions, and none others abide in the pure understanding. It was a design worthy of an acute thinker like Aristotle, to search for these fundamental conceptions. Destitute, however, of any guiding principle, he picked them up just as they occurred to him, and at first hunted out ten, which he called *categories* (*predicaments*). Afterwards he believed that he had discovered five others, which were added under the name of *post predicaments*. But his catalogue still remained defective. Besides, there are to be found among them some of the modes of pure sensibility (*quando, ubi, situs,* also *prius, simul*), and likewise an empirical conception (*motus*)—which can by no means belong to this genealogical register of the pure understanding. Moreover, there are deduced conceptions (*actio, passio*), enumerated among the original conceptions, and of the latter, some are entirely wanting.

With regard to these, it is to be remarked, that the categories, as the true primitive conceptions of the pure understanding, have also their pure deduced conceptions, which, in a complete system of transcendental philosophy, must by no means be passed over; though in a merely critical essay we must be contented with the simple mention of the fact.

Let it be allowed me to call these pure, but deduced conceptions of the understanding, the *predicables* of the pure understanding, in contradistinction to predicaments. If we are in possession of the original and primitive, the deduced and subsidiary conceptions can easily be added, and the genealogical tree of the understanding completely delineated. As my present aim is not to set forth a complete system, but merely the principles of one, I reserve this task for another time. It may be easily executed by anyone who will refer to the ontological manuals, and subordinate to the category of causality, for example, the predicables of force, action, passion; to that of community, those of presence and resistance; to the categories of modality, those of origination, extinction, change; and so with the rest. The categories combined with the modes of pure sensibility, or with one another, afford a great number of deduced à *priori* conceptions; a complete enumeration of which would be a useful and not unpleasant, but in this place a perfectly dispensable, occupation.

I purposely omit the definitions of the categories in this treatise. I shall analyze these conceptions only so far as is necessary for the doctrine of method, which is to form a part of this critique. In a system of pure reason, definitions of them would be with justice demanded of me, but to give them here would only hide from our view the main aim of our investigation, at the same time raising doubts and objections, the consideration of which, without injustice to our main purpose, may be very well postponed till another opportunity. Meanwhile, it ought to be sufficiently clear, from the little we have already said on this subject, that the formation of a complete vocabulary of pure conceptions, accompanied by all the requisite explanations, is not only a possible but an easy undertaking. The compartments already exist; it is only necessary to fill them up; and a systematic topic like the present indicates with perfect precision the proper place to which each conception belongs, while it readily points out any that have not yet been filled up.

Our table of the categories suggests considerations of some importance, which may perhaps have significant results in regard to the scientific form of all rational cognitions. For, that this table is useful in the theoretical part of philosophy, nay, indispensable for the sketching of the complete plan of a science, so far as that science rests upon conceptions à priori, and for dividing it mathematically, according to fixed principles, is most manifest from the fact that it contains all the elementary conceptions of the understanding, nay, even the form of a system of these in the understanding itself, and consequently indicates all the momenta, and also the internal arrangement of a projected speculative science, as I have elsewhere shown.* Here follow some of these observations.

I. This table, which contains four classes of conceptions of the understanding, may, in the first instance, be divided into two classes, the first of which relates to objects of intuition—pure as well as empirical; the second, to the existence of these objects, either in relation to one another, or to the understanding.

The former of these classes of categories I would entitle the *mathematical,* and the latter the *dynamical* categories. The former, as we see, has no correlates; these are only to be found in the second class. This difference must have a ground in the nature of the human understanding.

II. The number of the categories in each class is always the same, namely, three;—a fact which also demands some consideration, because in all other cases division à priori through conceptions is necessarily dichotomy. It is to be added, that the third category in each triad always arises from the combination of the second with the first.

* In the " Metaphysical Principles of Natural Science."

Thus Totality is nothing else but Plurality contemplated as Unity; Limitation is merely Reality conjoined with Negation; Community is the Causality of a Substance, reciprocally determining, and determined by other substances; and finally, Necessity is nothing but Existence, which is given through the Possibility itself. Let it not be supposed, however, that the third category is merely a deduced, and not a primitive conception of the pure understanding. For the conjunction of the first and second, in order to produce the third conception, requires a particular function of the understanding, which is by, no means identical with those which are exercised in the first and second. Thus, the conception of a number (which belongs to the category of Totality), is not always possible, where the conceptions of multitude and unity exist (for example, in the representation of the infinite). Or, if I conjoin the conception of a cause with that of a substance, it does not follow that the conception of *influence*, that is, how one substance can be the cause of something in another substance, will be understood from that. Thus it is evident, that a particular act of the understanding is here necessary; and so in the other instances.

III. With respect to one category, namely, that of community, which is found in the third class, it is not so easy as with the others to detect its accordance with the form of the disjunctive judgment which corresponds to it in the table of the logical functions.

In order to assure ourselves of this accordance, we must observe: that in every disjunctive judgment, the sphere of the judgment (that is, the complex of all that is contained in it) is represented as a whole divided into parts; and, since one part cannot be contained in the other, they are cogitated as co-ordinated with, not subordinated to each other, so that they do not determine each other unilaterally, as in a linear series, but reciprocally, as in an aggregate—(if one member of the division is posited, all the rest are excluded; and conversely).

Now a like connection is cogitated in a whole of things; for one thing is not subordinated, as effect, to another as cause of its existence, but, on the contrary, is co-ordinated contemporaneously and reciprocally, as a cause in relation to the determination of the others (for example, in a body—the parts of which mutually attract and repel each other). And this is an entirely different kind of connection from that which we find in the mere relation of the cause to the effect (the principle to the consequence), for in such a connection the consequence does not in its turn determine the principle, and therefore does not constitute, with the latter, a whole—just as the Creator does not with the world make up a whole. The process of understanding by which it represents to itself the sphere of a divided conception, is employed also when we think of a thing as divisible; and, in the same manner as the members of the division in the former exclude one another, and yet are connected in one sphere, so the understanding represents to itself the parts of the latter, as having—each of them—an existence (as substances), independently of the others, and yet as united in one whole.

In the transcendental philosophy of the ancients, there exists one more leading division, which contains pure conceptions of the understanding, and which, although not numbered among the categories, ought, according to them, as conceptions *à priori,* to be valid of objects. But in this case they would augment the number of the categories; which cannot be. These are set forth in the proposition, so renowned among the schoolmen—" *Quodlibet ens est unum, verum, bonum.*" Now, though the inferences from this principle were mere tautological propositions, and though it is allowed only by courtesy to retain a place in modern metaphysics, yet a thought which maintained itself for such a length of time, however empty it seems to be, deserves an investigation of its origin, and justifies the conjecture that it must be grounded in some law of the understanding, which, as is often the case, has only been erroneously interpreted. These pretended transcendental predicates are, in fact, nothing but logical requisites and criteria of all cognition of objects, and they employ, as the basis for this cognition, the categories of Quantity, namely, Unity, Plurality, and Totality. But these, which must be taken as material conditions, that is, as belonging to the possibility of things themselves, they employed merely in a formal signification, as belonging to the logical requisites of all cognition, and yet most unguardedly changed these criteria of thought into properties of objects, as things in themselves. Now, in every cognition of an object, there is *unity* of conception, which may be called *qualitative unity,* so far as by this term we understand only the unity in our connection of the manifold; for example, unity of the theme in a play, an oration, or a story. Secondly, there is *truth* in respect of the deductions from it. The more true deductions we have from a given conception, the more criteria of its objective reality. This we might call the *qualitative plurality* of characteristic marks, which belong to a conception as to a common foundation, but are not cogitated as a quantity in it. Thirdly, there is *perfection*—which consists in this, that the plurality falls back upon the unity of the conception, and accords completely with that conception, and with no other. This we may denominate *qualitative completeness*. Hence it is evident that these logical criteria of the possibility of cognition are merely the three categories of Quantity modified and transformed to suit an unauthorized manner of applying them. That is to say, the three categories, in which the unity of the production of the quantum must be homogeneous throughout, are transformed solely with a view to the connection of heterogeneous parts of cognition in one act of consciousness, by means of the quality of the cognition, which is the principle of that connection. Thus the criterion of the possibility of a conception (not of its object) is the definition of it, in which the unity of the conception, the truth of all that may be immediately deduced from it, and finally, the completeness of what has been thus deduced, constitute the requisites for the reproduction of the whole conception. Thus, also, the criterion or test of an hypothesis is the intelligibility of the received principle of explanation, or its unity (without help from any subsidiary hypothesis)—the truth of our deductions from it (consistency with each other and with experience) —and lastly, the completeness of the principle of the explanation of these deductions, which refer to neither more nor less than what was admitted in the hypothesis, restoring analytically and *à posteriori*, what was cogitated synthetically and *à priori*. By the conceptions, therefore, of Unity, Truth, and Perfection, we have made no addition to the transcendental table of the categories, which is complete without them. We have, on the contrary, merely employed the three categories of quantity, setting aside their application to objects of experience, as general logical laws of the consistency of cognition with itself.

Chapter II

Of the Deduction of the Pure Conceptions of the Understanding

SECTION I

Of the Principles of a Transcendental Deduction in general

Teachers of jurisprudence, when speaking of rights and claims, distinguish in a cause the question of right (*quid juris*) from the question of fact (*quid facti*), and while they demand proof of both, they give to the proof of the former, which goes to establish right or claim in law, the name of *Deduction*. Now we make use of a great number of empirical conceptions, without opposition from anyone; and consider ourselves, even without any attempt at deduction, justified in attaching to them a sense, and a supposititious signification, because we have always experience at hand to demonstrate their objective reality. There exist also, however, usurped conceptions, such as *fortune, fate,* which circulate with almost universal indulgence, and yet are occasionally challenged by the question, *quid juris?* In such cases, we have great difficulty in discovering any deduction for these terms, inasmuch as we cannot produce any manifest ground of right, either from experience or from reason, on which the claim to employ them can be founded.

Among the many conceptions, which make up the very variegated web of human cognition, some are destined for pure use *à priori,* independent of all experience; and their title to be so employed always requires a deduction inasmuch as, to justify such use of them, proofs from experience are not sufficient; but it is necessary to know how these conceptions can apply to objects without being derived from experience. I term, therefore, an explanation of the manner in which conceptions can apply *à priori* to objects, the *transcendental deduction* of conceptions, and I distinguish it from the *empirical* deduction, which indicates the mode in which a conception is obtained through experience and reflection thereon; consequently, does not concern itself with the right, but only with the fact of our obtaining conceptions in such and such a manner. We have already seen that we are in possession of two perfectly different kinds of conceptions, which nevertheless agree with each other in this, that they both apply to objects completely *à priori*. These are the conceptions of space and time as forms of sensibility, and the categories as pure conceptions of the understanding. To attempt an empirical deduction of either of these classes would be labor in vain, because the distinguishing characteristic of their nature consists in this, that they apply to their objects, without having borrowed anything from experience towards the representation of them. Consequently, if a deduction of these conceptions is necessary, it must always be transcendental.

Meanwhile, with respect to these conceptions, as with respect to all our cognition, we certainly may discover in experience, if not the principle of their possibility, yet the occasioning causes of their production. It will be found that the impressions of sense give the first occasion for bringing into action the whole faculty of cognition, and for the production of experience, which contains two very dissimilar elements, namely, a matter for cognition, given by the senses, and a certain form for the arrangement of this matter, arising out of the inner fountain of pure intuition and thought; and these, on occasion given by sensuous impressions, are called into exercise and produce conceptions. Such an investigation into the first efforts of our faculty of cognition to mount from particular perceptions to general conceptions, is undoubtedly of great utility; and we have to thank the celebrated Locke, for having first opened the way for this inquiry. But a deduction of the pure *à priori* conceptions of course never can be made in this way, seeing that, in regard to their future employment, which must be entirely independent of experience, they must have a far different certificate of birth to show from that of a descent from experience. This attempted physiological derivation, which cannot properly be called deduction, because it relates merely to a *quæstio facti*, I shall entitle an explanation of the *possession* of a pure cognition. It is therefore manifest that there can only be a transcendental deduction of these conceptions, and by no means an empirical one; also, that all attempts at an empirical deduction, in regard to pure *à priori* conceptions, are vain, and can only be made by one who does not understand the altogether peculiar nature of these cognitions.

But although it is admitted that the only possible deduction of pure *à priori* cognition is a transcendental deduction, it is not, for that reason, perfectly manifest that such a deduction is absolutely necessary. We have already traced to their sources the conceptions of space and time, by means of a transcendental deduction, and we have explained and determined their objective validity *à priori*. Geometry, nevertheless, advances steadily and securely in the province of pure *à priori* cognitions, without needing to ask from Philosophy any certificate as to the pure and legitimate origin of its fundamental conception of space. But the use of the conception in this science extends only to the external world of sense, the pure form of the intuition of which is space; and in *this* world, therefore, all geometrical cognition, because it is founded upon *à priori* intuition, possesses immediate evidence, and the objects of this cognition are given *à priori* (as regards their form) in intuition by and through the cognition itself. With the pure conceptions of Understanding, on the contrary, commences the absolute necessity of seeking a transcendental deduction, not only of these conceptions themselves, but likewise of space, because, inasmuch as they make affirmations concerning objects not by means of the predicates of intuition and sensibility, but of pure thought *à priori*, they apply to objects without any of the conditions of sensibility. Besides, not being founded on experience, they are not presented with any object in *à priori* intuition upon which, antecedently to experience, they might base their synthesis. Hence results, not only doubt as to the objective validity and proper limits of their use, but that even our conception of space is rendered equivocal; inasmuch as we are very ready with the aid of the categories, to carry the use of this conception beyond the conditions of sensuous intuition;—and for this reason, we have already found a transcendental deduction of it needful. The reader, then, must be quite convinced of the absolute necessity of a transcendental deduction, before taking a single step in the field of pure reason; because otherwise he goes to work blindly, and after he has wandered about in all directions, returns to the state of utter ignorance from which he started. He ought, moreover, clearly to recognize beforehand, the unavoidable difficulties in his undertaking, so that he may not afterwards complain of the obscurity in which the subject itself is deeply involved, or become too soon impatient of the obstacles in his path;—because we have a choice of only two things—either at once to give up all pretensions to knowledge beyond the limits of possible experience, or to bring this critical investigation to completion.

We have been able, with very little trouble, to make it comprehensible how the conceptions of space and time, although *à priori* cognitions, must necessarily apply to external objects, and render a synthetical cognition of these possible, independently of all experience. For inasmuch as only by means of such pure form of sensibility an object can appear to us, that is, be an object of empirical intuition, space and time are pure intuitions, which contain *à priori* the condition of the possibility of objects as phenomena, and an *à priori* synthesis in these intuitions possesses objective validity.

On the other hand, the categories of the understanding do not represent the conditions under which objects are given to us in intuition; objects can consequently appear to us without necessarily connecting themselves with these, and consequently without any necessity binding on the understanding to contain *à priori* the conditions of these objects. Thus we find ourselves involved in a difficulty which did not present itself in the sphere of sensibility, that is to say, we cannot discover *how the subjective conditions of thought can have objective validity,* in other words, can become conditions of the possibility of all cognition of objects;—for phenomena may certainly be given to us in intuition without any help from the functions of the understanding. Let us take, for example, the conception of *cause,* which indicates a peculiar kind of synthesis, namely, that with something, A, something entirely different, B, is connected according to a law. It is not *à priori* manifest why phenomena should contain anything of this kind (we are of course debarred from appealing for proof to experience, for the objective validity of this conception must be demonstrated *à priori*), and it hence remains doubtful *à priori,* whether such a conception be not quite void, and without any corresponding object among phenomena. For that objects of sensuous intuition must correspond to the formal conditions of sensibility existing *à priori* in the mind, is quite evident, from the fact, that without these they could not be objects for us; but that they must also correspond to the conditions which understanding requires for the synthetical unity or thought, is an assertion, the grounds for which are not so easily to be discovered. For phenomena might be so constituted, as not to correspond to the conditions of the unity of thought; and all things might lie in such confusion, that, for example, nothing could be met with in the sphere of phenomena to suggest a law of synthesis, and so correspond to the conception of cause and effect; so that this conception would be quite void, null, and without significance. Phenomena would nevertheless continue to present objects to our intuition; for mere intuition does not in any respect stand in need of the functions of thought.

If we thought to free ourselves from the labor of these investigations by saying, " Experience is constantly offering us examples of the relation of cause and effect in phenomena, and presents us with abundant opportunity of abstracting the conception of cause, and so at the same time of corroborating the objective validity of this conception; "—we should in this case be overlooking the fact, that the conception of cause cannot arise in this way at all; that, on the contrary, it must either have an *à priori* basis in the understanding, or be rejected as a mere chimera. For this conception demands that something, A, should be of such a nature, that something else, B, should follow from it necessarily, and according to an absolutely universal law. We may certainly collect from phenomena a law, according to which this or that *usually* happens, but the element of necessity is not to be found in it. Hence it is evident that to the synthesis of cause and effect belongs a dignity, which is utterly wanting in any empirical synthesis; for it is no mere mechanical synthesis, by means of addition, but a dynamical one, that is to say, the effect is not to be cogitated as merely annexed to the cause, but as posited by and through the cause, and resulting from it. The strict universality of this law never can be a characteristic of empirical laws, which obtain through induction only a comparative universality, that is, an extended range of practical application. But the pure conceptions of the understanding would entirely lose all their peculiar character if we treated them merely as the productions of experience.

Transition to the Transcendental Deduction of the Categories

There are only two possible ways in which synthetical representation and its objects can coincide with and relate necessarily to each other, and, as it were, meet together. Either the object alone makes the representation possible, or the representation alone makes the object possible. In the former case, the relation between them is only empirical, and an *à priori* representation is impossible. And this is the case with phenomena, as regards that in them which is referable to mere sensation. In the latter case—although representation alone (for of its causality, by means of the will, we do not here speak), does not produce the object as to its existence, it must nevertheless be *à priori* determinative in regard to the object, if it is only by means of the representation that we can cognize anything as an object. Now there are only two conditions of the possibility of a cognition of objects; firstly, *Intuition*, by means of which the object, though only as phenomenon, is given; secondly, *Conception*, by means of which the object which corresponds to this intuition is thought. But it is evident from what has been said on æsthetic, that the first condition, under which alone objects can be intuited, must in fact exist, as a formal basis for them, *à priori* in the mind. With this formal condition of sensibility, therefore, all phenomena necessarily correspond, because it is only through it that they can be phenomena at all; that is, can be empirically intuited and given. Now the question is, whether there do not exist *à priori* in the mind, conceptions of understanding also, as conditions under which alone something, if not intuited, is yet thought as object. If this question be answered in the affirmative, it follows that all empirical cognition of objects is necessarily conformable to such conceptions, since, if they are not presupposed, it is impossible that anything can be an object of experience. Now all experience contains, besides the intuition of the senses through which an object is given, a *conception* also of an object that is given in intuition. Accordingly, conceptions of objects in general must lie as *à priori* conditions at the foundation of all empirical cognition; and consequently, the objective validity of the categories, as *à priori* conceptions, will rest upon *this*, that experience (as far as regards the form of thought) is possible only by their means. For in that case they apply necessarily and *à priori* to objects of experience, because only through them can an object of experience be thought.

The whole aim of the transcendental deduction of all *à priori* conceptions is to show that these conceptions are *à priori* conditions of the possibility of all experience. Conceptions which afford us the objective foundation of the possibility of experience, are for that very reason necessary. But the analysis of the experiences in which they are met with is not deduction, but only an illustration of them, because from experience they could never derive the attribute of necessity. Without their original applicability and relation to all possible experience, in which all objects of cognition present themselves, the relation of the categories to objects, of whatever nature, would be quite incomprehensible.

The celebrated Locke, for want of due reflection on these points, and because he met with pure conceptions of the understanding in experience, sought also to deduce them from experience, and yet proceeded so inconsequently as to attempt, with their aid, to arrive at cognitions which lie far beyond the limits of all experience. David Hume perceived that, to render this possible, it was necessary that the conceptions should have an *à priori* origin. But as he could not explain how it was possible that conceptions which are not connected with each other in the understanding, must nevertheless be thought as necessarily connected in the object—and it never occurred to him that the understanding itself might, perhaps, by means of these conceptions, be the author of the experience in which its objects were presented to it—he was forced to derive these conceptions from experience, that is from a subjective necessity arising from repeated association of experiences erroneously considered to be objective—in one word, from " *habit.*" But he proceeded with perfect consequence, and declared it to be impossible with such conceptions and the principles arising from them, to overstep the limits of experience. The empirical derivation, however, which both of these philosophers attributed to these conceptions, cannot possibly be reconciled with the fact that we do possess scientific *à priori* cognitions, namely, those of pure mathematics and general physics.

The former of these two celebrated men opened a wide door to extravagance—(for if reason has once undoubted right on its side, it will not allow itself to be confined to set limits, by vague recommendations of moderation) ; the latter gave himself up entirely to scepticism—a natural consequence, after having discovered, as he thought, that the faculty of cognition was not trustworthy. We now intend to make a trial whether it be not possible safely to conduct reason between these two rocks, to assign her determinate limits, and yet leave open for her the entire sphere of her legitimate activity.

I shall merely premise an explanation of what the categories are. They are conceptions of an object in general, by means of which its intuition is contemplated as determined in relation to one of the logical functions of judgment. The following will make this plain. The function of the categorical judgment is that of the relation of subject to predicate; for example, in the proposition, " All bodies are divisible." But in regard to the merely logical use of the understanding, it still remains undetermined to which of these two conceptions belongs the function of subject, and to which that of predicate. For we could also say, " Some divisible is a body." But the category of substance, when the conception of a body is brought under it, determines that; and its empirical intuition in experience must be contemplated always as subject, and never as mere predicate. And so with all the other categories.

SECTION II

Of the Possibility of a Conjunction of the Manifold Representations given by Sense

The manifold content in our representations can be given in an intuition which is merely sensuous—in other words, is nothing but susceptibility; and the form of this intuition can exist à priori in our faculty of representation, without being anything else but the mode in which the subject is affected. But the conjunction (conjunctio) of a manifold in intuition never can be given us by the senses; it cannot therefore be contained in the pure form of sensuous intuition, for it is a spontaneous act of the faculty of representation. And as we must, to distinguish it from sensibility, entitle this faculty understanding; so all conjunction—whether conscious or unconscious, be it of the manifold in intuition, sensuous or nonsensuous, or of several conceptions—is an act of the understanding. To this act we shall give the general appellation of synthesis, thereby to indicate, at the same time, that we cannot represent anything as conjoined in the object without having previously conjoined it ourselves. Of all mental notions, that of conjunction is the only one which cannot be given through objects, but can be originated only by the subject itself, because it is an act of its purely spontaneous activity. The reader will easily enough perceive that the possibility of conjunction must be grounded in the very nature of this act, and that it must be equally valid for all conjunction; and that analysis, which appears to be its contrary, must, nevertheless, always presuppose it; for where the understanding has not previously conjoined, it cannot dissect or analyze, because only as conjoined by it, must that which is to be analyzed have been given to our faculty of representation.

But the conception of conjunction includes, besides the conception of the manifold and of the synthesis of it, that of the unity of it also. Conjunction is the representation of the synthetical unity of the manifold.* This idea of unity, therefore, cannot arise out of that of conjunction; much rather does that idea, by combining itself with the representation of the manifold, render the conception of conjunction possible. This unity, which à priori precedes all conceptions of conjunction, is not the category of unity; for all the categories are based upon logical functions of judgment, and in these functions we already have conjunction, and consequently unity of given conceptions. It is therefore evident that the category of unity presupposes conjunction. We must therefore look still higher for this unity, in that, namely, which contains the ground of the unity of diverse conceptions in judgments, the ground, consequently, of the possibility of the existence of the understanding, even in regard to its logical use.

Of the Originally Synthetical Unity of Apperception

The *I think* must accompany all my representations, for otherwise something would be represented in me which could not be thought; in other words, the representation would either be impossible, or at least be, in relation to me, nothing. That representation which can be given previously to all thought, is called intuition. All the diversity or manifold content of intuition, has, therefore, a necessary relation to the *I think*, in the subject in which this diversity is found. But this repre-

* Whether the representations are in themselves identical, and consequently whether one can be thought analytically by means of and through the other, is a question which we need not at present consider. Our *consciousness* of the one, when we speak of the manifold, is always distinguishable from our consciousness of the other; and it is only respecting the synthesis of this (possible) consciousness that we here treat.

sentation, *I think,* is an act of *spontaneity;* that is to say, it cannot be regarded as belonging to mere sensibility. I call it pure apperception,* in order to distinguish it from empirical; or primitive apperception, because it is a self-consciousness which, while it gives birth to the representation *I think,* must necessarily be capable of accompanying all our representations. It is in all acts of consciousness one and the same, and unaccompanied by it, no representation can exist *for me.* The unity of this apperception I call the transcendental unity of self-consciousness, in order to indicate the possibility of *à priori* cognition arising from it. For the manifold representations which are given in an intuition would not all of them be my representations, if they did not all belong to one self-consciousness, that is, as my representations (even although I am not conscious of them as such), they must conform to the condition under which alone they can exist altogether in a common self-consciousness, because otherwise they would not all without exception belong to me. From this primitive conjunction follow many important results.

For example, this universal identity of the apperception of the manifold given in intuition, contains a synthesis of representations, and is possible only by means of the consciousness of this synthesis. For the empirical consciousness which accompanies different representations is in itself fragmentary and disunited, and without relation to the identity of the subject. This relation, then does not exist because I accompany every representation with consciousness, but because I join one representation to another, and am conscious of the synthesis of them. Consequently, only because I can connect a variety of given representations in one consciousness, is it possible that I can represent to myself the identity of consciousness in these representations; in other words, the analytical unity of apperception is possible only under the presupposition of a synthetical unity.† The thought, " These representations given in intui-

---

* *Apperception* simply means consciousness. But it has been considered better to employ this term, not only because Kant saw fit to have another word besides *Bewusstseyn,* but because the term *consciousness* denotes a *state, apperception* an *act* of the *ego;* and from this alone the superiority of the latter is apparent. J. M. D. M.

† All general conceptions—as such—depend, for their existence, on the analytical unity of consciousness. For example, when I think of *red* in general, I thereby think to myself a property which (as a characteristic mark) can be discovered somewhere, or can be united with other representations; consequently, it is only by means of a forethought possible synthetical unity that I can think to myself the analytical. A representation which is cogitated as common to *different* representations is regarded as belonging to such as, besides this common representation, contain something *different;* consequently it must be previously thought in syntheti-

tion, belong all of them to me," is accordingly just the same as, " I unite them in one self-consciousness, or can at least so unite them;" and although this thought is not itself the consciousness of the synthesis of representations, it presupposes the possibility of it; that is to say, for the reason alone, that I can comprehend the variety of my representations in one consciousness, do I call them my representations, for otherwise I must have as many-colored and various a self as are the representations of which I am conscious. Synthetical unity of the manifold in intuitions, as given *à priori,* is therefore the foundation of the identity of apperception itself, which antecedes *à priori* all determinate thought. But the conjunction of representations into a conception is not to be found in objects themselves, nor can it be, as it were, borrowed from them and taken up into the understanding by perception, but it is on the contrary an operation of the understanding itself, which is nothing more than the faculty of conjoining *à priori,* and of bringing the variety of given representations under the unity of apperception. This principle is the highest in all human cognition.

This fundamental principle of the necessary unity of apperception is indeed an identical, and therefore analytical proposition; but it nevertheless explains the necessity for a synthesis of the manifold given in an intuition, without which the identity of self-consciousness would be incogitable. For the Ego, as a simple representation, presents us with no manifold content; only in intuition, which is quite different from the representation Ego, can it be given us, and by means of conjunction, it is cogitated in one self-consciousness. An understanding, in which all the manifold should be given by means of consciousness itself, would be intuitive; our understanding can only think, and must look for its intuition to sense. I am, therefore, conscious of my identical self, in relation to all the variety of representations given to me in an intuition, because I call all of them my representations   In other words, I am conscious myself of a necessary *à priori* synthesis of my representations, which is called the original synthetical unity of apperception, under which rank all the representations presented to me, but that only by means of a synthesis.

cal unity with other although only possible representations, before I can think in it he analytical unity of consciousness which makes it a *conceptas communis.* And thus the synthetical unity of apperception is the highest point with which we must connect every operation of the understanding, even the whole of logic, and after it our transcendental philosophy; indeed, this faculty is the understanding itself.

The principle of the Synthetical Unity of Apperception is the highest principle of all exercise of the Understanding

The supreme principle of the possibility of all intuition in relation to sensibility was, according to our transcendental æsthetic, that all the manifold in intuition be subject to the formal conditions of Space and Time. The supreme principle of the possibility of it in relation to the Understanding is: that all the manifold in it be subject to conditions of the originally synthetical Unity of Apperception.* To the former of these two principles are subject all the various representations of Intuition, in so far as they are given to us; to the latter, in so far as they must be capable of conjunction in one consciousness; for without this nothing can be thought or cognized, because the given representations would not have in common the act of the apperception *I think;* and therefore could not be connected in one self-consciousness.

Understanding is, to speak generally, *the faculty of Cognitions.* These consist in the determined relation of given representations to an object. But an object is that in the conception of which the manifold in a given intuition is united. Now all union of representations requires unity of consciousness in the synthesis of them. Consequently, it is the unity of consciousness alone that constitutes the possibility of representations relating to an object, and therefore of their objective validity, and of their becoming cognitions, and consequently, the possibility of the existence of the understanding itself.

The first pure cognition of understanding, then, upon which is founded all its other exercise, and which is at the same time perfectly independent of all conditions of mere sensuous intuition, is the principle of the original synthetical unity of apperception. Thus the mere form of external sensuous intuition, namely, space, affords us, *per se,* no cognition; it merely contributes the manifold à *priori* intuition to a possible cognition. But, in order to cognize something in space (for example, a line), I must draw it, and thus produce synthetically a deter-

---

* Space and Time, and all portions thereof, are *Intuitions;* consequently are, with a manifold for their content, single representations. (See the *Transcendental Æsthetic.*) Consequently, they are not pure conceptions, by means of which the same consciousness is found in a great number of representations; but, on the contrary, they are many representations contained in one, the consciousness of which is, so to speak, compounded. The unity of consciousness is nevertheless *synthetical,* and therefore primitive. From this peculiar character of consciousness follow many important consequences.

mined conjunction of the given manifold, so that the unity of this act is at the same time the unity of consciousness (in the conception of a line), and by this means alone is an object (a determinate space) cognized. The synthetical unity of consciousness is, therefore, an objective condition of all cognition, which I do not merely require in order to cognize an object, but to which every intuition must necessarily be subject, in order to become an object for me; because in any other way, and without this synthesis, the manifold in intuition could not be united in one consciousness.

This proposition is, as already said, itself analytical, although it constitutes the synthetical unity, the condition of all thought; for it states nothing more than that all my representations in any given intuition must be subject to the condition which alone enables me to connect them, as my representation with the identical self, and so to unite them synthetically in one apperception, by means of the general expression, *I think*.

But this principle is not to be regarded as a principle for every possible understanding, but only for that understanding by means of whose pure apperception in the thought *I am*, no manifold content is given. The understanding or mind which contained the manifold in intuition, in and through the act itself of its own self-consciousness, in other words, an understanding by and in the representation of which the objects of the representation should at the same time exist, would not require a special act of synthesis of the manifold as the condition of the unity of its consciousness, an act of which the human understanding, which thinks only and cannot intuite, has absolute need. But this principle is the first *principle* of all the operations of our understanding, so that we cannot form the least conception of any other possible understanding, either of one such as should be itself intuition, or possess a sensuous intuition, but with forms different from those of space and time.

What Objective Unity of Self-consciousness is

It is by means of the transcendental unity of apperception that all the manifold given in an intuition is united into a conception of the object. On this account it is called objective, and must be distinguished from the *subjective unity* of consciousness, which is a *determination of the internal sense,* by means of which the said manifold in intuition is given empirically to be so united. Whether I can be *empirically* conscious of the manifold as co-existent or as successive, depends upon circumstances, or empirical conditions. Hence the empirical unity of consciousness by means of association of representations, itself relates to a phenomenal world, and is wholly contingent. On the contrary, the pure form of intuition in time, merely as an intuition, which contains a given manifold, is subject to the original unity of consciousness, and that solely by means of the necessary relation of the manifold in intuition to the *I think*, consequently by means of the pure synthesis of the understanding, which lies *à priori* at the foundation of all empirical synthesis. The transcendental unity of apperception is alone objectively valid; the empirical which we do not consider in this essay, and which is merely a unity deduced from the former under given conditions *in concreto*, possesses only subjective validity. One person connects the notion conveyed in a word with one thing, another with another thing; and the unity of consciousness in that which is empirical, is, in relation to that which is given by experience, not necessarily and universally valid.

The Logical Form of all Judgments consists in the Objective Unity of Apperception of the Conceptions contained therein

I could never satisfy myself with the definition which logicians give of a judgment. It is, according to them, the representation of a relation between two conceptions. I shall not dwell here on the faultiness of this definition, in that it suits only for categorical and not for hypothetical or disjunctive judgments, these latter containing a relation not of conceptions but of judgments themselves;—a blunder from which many evil results have followed.* It is more important for our present purpose to observe, that this definition does not determine in what the said relation consists.

But if I investigate more closely the relation of given cognitions in every judgment, and distinguish it, as belonging to

* The tedious doctrine of the four syllogistic figures concerns only categorical syllogisms; and although it is nothing more than an artifice by surreptitiously introducing immediate conclusions (*consequentiæ immediatæ*) among the premises of a pure syllogism, to give rise to an appearance of more modes of drawing a conclusion than that in the first figure, the artifice would not have had much success had not its authors succeeded in bringing categorical judgments into exclusive respect, as those to which all others must be referred—a doctrine, however, which is utterly false.

the understanding, from the relation which is produced according to laws of the reproductive imagination (which has only subjective validity), I find that a judgment is nothing but the mode of bringing given cognitions under the objective unity of apperception. This is plain from our use of the term of relation *is* in judgments, in order to distinguish the objective unity of given representations from the subjective unity. For this term indicates the relation of these representations to the original apperception, and also their *necessary unity,* even although the judgment is empirical, therefore contingent, as in the judgment, " All bodies are heavy." I do not mean by this, that these representations do *necessarily* belong to each other in empirical intuition, but that by means of the *necessary unity* of apperception they belong to each other in the synthesis of intuitions, that is to say, they belong to each other according to principles of the objective determination of all our representations, in so far as cognition can arise from them, these principles being all deduced from the main principle of the transcendental unity of apperception. In this way alone can there arise from this relation a *judgment,* that is, a relation which has objective validity, and is perfectly distinct from that relation of the very same representations which has only subjective validity—a relation, to-wit, which is produced according to laws of association. According to these laws, I could only say: " When I hold in my hand or carry a body, I feel an impression of weight;" but I could not say: " It, the body, is heavy;" for this is tantamount to saying both these representations are conjoined in the object, that is, without distinction as to the condition of the subject, and do not merely stand together in my perception, however frequently the perceptive act may be repeated.

All Sensuous Intuitions are subject to the Categories, as Conditions under which alone the manifold Content of them can be united in one Consciousness

The manifold content given in a sensuous intuition comes necessarily under the original synthetical unity of apperception, because thereby alone is the *unity* of intuition possible. But that act of the understanding, by which the manifold content of given representations (whether intuitions or conceptions), is brought under one apperception, is the logical function of judgments. All the manifold therefore, in so far as it is given in one empirical intuition, is *determined* in relation to one of the logical functions of judgment, by means of which it is brought into union in one consciousness. Now the categories are nothing else than these functions of judgment, so far as the manifold in a given intuition is determined in relation to them. Consequently, the manifold in a given intuition is necessarily subject to the categories of the understanding.

Observation

The manifold in an intuition, which I call mine, is represented by means of the synthesis of the understanding, as belonging to the necessary unity of self-consciousness, and this takes place by means of the category.* The category indicates accordingly, that the empirical consciousness of a given manifold in an intuition is subject to a pure self-consciousness *à priori*, in the same manner as an empirical intuition is subject to a pure sensuous intuition, which is also *à priori*.—In the above proposition, then, lies the beginning of a deduction of the pure conceptions of the understanding. Now, as the categories have their origin in the understanding alone, independently of sensibility, I must in my deduction make abstraction of the mode in which the manifold of an empirical intuition is given, in order to fix my attention exclusively on the unity which is brought by the understanding into the intuition by means of the category. In what follows, it will be shown from the mode in which the empirical intuition is given in the faculty of sensibility, that the unity which belongs to it is no other than that which the category imposes on the manifold in a given intuition, and thus its *à priori* validity in regard to all objects of sense being established, the purpose of our deduction will be fully attained.

But there is one thing in the above demonstration, of which I could not make abstraction, namely, that the manifold to be intuited must be given previously to the synthesis of the understanding, and independently of it. How this takes place remains here undetermined. For if I cogitate an understanding which was itself intuitive (as, for example, a divine un-

* The proof of this rests on the represented *unity of intuition*, by means of which an object is given, and which always includes in itself a synthesis of the manifold to be intuited, and also the relation of this latter to unity of apperception.

derstanding which should not represent given objects, but by whose representation the objects themselves should be given or produced)—the categories would possess no signification in relation to such a faculty of cognition. They are merely rules for an understanding, whose whole power consists in thought, that is, in the act of submitting the synthesis of the manifold which is presented to it in intuition from a very different quarter, to the unity of apperception; a faculty, therefore, which cognizes nothing *per se*, but only connects and arranges the material of cognition, the intuition, namely, which must be presented to it by means of the object. But to show reasons for this peculiar character of our understandings, that it produces unity of apperception *à priori* only by means of categories and a certain kind and number thereof, is as impossible as to explain why we are endowed with precisely so many functions of judgment and no more, or why time and space are the only forms of our intuition.

In Cognition, its Application to Objects of Experience is the only legitimate use of the Category

To think an object and to cognize an object are by no means the same thing. In cognition there are two elements: firstly, the conception, whereby an object is cogitated (the category); and, secondly, the intuition, whereby the object is given. For supposing that to the conception a corresponding intuition could not be given, it would still be a thought as regards its form, but without any object, and no cognition of anything would be possible by means of it, inasmuch as, so far as I knew, there existed and could exist nothing to which my thought could be applied. Now all intuition possible to us is sensuous; consequently, our thought of an object by means of a pure conception of the understanding, can become cognition for us, only in so far as this conception is applied to objects of the senses. Sensuous intuition is either pure intuition (space and time) or empirical intuition—of that which is immediately represented in space and time by means of sensation as real. Through the determination of pure intuition we obtain *à priori* cognitions of objects, as in mathematics, but only as regards their form as phenomena; whether there can exist things which must be intuited in this form is not thereby established. All mathematical conceptions, therefore, are not *per se* cognition, except in so far as we presuppose that there exist things, which can only be represented conformably to the form of our pure sensuous intuition. But things in space and time are given, only in so far as they are perceptions (representations accompanied with sensation), therefore only by empirical representation. Consequently the pure conceptions of the understanding, even when they are applied to intuitions à priori (as in mathematics), produce cognition only in so far as these (and therefore the conceptions of the understanding by means of them), can be applied to empirical intuitions. Consequently the categories do not, even by means of pure intuition, afford us any cognition of things; they can only do so in so far as they can be applied to empirical intuition. That is to say, the categories serve only to render empirical cognition possible. But this is what we call experience. Consequently, in cognition, their application to objects of experience is the only legitimate use of the categories.

The foregoing proposition is of the utmost importance, for it determines the limits of the exercise of the pure conceptions of the understanding in regard to objects, just as transcendental æsthetic determined the limits of the exercise of the pure form of our sensuous intuition. Space and time, as conditions of the possibility of the presentation of objects to us, are valid no further than for objects of sense, consequently, only for experience. Beyond these limits they represent to us nothing, for they belong only to sense, and have no reality apart from it. The pure conceptions of the understanding are free from this limitation, and extend to objects of intuition in general, be the intuition like or unlike to ours, provided only it be sensuous, and not intellectual. But this extension of conceptions beyond the range of our intuition is of no advantage; for they are then mere empty conceptions of objects, as to the possibility or impossibility of the existence of which they furnish us with no means of discovery. They are mere forms of thought, without objective reality, because we have no intuition to which the synthetical unity of apperception, which alone the categories contain, could be applied, for the purpose of determining an object. Our sensuous and empirical intuition can alone give them significance and meaning.

If, then, we suppose an object of a non-sensuous intuition to be given, we can in that case represent it by all those predicates, which are implied in the presupposition that nothing *appertaining to sensuous intuition belongs to it;* for example, that it is not extended, or in space; that its duration is not time; that in it no change (the effect of the determination in time) is to be met with, and so on. But it is no proper knowledge if I merely indicate what the intuition of the object *is not,* without being able to say what is contained in it, for I have not shown the possibility of an object to which my pure conception of understanding could be applicable, because I have not been able to furnish any intuition corresponding to it, but am only to say that our intuition is not valid for it. But the most important point is this, that to a *something* of this kind not one category can be found applicable. Take, for example, the conception of substance, that is something that can exist as subject, but never as mere predicate; in regard to this conception I am quite ignorant whether there can really be anything to correspond to such a determination of thought, if empirical intuition did not afford me the occasion for its application. But of this more in the sequel.

Of the Application of the Categories to Objects of the Senses in general

The pure conceptions of the understanding apply to objects of intuition in general, through the understanding alone, whether the intuition be our own or some other, provided only it be sensuous, but are, for this very reason, mere forms of thought, by means of which alone no determined object can be cognized. The synthesis or conjunction of the manifold in these conceptions relates, we have said, only to the unity of apperception, and is for this reason the ground of the possibility of *à priori* cognition, in so far as this cognition is dependent on the understanding. This synthesis is, therefore, not merely transcendental, but also purely intellectual. But because a certain form of sensuous intuition exists in the mind *à priori* which rests on the receptivity of the representative faculty (sensibility), the understanding, as a spontaneity, is able to determine the internal sense by means of the diversity of given representations, conformably to the synthetical unity of apperception, and thus to cogitate the synthetical unity of the apperception of the manifold of sensuous intuition *à priori,* as the condition to which must necessarily be submitted all objects of human intuition. And in this manner the categories as mere

forms of thought receive objective reality, that is application
to objects which are given to us in intuition, but that only as
phenomena, for it is only of phenomena that we are capable
of *à priori* intuition.

This synthesis of the manifold of sensuous intuition, which
is possible and necessary *à priori,* may be called figurative (*synthesis speciosa*), in contradistinction to that which is cogitated
in the mere category in regard to the manifold of an intuition
in general, and is called connection or conjunction of the understanding (*synthesis intellectualis*). Both are transcendental, not merely because they themselves precede *à priori* all
experience, but also because they form the basis for the possibility of other cognition *à priori.*

But the figurative synthesis, when it has relation only to the
originally synthetical unity of apperception, that is to the transcendental unity cogitated in the categories, must, to be distinguished from the purely intellectual conjunction, be entitled
the *transcendental synthesis of imagination. Imagination* is
the faculty of representing an object even without its presence
in intuition. Now, as all our intuition is sensuous, imagination, by reason of the subjective condition under which alone
it can give a corresponding intuition to the conceptions of the
understanding, belongs to sensibility. But in so far as the synthesis of the imagination is an act of spontaneity, which is
determinative, and not, like sense, merely determinable, and
which is consequently able to determine sense *à priori,* according
to its form, conformably to the unity of apperception, in so far
is the imagination a faculty of determining sensibility *à priori,*
and its synthesis of intuitions according to the categories, must
be the transcendental synthesis of the imagination. It is an operation of the understanding on sensibility, and the first application of the understanding to objects of possible intuition, and
at the same time the basis for the exercise of the other functions
of that faculty. As figurative, it is distinguished from the
merely intellectual synthesis, which is produced by the understanding alone, without the aid of imagination. Now, in so
far as imagination is spontaneity, I sometimes call it also the
productive imagination, and distinguish it from the *reproductive,* the synthesis of which is subject entirely to empirical laws,
those of association, namely, and which, therefore, contributes
nothing to the explanation of the possibility of *à priori* cogni-

tion, and for this reason belongs not to transcendental philosophy, but to psychology.

*   *   *   *   *   *   *

We have now arrived at the proper place for explaining the paradox, which must have struck everyone in our exposition of the internal sense, namely—how this sense represents us to our own consciousness, only as we appear to ourselves, not as we are in ourselves, because, to-wit, we intuite ourselves only as we are inwardly affected. Now this appears to be contradictory, inasmuch as we thus stand in a passive relation to ourselves; and therefore in the systems of psychology, the internal sense is commonly held to be one with the faculty of apperception, while we, on the contrary, carefully distinguish them.

That which determines the internal sense is the understanding, and its original power of conjoining the manifold of intuition, that is, of bringing this under an apperception (upon which rests the possibility of the understanding itself). Now, as the human understanding is not in itself a faculty of intuition, and is unable to exercise such a power, in order to conjoin, as it were, the manifold of its own intuition, the synthesis of understanding is, considered *per se*, nothing but the unity of action, of which, as such, it is self-conscious, even apart from sensibility, by which, moreover, it is able to determine our internal sense in respect of the manifold which may be presented to it according to the form of sensuous intuition. Thus, under the name of a transcendental synthesis of imagination, the understanding exercises an activity upon the passive subject, whose faculty it is; and so we are right in saying that the internal sense is affected thereby. Apperception and its synthetical unity are by no means one and the same with the internal sense. The former, as the source of all our synthetical conjunction, applies, under the name of the categories, to the manifold of intuition in general, prior to all sensuous intuition of objects. The internal sense, on the contrary, contains merely the form of intuition, but without any synthetical conjunction of the manifold therein, and consequently does not contain any determined intuition, which is possible only through consciousness of the determination of the manifold by the transcendental act of the imagination (synthetical influence of the understanding on the internal sense), which I have named figurative synthesis.

This we can indeed always perceive in ourselves. We cannot cogitate a geometrical line without *drawing* it in thought, nor a circle without *describing* it, nor represent the three dimensions of space without drawing three lines from the same point perpendicular to one another. We cannot even cogitate time, unless, in drawing a straight line (which is to serve as the external figurative representation of time), we fix our attention on the act of the synthesis of the manifold, whereby we determine successively the internal sense, and thus attend also to the succession of this determination. Motion as an act of the subject (not as a determination of an object),* consequently the synthesis of the manifold in space, if we make abstraction of space and attend merely to the act by which we determine the internal sense according to its form, is that which produces the conception of succession. The understanding, therefore, does by no means *find* in the internal sense any such synthesis of the manifold, but *produces* it, in that it affects this sense. At the same time how [the] *I* who think is distinct from the *I* which intuits itself (other modes of intuition being cogitable as at least possible), and yet one and the same with this latter as the same subject; how, therefore, I am able to say: "I, as an intelligence and *thinking* subject, cognize myself as an object *thought,* so far as I am, moreover, given to myself in intuition—only, like other phenomena, not as I am in myself, and as considered by the understanding, but merely as I appear"—is a question that has in it neither more nor less difficulty than the question—" How can I be an object to myself?" or this—" How I can be an object of my own intuition and internal perception?" But that such must be the fact, if we admit that space is merely a pure form of the phenomena of external sense, can be clearly proved by the consideration that we cannot represent time, which is not an object of external intuition, in any other way than under the image of a line, which we draw in thought, a mode of represei tation without which we could not cognize the unity of its dimension, and also

---

* Motion of an *object* in space does not belong to a pure science, consequently not to geometry; because, that a thing is movable cannot be known *à priori,* but only from experience. But motion, considered as the *description* of a space, is a pure act of the successive synthesis of the manifold in external intuition by means of productive imagination, and belongs not only to geometry, but even to transcendental philosophy.

that we are necessitated to take our determination of periods of time, or of points of time, for all our internal perceptions from the changes which we perceive in outward things. It follows that we must arrange the determinations of the internal sense, as phenomena in time, exactly in the same manner as we arrange those of the external senses in space. And consequently, if we grant respecting this latter, that by means of them we know objects only in so far as we are affected externally, we must also confess, with regard to the internal sense, that by means of it we intuite ourselves only as we are internally affected by ourselves; in other words, as regards internal intuition, we cognize our own subject only as phenomenon, and not as it is in itself.*

On the other hand, in the transcendental synthesis of the manifold content of representations, consequently in the synthetical unity of apperception, I am conscious of myself, not as I appear to myself, nor as I am in myself, but only that *I am*. This representation is a *Thought,* not an *Intuition.* Now, as in order to cognize ourselves, in addition to the act of thinking, which subjects the manifold of every possible intuition to the unity of apperception, there is necessary a determinate mode of intuition, whereby this manifold is given; although my own existence is certainly not mere phenomenon (much less mere illusion), the determination of my existence † can only take place conformably to the form of the internal sense, according to the particular mode in which the manifold which I conjoin is given in internal intuition, and I have therefore no knowledge of myself as I am, but merely as I appear to myself. The consciousness of self is thus very far from a knowledge of self,

---

* I do not see why so much difficulty should be found in admitting that our internal sense is affected by ourselves. Every act of attention exemplifies it. In such an act the understanding determines the internal sense by the synthetical conjunction which it cogitates, conformably to the internal intuition which corresponds to the manifold in the synthesis of the understanding. How much the mind is usually affected thereby every one will be able to perceive in himself.

† The *I think* expresses the act of determining my own existence. My existence is thus already given by the act of consciousness; but the mode in which I must determine my existence, that is, the mode in which I must place the manifold belonging to my existence, is not thereby given. For this purpose intuition of self is required, and this intuition possesses a form given *à priori*, namely, time, which is sensuous, and belongs to our receptivity of the determinable. Now, as I do not possess another intuition of self which gives the *determining* in me (of the spontaneity of which I am conscious), prior to the act of *determination,* in the same manner as time gives the determinable, it is clear that I am unable to determine my own existence as that of a spontaneous being, but I am only able to represent to myself the spontaneity of my thought, that is, of my determination, and my existence remains ever determinable in a purely sensuous manner, that is to say, like the existence of a phenomenon. But it is because of this spontaneity that I call myself an *intelligence.*

in which I do not use the categories, whereby I cogitate an object, by means of the conjunction of the manifold in one apperception. In the same way as I require, in order to the cognition of an object distinct from myself, not only the thought of an object in general (in the category), but also an intuition by which to determine that general conception, in the same way do I require, in order to the cognition of myself, not only the consciousness of myself or the thought that I think myself, but in addition an intuition of the manifold in myself, by which to determine this thought. It is true that I exist as an intelligence which is conscious only of its faculty of conjunction or synthesis, but subjected in relation to the manifold which this intelligence has to conjoin to a limitative conjunction called the internal sense. My intelligence (that is, I) can render that conjunction or synthesis perceptible only according to the relations of time, which are quite beyond the proper sphere of the conceptions of the understanding, and consequently cognize itself in respect to an intuition (which cannot possibly be intellectual, nor given by the understanding), only as it appears to itself, and not as it would cognize itself, if its intuition were intellectual.

Transcendental Deduction of the universally possible employment in experience of the Pure Conceptions of the Understanding

In the metaphysical deduction, the *à priori* origin of the categories was proved by their complete accordance with the general logical functions of thought; in the *transcendental* deduction was exhibited the possibility of the categories as *à priori* cognitions of objects of an intuition in general. At present we are about to explain the possibility of cognizing, *à priori*, by means of the categories, all objects which can possibly be presented to our senses, not, indeed, according to the form of their intuition, but according to the laws of their conjunction or synthesis, and thus, as it were, of prescribing laws to nature, and even of rendering nature possible. For if the categories were adequate to this task, it would not be evident to us why everything that is presented to our senses must be subject to those laws which have an *à priori* origin in the understanding itself.

I premise, that by the term *synthesis of apprehension*, I understand the combination of the manifold in an empirical intuition, whereby perception, that is, empirical consciousness of the intuition (as phenomenon), is possible.

We have *à priori* forms of the external and internal sensuous intuition in the representations of space and time, and to these must the synthesis of apprehension of the manifold in a phenomenon be always conformable, because the synthesis itself can only take place according to these forms. But space and time are not merely forms of sensuous intuition, but *intuitions* themselves (which contain a manifold), and therefore contain *à priori* the determination of the *unity* of this manifold.* (See the *Trans. Æsthetic.*) Therefore is *unity of the synthesis* of the manifold without or within us, consequently also a conjunction to which all that is to be represented as determined in space or time must correspond, given *à priori* along with (not in) these intuitions, as the condition of the synthesis of all apprehension of them. But this synthetical unity can be no other than that of the conjunction of the manifold of a given intuition in general, in a primitive act of consciousness, according to the categories, but applied to our sensuous intuition. Consequently all synthesis, whereby alone is even perception possible, is subject to the categories. And, as experience is cognition by means of conjoined perceptions, the categories are conditions of the possibility of experience, and are therefore valid *à priori* for all objects of experience.

*   *   *   *   *   *   *

When, then, for example, I make the empirical intuition of a house by apprehension of the manifold contained therein into a perception, the *necessary unity* of space and of my external sensuous intuition lies at the foundation of this act, and I, as it were, draw the form of the house conformably to this synthetical unity of the manifold in space. But this very synthetical unity remains, even when I abstract the form of space, and has its seat in the understanding, and is in fact the category

* Space represented as an *object* (as geometry really requires it to be) contains more than the mere form of the intuition; namely, a combination of the manifold given according to the form of sensibility into a representation that can be intuited; so that the *form of the intuition* gives us merely the manifold, but the *formal intuition* gives unity of representation. In the Æsthetic I regarded this unity as belonging entirely to sensibility, for the purpose of indicating that it antecedes all conceptions, although it presupposes a synthesis which does not belong to sense, through which alone, however, all our conceptions of space and time are possible. For as by means of this unity alone (the understanding determining the sensibility) space and time are given as intuitions, it follows that the unity of this intuition *à priori* belongs to space and time, and not to the conception of the understanding.

of the synthesis of the homogeneous in an intuition; that is to say, the category of *quantity*, to which the aforesaid synthesis of apprehension, that is, the perception, must be completely conformable.*

To take another example, when I perceive the freezing of water, I apprehend two states (fluidity and solidity), which as such, stand towards each other mutually in a relation of time. But in the time, which I place as an internal intuition, at the foundation of this phenomenon, I represent to myself synthetical *unity* of the manifold, without which the aforesaid relation could not be given in an intuition as *determined* (in regard to the succession of time). Now this synthetical unity, as the *à priori* condition under which I conjoin the manifold of an intuition, is, if I make abstraction of the permanent form of my internal intuition (that is to say, of time), the category of *cause*, by means of which, when applied to my sensibility, *I determine everything that occurs according to relations of time.* Consequently apprehension in such an event, and the event itself, as far as regards the possibility of its perception, stands under the conception of the relation of cause and effect: and so in all other cases.

*   *   *   *   *   *   *

Categories are conceptions which prescribe laws *à priori* to phenomena, consequently to nature as the complex of all phenomena (*natura materialiter spectata*). And now the question arises—inasmuch as these categories are not derived from nature, and do not regulate themselves according to her as their model (for in that case they would be empirical)—how it is conceivable that nature must regulate herself according to them, in other words, how the categories can determine *à priori* the synthesis of the manifold of nature, and yet not derive their origin from her. The following is the solution of this enigma.

It is not in the least more difficult to conceive how the laws of the phenomena of nature must harmonize with the understanding and with its *à priori* form—that is, its faculty of conjoining the manifold—than it is to understand how the phenomena themselves must correspond with the *à priori* form of

---

* In this manner it is proved that the synthesis of apprehension, which is empirical, must necessarily be conformable to the synthesis of apperception, which is intellectual, and contained *à priori* in the category. It is one and the same spontaneity which at one time, under the name of imagination, at another under that of understanding, produces conjunction in the manifold of intuition.

our sensuous intuition. For laws do not exist in the phenomena any more than the phenomena exist as things in themselves. Laws do not exist except by relation to the subject in which the phenomena inhere, in so far as it possesses understanding, just as phenomena have no existence except by relation to the same existing subject in so far as it has senses. To things as things in themselves, conformability to law must necessarily belong independently of an understanding to cognize them. But phenomena are only representations of things which are utterly unknown in respect to what they are in themselves. But as mere representations, they stand under no law of conjunction except that which the conjoining faculty prescribes. Now that which conjoins the manifold of sensuous intuition is imagination, a mental act to which understanding contributes unity of intellectual synthesis, and sensibility, manifoldness of apprehension. Now as all possible perception depends on the synthesis of apprehension, and this empirical synthesis itself on the transcendental, consequently on the categories, it is evident that all possible perceptions, and therefore everything that can attain to empirical consciousness, that is, all phenomena of nature, must, as regards their conjunction, be subject to the categories. And nature (considered merely as nature in general) is dependent on them as the original ground of her necessary conformability to law (as *natura formaliter spectata*). But the pure faculty (of the understanding) of prescribing laws *à priori* to phenomena by means of mere categories, is not competent to enounce other or more laws than those on which a *nature* in general, as a conformability to law of phenomena of space and time, depends. Particular laws, inasmuch as they concern empirically determined phenomena, cannot be entirely deduced from pure laws, although they all stand under them. Experience must be superadded in order to know these particular laws; but in regard to experience in general, and everything that can be cognized as an object thereof, these *à priori* laws are our only rule and guide.

Result of this Deduction of the Conceptions of the Understanding

We cannot think any object except by means of the categories; we cannot cognize any thought except by means of intuitions corresponding to these conceptions. Now all our intuitions are sensuous, and our cognition, in so far as the object of it is given, is empirical. But empirical cognition is experience; consequently no *à priori cognition* is possible for us, except of objects of possible *experience*.*

But this cognition, which is limited to objects of experience, is not for that reason derived entirely from experience, but—and this is asserted of the pure intuitions and the pure conceptions of the understanding—there are, unquestionably, elements of cognition, which exist in the mind *à priori*. Now there are only two ways in which a necessary harmony of experience with the conceptions of its objects can be cogitated. Either experience makes these conceptions possible, or the conceptions make experience possible. The former of these statements will not hold good with respect to the categories (nor in regard to pure sensuous intuition), for they are *à priori* conceptions, and therefore independent of experience. The assertion of an empirical origin would attribute to them a sort of *generatio æquivoca*. Consequently, nothing remains but to adopt the second alternative (which presents us with a system, as it were, of the *Epigenesis* of pure reason), namely, that on the part of the understanding the categories do contain the grounds of the possibility of all experience. But with respect to the questions how they make experience possible, and what are the principles of the possibility thereof with which they present us in their application to phenomena, the following section on the transcendental exercise of the faculty of judgment will inform the reader.

It is quite possible that someone may propose a species of *præformation-system* of pure reason—a middle way between the two—to-wit, that the categories are neither innate and first *à priori* principles of cognition, nor derived from experience, but are merely subjective aptitudes for thought implanted in us contemporaneously with our existence, which were so ordered and disposed by our Creator, that their exercise perfectly harmonizes with the laws of nature which regulate experience.

* Lest my readers should stumble at this assertion, and the conclusions that may be too rashly drawn from it, I must remind them that the categories in the *act of thought* are by no means limited by the conditions of our sensuous intuition, but have an unbounded sphere of action. It is only the cognition of the object of thought, the determining of the object, which requires intuition. In the absence of intuition, our thought of an object may still have true and useful consequences in regard to the exercise of reason by the subject. But as this exercise of reason is not always directed on the determination of the object, in other words, on cognition thereof, but also on the determination of the subject and its volition, I do not intend to treat of it in this place.

Now, not to mention that with such an hypothesis it is impossible to say at what point we must stop in the employment of predetermined aptitudes, the fact that the categories would in this case entirely lose that character of *necessity* which is essentially involved in the very conception of them, is a conclusive objection to it. The conception of cause, for example, which expresses the necessity of an effect under a presupposed condition, would be false, if it rested only upon such an arbitrary subjective necessity of uniting certain empirical representations according to such a rule of relation. I could not then say—" The effect is connected with its cause in the object (that is, necessarily)," but only, " I am so constituted that I can think this representation as so connected, and not otherwise." Now this is just what the sceptic wants. For in this case, all our knowledge, depending on the supposed objective validity of our judgment, is nothing but mere illusion; nor would there be wanting people who would deny any such subjective necessity in respect to themselves, though they must feel it. At all events, we could not dispute with anyone on that which merely depends on the manner in which his subject is organized.

Short view of the above Deduction

The foregoing deduction is an exposition of the pure conceptions of the understanding (and with them of all theoretical *à priori* cognition), as principles of the possibility of experience, but of experience as the *determination* of all phenomena in space and time *in general*—of experience, finally, from the principle of the *original* synthetical unity of apperception, as the form of the understanding in relation to time and space as original forms of sensibility.

* * * * * * *

I consider the division by paragraphs to be necessary only up to this point, because we had to treat of the elementary conceptions. As we now proceed to the exposition of the employment of these, I shall not designate the chapters in this manner any further.

BOOK II

Analytic of Principles

General logic is constructed upon a plan which coincides exactly with the division of the higher faculties of cognition. These are, *Understanding, Judgment,* and *Reason.* This science, accordingly, treats in its analytic of *Conceptions, Judgments,* and *Conclusions* in exact correspondence with the functions and order of those mental powers which we include generally under the generic denomination of understanding.

As this merely formal logic makes abstraction of all content of cognition, whether pure or empirical, and occupies itself with the mere form of thought (discursive cognition), it must contain in its analytic a canon for reason. For the form of reason has its law, which, without taking into consideration the particular nature of the cognition about which it is employed, can be discovered *à priori,* by the simple analysis of the action of reason into its momenta.

Transcendental logic, limited as it is to a determinate content, that of pure *à priori* cognitions, to-wit, cannot imitate general logic in this division. For it is evident that the *transcendental employment of reason* is not objectively valid, and therefore does not belong to the *logic of truth* (that is, to analytic), but as a *logic of illusion* occupies a particular department in the scholastic system under the name of transcendental *Dialectic.*

Understanding and judgment accordingly possess in transcendental logic a canon of objectively valid, and therefore true, exercise, and are comprehended in the analytical department of that logic. But reason, in her endeavors to arrive by *à priori* means at some true statement concerning objects, and to extend cognition beyond the bounds of possible experience, is altogether dialectic, and her illusory assertions cannot be constructed into a canon such as an analytic ought to contain.

Accordingly, the analytic of principles will be merely a canon for the *faculty of judgment,* for the instruction of this faculty in its application to phenomena of the pure conceptions of the understanding, which contain the necessary condition for the establishment of *à priori* laws. On this account, although the subject of the following chapters is the especial principles of *understanding,* I shall make use of the term " *Doctrine of the faculty of judgment,*" in order to define more particularly my present purpose.

Of the Transcendental Faculty of Judgment in General

If understanding in general be defined as the faculty of laws or rules, the faculty of judgment may be termed the faculty of *subsumption* under these rules; that is, of distinguishing whether this or that does or does not stand under a given rule (*casus datæ legis*). General logic contains no directions or precepts for the faculty of judgment, nor can it contain any such. For as *it makes abstraction of all content of cognition,* no duty is left for it, except that of exposing analytically the mere form of cognition in conceptions, judgments and conclusions, and of thereby establishing formal rules for all exercise of the understanding. Now if this logic wished to give some general direction how we should subsume under these rules, that is, how we should distinguish whether this or that did or did not stand under them, this again, could not be done otherwise than by means of a rule. But this rule, precisely because it is a rule, requires for itself direction from the faculty of judgment. Thus, it is evident, that the understanding is capable of being instructed by rules, but that the judgment is a peculiar talent, which does not, and cannot require tuition, but only exercise. This faculty is therefore the specific quality of the so-called mother-wit, the want of which no scholastic discipline can compensate. For although education may furnish, and, as it were, ingraft upon a limited understanding rules borrowed from other minds, yet the power of employing these rules correctly must belong to the pupil himself; and no rule which we can prescribe to him with this purpose, is, in the absence or deficiency of this gift of nature, secure from misuse.* A physician, therefore, a judge or a statesman, may have in his head many admirable pathological, juridical, or political rules, in a degree that may enable him to be a pro-

* **Deficiency** in judgment is properly that which is called stupidity; and for such a thing we know no remedy. A dull or narrow-minded person, to whom nothing is wanting but a proper degree of understanding, may be improved by tuition, even so far as to deserve the epithet of *learned.* But as such persons frequently labor under a deficiency in the faculty of judgment, it is not uncommon to find men extremely learned, who in the application of their science betray to a lamentable degree this irremediable want.

found teacher in his particular science, and yet in the application of these rules, he may very possibly blunder—either because he is wanting in natural judgment (though not in understanding), and while he can comprehend the general *in abstracto,* cannot distinguish whether a particular case *in concreto* ought to rank under the former; or because his faculty of judgment has not been sufficiently exercised by examples and real practice. Indeed, the grand and only use of examples, is.to sharpen the judgment. For as regards the correctness and precision of the insight of the understanding, examples are commonly injurious rather than otherwise, because, as *casus in terminis,* they seldom adequately fulfil the conditions of the rule. Besides, they often weaken the power of our understanding to apprehend rules or laws in their universality, independently of particular circumstances of experience; and hence, accustom us to employ them more as formulæ than as principles. Examples are thus the go-cart of the judgment, which he who is naturally deficient in that faculty, cannot afford to dispense with.

But although general logic cannot give directions to the faculty of judgment, the case is very different as regards transcendental logic, insomuch that it appears to be the especial duty of the latter to secure and direct, by means of determinate rules, the faculty of judgment in the employment of the pure understanding. For, as a doctrine, that is, as an endeavor to enlarge the sphere of the understanding in regard to pure *à priori* cognitions, philosophy is worse than useless, since from all the attempts hitherto made, little or no ground has been gained. But, as a critique, in order to guard against the mistakes of the faculty of judgment (*lapsus judicii*) in the employment of the few pure conceptions of the understanding which we possess, although its use is in this case purely negative, philosophy is called upon to apply all its acuteness and penetration.

But transcendental philosophy has this peculiarity, that besides indicating the rule, or rather the general condition for rules, which is given in the pure conception of the understanding, it can, at the same time, indicate *à priori* the case to which the rule must be applied. The cause of the superiority which, in this respect, transcendental philosophy possesses above all other sciences except mathematics, lies in this:—it treats of conceptions which must relate *à priori* to their objects, whose objective validity consequently cannot be demonstrated *à posteriori*, and is, at the same time, under the obligation of presenting in general but sufficient tests, the conditions under which objects can be given in harmony with those conceptions; otherwise they would be mere logical forms, without content, and not pure conceptions of the understanding.

Our transcendental doctrine of the faculty of judgment will contain two chapters. The first will treat of the sensuous condition under which alone pure conceptions of the understanding can be employed—that is, of the *schematism* of the pure understanding. The second will treat of those synthetical judgments which are derived *à priori* from pure conceptions of the understanding under those conditions, and which lie *à priori* at the foundation of all other cognitions, that is to say, it will treat of the principles of the pure understanding.

CHAPTER I

Of the Schematism of the Pure Conceptions of the Understanding

In all subsumptions of an object under a conception, the representation of the object must be homogeneous with the conception; in other words, the conception must contain that which is represented in the object to be subsumed under it. For this is the meaning of the expression, An object is contained under a conception. Thus the empirical conception of a *plate* is homogeneous with the pure geometrical conception of a *circle*, inasmuch as the roundness which is cogitated in the former is intuited in the latter.

But pure conceptions of the understanding, when compared with empirical intuitions, or even with sensuous intuitions in general, are quite heterogeneous, and never can be discovered in any intuition. How then is the *subsumption* of the latter under the former, and consequently the application of the categories to phenomena, possible?—For it is impossible to say, for example, Causality can be intuited through the senses, and is contained in the phenomenon.—This natural and important question forms the real cause of the necessity of a transcendental doctrine of the faculty of judgment, with the purpose, to-wit, of showing how pure conceptions of the understanding can be applied to phenomena. In all other sciences, where the conceptions by which the object is thought in the general are not so different and heterogeneous from those which represent the object *in concreto*—as it is given, it is quite unnecessary to institute any special inquiries concerning the application of the former to the latter.

Now it is quite clear, that there must be some third thing, which on the one side is homogeneous with the category, and with the phenomenon on the other, and so makes the application of the former to the latter possible. This mediating representation must be pure (without any empirical content), and yet must on the one side be *intellectual,* on the other *sensuous.* Such a representation is the *transcendental schema.*

The conception of the understanding contains pure synthetical unity of the manifold in general. Time, as the formal condition of the manifold of the internal sense, consequently of the conjunction of all representations, contains *à priori* a manifold of the pure intuition. Now a transcendental determination of time is so far homogeneous with the *category,* which constitutes the unity thereof, that it is universal, and rests upon a rule *à priori.* On the other hand, it is so far homogeneous with the *phenomenon,* inasmuch as time   contained in every empirical representation of the manifold. Thus an application of the category to phenomena becomes possible, by means of the transcendental determination of time, which, as the schema of the conceptions of the understanding, mediates the subsumption of the latter under the former.

After what has been proved in our deduction of the categories, no one, it is to be hoped, can hesitate as to the proper decision of the question, whether the employment of these pure conceptions of the understanding ought to be merely empirical or also transcendental; in other words, whether the categories, as conditions of a possible experience, relate *à priori* solely to phenomena, or whether, as conditions of the possibility of things in general, their application can be extended to objects as things in themselves. For we have there seen that conceptions are quite impossible, and utterly without signification, unless either to them, or at least to the elements of which they consist, an object be given; and that, consequently, they cannot possibly apply to objects as things in themselves without re gard to the question whether and how these may be given to us; and further, that the only manner in which objects can be given to us, is by means of the modification of our sensibility; and finally, that pure *à priori* conceptions, in addition to the function of the understanding in the category, must contain *à priori* formal conditions of sensibility (of the internal sense, namely), which again contain the general condition under which alone the category can be applied to any object. This formal and pure condition of sensibility, to which the conception of the understanding is restricted in its employment, we shall name the *schema* of the conception of the understanding, and the procedure of the understanding with these schemata, we shall call the *Schematism* of the pure understanding.

The Schema is, in itself, always a mere product of the imagination. But as the synthesis of imagination has for its aim no single intuition, but merely unity in the determination of sensibility, the schema is clearly distinguishable from the image. Thus, if I place five points one after another, ... this is an image of the number five. On the other hand, if I only think a number in general, which may be either five or a hundred, this thought is rather the representation of a method of representing in an image a sum (*e.g.* a thousand) in conformity with a conception, than the image itself, an image which I should find some little difficulty in reviewing, and comparing with the conception. Now this representation of a general procedure of the imagination to present its image to a conception, I call the schema of this conception.

In truth, it is not images of objects, but schemata, which lie at the foundation of our pure sensuous conception. No image could ever be adequate to our conception of a triangle in general. For the generalness of the conception it never could attain to, as this includes under itself all triangles, whether right-angled, acute-angled, etc., while the image would always be limited to a single part of this sphere. The schema of the triangle can exist nowhere else than in thought, and it indicates a rule of the synthesis of the imagination in regard to pure figures in space. Still less is an object of experience, or an image of the object, ever adequate to the empirical conception. On the contrary, the conception always relates immediately to the schema of the imagination, as a rule for the determination of our intuition, in conformity with a certain general conception. The conception of a dog indicates a rule, according to which my imagination can delineate the figure of a four-footed animal in general, without being limited to any particular individual form which experience presents to me, or indeed to any possible image that I can represent to myself *in concreto*. This schematism of our understanding in regard to phenomena and their mere form, is an art, hidden in the depths of the human soul, whose true modes of action we shall only with difficulty discover and unveil. Thus much only can we say:—The *image* is a product of the empirical faculty of the productive imagination—the *schema* of sensuous conceptions (of figures in space, for example) is a product, and, as it were, a monogram of the pure imagination *à priori*, whereby and according to which images first become possible, which, however, can be connected with the conception only mediately by means of the schema which they indicate, and are in themselves never fully adequate to it. On the other hand, the schema of a pure conception of the understanding is something that cannot be reduced into any image—it is nothing else than the pure synthesis expressed by the category, conformably to a rule of unity according to conceptions. It is a transcendental product of the imagination, a product which concerns the determination of the internal sense, according to conditions of its form (time) in respect to all representations, in so far as these representations must be conjoined *à priori* in one conception, conformably to the unity of apperception.

Without entering upon a dry and tedious analysis of the essential requisites of transcendental schemata of the pure conceptions of the understanding, we shall rather proceed at once to give an explanation of them according to the order of the categories, and in connection therewith.

For the external sense the pure image of all quantities (*quantorum*) is space; the pure image of all objects of sense in general, is time. But the pure *schema of quantity* (*quantitatis*) as a conception of the understanding is *number*, a representation which comprehends the successive addition of one to one (homogeneous quantities). Thus, number is nothing else than the unity of the synthesis of the manifold in a homogeneous intuition, by means of my generating time itself in my apprehension of the intuition.

Reality, in the pure conception of the understanding, is that which corresponds to a sensation in general; that, consequently, the conception of which indicates a being (in time). Negation is that the conception of which represents a not-being (in time). The opposition of these two consists therefore in the difference of one and the same time, as a time filled or a time empty. Now as time is only the form of intuition, consequently of objects as phenomena, that which in objects corresponds to sensation is the transcendental matter of all objects as things in themselves (*Sachheit,* reality). Now every sensation has a degree or quantity by which it can fill time, that is to say, the internal sense in respect of the representation of an object, more or less, until it vanishes into nothing ($= 0 = negatio$). Thus there is a relation and connection between reality and negation, or rather a transition from the former to the latter, which makes every reality representable to us as a quantum; and the schema of a reality as the quantity of something in so far as it fills time, is exactly this continuous and uniform generation of the reality in time, as we descend in time from the sensation which has a certain degree, down to the vanishing thereof, or gradually ascend from negation to the quantity thereof.

The schema of substance is the permanence of the real in time; that is, the representation of it as a substratum of the empirical determination of time; a substratum which therefore remains, while all else changes. (Time passes not, but in it passes the existence of the changeable. To time, therefore, which is itself unchangeable and permanent, corresponds that which is in the phenomenon is unchangeable in existence, that is, substance, and it is only by it that the succession and coexistence of phenomena can be determined in regard to time.)

The schema of cause and of the causality of a thing is the real which, when posited, is always followed by something else. It consists, therefore, in the succession of the manifold, in so far as that succession is subjected to a rule.

The schema of community (reciprocity of action and reaction), or the reciprocal causality of substances in respect of their accidents, is the coexistence of the determinations of the one with those of the other, according to a general rule.

The schema of possibility is the accordance of the synthesis of different representations with the conditions of time in general (as, for example, opposites cannot exist together at the same time in the same thing, but only after each other), and is therefore the determination of the representation of a thing at *any* time.

The schema of reality is existence in a determined time.

The schema of necessity is the existence of an object in all time.

It is clear, from all this, that the schema of the category of quantity contains and represents the generation (synthesis) of time itself, in the successive apprehension of an object; the schema of quality the synthesis of sensation with the representation of time, or the filling up of time; the schema of relation the relation of perceptions to each other in all time (that is, according to a rule of the determination of time) : and finally, the schema of modality and its categories, time itself, as the correlative of the determination of an object— whether it does belong to time, and how. The schemata, therefore, are nothing but *à priori determinations of time* according to rules, and these, in regard to all possible objects, following the arrangement of the categories, relate to *the series in time, the content in time, the order in time,* and finally, *to the complex or totality in time.*

Hence it is apparent that the schematism of the understanding, by means of the transcendental synthesis of the imagination, amounts to nothing else than the unity of the manifold of intuition in the internal sense, and thus indirectly to the unity of apperception, as a function corresponding to the internal sense (a receptivity). Thus, the schemata of the pure conceptions of the understanding are the true and only conditions whereby our understanding receives an application to objects, and consequently *significance.* Finally, therefore, the categories are only capable of empirical use, inasmuch as they serve merely to subject phenomena to the universal rules of synthesis, by means of an *à priori* necessary unity (on account of the necessary union of all consciousness in one original apperception) ; and so to render them susceptible of a complete connection in one experience. But within this whole of possible experience lie all our cognitions, and in the universal relation to this experience consists transcendental truth, which antecedes all empirical truth, and renders the latter possible.

It is, however, evident at first sight, that although the schemata of sensibility are the sole agents in realizing the categories, they do, nevertheless, also restrict them, that is, they limit the categories by conditions which lie beyond the sphere of understanding—namely, in sensibility. Hence the schema is properly only the phenomenon, or the sensuous conception of an object in harmony with the category. (*Numerus* est quantitas phænomenon—*sensatio* realitas phænomenon; *constans* et perdurabile rerum substantia phænomenon—*æternitas, necessitas,* phænomena, etc.) Now, if we remove a restrictive condition, we thereby amplify, it appears, the formerly limited conception. In this way, the categories in their pure signification, free from all conditions of sensibility, ought to be valid of things *as they are,* and not, as the schemata represent them, merely as they appear, and consequently the categories must have a significance far more extended, and wholly independent of all schemata. In truth, there does always remain to the pure conceptions of the understanding, after abstracting every sensuous condition, a value and significance, which is, however, merely logical. But in this case, no object is given them, and therefore they have no meaning sufficient to afford us a conception of an object. The notion of substance, for example, if we leave out the sensuous determination of permanence, would mean nothing more than a something which can be cogitated as subject, without the possibility of becoming a predicate to anything else. Of this representation I can make nothing, inasmuch as it does not indicate to me what determinations the thing possesses which must thus be valid as *premier* subject. Consequently, the categories, without schemata, are merely functions of the understanding for the production of conceptions, but do not represent any object. This significance they derive from sensibility, which at the same time realizes the understanding and restricts it.

Chapter II

System of all Principles of the Pure Understanding

In the foregoing chapter we have merely considered the general conditions under which alone the transcendental faculty of judgment is justified in using the pure conceptions of the understanding for synthetical judgments. Our duty at present is to exhibit in systematic connection those judgments which the understanding really produces *à priori.* For this purpose, our table of the categories will certainly afford us the natural and safe guidance. For it is precisely the categories whose application to possible experience must constitute all pure *à priori* cognition of the understanding; and the relation of which to sensibility will, on that very account, present us with a complete and systematic catalogue of all the transcendental principles of the use of the understanding.

Principles *à priori* are so called, not merely because they contain in themselves the grounds of other judgments, but also because they themselves are not grounded in higher and more general cognitions. This peculiarity, however, does not raise them altogether above the need of a proof. For although there could be found no higher cognition, and therefore no objective proof, and although such a principle rather serves as the foundation of all cognition of the object, this by no means hinders us from drawing a proof from the subjective sources of the possibility of the cognition of an object. Such a proof is necessary moreover, because without it the principle might be liable to the imputation of being a mere gratuitous assertion.

In the second place, we shall limit our investigations to those principles which relate to the categories. For as to the principles of transcendental æsthetic, according to which space and time are the conditions of the possibility of things as phenomena, as also the restriction of these principles, namely, that they cannot be applied to objects as things in themselves;—these, of course, do not fall within the scope of our present inquiry. In like manner, the principles of mathematical science form no part of this system, because they are all drawn from intuition, and not from the pure conception of the understanding. The possibility of these principles, however, will necessarily be considered here, inasmuch as they are synthetical judgments *à priori,* not indeed for the purpose of proving their accuracy and apodictic certainty, which is unnecessary, but merely to render conceivable and deduce the possibility of such evident *à priori* cognitions.

But we shall have also to speak of the principle of analytical judgments, in opposition to synthetical judgments, which is the proper subject of our inquiries, because this very opposition will free the theory of the latter from all ambiguity, and place it clearly before our eyes in its true nature.

Section I.—Of the Supreme Principle of all Analytical Judgments

Whatever may be the content of our cognition, and in whatever manner our cognition may be related to its object, the universal, although only negative condition of all our judgments is that they do not contradict themselves; otherwise these judgments are in themselves (even without respect to the object) nothing. But although there may exist no contradiction in our judgment, it may nevertheless connect conceptions in such a manner, that they do not correspond to the object, or without any grounds either *à priori* or *à posteriori* for arriving at such a judgment, and thus, without being self-contradictory, a judgment may nevertheless be either false or groundless.

Now, the proposition, "No subject can have a predicate that contradicts it," is called the principle of contradiction, and is an universal but purely negative criterion of all truth. But it belongs to logic alone, because it is valid of cognitiohs, merely as cognitions, and without respect to their content, and declares that the contradiction entirely nullifies them. We can also, however, make a positive use of this principle, that is, not merely to banish falsehood and error (in so far as it rests upon contradiction), but also for the cognition of truth. For *if the judgment is analytical,* be it affirmative or negative, its truth must always be recognizable by means of the principle of contradiction. For the contrary of that which lies and is cogitated as conception in the cognition of the object will be always properly negatived, but the conception itself must always be affirmed of the object, inasmuch as the contrary thereof would be in contradiction to the object.

We must therefore hold the *principle of contradiction* to be the universal and fully sufficient *principle of all analytical cognition.* But as a sufficient criterion of truth, it has no further utility or authority. For the fact that no cognition can be at variance with this principle without nullifying itself constitutes this principle the *sine qua non,* but not the determining ground of the truth of our cognition. As our business at present is properly with the synthetical part of our knowledge only, we shall always be on our guard not to transgress this inviolable principle; but at the same time not to expect from it any direct assistance in the establishment of the truth of any synthetical proposition.

There exists, however, a formula of this celebrated principle —a principle merely formal and entirely without content—which contains a synthesis that has been inadvertently and quite unnecessarily mixed up with it. It is this:—" It is impossible for a thing to be and not to be at the same time." Not to mention the superfluousness of the addition of the word *impossible* to indicate the apodictic certainty, which ought to be self-evident from the proposition itself, the proposition is affected by the condition of time, and as it were says: "A thing $= A$, which is something $= B$, cannot at the same time be *non-B*." But both, B as well as *non-B*, may quite well exist in succession. For example, a man who is young cannot at the same time be old; but the same man can very well be at one time young, and at another not young, that is, old. Now the principle of contradiction as a merely logical proposition must not by any means limit its application merely to relations of time, and consequently a formula like the preceding is quite foreign to its true purpose. The misunderstanding arises in this way. We first of all separate a predicate of a thing from the conception of the thing, and afterwards connect with this predicate its opposite, and hence do not establish any contradiction with the subject, but only with its predicate, which has been conjoined with the subject synthetically,—a contradiction, moreover, which obtains only when the first and second predicate are affirmed in the same time. If I say: " A man who is ignorant is not learned," the condition " at the same time " must be added, for he who is at one time ignorant, may at another be learned. But if I say: " No ignorant man is a learned man," the proposition is analytical, because the characteristic *ignorance* is now a constituent part of the conception of the subject; and in this case the negative proposition is evident immediately from the proposition of contradiction, without the necessity of adding the condition " at the same time."—This is the reason why I have altered the formula of this principle—an alteration which shows very clearly the nature of an analytical proposition.

Section II.—Of the Supreme Principle of all Synthetical Judgments

The explanation of the possibility of synthetical judgments is a task with which general Logic has nothing to do; indeed she needs not even be acquainted with its name. But in transcendental Logic it is the most important matter to be dealt with,—indeed the only one, if the question is of the possibility of synthetical judgments *à priori*, the conditions and extent of their validity. For when this question is fully decided, it can reach its aim with perfect ease, the determination, to wit, of the extent and limits of the pure understanding.

In an analytical judgment I do not go beyond the given conception, in order to arrive at some decision respecting it. If the judgment is affirmative, I predicate of the conception only that which was already cogitated in it; if negative, I merely exclude from the conception its contrary. But in synthetical judgments, I must go beyond the given conception, in order to cogitate, in relation with it, something quite different from that which was cogitated in it, a relation which is consequently never one either of identity or contradiction, and by means of which the truth or error of the judgment cannot be discerned merely from the judgment itself.

Granted then, that we must go out beyond a given conception, in order to compare it synthetically with another, a third thing is necessary, in which alone the synthesis of two conceptions can originate. Now what is this *tertium quid,* that is to be the medium of all synthetical judgments? It is only a complex, in which all our representations are contained, the internal sense to wit, and its form *à priori*, Time.

The synthesis of our representations rests upon the imagination; their synthetical unity (which is requisite to a judgment), upon the unity of apperception. In this, therefore, is to be sought the possibility of synthetical judgments, and as all three contain the sources of *à priori* representations, the possibility of pure synthetical judgments also; nay, they are necessary upon these grounds, if we are to possess a knowledge of objects, which rests solely upon the synthesis of representations.

If a cognition is to have objective reality, that is, to relate to an object, and possess sense and meaning in respect to it, it is necessary that the object be given in some way or another.

Without this, our conceptions are empty, and we may indeed have thought by means of them, but by such thinking, we have not, in fact, cognized anything, we have merely played with representation.   To give an object, if this expression be understood in the sense of to present the object, not mediately but immediately in intuition, means nothing else than to apply the representation of it to experience, be that experience real or only possible.   Space and time themselves, pure as these conceptions are from all that is empirical, and certain as it is that they are represented fully à *priori* in the mind, would be completely without objective validity, and without sense and significance, if their necessary use in the objects of experience were not shown.   Nay, the representation of them is a mere schema, that always relates to the reproductive imagination, which calls up the objects of experience, without which they have no meaning.   And so is it with all conceptions without distinction.

The *possibility of experience* is, then, that which gives objective reality to all our à *priori* cognitions.   Now experience depends upon the synthetical unity of phenomena, that is, upon a synthesis according to conceptions of the object of phenomena in general, a synthesis without which experience never could become knowledge, but would be merely a rhapsody of perceptions, never fitting together into any connected text, according to rules of a thoroughly united (possible) consciousness, and therefore never subjected to the transcendental and necessary unity of apperception.   Experience has therefore for a foundation à *priori* principles of its form, that is to say, general rules of unity in the synthesis of phenomena, the objective reality of which rules, as necessary conditions—even of the possibility of experience—can always be shown in experience.   But apart from this relation, à *priori* synthetical propositions are absolutely impossible, because they have no third term, that is, no pure object in which the synthetical unity can exhibit the objective reality of its conceptions.

Although, then, respecting space, or the forms which productive imagination describes therein, we do cognize much à *priori* in synthetical judgments, and are really in no need of experience for this purpose, such knowledge would nevertheless amount to nothing but a busy trifling with a mere chimera, were not space to be considered as the condition of the phenomena which constitute the material of external experience.   Hence

those pure synthetical judgments do relate, though but mediately, to possible experience, or rather to the possibility of experience, and upon that alone is founded the objective validity
of their synthesis.

While then, on the one hand, experience, as empirical synthesis, is the only possible mode of cognition which gives reality
to all other synthesis; on the other hand, this latter synthesis, as
cognition *à priori*, possesses truth, that is, accordance with its
object, only in so far as it contains nothing more than what is
necessary to the synthetical unity of experience.

Accordingly, the supreme principle of all synthetical judgments is: Every object is subject to the necessary conditions of
the synthetical unity of the manifold of intuition in a possible
experience.

A priori synthetical judgments are possible, when we apply
the formal conditions of the *à priori* intuition, the synthesis of
the imagination, and the necessary unity of that synthesis in a
transcendental apperception, to a possible cognition of experience, and say: The conditions of the *possibility* of *experience* in
general, are at the same time conditions of the *possibility* of the
objects of *experience*, and have, for that reason, objective validity in an *à priori* synthetical judgment.

Section III.—Systematic Representation of all Synthetical Principles thereof

That principles exist at all is to be ascribed solely to the pure
understanding, which is not only the faculty of rules in regard
to that which happens, but is even the source of principles according to which everything that can be presented to us as an
object is necessarily subject to rules, because without such rules
we never could attain to cognition of an object.   Even the laws
of nature, if they are contemplated as principles of the empirical
use of the understanding, possess also a characteristic of necessity, and we may therefore at least expect them to be determined upon grounds which are valid *à priori* and antecedent to
all experience.   But all laws of nature, without distinction, are
subject to higher principles of the understanding, inasmuch as
the former are merely applications of the latter to particular
cases of experience.   These higher principles alone therefore
give the conception, which contains the necessary condition,

and, as it were, the exponent of a rule; experience, on the other hand, gives the case which comes under the rule.

There is no danger of our mistaking merely empirical principles for principles of the pure understanding, or conversely; for the character of necessity, according to conceptions which distinguishes the latter, and the absence of this in every empirical proposition, how extensively valid soever it may be, is a perfect safeguard against confounding them. There are, however, pure principles *à priori*, which nevertheless I should not ascribe to the pure understanding—for this reason, that they are not derived from pure conceptions, but (although by the mediation of the understanding) from pure intuitions. But understanding is the faculty of conceptions. Such principles mathematical science possesses, but their application to experience, consequently their objective validity, nay the possibility of such *à priori* synthetical cognitions (the deduction thereof) rests entirely upon the pure understanding.

On this account, I shall not reckon among my principles those of mathematics; though I shall include those upon the possibility and objective validity *à priori*, of principles of the mathematical science, which, consequently, are to be looked upon as the principle of these, and which proceed from conceptions to intuition, and not from intuition to conceptions.

In the application of the pure conceptions of the understanding to possible experience, the employment of their synthesis is either *mathematical* or *dynamical,* for it is directed partly on the *intuition* alone, partly on the *existence* of a phenomenon. But the *à priori* conditions of intuition are in relation to a possible experience absolutely necessary, those of the existence of objects of a possible empirical intuition are in themselves contingent. Hence the principles of the mathematical use of the categories will possess a character of absolute necessity, that is, will be apodictic; those, on the other hand, of the dynamical use, the character of an *à priori* necessity indeed, but only under the condition of empirical thought in an experience, therefore only mediately and indirectly. Consequently they will not possess that immediate evidence which is peculiar to the former, although their application to experience does not, for that reason, lose its truth and certitude. But of this point we shall be better able to judge at the conclusion of this system of principles.

The table of the categories is naturally our guide to the table of principles, because these are nothing else than rules for the objective employment of the former. Accordingly, all principles of the pure understanding are—

I

Axioms of
Intuition.

II

Anticipations
of
Perception.

III

Analogies
of
Experience.

IV

Postulates of
Empirical Thought
in general.

These appellations I have chosen advisedly, in order that we might not lose sight of the distinctions in respect of the evidence and the employment of these principles. It will, however, soon appear that—a fact which concerns both the evidence of these principles, and the *à priori* determination of phenomena—according to the categories of *Quantity* and *Quality* (if we attend merely to the form of these), the principles of these categories are distinguishable from those of the two others, inasmuch as the former are possessed of an intuitive, but the latter of a merely discursive, though in both instances a complete certitude. I shall therefore call the former *mathematical*, and the latter *dynamical* principles.* It must be observed, however, that by these terms I mean, just as little in the one case the principles of mathematics, as those of general (physical) dynamics, in the other. I have here in view merely the principles of the pure un-

---

* All *combination (conjunctio)* is either *composition (compositio)* or *connection (nexus)*. The former is the synthesis of a manifold, the parts of which do not necessarily belong to each other. For example, the two triangles into which a square is divided by a diagonal do not necessarily belong to each other, and of this kind is the synthesis of the *homogeneous* in everything that can be *mathematically* considered. This synthesis can be divided into those of *aggregation* and *coalition*, the former of which is applied to *extensive*, the latter to *intensive* quantities. The second sort of combination (*nexus*) is the synthesis of a manifold, in so far as its parts do belong necessarily to each other; for example, the accident to a substance, or the effect to the cause. Consequently it is a synthesis of that which, though *heterogeneous*, is represented as connected, *à priori*. This combination—not an arbitrary one —I entitle *dynamical*, because it concerns the connection of the *existence* of the manifold. This, again, may be divided into the *physical* synthesis of the phenomena among each other, and the *metaphysical* synthesis, or the connection of phenomena *à priori* in the faculty of cognition.

derstanding, in their application to the internal sense (without distinction of the representations given therein), by means of which the sciences of mathematics and dynamics become possible. Accordingly, I have named these principles rather with reference to their application, than their content; and I shall now proceed to consider them in the order in which they stand in the table.

I.—Axioms of Intuition

The Principle of these is, "All Intuitions are Extensive Quantities"

PROOF

All phenomena contain, as regards their form, an intuition in space and time, which lies à priori at the foundation of all without exception. Phenomena, therefore, cannot be apprehended, that is, received into empirical consciousness otherwise than through the synthesis of a manifold, through which the representations of a determinate space or time are generated; that is to say, through the composition of the homogeneous, and the consciousness of the synthetical unity of this manifold (homogeneous). Now the consciousness of a homogeneous manifold in intuition, in so far as thereby the representation of an object is rendered possible, is the conception of a quantity (quanti). Consequently, even the perception of an object as phenomenon is possible only through the same synthetical unity of the manifold of the given sensuous intuition, through which the unity of the composition of the homogeneous manifold in the conception of a quantity is cogitated; that is to say, all phenomena are quantities, and extensive quantities, because as intuitions in space or time, they must be represented by means of the same synthesis, through which space and time themselves are determined.

An extensive quantity I call that wherein the representation of the parts renders possible (and therefore necessarily antecedes) the representation of the whole. I cannot represent to myself any line, however small, without drawing it in thought, that is, without generating from a point all its parts one after another, and in this way alone producing this intuition. Precisely the same is the case with every, even the smallest portion of time. I cogitate therein only the successive progress from one moment to another, and hence, by means of the different portions of time and the addition of them, a determinate quantity of time is produced. As the pure intuition in all phenomena is either time or space, so is every phenomenon in its character of intuition an extensive quantity, inasmuch as it can only be cognized in our apprehension by successive synthesis (from part to part). All phenomena are, accordingly, to be considered as aggregates, that is, as a collection of previously given parts; which is not the case with every sort of quantities, but only with those which are represented and apprehended by us as extensive.

On this successive synthesis of the productive imagination, in the generation of figures, is founded the mathematics of extension, or geometry, with its axioms, which express the conditions of sensuous intuition *à priori*, under which alone the schema of a pure conception of external intuition can exist; for example, " between two points only one straight line is possible," " two straight lines cannot inclose a space," etc. These are the axioms which properly relate only to quantities (*quanta*) as such.

But, as regards the quantity of a thing (*quantitas*), that is to say, the answer to the question, How large is this or that object? although, in respect to this question, we have various propositions synthetical and immediately certain (*indemonstrabilia*); we have, in the proper sense of the term, no axioms. For example, the propositions, " If equals be added to equals, the wholes are equal; " " If equals be taken from equals, the remainders are equal; " are analytical, because I am immediately conscious of the identity of the production of the one quantity with the production of the other; whereas axioms must be *à priori* synthetical propositions. On the other hand, the self-evident propositions as to the relation of numbers, are certainly synthetical, but not universal, like those of geometry, and for this reason cannot be called axioms, but numerical formulæ That $7 + 5 = 12$, is not an analytical proposition. For neither in the representation of seven, nor of five, nor of the composition of the two numbers, do I cogitate the number twelve. (Whether I cogitate the number in the *addition* of both, is not at present the question; for in the case of an analytical proposition, the only point is, whether I really cogitate the predicate in the representation of the subject.) But although the proposition is synthetical, it is nevertheless only a singular proposition. In so far as regard is here had merely to the synthesis of the homogeneous (the units), it cannot take place except in one manner, although our *use* of these numbers is afterwards general. If I say, " A triangle can be constructed with three lines, any two of which taken together are greater than the third," I exercise merely the pure function of the productive imagination, which may draw the lines longer or shorter, and construct the angles at its pleasure. On the contrary, the number seven is possible only in one manner, and so is likewise the number twelve, which results from the synthesis of seven and five. Such propositions, then, cannot be termed axioms (for in that case we should have an affinity of these), but numerical formulæ.

This transcendental principle of the mathematics of phenomena greatly enlarges our *à priori* cognition. For it is by this principle alone that pure mathematics is rendered applicable in all its precision to objects of experience, and without it the validity of this application would not be so self-evident; on the contrary, contradictions and confusions have often arisen on this very point. Phenomena are not things in themselves. Empirical intuition is possible only through pure intuition (of space and time); consequently, what geometry affirms of the latter, is indisputably valid of the former. All evasions, such as the statement that objects of sense do not conform to the rules of construction in space (for example, to the rule of the infinite divisibility of lines or angles), must fall to the ground. For, if these objections hold good, we deny to space, and with it to all mathematics, objective validity, and no longer know, wherefore, and how far, mathematics can be applied to phenomena. The synthesis of spaces and times as the essential form of all intuition, is that which renders possible the apprehension of a phenomenon, and therefore every external experience, consequently all cognition of the objects of experience; and whatever mathematics in its pure use proves of the former, must necessarily hold good of the latter. All objections are but the chicaneries of an ill-instructed reason, which erroneously thinks to liberate the objects of sense from the formal conditions of our sensibility, and represents these, although mere phenomena, as things in themselves, presented as such to our understandings. But in this case, no *à priori* synthetical cognition of them could be possible, consequently not through pure conceptions of space, and the science which determines these conceptions, that is to say, geometry, would itself be impossible.

II.—Anticipations of Perception

The principle of these is: In all phenomena the Real, that which is an object of sensation, has Intensive Quantity, that is, has a Degree

PROOF

Perception is empirical consciousness, that is to say, a consciousness, which contains an element of sensation. Phenomena as objects of perception are not pure, that is, merely formal intuitions, like space and time, for they cannot be perceived in themselves. They contain, then, over and above the intuition, the materials for an object (through which is represented something existing in space or time), that is to say, they contain the real of sensation, as a representation merely subjective, which gives us merely the consciousness that the subject is affected, and which we refer to some external object. Now, a gradual transition from empirical consciousness to pure consciousness is possible, inasmuch as the real in this consciousness entirely evanishes, and there remains a merely formal consciousness (*à priori*) of the manifold in time and space; consequently there is possible a synthesis also of the production of the quantity of a sensation from its commencement, that is, from the pure intuition $= o$ onwards, up to a certain quantity of the sensation. Now as sensation in itself is not an objective representation, and in it is to be found neither the intuition of space nor of time, it cannot possess any extensive quantity, and yet there does belong to it a quantity (and that by means of its apprehension, in which empirical consciousness can within a certain time rise from nothing $= o$ up to its given amount), consequently an *intensive quantity*. And thus we must ascribe intensive quantity, that is, a degree of influence on sense to all objects of perception, in so far as this perception contains sensation.

All cognition, by means of which I am enabled to cognize and determine *à priori* what belongs to empirical cognition, may be called an Anticipation; and without doubt this is the sense in which Epicurus employed his expression προληψις. But as there is in phenomena some-

thing which is never cognized *à priori*, which on this account constitutes
the proper difference between pure and empirical cognition, that is to
say, sensation (as the matter of perception), it follows, that sensation
is just that element in cognition which cannot be at all anticipated.
On the other hand, we might very well term the pure determinations
in space and time, as well in regard to figure as to Quantity, anticipations of phenomena, because they represent *à priori* that which may
always be given *à posteriori* in experience.   But suppose that in every
sensation, as sensation in general, without any particular sensation being thought of, there existed something which could be cognized *à
priori*, this would deserve to be called anticipation in a special sense—
special, because it may seem surprising to forestall experience, in that
which concerns the matter of experience, and which we can only derive
from itself.   Yet such really is the case here.

Apprehension, by means of sensation alone, fills only one moment,
that is, if I do not take into consideration a succession of many sensations.   As that in the phenomenon, the apprehension of which is not
a successive synthesis advancing from parts to an entire representation,
sensation has therefore no extensive quantity; the want of sensation
in a moment of time would represent it as empty, consequently = o.
That which in the empirical intuition corresponds to sensation is reality
(*realitas phænomenon*); that which corresponds to the absence of it,
negation = o.   Now every sensation is capable of a diminution, so that
it can decrease, and thus gradually disappear.   Therefore, between
reality in a phenomenon and negation, there exists a continuous con-
catenation of many possible intermediate sensations, the difference of
which from each other is always smaller than that between the given
sensation and zero, or complete negation.   That is to say, the real in a
phenomenon has always a quantity, which however is not discoverable
in Apprehension, inasmuch as Apprehension takes place by means of
mere sensation in one instant, and not by the successive synthesis of
many sensations, and therefore does not progress from parts to the
whole.   Consequently it has a quantity, but not an extensive quantity.

Now that quantity which is apprehended only as unity, and in which
plurality can be represented only by approximation to negation = o, I
term *intensive quantity*.   Consequently, reality in a phenomenon has intensive quantity, that is, a degree.   If we consider this reality as cause
(be it of sensation or of another reality in the phenomenon, for example, a change); we call the degree of reality in its character of cause
a momentum, for example, the momentum of weight; and for this
reason, that the degree only indicates that quantity the apprehension
of which is not successive, but instantaneous.   This, however, I touch
upon only in passing, for with Causality I have at present nothing to do.

Accordingly, every sensation, consequently every reality in phenom-
enₐ, however small it may be, has a degree, that is, an intensive quantity, which may always be lessened, and between reality and negation
there exists a continuous connection of possible realities, and possible
smaller perceptions.   Every color—for example, red—has a degree,
which, be it ever so small, is never the smallest, and so is it always with
heat, the momentum of weight, etc.

This property of quantities, according to which no part of them is the smallest possible (no part simple), is called their continuity. Space and time are *quanta continua*, because no part of them can be given, without enclosing it within boundaries (points and moments), consequently, this given part is itself a space or a time. Space, therefore, consists only of spaces, and time of times. Points and moments are only boundaries, that is, the mere places or positions of their limitation. But places always presuppose intuitions which are to limit or determine them; and we cannot conceive either space or time composed of constituent parts which are given before space or time. Such quantities may also be called *flowing*, because the synthesis (of the productive imagination) in the production of these Quantities is a progression in time, the continuity of which we are accustomed to indicate by the expression *flowing*.

All phenomena, then, are continuous quantities, in respect both to intuition and mere perception (sensation, and with it reality). In the former case they are extensive quantities; in the latter, intensive. When the synthesis of the manifold of a phenomenon is interrupted, there results merely an aggregate of several phenomena, and not properly a phenomenon as a quantity, which is not produced by the mere continuation of the productive synthesis of a certain kind, but by the repetition of a synthesis always ceasing. For example, if I call thirteen dollars a sum or quantity of money, I employ the term quite correctly, inasmuch as I understand by thirteen dollars the value of a mark in standard silver, which is, to be sure, a continuous quantity, in which no part is the smallest, but every part might constitute a piece of money, which would contain material for still smaller pieces. If, however, by the words thirteen dollars I understand so many coins (be their value in silver what it may), it would be quite erroneous to use the expression a quantity of dollars; on the contrary, I must call them aggregate, that is, a number of coins. And as in every number we must have unity as the foundation, so a phenomenon taken as unity is a quantity, and as such always a continuous quantity (*quantum continuum*).

Now, seeing all phenomena, whether considered as extensive or intensive, are continuous quantities, the proposition, "All change (transition of a thing from one state into another) is continuous," might be proved here easily, and with mathematical evidence, were it not that the causality of a change lies entirely beyond the bounds of a transcendental philosophy, and presupposes empirical principles. For of the possibility of a cause which changes the condition of things, that is, which determines them to the contrary of a certain given state, the understanding gives us *à priori* no knowledge; not merely because it has no insight into the possibility of it (for such insight is absent in several *à priori* cognitions), but because the notion of change concerns only certain determinations of phenomena, which experience alone can acquaint us with, while their cause lies in the unchangeable. But seeing that we have nothing which we could here employ but the pure fundamental conceptions of all possible experience, among which of course nothing empirical can be admitted, we dare not, without injuring the unity of our system, anticipate general physical science, which is built upon certain fundamental experiences.

Nevertheless, we are in no want of proofs of the great influence which the principle above developed exercises in the anticipation of perceptions, and even in supplying the want of them, so far as to shield us against the false conclusions which otherwise we might rashly draw.

If all reality in perception has a degree, between which and negation there is an endless sequence of ever smaller degrees, and if nevertheless every sense must have a determinate degree of receptivity for sensations; no perception, and consequently no experience is possible, which can prove, either immediately or mediately, an entire absence of all reality in a phenomenon; in other words, it is impossible ever to draw from experience a proof of the existence of empty space or of empty time. For in the first place, an entire absence of reality in a sensuous intuition cannot of course be an object of perception; secondly, such absence cannot be deduced from the contemplation of any single phenomenon, and the difference of the degrees in its reality; nor ought it ever to be admitted in explanation of any phenomenon. For if even the complete intuition of a determinate space or time is thoroughly real, that is, if no part thereof is empty, yet because every reality has its degree, which, with the extensive quantity of the phenomena unchanged, can diminish through endless gradations down to nothing (the void), there must be infinitely graduated degrees, with which space or time is filled, and the intensive quantity in different phenomena may be smaller or greater, although the extensive quantity of the intuition remains equal and unaltered.

We shall give an example of this. Almost all natural philosophers, remarking a great difference in the quantity of the matter of different kinds in bodies with the same volume (partly on account of the momentum of gravity or weight, partly on account of the momentum of resistance to other bodies in motion), conclude unanimously, that this volume (extensive quantity of the phenomenon) must be void in all bodies, although in different proportion. But who would suspect that these for the most part mathematical and mechanical inquirers into nature should ground this conclusion solely on a metaphysical hypothesis—a sort of hypothesis which they profess to disparage and avoid? Yet this they do, in assuming that the real in space (I must not here call it impenetrability or weight, because these are empirical conceptions) is always identical, and can only be distinguished according to its extensive quantity, that is, multiplicity. Now to this presupposition, for which they can have no ground in experience, and which consequently is merely metaphysical, I oppose a transcendental demonstration, which it is true will not explain the difference in the filling up of spaces, but which nevertheless completely does away with the supposed necessity of the above-mentioned presupposition that we cannot explain the said difference otherwise than by the hypothesis of empty spaces. This demonstration, moreover, has the merit of setting the understanding at liberty to conceive this distinction in a different manner, if the explanation of the fact requires any such hypothesis. For we perceive that although two equal spaces may be completely filled by matters altogether different, so that in neither of them is there left a single point wherein matter is not present, nevertheless, every reality has its degree (of resistance or of weight), which, without diminution of the extensive quantity, can become less and less *ad infinitum*, before it passes into nothingness and disappears. Thus an expansion which fills a space —for example, caloric, or any other reality in the phenomenal world— can decrease in its degrees to infinity, yet without leaving the smallest part of the space empty; on the contrary, filling it with those lesser degrees, as completely as another phenomenon could with greater. My intention here is by no means to maintain that this is really the case with the difference of matters, in regard to their specific gravity; I wish only to prove, from a principle of pure understanding, that the nature of our perceptions makes such a mode of explanation possible, and that it is erroneous to regard the real in a phenomenon as equal *quoad* its degree, and different only *quoad* its aggregation and extensive quantity, and this, too, on the pretended authority of an *à priori* principle of the understanding.

Nevertheless, this principle of the anticipation of perception must somewhat startle an inquirer whom initiation into transcendental philosophy has rendered cautious. We may naturally entertain some doubt whether or not the understanding can enounce any such synthetical proposition as that respecting the degree of all reality in phenomena, and consequently the possibility of the internal difference of sensation itself—abstraction being made of its empirical quality. Thus it is a question not unworthy of solution: How the understanding can pronounce synthetically and *à priori* respecting phenomena, and thus anticipate these, even in that which is peculiarly and merely empirical, that, namely, which concerns sensation itself?

The quality of sensation is in all cases merely empirical, and cannot be represented *à priori* (for example, colors, taste, etc.). But the real —that which corresponds to sensation—in opposition to negation $= o$, only represents something the conception of which in itself contains a being (ein seyn), and signifies nothing but the synthesis in an empirical consciousness. That is to say, the empirical consciousness in the internal sense can be raised from o to every higher degree, so that the very same extensive quantity of intuition, an illuminated surface, for example, excites as great a sensation as an aggregate of many other surfaces less illuminated. We can therefore make complete abstraction of the extensive quantity of a phenomenon, and represent to ourselves in the mere sensation in a certain momentum, a synthesis of homogeneous ascension from o up to the given empirical consciousness. All sensations therefore as such are given only *à posteriori*, but this property thereof, namely, that they have a degree, can be known *à priori*. It is worthy of remark, that in respect to quantities in general, we can cognize *à priori* only a single quality, namely, continuity; but in respect to all quality (the real in phenomena), we cannot cognize *à priori* anything more than the intensive quantity thereof, namely, that they have a degree. All else is left to experience.

III.—Analogies of Experience

The principle of these is: Experience is possible only through the representation of a necessary connection of perceptions

PROOF

Experience is an empirical cognition; that is to say, a cognition which determines an object by means of perceptions. It is therefore a synthesis of perceptions, a synthesis which is not itself contained in perception, but which contains the synthetical unity of the manifold of perception in a consciousness; and this unity constitutes the essential of our cognition of *objects* of the senses, that is, of experience (not merely of intuition or sensation). Now in experience our perceptions come together contingently, so that no character of necessity in their connection appears, or can appear from the perceptions themselves, because apprehension is only a placing together of the manifold of empirical intuition, and no representation of a necessity in the connected existence of the phenomena which apprehension brings together, is to be discovered therein. But as experience is a cognition of objects by means of perceptions, it follows that the relation of the existence of the manifold must be represented in experience not as it is put together in time, but as it is objectively in time. And as time itself cannot be perceived, the determination of the existence of objects in time can only take place by means of their connection in time in general, consequently only by means of *à priori* connecting conceptions. Now as these conceptions always possess the character of necessity, experience is possible only by means of a representation of the necessary connection of perception.

The three *modi* of time are *permanence, succession, and co-existence.* Accordingly, there are three rules of all relations of time in phenomena, according to which the existence of every phenomenon is determined in respect of the unity of all time, and these antecede all experience, and render it possible.

The general principle of all three analogies rests on the necessary *unity* of apperception in relation to all possible empirical consciousness (perception) *at every time,* consequently, as this unity lies *à priori* at the foundation of all mental operations, the principle rests on the synthetical unity of all phenomena according to their relation in time. For the original apperception relates to our internal sense (the complex of all representations), and indeed relates *à priori* to its form, that is to say, the relation of the manifold empirical consciousness in time. Now this manifold must be combined in original apperception according to relations of time—a necessity imposed by the *à priori* transcendental unity of apperception, to which is subjected all that can belong to my (*i.e.* my own) cognition, and therefore all that can become an object for me. This synthetical and *à priori* determined unity in relation of perceptions in time is therefore the rule: " All empirical determinations of time must be subject to rules of the general deter-

mination of time;" and the analogies of experience, of which we are
now about to treat, must be rules of this nature.

These principles have this peculiarity, that they do not concern phenomena, and the synthesis of the empirical intuition thereof, but merely
the *existence* of phenomena and their *relation* to each other in regard
to this existence. Now the mode in which we apprehend a thing in a
phenomenon can be determined *à priori* in such a manner, that the rule
of its synthesis can give, that is to say, can produce this *à priori* intuition in every empirical example. But the existence of phenomena cannot be known *à priori,* and although we could arrive by this path at a
conclusion of the fact of some existence, we could not cognize that
existence determinately, that is to say, we should be incapable of antici-
pating in what respect the empirical intuition of it would be distinguishable from that of others.

The two principles above mentioned, which I called mathematical,
in consideration of the fact of their authorizing the application of
mathematics to phenomena, relate to these phenomena only in regard
to their possibility, and instruct us how phenomena, as far as regards
their intuition or the real in their perception, can be generated according to the rules of a mathematical synthesis. Consequently, numerical
quantities, and with them the determination of a phenomenon as a
quantity, can be employed in the one case as well as in the other. Thus,
for example, out of 200,000 illuminations by the moon, I might com-
pose, and give *à priori,* that is, construct, the degree of our sensations
of the sunlight. We may therefore entitle these two principles
constitutive.

The case is very different with those principles whose province it is
to subject the existence of phenomena to rules *à priori.* For as existence does not admit of being constructed, it is clear that they must
only concern the relations of existence, and be merely *regulative* principles. In this case, therefore, neither axioms nor anticipations are to
be thought of. Thus, if a perception is given us, in a certain relation
of time to other (although undetermined) perceptions, we cannot then
say *à priori, what* and *how great* (in quantity) the other perception
necessarily connected with the former is, but only *how* it is connected,
quoad its existence, in this given modus of time. Analogies in philosophy mean something very different from that which they represent in
mathematics. In the latter they are formulæ, which enounce the equality of two relations of quantity, and are always *constitutive,* so that if
two terms of the proportion are given, the third is also given, that is,
can be constructed by the aid of these formulæ. But in philosophy,
analogy is not the equality of two *quantitative* but of two *qualitative*
relations. In this case, from three given terms, I can give *à priori* and
cognize the *relation* to a fourth member, but not this fourth term itself,
although I certainly possess a rule to guide me in the search for this
fourth term in experience, and a mark to assist me in discovering it.
An analogy of experience is therefore only a rule according to which
unity of experience must arise out of perceptions in respect to objects
(phenomena) not as a *constitutive,* but merely as a *regulative* principle. The same holds good also of the postulates of empirical thought

in general, which relate to the synthesis of mere intuition (which concerns the form of phenomena), the synthesis of perception (which concerns the matter of phenomena), and the synthesis of experience (which concerns the relation of these perceptions). For they are only regulative principles, and clearly distinguishable from the mathematical, which are constitutive, not indeed in regard to the certainty which both possess *à priori,* but in the mode of evidence thereof, consequently also in the manner of demonstration.

But what has been observed of all synthetical propositions, and must be particularly remarked in this place, is this, that these analogies possess significance and validity, not as principles of the transcendental, but only as principles of the empirical use of the understanding, and their truth can therefore be proved only as such, and that consequently the phenomena must not be subjoined directly under the categories, but only under their schemata. For if the objects to which those principles must be applied were things in themselves, it would be quite impossible to cognize aught concerning them synthetically *à priori.* But they are nothing but phenomena; a complete knowledge of which—a knowledge to which all principles *à priori* must at last relate—is the only possible experience. It follows that these principles can have nothing else for their aim, than the conditions of the unity of empirical cognition in the synthesis of phenomena. But this synthesis is cogitated only in the schema of the pure conception of the understanding, of whose unity, as that of a synthesis in general, the category contains the function unrestricted by any sensuous condition. These principles will therefore authorize us to connect phenomena according to an analogy, with the logical and universal unity of conceptions, and consequently to employ the categories in the principles themselves; but in the application of them to experience, we shall use only their schemata, as the key to their proper application, instead of the categories, or rather the latter as restricting conditions, under the title of formulæ of the former.

A

First Analogy

Principle of the Permanence of Substance

In all changes of phenomena, substance is permanent, and the quantum thereof in nature is neither increased nor diminished

PROOF

All phenomena exist in time, wherein alone as substratum, that is, as the permanent form of the internal intuition, co-existence and succession can be represented. Consequently time, in which all changes of phenomena must be cogitated, remains and changes not, because it is that in which succession and co-existence can be represented only as determinations thereof. Now, time in itself cannot be an object of perception. It follows that in objects of perception, that is, in phenomena, there must be found a substratum which represents time in general, and in which all change or co-existence can be perceived by means of the relation of phenomena to it. But the substratum of all reality, that is, of all that pertains to the existence of things, is substance; all that pertains to existence can be cogitated only as a determination of substance. Consequently, the permanent, in relation to which alone can all relations of time in phenomena be determined, is substance in the world of phenomena, that is, the real in phenomena, that which, as the substratum of all change, remains ever the same. Accordingly, as this cannot change in existence, its quantity in nature can neither be increased nor diminished.

Our *apprehension* of the manifold in a phenomenon is always successive, is consequently always changing. By it alone we could, therefore, never determine whether this manifold, as an object of experience, is co-existent or successive, unless it had for a foundation something that exists *always,* that is, something *fixed* and *permanent,* of the existence of which all succession and co-existence are nothing but so many modes (*modi* of time). Only in the permanent, then, are relations of time possible (for simultaneity and succession are the only relations in time); that is to say, the permanent is the *substratum* of our empirical representation of time itself, in which alone all determination of time is possible. Permanence is, in fact, just another expression for time, as the abiding correlate of all existence of phenomena, and of all change, and of all co-existence. For change does not affect time itself, but only the phenomena in time (just as co-existence cannot be regarded as a *modus* of time itself, seeing that in time no parts are co-existent, but all successive). If we were to attribute succession to time itself, we should be obliged to cogitate another time, in which this succession would be possible. It is only by means of the permanent that existence in different parts of the successive series of time receives a *quantity,* which we entitle *duration.* For in mere succession, existence is perpetually vanishing and recommencing, and therefore never has even the least quantity. Without the permanent, then, no relation in time is possible. Now, time in itself is not an object of perception; consequently the permanent in phenomena must be regarded as the substratum of all determination of time, and consequently also as the condition as the possibility of all synthetical unity of perceptions, that is, of experience; and all existence and all change in time can only be regarded as a mode in the existence of that which abides unchangeably. Therefore, in all phenomena, the permanent is the object *in itself,* that is, the substance (phenomenon); but all that changes or can change belongs only to the mode of the existence of this substance or substances, consequently to its determinations.

I find that in all ages not only the philosopher, but even the common understanding, has preposited this permanence as a substratum of all change in phenomena; indeed, I am compelled to believe that they will always accept this as an indubitable fact. Only the philosopher expresses himself in a more precise and definite manner, when he says: " In all changes in the world, the *substance* remains, and the *accidents* alone are changeable." But of this decidedly synthetical proposition, I nowhere meet with even an attempt at proof; nay, it very rarely has the good fortune to stand, as it deserves to do, at the head of the pure and entirely *à priori* laws of nature. In truth, the statement that substance is permanent, is tautological. For this very permanence is the ground on which we apply the category of substance to the phenomenon; and we should have been obliged to prove that in all phenomena there is something permanent, of the existence of which the changeable is nothing but a determination. But because a proof of this nature cannot be dogmatical, that is, cannot be drawn from conceptions, inasmuch as it concerns a synthetical proposition *à priori*, and as philosophers never reflected that such propositions are valid only in relation to possible experience, and therefore cannot be proved except by means of a deduction of the possibility of experience, it is no wonder that while it has served as the foundation of all experience (for we feel the need of it in empirical cognition), it has never been supported by proof.

A philosopher was asked, "What is the weight of smoke?" He answered, "Subtract from the weight of the burnt wood the weight of the remaining ashes, and you will have the weight of the smoke." Thus he presumed it to be incontrovertible that even in fire the matter (substance) does not perish, but that only the form of it undergoes a change. In like manner was the saying, "From nothing comes nothing," only another inference from the principle of permanence, or rather of the ever-abiding existence of the true subject in phenomena. For if that in the phenomenon which we call substance is to be the proper substratum of all determination of time, it follows that all existence in past as well as in future time, must be determinable by means of it alone. Hence we are entitled to apply the term substance to a phenomenon, only because we suppose its existence in all time, a notion which the word permanence does not fully express, as it seems rather to be referable to future time. However, the internal necessity perpetually to be, is inseparably connected with the necessity always to have been, and so the expression may stand as it is. "*Gigni de nihilo nihil,*"—"*in nihilum nil posse reverti,*" are two propositions which the ancients never parted, and which people nowadays sometimes mistakenly disjoin, because they imagine that the propositions apply to objects as things in themselves, and that the former might be inimical to the dependence (even in respect of its substance also) of the world upon a supreme cause. But this apprehension is entirely needless, for the question in this case is only of phenomena in the sphere of experience, the unity of which never could be possible, if we admitted the possibility that new things (in respect of their substance) should arise. For in that case, we should lose altogether that which alone can represent the unity of time, to wit, the identity of the substratum, as that through which alone all change possesses complete and thorough unity. This permanence is, however, nothing but the manner in which we represent to ourselves the existence of things in the phenomenal world.

The determinations of a substance, which are only particular modes of its existence, are called *accidents*. They are always real, because they concern the existence of substance (negations are only determinations, which express the non-existence of something in the substance). Now, if to this real in the substance we ascribe a particular existence (for example, to motion as an accident of matter), this existence is called inherence, in contradistinction to the existence of substance, which we call subsistence. But hence arise many misconceptions, and it would be a more accurate and just mode of expression to designate the accident only as the mode in which the existence of a substance is positively determined. Meanwhile, by reason of the conditions of the logical exercise of our understanding, it is impossible to avoid separating, as it were, that which in the existence of a substance is subject to change, while the substance remains, and regarding it in relation to that which is properly permanent and radical. On this account, this category of substance stands under the title of relation, rather because it is the condition thereof, than because it contains in itself any relation.

Now, upon this notion of permanence rests the proper notion of the conception of *change*. Origin and extinction are not changes of that which originates or becomes extinct. Change is but a mode of existence, which follows on another mode of existence of the same object; hence all that changes is permanent, and only the condition thereof changes. Now since this mutation affects only determinations, which can have a beginning or an end, we may say, employing an expression which seems somewhat paradoxical, " Only the *permanent* (substance) is subject to change; the mutable suffers no change, but rather *alternation*, that is, when certain determinations cease others begin."

Change, then, cannot be perceived by us except in substances, and origin or extinction in an absolute sense, that does not concern merely a determination of the permanent, cannot be a possible perception, for it is in this very notion of the permanent which renders possible the representation of a transition from one state into another, and from non-being to being, which, consequently, can be empirically cognized only as alternating determinations of that which is permanent. Grant that a thing absolutely begins to be; we must then have a point of time in which it was not. But how and by what can we fix and determine this point of time, unless by that which already exists? For a void time —preceding—is not an object of perception; but if we connect this beginning with objects which existed previously, and which continue to exist till the object in question begins to be, then the latter can only be a determination of the former as the permanent. The same holds good of the notion of extinction, for this presupposes the empirical representation of a time, in which a phenomenon no longer exists.

Substances (in the world of phenomena) are the substratum of all determinations of time. The beginning of some, and the ceasing to be of other substances, would utterly do away with the only condition of the empirical unity of time; and in that case phenomena would relate to two different times, in which, side by side, existence would pass; which is absurd. For there is only *one* time in which all different times must be placed, not as co-existent, but as successive.

Accordingly, permanence is a necessary condition under which alone phenomena, as things or objects, are determinable in a possible experience. But as regards the empirical criterion of this necessary permanence, and with it of the substantiality of phenomena, we shall find sufficient opportunity to speak in the sequel.

B

SECOND ANALOGY

Principle of the Succession of Time According to the Law of Causality

All changes take place according to the law of the connection of Cause and Effect

PROOF

That all phenomena in the succession of time are only changes, that is, a successive being and non-being of the determinations of substance, which is permanent; consequently that a being of substance itself which follows on the non-being thereof, or a non-being of substance which follows on the being thereof, in other words, that the origin or extinction of substance itself, is impossible—all this has been fully established in treating of the foregoing principle. This principle might have been expressed as follows: "*All alteration (succession) of phenomena is merely change;*" for the changes of substance are not origin or extinction, because the conception of change presupposes the same subject as existing with two opposite determinations, and consequently as permanent. After this premonition, we shall proceed to the proof.

I perceive that phenomena succeed one another, that is to say, a state of things exists at one time, the opposite of which existed in a former state. In this case then, I really connect together two perceptions in time. Now connection is not an operation of mere sense and intuition, but is the product of a synthetical faculty of imagination, which determines the internal sense in respect of a relation of time. But imagination can connect these two states in two ways, so that either the one or the other may antecede in time; for time in itself cannot be an object of perception, and what in an object precedes and what follows cannot be empirically determined in relation to it. I am only conscious then, that my imagination places one state before, and the other after; not that the one state antecedes the other in the object. In other words, the objective relation of the successive phenomena remains quite undetermined by means of mere perception. Now in order that this relation may be cognized as determined, the relation between the two states must be so cogitated that it is thereby determined as necessary, which of them must be placed before and which after, and not conversely. But the conception which carries with it a necessity of synthetical unity, can be none other than a pure conception of the understanding which does not lie in mere perception; and in this case it is the conception of the *relation of cause and effect,* the former of which determines the latter in time, as its necessary consequence, and not as something which might possibly antecede (or which might in some cases not be perceived to follow). It follows that it is only because we subject the sequence of phenomena, and consequently all change to the law of causality, that experience itself, that is, empirical cognition of phenomena, becomes possible; and consequently, that phenomena themselves, as objects of experience, are possible only by virtue of this law.

Our apprehension of the manifold of phenomena is always successive. The representations of parts succeed one another. Whether they succeed one another in the object also, is a second point for reflection, which was not contained in the former. Now we may certainly give the name of object to everything, even to every representation, so far as we are conscious thereof; but what this word may mean in the case of phenomena, not merely in so far as they (as representations) are objects, but only in so far as they indicate an object, is a question requiring deeper consideration. In so far as they, regarded merely as representations, are at the same time objects of consciousness, they are not to be distinguished from apprehension, that is, reception into the synthesis of imagination, and we must therefore say: " The manifold of phenomena is always produced successively in the mind." If phenomena were things in themselves, no man would be able to conjecture from the succession of our representations how this manifold is connected in the object; for we have to do only with our representations. How things may be in themselves, without regard to the representations through which they affect us, is utterly beyond the sphere of our cognition. Now although phenomena are not things in themselves, and are nevertheless the only thing given to us to be cognized, it is my duty to show what sort of connection in time belongs to the manifold in phenomena themselves, while the representation of this manifold in apprehension is always successive. For example, the apprehension of the manifold in the phenomenon of a house which stands before me, is successive. Now comes the question, whether the manifold of this house is in itself also successive;—which no one will be at all willing to grant. But, so soon as I raise my conception of an object to the transcendental signification thereof, I find that the house is not a thing in itself, but only a phenomenon, that is, a representation, the transcendental object of which remains utterly unknown. What then am I to understand by the question, How can the manifold be connected in the phenomenon itself—not considered as a thing in itself, but merely as a phenomenon? Here that which lies in my successive apprehension is regarded as representation, while the phenomenon which is given me, notwithstanding that it is nothing more than a complex of these representations, is regarded as the object thereof, with which my conception, drawn from the representations of apprehension, must harmonize. It is very soon seen that, as accordance of the cognition with its object constitutes truth, the question now before us can only relate to the formal conditions of empirical truth, and that the phenomenon, in opposition to the representations of apprehension, can only be distinguished therefrom as the object of them, if it is subject to a rule, which distinguishes it from every other apprehension, and which renders necessary a mode of connection of the manifold. That in the phenomenon which contains the condition of this necessary rule of apprehension is the object.

Let us now proceed to our task. That something happens, that is to say, that something or some state exists which before was not, cannot be empirically perceived, unless a phenomenon precedes, which does not contain in itself this state. For a reality which should follow upon a void time, in other words, a beginning, which no state of things precedes, can just as little be apprehended as the void time itself. Every apprehension of an event is therefore a perception which follows upon another perception. But as this is the case with all synthesis of apprehension, as I have shown above in the example of a house, my apprehension of an event is not yet sufficiently distinguished from other apprehensions. But I remark also, that if in a phenomenon which contains an occurrence, I call the antecedent state of my perception, A, and the following state, B, the perception B can only follow A in apprehension, and the perception A cannot follow B, but only precede it. For example, I see a ship float down the stream of a river. My perception of its place lower down follows upon my perception of its place higher up the course of the river, and it is impossible that in the apprehension of this phenomenon, the vessel should be perceived first below and afterwards higher up the stream. Here, therefore, the order in the sequence of perceptions in apprehension is determined; and by this order apprehension is regulated. In the former example, my perceptions in the apprehension of a house, might begin at the roof and end at the foundation, or *vice versâ;* or I might apprehend the manifold in this empirical intuition by going from left to right, and from right to left. Accordingly, in the series of these perceptions, there was no determined order, which necessitated my beginning at a certain point, in order empirically to connect the manifold. But this rule is always to be met with in the perception of that which happens, and it makes the order of the successive perceptions in the apprehension of such a phenomenon *necessary.*

I must therefore, in the present case, deduce the *subjective sequence* of apprehension from the *objective sequence* of phenomena, for otherwise the former is quite undetermined, and one phenomenon is not distinguishable from another. The former alone proves nothing as to the connection of the manifold in an object, for it is quite arbitrary. The latter must consist in the order of the manifold in a phenomenon, according to which order the apprehension of one thing (that which happens) follows that of another thing (which precedes), in conformity with a rule. In this way alone can I be authorized to say of the phenomenon itself, and not merely of my own apprehension, that a certain order or sequence is to be found therein. That is, in other words, I cannot arrange my apprehension otherwise than in this order.

In conformity with this rule, then, it is necessary that in that which antecedes an event there be found the condition of a rule, according to which this event follows always and necessarily; but I cannot reverse this and go back from the event, and determine (by apprehension) that which antecedes it. For no phenomenon goes back from the succeeding point of time to the preceding point, although it does certainly, relate to a preceding point of time; from a given time, on the other hand, there is always a necessary progression to the determined succeeding time. Therefore, because there certainly is something that follows, I must of necessity connect it with something else, which antecedes, and upon which it follows, in conformity with a rule, that is necessarily, so that the event, as conditioned, affords certain indication of a condition, and this condition determines the event.

Let us suppose that nothing precedes an event, upon which this event must follow in conformity with a rule. All sequence of perception would then exist only in apprehension, that is to say, would be merely subjective, and it could not thereby be objectively determined what thing ought to precede, and what ought to follow in perception. In such a case, we should have nothing but a play of representations, which would possess no application to any object. That is to say, it would not be possible through perception to distinguish one phenomenon from another, as regards relations of time; because the succession in the act of apprehension would always be of the same sort, and therefore there would be nothing in the phenomenon to determine the succession, and to render a certain sequence objectively necessary. And, in this case, I cannot say that two states in a phenomenon would follow one upon the other, but only that one apprehension follows upon another. But this is merely subjective, and does not determine an object, and consequently cannot be held to be cognition of an object—not even in the phenomenal world.

Accordingly, when we know in experience that something happens, we always presuppose that something precedes, whereupon it follows in conformity with a rule. For otherwise I could not say of the object, that it follows; because the mere succession in my apprehension, if it be not determined by a rule in relation to something preceding, does not authorize succession in the object. Only therefore, in reference to a rule, according to which phenomena are determined in their sequence, that is, as they happen, by the preceding state, can I make my subjective synthesis (of apprehension) objective, and it is only under this presupposition that even the experience of an event is possible.

No doubt it appears as if this were in thorough contradiction to all the notions which people have hitherto entertained in regard to the procedure of the human understanding. According to these opinions, it is by means of the perception and comparison of similar consequences following upon certain antecedent phenomena, that the understanding is led to the discovery of a rule, according to which certain events always follow certain phenomena, and it is only by this process that we attain to the conception of cause. Upon such a basis, it is clear that this conception must be merely empirical, and the rule which it furnishes us with—" Everything that happens must have a cause "—would be just as contingent as experience itself. The universality and necessity of the rule or law would be perfectly spurious attributes of it. Indeed, it could not possess universal validity, inasmuch as it would not in this case be *à priori*, but founded on deduction. But the same is the case with this law as with other pure *à priori* representations (*e. g.* space and time), which we can draw in perfect clearness and completeness from experience, only because we had already placed them therein, and by that means, and by that alone, had rendered experience possible. Indeed, the logical clearness of this representation of a rule, determining the series of events, is possible only when we have made use thereof in experience. Nevertheless, the recognition of this rule, as a condition of the synthetical unity of phenomena in time, was the ground of experience itself, and consequently preceded it *à priori*.

It is now our duty to show by an example, that we never, even in experience, attribute to an object the notion of succession or effect (of an event—that is, the happening of something that did not exist before), and distinguish it from the subjective succession of apprehension, unless when a rule lies at the foundation, which compels us to observe this order of perception in preference to any other, and that, indeed, it is this necessity which first renders possible the representation of a succession in the object.

We have representations within us, of which also we can be conscious. But, however widely extended, however accurate and thorough-going this consciousness may be, these representations are still nothing more than representations, that is, internal determinations of the mind in this or that relation of time. Now how happens it, that to these representations we should set an object, or that, in addition to their subjective reality, as modifications, we should still further attribute to them a certain unknown objective reality? It is clear that objective significancy cannot exist in a relation to another representation (of that which we desire to term object), for in that case the question again arises: " How does this other representation go out of itself, and obtain objective significancy over and above the subjective, which is proper to it, as a determination of a state of mind? " If we try to discover what sort of new property the *relation to an object* gives to our subjective representations, and what new importance they thereby receive, we shall find that this relation has no other effect than that of rendering necessary the connection of our representations in a certain manner, and of subjecting them to a rule; and that conversely, it is only because a certain order is necessary in the relations of time of our representations, that objective significancy is ascribed to them.

In the synthesis of phenomena, the manifold of our representations is always successive. Now hereby is not represented an object, for by means of this succession, which is common to all apprehension, no one thing is distinguished from another. But so soon as I perceive or assume, that in this succession there is a relation to a state antecedent, from which the representation follows in accordance with a rule, so soon do I represent something as an event, or as a thing that happens; in other words, I cognize an object to which I must assign a certain determinate position in time, which cannot be altered, because of the preceding state in the object. When, therefore, I perceive that something happens, there is contained in this representation, in the first place, the fact, that something antecedes; because it is only in relation to this, that the phenomena obtains its proper relation of time, in other words, exists after an antecedent time, in which it did not exist. But it can receive its determined place in time, only by the presupposition that something existed in the foregoing state, upon which it follows inevitably and always, that is, in conformity with a rule. From all this it is evident that, in the first place, I cannot reverse the order of succession, and make that which happens precede that upon which it follows; and that, in the second place, if the antecedent state be posited, a certain determinate event inevitably and necessarily follows. Hence it follows that there exists a certain order in our representations, whereby the present gives a sure indication of some previously existing state, as a correlate, though still undetermined, of the existing event which is given—a correlate which itself relates to the event as its consequence, conditions it, and connects it necessarily with itself in the series of time.

If then it be admitted as a necessary law of sensibility, and consequently a formal condition of all perception, that the preceding necessarily determines the succeeding time (inasmuch as I cannot arrive at the succeeding except through the preceding), it must likewise be an indispensable law of empirical representation of the series of time, that the phenomena of the past determine all phenomena in the succeeding time, and that the latter, as events, cannot take place, except in so far as the former determine their existence in time, that is to say, establish it according to a rule. For it is of course only in phenomena that we can empirically cognize this continuity in the connection of times.

For all experience and for the possibility of experience, understanding is indispensable, and the first step which it takes in this sphere is not to render the representation of objects clear, but to render the representation of an object in general, possible. It does this by applying the order of time to phenomena, and their existence. In other words, it assigns to each phenomenon, as a consequence, a place in relation to preceding phenomena, determined à priori in time, without which it could not harmonize with time itself, which determines a place à priori to all its parts. This determination of place cannot be derived from the relation of phenomena to absolute time (for it is not an object of perception); but, on the contrary, phenomena must reciprocally determine the places in time of one another, and render these necessary in the order of time. In other words, whatever follows or happens, must follow in conformity with an universal rule upon that which was contained in the foregoing state. Hence arises a series of phenomena, which, by means of the understanding, produces and renders necessary exactly the same order and continuous connection in the series of our possible perceptions, as is found à priori in the form of internal intuition (time), in which all our perceptions must have place.

That something happens, then, is a perception which belongs to a possible experience, which becomes real, only because I look upon the phenomenon as determined in regard to its place in time, consequently as an object, which can always be found by means of a rule in the connected series of my perceptions. But this rule of the determination of a thing according to succession in time is as follows: "In what precedes may be found the condition, under which an event always (that is, necessarily) follows." From all this it is obvious that the principle of cause and effect is the principle of possible experience, that is, of objective cognition of phenomena, in regard to their relations in the succession of time.

The proof of this fundamental proposition rests entirely on the following momenta of argument. To all empirical cognition belongs the synthesis of the manifold by the imagination, a synthesis which is always successive, that is, in which the representations therein always follow one another. But the order of succession in imagination is not determined, and the series of successive representations may be taken retrogressively as well as progressively. But if this synthesis is a synthesis of apprehension (of the manifold of a given phenomenon), then the order is determined in the object, or, to speak more accurately, there is therein an order of successive synthesis which determines an object, and according to which something necessarily precedes, and when this is posited, something else necessarily follows. If, then, my perception is to contain the cognition of an event, that is, of something which really happens, it must be an empirical judgment, wherein we think that the succession is determined; that is, it presupposes another phenomenon, upon which this event follows necessarily, or in conformity, with a rule. If, on the contrary, when I posited the antecedent, the event did not necessarily follow, I should be obliged to consider it merely as a subjective play of my imagination, and if in this I represented to myself anything as objective, I must look upon it as a mere dream. Thus the relation of phenomena (as possible perceptions), according to which that which happens, is, as to its existence, necessarily determined in time by something which antecedes, in conformity with a rule—in other words, the relation of cause and effect—is the condition of the objective validity of our empirical judgments in regard to the sequence of perceptions, consequently of their empirical truth, and therefore of experience. The principle of the relation of causality in the succession of phenomena is therefore valid for all objects of experience, because it is itself the ground of the possibility of experience.

Here, however, a difficulty arises, which must be resolved. The principle of the connection of causality among phenomena is limited in our formula to the succession thereof, although in practice we find that the principle applies also when the phenomena exist together in the same time, and that cause and effect may be simultaneous. For example, there is heat in a room, which does not exist in the open air. I look about for the cause, and find it to be the fire. Now the fire as the cause, is simultaneous with its effect, the heat of the room. In this case, then, there is no succession as regards time, between cause and effect, but they are simultaneous; and still the law holds good. The greater part of operating causes in nature are simultaneous with their effects, and the succession in time of the latter is produced only because the cause cannot achieve the total of its effect in one moment. But at the moment when the effect *first* arises, it is always simultaneous with the causality of its cause, because if the cause had but a moment before ceased to be, the effect could not have arisen. Here it must be specially remembered, that we must consider the *order* of time, and not the *lapse* thereof. The relation remains, even though no time has elapsed. The time between the causality of the cause and its immediate effect may entirely vanish, and the cause and effect be thus simultaneous, but the relation of the one to the other remains always determinable according to time. If, for example, I consider a leaden ball, which lies upon a cushion and makes a hollow in it, as a cause, then it is simultaneous with the effect. But I distinguish the two through the relation of time of the dynamical connection of both. For if I lay the ball upon the cushion, then the hollow follows upon the before smooth surface; but supposing the cushion has, from some cause or another, a hollow, there does not thereupon follow a leaden ball.

Thus, the law of the succession of time is in all instances the only empirical criterion of effect in relation to the causality of the antecedent cause. The glass is the cause of the rising of the water above its horizontal surface, although the two phenomena are contemporaneous. For, as soon as I draw some water with the glass from a larger vessel, an effect follows thereupon, namely, the change of the horizontal state which the water had in the large vessel into a concave, which it assumes in the glass.

This conception of causality leads us to the conception of action; that of action, to the conception of force; and through it, to the conception of substance. As I do not wish this critical essay, the sole purpose of which is to treat of the sources of our synthetical cognition à priori, to be crowded with analyses which merely explain, but do not enlarge the sphere of our conceptions, I reserve the detailed explanation of the above conceptions for a future system of pure reason. Such an analysis, indeed, executed with great particularity, may already be found in well-known works on this subject. But I cannot at present refrain from making a few remarks on the empirical criterion of a substance, in so far as it seems to be more evident and more easily recognized through the conception of action, than through that of the permanence of a phenomenon.

Where action (consequently activity and force) exists, substance also must exist, and in it alone must be sought the seat of that fruitful source of phenomena. Very well. But if we are called upon to explain what we mean by substance, and wish to avoid the vice of reasoning in a circle, the answer is by no means so easy. How shall we conclude immediately from the action to the *permanence* of that which acts, this being nevertheless an essential and peculiar criterion of substance (phenomenon)? But after what has been said above, the solution of this question becomes easy enough, although by the common mode of procedure—merely analyzing our conceptions—it would be quite impossible. The conception of an action indicates the relation of the subject of causality to the effect. Now because all effect consists in that which happens, therefore in the changeable, the last subject thereof is the *permanent*, as the substratum of all that changes, that is, substance. For according to the principle of causality, actions are always the first ground of all change in phenomena, and consequently cannot be a property of a subject which itself changes, because if this were the case, other actions and another subject would be necessary to determine this change. From all this it results that action alone, as an empirical criterion, is a sufficient proof of the presence of substantiality, without any necessity on my part of endeavoring to discover the permanence of substance by a comparison. Besides, by this mode of induction we could not attain to the completeness which the magnitude and strict universality of the conception requires. For that the primary subject of the causality of all arising and passing away, all origin and extinction, cannot itself (in the sphere of phenomena) arise and pass away, is a sound and safe conclusion, a conclusion which leads us to the conception of empirical necessity and permanence in existence, and consequently to the conception of a substance as phenomenon.

When something happens, the mere fact of the occurrence, without regard to that which occurs, is an object requiring investigation. The transition from the non-being of a state into the existence of it, supposing that this state contains no quality which previously existed in the phenomenon, is a fact of itself demanding inquiry. Such an event, as has been shown in No. A, does not concern substance (for substance does not thus originate), but its condition or state. It is therefore only change, and not origin from nothing. If this origin be regarded as the effect of a foreign cause, it is termed creation, which cannot be admitted as an event among phenomena, because the very possibility of it would annihilate the unity of experience. If, however, I regard all things not as phenomena, but as things in themselves, and objects of understanding alone, they, although substances, may be considered as dependent, in respect of their existence, on a foreign cause. But this would require a very different meaning in the words, a meaning which could not apply to phenomena as objects of possible experience.

How a thing can be changed, how it is possible that upon one state existing in one point of time, an opposite state should follow in another point of time—of this we have not the smallest conception *à priori*. There is requisite for this the knowledge of real powers, which can only be given empirically; for example, knowledge of moving forces, or, in other words, of certain successive phenomena (as movements) which indicate the presence of such forces. But the form of every change, the condition under which alone it can take place as the coming into existence of another state (be the content of the change, that is, the state which is changed, what it may), and consequently the succession of the states themselves, can very well be considered *à priori*, in relation to the law of causality and the conditions of time.*

When a substance passes from one state, a, into another state, b, the point of time in which the latter exists is different from, and subsequent to that in which the former existed. In like manner, the second state, as reality (in the phenomenon), differs from the first, in which the reality of the second did not exist, as b from zero. That is to say, if the state, b, differs from the state, a, only in respect to quantity, the change is a coming into existence of $b-a$, which in the former state did not exist, and in relation to which that state is $= 0$.

Now the question arises, how a thing passes from one state $= a$, into

* It must be remarked, that I do not speak of the change of certain relations, but of the change of the state. Thus, when a body moves in an uniform manner, it does not change its state (of motion); but only when its motion increases or decreases.

another state $= b$. Between two moments there is always a certain time, and between two states existing in these moments, there is always a difference having a certain quantity (for all parts of phenomena are in their turn quantities). Consequently, every transition from one state into another, is always effected in a time contained between two moments, of which the first determines the state which the thing leaves, and the second determines the state into which the thing passes. Both moments, then, are limitations of the time of a change, consequently of the intermediate state between both, and as such they belong to the total of the change. Now every change has a cause, which evidences its causality in the whole time during which the change takes place. The cause, therefore, does not produce the change all at once or in one moment, but in a time, so that, as the time gradually increases from the commencing instant, a, to its completion at b, in like manner also, the quantity of the reality $(b - a)$ is generated through the lesser degrees which are contained between the first and last. All change is therefore possible only through a continuous action of the causality, which, in so far as it is uniform, we call a momentum. The change does not consist of these momenta, but is generated or produced by them as their effect.

Such is the law of the continuity of all change, the ground of which is, that neither time itself nor any phenomenon in time consists of parts which are the smallest possible, but that, notwithstanding, the state of a thing passes in the process of a change through all these parts, as elements, to its second state. There is no smallest degree of reality in a phenomenon, just as there is no smallest degree in the quantity of time; and so the new state of the reality grows up out of the former state, through all the infinite degrees thereof, the differences of which one from another, taken all together, are less than the difference between o and a.

It is not our business to inquire here into the utility of this principle in the investigation of nature. But how such a proposition, which appears so greatly to extend our knowledge of nature, is possible completely *à priori*, is indeed a question which deserves investigation, although the first view seems to demonstrate the truth and reality of the principle, and the question, how it is possible, may be considered superfluous. For there are so many groundless pretensions to the enlargement of our knowledge by pure reason, that we must take it as a general rule to be mistrustful of all such, and without a thorough-going and radical deduction, to believe nothing of the sort even on the clearest dogmatical evidence.

Every addition to our empirical knowledge, and every advance made in the exercise of our perception, is nothing more than an extension of the determination of the internal sense, that is to say, a progression in time, be objects themselves what they may, phenomena, or pure intuitions. This progression in time determines everything, and is itself determined by nothing else. That is to say, the parts of the progression exist only in time, and by means of the synthesis thereof, and are not given antecedently to it. For this reason, every transition in perception to anything which follows upon another in time, is a determination of time by means of the production of this perception. And as this determination of time is, always and in all parts, a quantity, the perception produced is to be considered as a quantity which proceeds through all its degrees—no one of which is the smallest possible—from zero up to its determined degree. From this we perceive the possibility of cognizing *à priori* a law of changes—a law, however, which concerns their form merely. We merely anticipate our own apprehension, the formal condition of which, inasmuch as it is itself to be found in the mind antecedently to all given phenomena, must certainly be capable of being cognized *à priori*.

Thus, as time contains the sensuous condition *à priori* of the possibility of a continuous progression of that which exists to that which follows it, the understanding, by virtue of the unity of apperception, contains the condition *à priori* of the possibility of a continuous determination of the position in time of all phenomena, and this by means of the series of causes and effects, the former of which necessitate the sequence of the latter, and thereby render universally and for all time, and by consequence, objectively, valid the empirical cognition of the relations of time.

C

Third Analogy

Principle of Co-existence, According to the Law of Reciprocity or Community

All substances, in so far as they can be perceived in space at the same time, exist in a state of complete reciprocity of action

PROOF

Things are co-existent, when in empirical intuition the perception of the one can follow upon the perception of the other, and *vice versâ*—which cannot occur in the succession of phenomena, as we have shown in the explanation of the second principle. Thus I can perceive the moon and then the earth, or conversely, first the earth and then the moon; and for the reason that my perception of these objects can reciprocally follow each other, I say, they exist contemporaneously. Now co-existence is the existence of the manifold in the same time. But time itself is not an object of perception; and therefore we cannot conclude from the fact that things are placed in the same time, the other fact, that the perceptions of these things can follow each other reciprocally. The synthesis of the imagination in apprehension would only present to us each of these perceptions as present in the subject when the other is not present, and contrariwise; but would not show that the objects are co-existent, that is to say, that, if the one exists, the other also exists in the same time, and that this is necessarily so, in order that the perceptions may be capable of following each other reciprocally. It follows that a conception of the understanding or category of the reciprocal sequence of the determinations of phenomena (existing as they do, apart from each other, and yet contemporaneously), is requisite to justify us in saying that the reciprocal succession of perceptions has its foundation in the object, and to enable us to represent co-existence as objective. But that relation of substances in which the one contains determinations the ground of which is in the other substance, is the relation of influence. And, when this influence is reciprocal, it is the relation of community or reciprocity. Consequently the co-existence of substances in space cannot be cognized in experience otherwise than under the precondition of their reciprocal action. This is therefore the condition of the possibility of things themselves as objects of experience.

Things are co-existent, in so far as they exist in one and the same time. But how can we know that they exist in one and the same time? Only by observing that the order in the synthesis of apprehension of the manifold is arbitrary and a matter of indifference, that is to say, that it can proceed from A, through B, C, D, to E, or contrariwise from E to A. For if they were successive in time (and in the order, let us suppose, which begins with A), it is quite impossible for the apprehension in perception to begin with E and go backwards to A, inasmuch as A belongs to past time, and therefore cannot be an object of apprehension.

Let us assume that in a number of substances considered as phenomena each is completely isolated, that is, that no one acts upon another. Then I say that the *co-existence* of these cannot be an object of possible perception, and that the existence of one cannot, by any mode of empirical synthesis, lead us to the existence of another. For we imagine them in this case to be separated by a completely void space, and thus perception, which proceeds from the one to the other in time, would indeed determine their existence by means of a following perception, but would be quite unable to distinguish whether the one phenomenon follows objectively upon the first, or is co-existent with it.

Besides the mere fact of existence then, there must be something by means of which A determines the position of B in time, and conversely, B the position of A; because only under this condition can substances be empirically represented as existing contemporaneously. Now that alone determines the position of another thing in time, which is the cause of it or of its determinations. Consequently every substance (inasmuch as it can have succession predicated of it only in respect of its determinations) must contain the causality of certain determinations in another substance, and at the same time the effects of the causality of the other in itself. That is to say, substances must stand (mediately or immediately) in dynamical community with each other, if co-existence is to be cognized in any possible experience. But, in regard to objects of experience, that is absolutely necessary, without which the experience of these objects would itself be impossible. Consequently it is absolutely necessary that all substances in the world of phenomena, in so far as they are co-existent, stand in a relation of complete community of reciprocal action to each other.

The word community has in our language* two meanings, and contains the two notions conveyed in the Latin *communio*, and *commercium*. We employ it in this place in the latter sense—that of a dynamical community, without which even the community of place (*communio spatii*) could not be empirically cognized. In our experiences it is easy to observe, that it is only the continuous influences in all parts of space that can conduct our senses from one object to another; that the light which plays between our eyes and the heavenly bodies produces a mediating community between them and us, and thereby evidences their co-existence with us; that we cannot empirically change our position (perceive this change), unless the existence of matter throughout the whole of space rendered possible the perception of the positions we occupy; and that this perception can prove the contemporaneous existence of these places only through their reciprocal influence, and thereby also the co-existence of even the most remote objects—although in this case the proof is only mediate. Without community, every perception (of a phenomenon in space) is separated from every other and isolated, and the chain of empirical representations, that is, of experience, must, with the appearance of a new object, begin entirely *de novo*, without the least connection with preceding representations, and without standing towards these even in the relation of time. My intention here is by no means to combat the notion of empty space; for it may exist where our perceptions cannot exist, inasmuch as they cannot reach thereto, and where, therefore, no empirical perception of co-existence takes place. But in this place it is not an object of possible experience.

The following remarks may be useful in the way of explanation. In the mind, all phenomena, as contents of a possible experience, must exist in community (communio) of apperception or consciousness, and in so far as it is requisite that objects be represented as co-existent and connected, in so far must they reciprocally determine the position in time of each other, and thereby constitute a whole. If this subjective community is to rest upon an objective basis, or to be applied to substances as phenomena, the perception of one substance must render possible the perception of another, and conversely. For otherwise succession, which is always found in perceptions as apprehensions, would be predicated of external objects, and their representation of their co-existence be thus impossible. But this is a reciprocal influence, that is to say, a real community (commercium) of substances, without which therefore the empirical relation of co-existence would be a notion beyond the reach of our minds. By virtue of this commercium, phenomena, in so far as they are apart from, and nevertheless in connection with each other, constitute a *compositum reale*. Such *composita* are possible in many different ways. The three dynamical relations then, from which all others spring, are those of Inherence, Consequence, and Composition.

* * * * * * *

These, then, are the three analogies of experience. They are nothing more than principles of the determination of the existence of phe-

* German.

nomena in time, according to the three *modi* of this determination; to wit, the relation to time itself as a quantity (the quantity of existence, that is, duration), the relation in time as a series or succession, finally, the relation in time as the complex of all existence (simultaneity). This unity of determination in regard to time is thoroughly dynamical; that is to say, time is not considered as that in which experience determines immediately to every existence its position; for this is impossible, inasmuch as absolute time is not an object of perception, by means of which phenomena can be connected with each other. On the contrary, the rule of the understanding, through which alone the existence of phenomena can receive synthetical unity as regards relations of time, determines for every phenomenon its position in time, and consequently *à priori,* and with validity for all and every time.

By nature, in the empirical sense of the word, we understand the totality of phenomena connected, in respect of their existence, according to necessary rules, that is, laws. There are therefore certain laws (which are moreover *à priori*) which make nature possible; and all empirical laws can exist only by means of experience, and by virtue of those primitive laws through which experience itself becomes possible. The purpose of the analogies is therefore to represent to us the unity of nature in the connection of all phenomena under certain exponents, the only business of which is to express the relation of time (in so far as it contains all existence in itself) to the unity of apperception, which can exist in synthesis only according to rules. The combined expression of all this is: All phenomena exist in one nature, and must so exist, inasmuch as without this *à priori* unity, no unity of experience, and consequently no determination of objects in experience, is possible.

As regards the mode of proof which we have employed in treating of these transcendental laws of nature, and the peculiar character of it, we must make one remark, which will at the same time be important as a guide in every other attempt to demonstrate the truth of intellectual and likewise synthetical propositions *à priori.* Had we endeavored to prove these analogies dogmatically, that is, from conceptions; that is to say, had we employed this method in attempting to show that everything which exists, exists only in that which is permanent—that every thing or event presupposes the existence of something in a preceding state, upon which it follows in conformity with a rule—lastly, that in the manifold, which is co-existent, the states co-exist in connection with each other according to a rule—all our labor would have been utterly in vain. For mere conceptions of things, analyze them as we may, cannot enable us to conclude from the existence of one object to the existence of another. What other course was left for us to pursue? This only, to demonstrate the possibility of experience as a cognition in which at last all objects must be capable of being presented to us, if the representation of them is to possess any objective reality. Now in this third, this mediating term, the essential form of which consists in the synthetical unity of the apperception of all phenomena, we found *à priori* conditions of the universal and necessary determination as to time of all existences in the world of phenomena, without which the empirical determination thereof as to time would itself be impossible, and we also discovered rules of synthetical unity *à priori,* by means of which we could anticipate experience. For want of this method, and from the fancy that it was possible to discover a dogmatical proof of the synthetical propositions which are requisite in the empirical employment of the understanding, has it happened, that a proof of the principle of sufficient reason has been so often attempted, and always in vain. The other two analogies nobody has ever thought of, although they have always been silently employed by the mind,* because the guiding thread furnished by the categories was wanting, the guide which alone can enable us to discover every hiatus, both in the system of conceptions and of principles.

IV. The Postulates of Empirical Thought

1. That which agrees with the formal conditions (intuition and conception) of experience, is possible.

2. That which coheres with the material conditions of experience (sensation) is real.

3. That whose coherence with the real is determined according to universal conditions of experience is (exists) necessary.

EXPLANATION

The categories of modality possess this peculiarity, that they do not in the least determine the object, or enlarge the conception to which they are annexed as predicates, but only express its relation to the faculty of cognition. Though my conception of a thing is in itself complete, I am still entitled to ask whether the object of it is merely possible, or whether it is also real, or, if the latter, whether it is also necessary. But hereby the object itself is not more definitely determined in thought, but the question is only in what relation it, including all its determinations, stands to the understanding and its employment in experience, to the empirical faculty of judgment, and to the reason in its application to experience.

For this very reason, too, the categories of modality are nothing more than explanations of the conceptions of possibility, reality, and necessity, as employed in experience, and at

---

* The unity of the universe, in which all phenomena must be connected, is evidently a mere consequence of the tacitly admitted principle of the community of all substances which are co-existent. For were substances isolated, they could not as parts constitute a whole, and were their connection (reciprocal action of the manifold) not necessary from the very fact of co-existence, we could not conclude from the fact of the latter as a merely ideal relation to the former as a real one. We have, however, shown in its place, that community is the proper ground of the possibility of an empirical cognition of co-existence, and that we may therefore properly reason from the latter to the former as its condition.

the same time, restrictions of all the categories to empirical use alone, not authorizing the transcendental employment of them. For if they are to have something more than a merely logical significance, and to be something more than a mere analytical expression of the form of *thought,* and to have a relation to *things* and their possibility, reality or necessity, they must concern possible experience and its synthetical unity, in which alone objects of cognition can be given.

The postulate of the possibility of things requires also, that the conception of the things agree with the formal conditions of our experience in general. But this, that is to say, the objective form of experience, contains all the kinds of synthesis which are requisite for the cognition of objects. A conception which contains a synthesis must be regarded as empty and without reference to an object, if its synthesis does not belong to experience—either as borrowed from it, and in this case it is called an *empirical conception,* or such as is the ground and *à priori* condition of experience (its form), and in this case it is a *pure conception,* a conception which nevertheless belongs to experience, inasmuch as its object can be found in this alone. For where shall we find the criterion or character of the possibility of an object which is cogitated by means of an *à priori* synthetical conception, if not in the synthesis which constitutes the form of empirical cognition of objects? That in such a conception no contradiction exists is indeed a necessary logical condition, but very far from being sufficient to establish the objective reality of the conception, that is, the possibility of such an object as is thought in the conception. Thus, in the conception of a figure which is contained within two straight lines, there is no contradiction, for the conceptions of two straight lines and of their junction contain no negation of a figure. The impossibility in such a case does not rest upon the conception in itself, but upon the construction of it in space, that is to say, upon the conditions of space and its determinations. But these have themselves objective reality, that is, they apply to possible things, because they contain *à priori* the form of experience in general.

And now we shall proceed to point out the extensive utility and influence of this postulate of possibility. When I represent to myself a thing that is permanent, so that everything in it which changes belongs merely to its state or condition, from such a conception alone I never can cognize that such a thing is possible. Or, if I represent to myself something which is so constituted that, when it is posited, something else follows always and infallibly, my thought contains no self-contradiction; but whether such a property as causality is to be found in any possible thing, my thought alone affords no means of judging. Finally, I can represent to myself different things (substances) which are so constituted, that the state or condition of one causes a change in the state of the other, and reciprocally; but whether such a relation is a property of things cannot be perceived from these conceptions, which contain a merely arbitrary synthesis. Only from the fact, therefore, that these conceptions express à priori the relations of perceptions in every experience, do we know that they possess objective reality, that is, transcendental truth; and that independent of experience, though not independent of all relation to the form of an experience in general and its synthetical unity, in which alone objects can be empirically cognized.

But when we fashion to ourselves new conceptions of substances, forces, action and reaction, from the material presented to us by perception, without following the example of experience in their connection, we create mere chimeras, of the possibility of which we cannot discover any criterion, because we have not taken experience for our instructress, though we have borrowed the conceptions from her. Such fictitious conceptions derive their character of possibility, not, like the categories, à priori, as conceptions on which all experience depends, but only, à posteriori, as conceptions given by means of experience itself, and their possibility must either be cognized à posteriori and empirically, or it cannot be cognized at all. A substance, which is permanently present in space, yet without filling it (like that tertium quid between matter and the thinking subject which some have tried to introduce into metaphysics), or a peculiar fundamental power of the mind of intuiting the future by anticipation (instead of merely inferring from past and present events), or, finally, a power of the mind to place itself in community of thought with other men, however distant they may be—these are conceptions, the possibility of which has no ground to rest upon. For they are not based upon experience and its known laws; and without experience, they are a merely arbitrary conjunction of thoughts, which, though containing no internal contradiction, has no claim to objective reality, neither, consequently, to the possibility of such an object as is thought in these conceptions. As far as concerns reality, it is self-evident that we cannot cogitate such a possibility *in concreto* without the aid of experience; because reality is concerned only with sensation, as the matter of experience, and not with the form of thought, with which we can no doubt indulge in shaping fancies.

But I pass by everything which derives its possibility from reality in experience, and I purpose treating here merely of the possibility of things by means of *à priori* conceptions. I maintain, then, that the possibility of things is not derived from such conceptions *per se,* but only when considered as formal and objective conditions of an experience in general.

It seems, indeed, as if the possibility of a triangle could be cognized from the conception of it alone (which is certainly independent of experience); for we can certainly give to the conception a corresponding object completely *à priori,* that is to say, we can construct it. But as a triangle is only the form of an object, it must remain a mere product of the imagination, and the possibility of the existence of an object corresponding to it must remain doubtful, unless we can discover some other ground, unless we know that the figure can be cogitated under the conditions upon which all objects of experience rest. Now, the facts that space is a formal condition *à priori* of external experience, that the formative synthesis, by which we construct a triangle in imagination, is the very same as that we employ in the apprehension of a phenomenon for the purpose of making an empirical conception of it, are what alone connect the notion of the possibility of such a thing with the conception of it. In the same manner, the possibility of continuous quantities, indeed of quantities in general, for the conceptions of them are without exception synthetical, is never evident from the conceptions in themselves, but only when they are considered as the formal conditions of the determination of objects in experience. And where, indeed, should we look for objects to correspond to our conceptions, if not in experience, by which alone objects are presented to us? It is, however, true that without antecedent experience we can cognize and characterize the possibility of things, relatively to the formal conditions, under something is determined in experience as an object, consequently completely *à priori*. But still this is possible only in relation to experience and within its limits.

The postulate concerning the cognition of the *reality* of things requires *perception,* consequently conscious sensation, not indeed immediately, that is, of the object itself, whose existence is to be cognized, but still that the object have some connection with a real perception, in accordance with the analogies of experience, which exhibit all kinds of real connection in experience.

From the *mere conception* of a thing it is impossible to conclude its existence. For, let the conception be ever so complete, and containing a statement of all the determinations of the thing, the existence of it has nothing to do with all this, but only with the question—whether such a thing is given, so that the perception of it can in every case precede the conception. For the fact that the conception of it precedes the perception, merely indicates the possibility of its existence; it is perception, which presents matter to the conception, that is the sole criterion of reality. Prior to the perception of the thing, however, and therefore comparatively *à priori,* we are able to cognize its existence, provided it stands in connection with some perceptions according to the principles of the empirical conjunction of these, that is, in conformity with the analogies of perception. For, in this case, the existence of the supposed thing is connected with our perceptions in a possible experience, and we are able, with the guidance of these analogies, to reason in the series of possible perceptions from a thing which we do really perceive to the thing we do not perceive. Thus, we cognize the existence of a magnetic matter penetrating all bodies from the perception of the attraction of the steel-filings by the magnet, although the constitution of our organs renders an immediate perception of this matter impossible for us. For, according to the laws of sensibility and the connected context of our perceptions, we should in an experience come also on an immediate empirical intuition of this matter, if our senses were more acute—but this obtuseness has no influence upon and cannot alter the *form* of possible experience in general. Our knowledge of the existence of things reaches as far as our perceptions, and what may be inferred from them according to empirical laws, extend. If we do not set out from experience, or do not proceed according to the laws of the empirical connection of phenomena, our pretensions to discover the existence of a thing which we do not immediately perceive are vain. *Idealism*, however, brings forward powerful objections to these rules for proving existence mediately. This is, therefore, the proper place for its refutation.

Refutation of Idealism

Idealism—I mean *material* idealism—is the theory which declares the existence of objects in space without us to be either (1) doubtful and indemonstrable, or (2) false and impossible. The first is the *problematical* idealism of Descartes, who admits the undoubted certainty of only one empirical assertion (*assertio*), to wit, *I am*. The second is the *dogmatical* idealism of Berkeley, who maintains that space, together with all the objects of which it is the inseparable condition, is a thing which is in itself impossible, and that consequently the objects in space are mere products of the imagination. The dogmatical theory of idealism is unavoidable, if we regard space as a property of things in themselves; for in that case it is, with all to which it serves as condition, a nonentity. But the foundation for this kind of idealism we have already destroyed in the transcendental æsthetic. Problematical idealism, which makes no such assertion, but only alleges our incapacity to prove the existence of anything besides ourselves by means of immediate experience, is a theory rational and evidencing a thorough and philosophical mode of thinking, for it observes the rule, not to form a decisive judgment before sufficient proof be shown. The desired proof must therefore demonstrate that we have *experience* of external things, and not mere *fancies*. For this purpose, we must prove, that our internal and, to Descartes, indubitable experience is itself possible only under the previous assumption of external experience.

Theorem

The simple but empirically determined consciousness of my own existence proves the existence of external objects in space

PROOF

I am conscious of my own existence as determined in time. All determination in regard to time presupposes the existence of *something permanent* in perception. But this permanent something cannot be something in me, for the very reason that my existence in time is itself determined by this permanent something. It follows that the perception of this permanent existence is possible only through a *thing* without me, and not through the mere *representation* of a thing without me. Consequently, the determination of my existence in time is possible only through the existence of real things external to me. Now, consciousness in time is necessarily connected with the consciousness of the possibility of this determination in time. Hence it follows, that consciousness in time is necessarily connected also with the existence of things without me, inasmuch as the existence of these things is the condition of determination in time. That is to say, the consciousness of my own existence is at the same time an immediate consciousness of the existence of other things without me.

Remark I. The reader will observe that, in the foregoing proof, the game which idealism plays is retorted upon itself, and with more justice. It assumed, that the only immediate experience is internal, and that from this we can only *infer* the existence of external things. But, as always happens, when we reason from given effects to *determined* causes, idealism has reasoned with too much haste and uncertainty, for it is quite possible that the cause of our representations may lie in ourselves, and that we ascribe it falsely to external things. But our proof shows that external experience is properly immediate,* that only by virtue of it—not, indeed, the consciousness of our own existence, but certainly the determination of our existence in time, that is, internal experience—is possible. It is true that the representation *I am,* which is the expression of the consciousness which can accompany all my thoughts, is that which immediately includes the existence of a subject. But in this representation we cannot find any knowledge of the subject, and therefore also no empirical knowledge, that is, experience. For experience contains, in addition to the thought of something existing, intuition, and in this case it must be internal intuition, that is, time, in relation to which the subject must be determined. But the existence of external things is absolutely requisite for this purpose, so that it follows that internal experience is itself possible only mediately and through external experience.

Remark II. Now with this view all empirical use of our faculty of cognition in the determination of time is in perfect accordance. Its truth is supported by the fact, that it is possible to perceive a determination of time only by means of a change in external relations (motion) to the permanent in space (for example, we become aware of the sun's motion, by observing the changes of his relation to the objects of this earth). But this is not all. We find that we possess nothing permanent

---

* The *immediate* consciousness of the existence of external things is, in the preceding theorem, not presupposed, but proved, be the possibility of this consciousness understood by us or not. The question as to the possibility of it would stand thus: Have we an internal sense, but no external sense, and is our belief in external perception a mere delusion? But it is evident that, in order merely to fancy to ourselves anything as external, that is, to present it to the sense in intuition, we must already possess an external sense, and must thereby distinguish immediately the mere receptivity of an external intuition from the spontaneity which characterizes every act of imagination. For merely to imagine also an external sense, would annihilate the faculty of intuition itself which is to be determined by the imagination.

that can correspond and be submitted to the conception of a substance as intuition, except *matter*. This idea of permanence is not itself derived from external experience, but is an *à priori* necessary condition of all determination of time, consequently also of the internal sense in reference to our own existence, and that through the existence of external things. In the representation *I*, the consciousness of myself is not an intuition, but a merely intellectual representation produced by the spontaneous activity of a thinking subject. It follows, that this *I* has not any predicate of intuition, which, in its character of permanence, could serve as correlate to the determination of time in the internal sense—in the same way as impenetrability is the correlate of matter as an empirical intuition.

Remark III. From the fact that the existence of external things is a necessary condition of the possibility of a determined consciousness of ourselves, it does not follow that every intuitive representation of external things involves the existence of these things, for their representations may very well be the mere products of the imagination (in dreams as well as in madness); though, indeed, these are themselves created by the reproduction of previous external perceptions, which, as has been shown, are possible only through the reality of external objects. The sole aim of our remarks has, however, been to prove that internal experience in general is possible only through external experience in general. Whether this or that supposed experience be purely imaginary, must be discovered from its particular determinations, and by comparing these with the criteria of all real experience.

Finally, as regards the third postulate, it applies to material necessity in existence, and not to merely formal and logical necessity in the connection of conceptions. Now as we cannot cognize completely *à priori* the existence of any object of sense, though we can do so comparatively *à priori*, that is, relatively to some other previously given existence—a cognition, however, which can only be of such an existence as must be contained in the complex of experience, of which the previously given perception is a part—the necessity of existence can never be cognized from conceptions, but always, on the contrary, from its connection with that which is an object of perception. But the only existence cognized, under the condition of other given phenomena, as necessary, is the existence of effects from given causes in conformity with the laws of causality. It is consequently not the necessity of the existence of things (as substances), but the necessity of the state of things that we cognize, and that not immediately, but by means of the existence of other states given in perception, according to empirical laws of causality. Hence it follows, that the criterion of necessity is to be found only in the law of a possible experience—that everything which happens is determined *à priori* in the phenomenon by its cause. Thus we cognize only the necessity of *effects* in nature, the causes of which are given us. Moreover, the criterion of necessity in existence possesses no application beyond the field of possible experience, and even in this it is not valid of the existence of things as substances, because these can never be considered as empirical effects, or as something that happens and has a beginning. Necessity, therefore, regards only the relations of phenomena according to the dynamical law of causality, and the possibility grounded thereon, of reasoning from some given existence (of a cause) *à priori* to another existence (of an effect). *Everything that happens is hypothetically necessary,* is a principle which subjects the changes that take place in the world to a law, that is, to a rule of necessary existence, without which nature herself could not possibly exist. Hence the proposition, *Nothing happens by blind chance (in mundo non datur casus),* is an *à priori* law of nature. The case is the same with the proposition, *Necessity in nature is not blind,* that is, it is conditioned, consequently intelligible necessity *(non datur fatum).* Both laws subject the play of change to *a nature of things* (as phenomena), or, which is the same thing, to the unity of the understanding, and through the understanding alone can changes belong to an experience, as the synthetical unity of phenomena. Both belong to the class of dynamical principles. The former is properly a consequence of the principle of causality—one of the analogies of experience. The latter belongs to the principles of modality, which to the determination of causality adds the conception of necessity, which is itself, however, subject to a rule of the understanding. The principle of continuity forbids any *leap* in the series of phenomena regarded as changes *(in mundo non datur saltus)*; and likewise, in the complex of all empirical intuitions in space, any break or hiatus between two phenomena *(non datur hiatus)* —for we can so express the principle, that experience can admit nothing which proves the existence of a vacuum, or which even admits it as a part of an empirical synthesis. For, as regards a vacuum or void, which we may cogitate as out of and beyond the field of possible experience (the world), such a question cannot come before the tribunal of mere understanding, which decides only upon questions that concern the employment of given phenomena for the construction of empirical cognition. It is rather a problem for ideal reason, which passes beyond the sphere of a possible experience, and aims at forming a judgment of that which surrounds and circumscribes it, and the proper place for the consideration of it is the transcendental dialectic. These four propositions, *In mundo non datur hiatus, non datur saltus, non datur casus, non datur fatum,* as well as all principles of transcendental origin, we could very easily exhibit in their proper order, that is, in conformity with the order of the categories, and assign to each its proper place. But the already practised reader will do this for himself, or discover the clue to such an arrangement. But the combined result of all is simply this, to admit into the empirical synthesis nothing which might cause a break in or be foreign to the understanding and the continuous connection of all phenomena, that is, the unity of the conceptions of the understanding. For in the understanding alone is the unity of experience, in which all perceptions must have their assigned place, possible.

Whether the field of possibility be greater than that of reality, and whether the field of the latter be itself greater than that of necessity, are interesting enough questions, and quite capable of synthetical solution, questions, however, which come under the jurisdiction of reason alone. For they are tantamount to asking, whether all things as phenomena do without exception belong to the complex and connected whole of a single experience, of which every given perception is a part, a part which therefore cannot be conjoined with any other phenomena —or, whether my perceptions can belong to more than one possible experience? The understanding gives to experience, according to the subjective and formal conditions, of sensibility as well as of apperception, the rules which alone make this experience possible. Other forms of intuition, besides those of space and time, other forms of understanding besides the discursive forms of thought, or of cognition by means of conceptions, we can neither imagine nor make intelligible to ourselves; and even if we could, they would still not belong to experience, which is the only mode of cognition by which objects are presented to us. Whether other perceptions besides those which belong to the total of our possible experience, and consequently whether some other sphere of matter exists, the understanding has no power to decide, its proper occupation being with the synthesis of that which is given. Moreover, the poverty of the usual arguments which go to prove the existence of a vast sphere of possibility, of which all that is real (every object of experience) is but a small part, is very remarkable. " All real is possible;" from this follows naturally, according to the logical laws of conversion, the particular proposition, " Some possible is real." Now this seems to be equivalent to " Much is possible that is not real." No doubt it does seem as if we ought to consider the sum of the possible to be greater than that of the real, from the fact that something must be added to the former to constitute the latter. But this notion of adding to the possible is absurd. For that which is not in the sum of the possible, and consequently requires to be added to it, is manifestly impossible. In addition to accordance with the formal conditions of experience, the understanding requires a connection with some perception; but that which is connected with this perception, is real, even though it is not immediately perceived. But that another series of phenomena, in complete coherence with that which is given in perception, consequently more than one all-embracing experience is possible, is an inference which cannot be concluded from the data given us by experience, and still less without any data at all. That which is possible only under conditions which are themselves merely possible, is not possible *in any respect*. And yet we can find no more certain ground on which to base the discussion of the question whether the sphere of possibility is wider than that of experience.

I have merely mentioned these questions, that in treating of the conception of understanding, there might be no omission of anything that, in the common opinion, belongs to them. In reality, however, the notion of absolute possibility (possibility which is valid in every respect) is not a mere conception of the understanding, which can be employed empirically, but belongs to reason alone, which passes the bounds of all empirical use of the understanding. We have, therefore, contented ourselves with a merely critical remark, leaving the subject to be explained in the sequel.

Before concluding this fourth section, and at the same time the system of all principles of the pure understanding, it seems proper to mention the reasons which induced me to term the principles of modality postulates. This expression I do not here use in the sense which some more recent philosophers, contrary to its meaning with mathematicians, to whom the word properly belongs, attach to it—that of a proposition, namely, immediately certain, requiring neither deduction nor proof. For if, in the case of synthetical propositions, however evident they may be, we accord to them without deduction, and merely on the strength of their own pretensions, unqualified belief, all critique of the understanding is entirely lost; and, as there is no want of bold pretensions, which the common belief (though for the philosopher this is no credential) does not reject, the understanding lies exposed to every delusion and conceit, without the power of refusing its assent to those assertions, which, though illegitimate, demand acceptance as veritable axioms. When, therefore, to the conception of a thing an *à priori* determination is synthetically added, such a proposition must obtain, if not a proof, at least a deduction of the legitimacy of its assertion.

The principles of modality are, however, not objectively synthetical, for the predicates of possibility, reality, and necessity do not in the least augment the conception of that of which they are affirmed, inasmuch as they contribute nothing to the representation of the object. But as they are, nevertheless, always synthetical, they are so merely subjectively. That is to say, they have a reflective power, and apply to the conception of a thing, of which, in other respects, they affirm nothing, the faculty of cognition in which the conception originates and has its seat. So that if the conception merely agree with the formal conditions of experience, its object is called possible; if it is in connection with perception, and determined thereby, the object is real; if it is determined according to conceptions by means of the connection of perceptions, the object is called necessary. The principles of modality therefore predicate of a conception nothing more than the procedure of the faculty of cognition which generated it. Now a postulate in mathematics is a practical proposition which contains nothing but the synthesis by which we present an object to ourselves, and produce the conception of it, for example—" With a given line, to describe a circle upon a plane, from a given point;" and such a proposition does not admit of proof, because the procedure, which it requires, is exactly that by which alone it is possible to generate the conception of such a figure. With the same right, accordingly, can we postulate the principles of modality, because they do not augment* the conception of a thing, but merely indicate the manner in which it is connected with the faculty of cognition.

* When I think the *reality* of a thing, I do really think more than the possibility, but not *in the thing;* for that can never contain more in reality than was contained in its complete possibility. But while the notion of possibility is merely the notion of a position of a thing in relation to the understanding (its empirical use), reality is the conjunction of the thing with perception.

General Remark of the System of Principles

It is very remarkable that we cannot perceive the possibility of a thing from the category alone, but must always have an intuition, by which to make evident the objective reality of the pure conception of the understanding. Take, for example, the categories of relation. How (1) a thing can exist only as a *subject*, and not as a mere determination of other things, that is, can be *substance*; or how (2), because something exists, some other thing must exist, consequently how a thing can be a cause; or (3) how, when several things exist, from the fact that one of these things exists, some consequence to the others follows, and reciprocally, and in this way a community of substances can be possible—are questions whose solution cannot be obtained from mere conceptions. The very same is the case with the other categories; for example, how a thing can be of the same sort with many others, that is, can be a quantity, and so on. So long as we have not intuition we cannot know, whether we do really think an object by the categories, and where an object can anywhere be found to cohere with them, and thus the truth is established, that the categories are not in themselves *cognitions*, but mere *forms of thought* for the construction of cognitions from given intuitions. For the same reason is it true that from categories alone no synthetical proposition can be made. For example, " In every existence there is substance," that is, something that can exist only as a subject and not as mere predicate; or, " everything is a quantity "—to construct propositions such as these, we require something to enable us to go out beyond the given conception and connect another with it. For the same reason the attempt to prove a synthetical proposition by means of mere conceptions, for example, " Everything that exists contingently has a cause," has never succeeded. We could never get further than proving that, without this relation to conceptions, we could *not conceive* the existence of the contingent, that is, could not *à priori* through the understanding cognize the existence of such a thing; but it does not hence follow that this is also the condition of the possibility of the thing itself that is said to be contingent. If, accordingly, we look back to our proof of the principle of causality, we shall find that we were able to prove it as valid only of objects of possible experience, and, indeed, only as itself the principle of the possibility of experience, consequently of the *cognition* of an object given in *empirical intuition,* and not from mere conceptions. That, however, the proposition, "Every-thing that is contingent must have a cause," is evident to every one merely from conceptions, is not to be denied. But in this case the conception of the contingent is cogitated as involving not the category of modality (as that the non-existence of which can be *conceived*), but that of relation (as that which can exist only as the consequence of something else), and so it is really an identical proposition, "That which can exist only as a con-sequence, has a cause." In fact, when we have to give examples of contingent existence, we always refer to *changes,* and not merely to the possibility of *conceiving the opposite.** But change is an event, which, as such, is possible only through a cause, and considered *per se* its non-existence is therefore pos-sible, and we become cognizant of its contingency from the fact that it can exist only as the effect of a cause. Hence, if a thing is assumed to be contingent, it is an analytical proposition to say, it has a cause.

But it is still more remarkable that, to understand the pos-sibility of things according to the categories, and thus to demon-strate the *objective reality* of the latter, we require not merely intuitions, but *external intuitions.* If, for example, we take the pure conceptions of relation, we find that (1) for the purpose of presenting to the conception of *substance* something *permanent* in intuition corresponding thereto, and thus of demonstrating the objective reality of this conception, we require an intuition (of matter) in *space,* because space alone is permanent and de-termines things as such, while time, and with it all that is in the internal sense, is in a state of continual flow; (2) in order to represent *change* as the intuition corresponding to the concep-tion of causality, we require the representation of motion as change in space; in fact, it is through it alone that changes, the possibility of which no pure understanding can perceive, are

---

* We can easily conceive the non-existence of matter; but the ancients did not thence infer its contingency. But even the alternation of the ex-istence and non-existence of a given state in a thing, in which all change con-sists, by no means proves the con-tingency of that state—the ground of proof being the reality of its opposite. For example, a body is in a state of rest after motion, but we cannot infer the contingency of the motion from the fact that the former is the opposite of the latter. For this opposite is merely a logical and not a real opposite to the other. If we wish to demonstrate the contingency of the motion, what we ought to prove is, that, *instead* of the motion which took place in the preced-ing point of time, it was possible for the body to have been *then* in rest, not that it is *afterwards* in rest; for, in this case, both opposites are perfectly con-sistent with each other.

capable of being intuited. Change is the connection of determinations contradictorily opposed to each other in the existence
of one and the same thing. Now, how it is possible that out of a
given state one quite opposite to it in the same thing should follow, reason without an example cannot only not conceive, but
cannot even make intelligible without intuition; and this intuition is the motion of a point in space; the existence of which
in different spaces (as a consequence of opposite determinations) alone makes the intuition of change possible. For, in
order to make even internal change cogitable, we require to
represent time, as the form of the internal sense, figuratively
by a line, and the internal change by the drawing of that line
(motion), and consequently are obliged to employ external intuition to be able to represent the successive existence of ourselves in different states. The proper ground of this fact is,
that all change to be perceived as change pre-supposes something permanent in intuition, while in the internal sense no
permanent intuition is to be found. Lastly, the objective possibility of the category of *community* cannot be conceived by
mere reason, and consequently its objective reality cannot be
demonstrated without an intuition, and that external in space.
For how can we conceive the possibility of community, that is,
when several substances exist, that some effect on the existence
of the one follows from the existence of the other, and reciprocally, and therefore that, because something exists in the latter,
something else must exist in the former, which could not be
understood from its own existence alone? For this is the very
essence of community—which is inconceivable as a property of
things which are perfectly isolated. Hence, Leibnitz, in attributing to the substances of the world—as cogitated by the understanding alone—a community, required the mediating aid of
a divinity; for, from their existence, such a property seemed
to him with justice inconceivable. But we can very easily conceive the possibility of community (of substances as phenomena) if we represent them to ourselves as in space, consequently in external intuition. For external intuition contains
in itself *à priori* formal external relations, as the conditions of
the possibility of the real relations of action and reaction, and
therefore of the possibility of community. With the same ease
can it be demonstrated, that the possibility of things as *quantities,* and consequently the objective reality of the category of

quantity, can be grounded only in external intuition, and that by its means alone is the notion of quantity appropriated by the internal sense. But I must avoid prolixity, and leave the task of illustrating this by examples to the reader's own reflection.

The above remarks are of the greatest importance, not only for the confirmation of our previous confutation of idealism, but still more, when the subject of *self-cognition* by mere internal consciousness and the determination of our own nature without the aid of external empirical intuitions is under discussion, for the indication of the grounds of the possibility of such a cognition.

The result of the whole of this part of the Analytic of Principles is, therefore—All principles of the pure understanding are nothing more than *à priori* principles of the possibility of experience, and to experience alone do all *à priori* synthetical propositions apply and relate—indeed, their possibility itself rests entirely on this relation.

Chapter III

Of the Ground of the Division of all Objects into Phenomena and Noumena

We have now not only traversed the region of the pure understanding, and carefully surveyed every part of it, but we have also measured it, and assigned to everything therein its proper place. But this land is an island, and inclosed by nature herself within unchangeable limits. It is the land of truth (an attractive word), surrounded by a wide and stormy ocean, the region of illusion, where many a fog-bank, many an iceberg, seems to the mariner, on his voyage of discovery, a new country, and while constantly deluding him with vain hopes, engages him in dangerous adventures, from which he never can' desist, and which yet he never can bring to a termination. But before venturing upon this sea, in order to explore it in its whole extent, and to arrive at a certainty whether anything is to be discovered there, it will not be without advantage if we cast our eyes upon the chart of the land that we are about to leave, and to ask ourselves, firstly, whether we cannot rest perfectly contented with what it contains, or whether we must not of necessity be contented with it, if we can find nowhere else a solid foundation to build upon; and, secondly, by what title we possess this land itself, and how we hold it secure against all hostile claims? Although, in the course of our analytic, we have already given sufficient answers to these questions, yet a summary recapitulation of these solutions may be useful in strengthening our conviction, by uniting in one point the momenta of the arguments.

We have seen that everything which the understanding draws from itself, without borrowing from experience, it nevertheless possesses only for the behoof and use of experience. The principles of the pure understanding, whether constitutive à priori (as the mathematical principles), or merely regulative (as the dynamical), contain nothing but the pure schema, as it were, of possible experience. For experience possesses its unity from the synthetical unity which the understanding, originally and from itself, imparts to the synthesis of the imagination in relation to apperception, and in à priori relation to and agreement with which phenomena, as data for a possible cognition, must stand. But although these rules of the understanding are not only à priori true, but the very source of all truth, that is, of the accordance of our cognition with objects, and on this ground, that they contain the basis of the possibility of experience, as the *ensemble* of all cognition, it seems to us not enough to propound what is true—we desire also to be told what we want to know. If, then, we learn nothing more by this critical examination, than what we should have practised in the merely empirical use of the understanding, without any such subtle inquiry, the presumption is, that the advantage we reap from it is not worth the labor bestowed upon it. It may certainly be answered, that no rash curiosity is more prejudicial to the enlargement of our knowledge than that which must know beforehand the utility of this or that piece of information which we seek, before we have entered on the needful investigations, and before one could form the least conception of its utility, even though it were placed before our eyes. But there is one advantage in such transcendental inquiries which can be made comprehensible to the dullest and most reluctant learner—this, namely, that the understanding which is occupied merely with empirical exercise, and does not reflect on the sources of its own cognition, may exercise its functions very well and very successfully, but is quite unable

to do one thing, and that of very great importance, to determine, namely, the bounds that limit its employment, and to
know what lies within or without its own sphere. This purpose can be obtained only by such profound investigations as
we have instituted. But if it cannot distinguish whether certain questions lie within its horizon or not, it can never be sure
either as to its claims or possessions, but must lay its account
with many humiliating corrections, when it transgresses, as if
unavoidably will, the limits of its own territory, and loses itself
in fanciful opinions and blinding illusions.

That the understanding, therefore, cannot make of its *à priori*
principles, or even of its conceptions other than an empirical
use, is a proposition which leads to the most important results.
A transcendental use is made of a conception in a fundamental
proposition or principle, when it is referred to things *in general*
and considered as things *in themselves;* an empirical use, when
it is referred merely to *phenomena,* that is to objects of a possible *experience.* That the latter use of a conception is the only
admissible one is evident from the reasons following. For
every conception are requisite, firstly, the logical form of a conception (of thought) in general; and, secondly, the possibility
of presenting to this an object to which it may apply. Failing
this latter, it has no sense, and is utterly void of content, although it may contain the logical function for constructing a
conception from certain data. Now object cannot be given to
a conception otherwise than by intuition, and, even if a pure
intuition antecedent to the object is *à priori* possible, this pure
intuition can itself obtain objective validity only from empirical
intuition, of which it is itself but the form. All conceptions,
therefore, and with them all principles, however high the degree of their *à priori* possibility, relate to empirical intuitions,
that is, to data towards a possible experience. Without this
they possess no objective validity, but are a mere play of imagination or of understanding with images or notions. Let
us take, for example, the conceptions of mathematics, and first
in its pure intuitions. "Space has three dimensions"—"Between two points there can be only one straight line," etc. Although all these principles, and the representation of the object
with which this science occupies itself, are generated in the mind
entirely *à priori,* they would nevertheless have no significance,
if we were not always able to exhibit their significance in and

by means of phenomena (empirical objects). Hence it is requisite that an abstract conception be *made sensuous*, that is, that an object corresponding to it in intuition be forthcoming, otherwise the conception remains, as we say, without *sense*, that is, without meaning. Mathematics fulfils this requirement by the construction of the figure, which is a phenomenon evident to the senses. The same science finds support and significance in number; this in its turn finds it in the fingers, or in counters, or in lines and points. The conception itself is always produced *à priori*, together with the synthetical principles or formulas from such conceptions; but the proper employment of them, and their application to objects, can exist nowhere but in experience, the possibility of which, as regards its form, they contain *à priori*.

That this is also the case with all of the categories and the principles based upon them, is evident from the fact, that we cannot render intelligible the possibility of an object corresponding to them, without having recourse to the conditions of sensibility, consequently, to the form of phenomena, to which, as their only proper objects, their use must therefore be confined, inasmuch as, if this condition is removed, all significance, that is, all relation to an object disappears, and no example can be found to make it comprehensible what sort of things we ought to think under such conceptions.

The conception of quantity cannot be explained except by saying that it is the determination of a thing whereby it can be cogitated how many times one is placed in it. But this "how many times" is based upon successive repetition, consequently upon time and the synthesis of the homogeneous therein. Reality, in contradistinction to negation, can be explained only by cogitating a time which is either filled therewith or is void. If I leave out the notion of permanence (which is existence in all time), there remains in the conception of substance nothing but the logical notion of subject, a notion of which I endeavor to realize by representing to myself something that can exist only as a subject. But not only am I perfectly ignorant of any conditions under which this logical prerogative can belong to a thing, I can make nothing out of the notion, and draw no inference from it, because no object to which to apply the conception is determined, and we consequently do not know whether it has any meaning at all. In like manner, if I leave out the notion of time, in which something follows upon some other thing in conformity with a rule, I can find nothing in the pure category, except that there is a something of such a sort that from it a conclusion may be drawn as to the existence of some other thing. But in this case it would not only be impossible to distinguish between a cause and an effect, but, as this power to draw conclusions requires conditions of which I am quite ignorant, the conception is not determined as to the mode in which it ought to apply to an object. The so-called principle, Everything that is contingent has a cause, comes with a gravity and self-assumed authority that seems to require no support from without. But, I ask, what is meant by contingent? The answer is, that the non-existence of which is possible. But I should like very well to know, by what means this possibility of non-existence is to be cognized, if we do not represent to ourselves a succession in the series of phenomena, and in this succession an existence which follows a non-existence, or conversely, consequently, change. For to say that the non-existence of a thing is not self-contradictory. is a lame appeal to a logical condition, which is no doubt a necessary condition of the existence of the conception, but is far from being sufficient for the real objective possibility of non-existence. I can annihilate in thought every existing substance without self-contradiction, but I cannot infer from this their objective contingency in existence, that is to say, the possibility of their non-existence in itself. As regards the category of community, it may easily be inferred that, as the pure categories of substance and causality are incapable of a definition and explanation sufficient to determine their object without the aid of intuition, the category of reciprocal causality in the relation of substances to each other (*commercium*) is just as little susceptible thereof. Possibility, Existence, and Necessity nobody has ever yet been able to explain without being guilty of manifest tautology, when the definition has been drawn entirely from the pure understanding. For the substitution of the logical possibility of the *conception*—the condition of which is that it be not self-contradictory, for the transcendental possibility of *things*—the condition of which is, that there be an object corresponding to the conception, is a trick which can only deceive the inexperienced.*

* In one word, to none of these conceptions belongs a corresponding object, and consequently their real possibility cannot be demonstrated, if we

It follows incontestably, that the pure conceptions of the understanding are incapable of *transcendental,* and must always be of *empirical* use alone, and that the principles of the pure understanding relate only to the general conditions of a possible experience, to objects of the senses, and never to things in general, apart from the mode in which we intuite them.

Transcendental Analytic has accordingly this important result, to-wit, that the understanding is competent to effect nothing *à priori,* except the anticipation of the form of a possible experience in general, and that, as that which is not phenomenon cannot be an object of experience, it can never overstep the limits of sensibility, within which alone objects are presented to us. Its principles are merely principles of the exposition of phenomena, and the proud name of an Ontology, which professes to present synthetical cognitions *à priori* of things in general in a systematic doctrine, must give place to the modest title of analytic of the pure understanding.

Thought is the act of referring a given intuition to an object. If the mode of this intuition is unknown to us, the object is merely transcendental, and the conception of the understanding is employed only transcendentally, that is, to produce unity in the thought of a manifold in general. Now a pure category, in which all conditions of sensuous intuition—as the only intuition we possess—are abstracted, does not determine an object, but merely expresses the thought of an object in general, according to different modes. Now, to employ a conception, the function of judgment is required, by which an object is subsumed under the conception, consequently the at least formal condition, under which something can be given in intuition. Failing this condition of judgment (schema), subsumption is impossible; for there is in such a case nothing given, which may be subsumed under the conception. The merely transcendental use of the categories is therefore, in fact, no use at all, and has no determined, or even, as regards its form, determinable object. Hence it follows, that the pure category is incompetent to establish a synthetical *à priori* principle, and that the principles of the pure understanding are only of empirical and never of transcendental use, and that beyond the

take away sensuous intuition—the only intuition which we possess, and there then remains nothing but the *logical* possibility, that is, the fact that the conception or thought is possible— which, however, is not the question; what we want to know being, whether it relates to an object and thus possesses any meaning.

sphere of possible experience no synthetical *à priori* principles are possible.

It may be advisable, therefore, to express ourselves thus. The pure categories, apart from the formal conditions of sensibility, have a merely transcendental *meaning*, but are nevertheless not of transcendental *use*, because this is in itself impossible, inasmuch as all the conditions of any employment or use of them (in judgments) are absent, to wit, the formal conditions of the subsumption of an object under these conceptions. As, therefore, in the character of pure categories, they must be employed empirically, and cannot be employed transcendentally, they are of no use at all, when separated from sensibility, that is, they cannot be applied to an object. They are merely the pure form of the employment of the understanding in respect of objects in general and of thought, without its being at the same time possible to think or to determine any object by their means.

But there lurks at the foundation of this subjejct an illusion which it is very difficult to avoid. The categories are not based, as regards their origin, upon sensibility, like the *forms of intuition*, space and time; they seem, therefore, to be capable of an application beyond the sphere of sensuous objects. But this is not the case. They are nothing but mere *forms of thought*, which contain only the logical faculty of uniting *à priori* in consciousness the manifold given in intuition. Apart, then, from the only intuition possible for us, they have still less meaning than the pure sensuous forms, space and time, for through them an object is at least given, while a mode of connection of the manifold, when the intuition which alone gives the manifold is wanting, has no meaning at all. At the same time, when we designate certain objects as phenomena or sensuous existence, thus distinguishing our mode of intuiting them from their own nature as things in themselves, it is evident that by this very distinction we as it were place the latter, considered in this their own nature, although we do not so intuite them, in opposition to the former, or, on the other hand, we do so place other possible things, which are not objects of our senses, but are cogitated by the understanding alone, and call them intelligible existences (noumena). Now the question arises, whether the pure conceptions of our understanding do possess significance in respect of these latter, and may possibly be a mode of cognizing them.

But we are met at the very commencement with an ambiguity, which may easily occasion great misapprehension.   The understanding, when it terms an object in a certain relation phenomenon, at the same time forms out of this relation a representation or notion of an *object in itself*, and hence believes that it can form also *conceptions* of such objects.   Now as the understanding possesses no other fundamental conceptions besides the categories, it takes for granted that an object considered as a thing in itself must be capable of being thought by means of these pure conceptions, and is thereby led to hold the perfectly undetermined conception of an intelligible existence, a something out of the sphere of our sensibility, for a *determinate* conception of an existence which we can cognize in some way or other by means of the understanding.

If, by the term noumenon, we understand a thing so far as it is *not an object of our sensuous intuition*, thus making abstraction of our mode of intuiting it, this is a noumenon in the *negative* sense of the word.   But if we understand by it an *object of a non-sensuous intuition*, we in this case assume a peculiar mode of intuition, an intellectual intuition, to wit, which does not, however, belong to us, of the very possibility of which we have no notion—and this is a noumenon in the *positive* sense.

The doctrine of sensibility is also the doctrine of noumena in the negative sense, that is, of things which the understanding is obliged to cogitate apart from any relation to our mode of intuition, consequently not as mere phenomena, but as things in themselves.   But the understanding at the same time comprehends that it cannot employ its categories for the consideration of things in themselves, because these possess significance only in relation to the unity of intuitions in space and time, and that they are competent to determine this unity by means of general *à priori* connecting conceptions only on account of the pure ideality of space and time.   Where this unity of time is not to be met with, as is the case with noumena, the whole use, indeed the whole meaning of the categories is entirely lost, for even the possibility of things to correspond to the categories, is in this case incomprehensible.   On this point, I need only refer the reader to what I have said at the commencement of the General Remark appended to the foregoing chapter.   Now, the possibility of a thing can never be proved from the fact that the conception of it is not self-contradictory, but only by means of an intuition corresponding to the conception. If, therefore, we wish to apply the categories to objects which cannot be regarded as phenomena, we must have an intuition different from the sensuous, and in this case the objects would be a noumena *in the positive sense* of the word. Now, as such an intuition, that is, an intellectual intuition, is no part of our faculty of cognition, it is absolutely impossible for the categories to possess any application beyond the limits of experience. It may be true that there are intelligible existences to which our faculty of sensuous intuition has no relation, and cannot be applied, but our conceptions of the understanding, as mere forms of thought for our sensuous intuition, do not extend to these. What, therefore, we call noumenon, must be understood by us as such in a *negative* sense.

If I take away from an empirical intuition all thought (by means of the categories), there remains no cognition of any object; for by means of mere intuition nothing is cogitated, and from the existence of such or such an affection of sensibility in me, it does not follow that this affection or representation has any relation to an object without me. But if I take away all intuition, there still remains the form of thought, that is, the mode of determining an object for the manifold of a possible intuition. Thus the categories do in some measure really extend further than sensuous intuition, inasmuch as they think objects in general, without regard to the mode (of sensibility) in which these objects are given. But they do not for this reason apply to and determine a wider sphere of objects, because we cannot assume that such can be given, without presupposing the possibility of another than the sensuous mode of intuition, a supposition we are not justified in making.

I call a conception problematical which contains in itself no contradiction, and which is connected with other cognitions as a limitation of given conceptions, but whose objective reality cannot be cognized in any manner. The conception of a *noumenon*, that is, of a thing which must be cogitated not as an object of sense, but as a thing in itself (solely through the pure understanding) is not self-contradictory, for we are not entitled to maintain that sensibility is the only possible mode of intuition. Nay, further, this conception is necessary to restrain sensuous intuition within the bounds of phenomena, and thus to limit the objective validity of sensuous cognition; for things in them-selves, which lie beyond its province, are called noumena, for the very purpose of indicating that this cognition does not ex-tend its application to all that the understanding thinks. But, after all, the possibility of such noumena is quite incompre-hensible, and beyond the sphere of phenomena, all is for us a mere void: that is to say, we possess an understanding whose province does *problematically* extend beyond this sphere, but we do not possess an intuition, indeed, not even the conception of a possible intuition, by means of which objects beyond the region of sensibility could be given us, and in reference to which the understanding might be employed *assertorically*. The con-ception of a noumenon is therefore merely a *limitative concep-tion*, and therefore only of negative use. But it is not an arbi-trary or fictitious notion, but is connected with the limitation of sensibility, without, however, being capable of presenting us with any positive datum beyond this sphere.

The division of objects into phenomena and noumena, and of the world into a *mundus sensibilis* and *intelligibilis* is therefore quite inadmissible in a *positive sense,* although conceptions do certainly admit of such a division; for the class of noumena have no determinate object corresponding to them, and cannot there-fore possess objective validity. If we abandon the senses, how can it be made conceivable that the categories (which are the only conceptions that could serve as conceptions for noumena) have any sense or meaning at all, inasmuch as something more than the mere unity of thought, namely, a possible intuition, is requisite for their application to an object? The conception of a noumenon, considered as merely problematical, is, however, not only admissible, but, as a limitative conception of sensibility, ab-solutely necessary. But, in this case, a noumenon is not a par-ticular *intelligible object* for our understanding; on the con-trary, the kind of understanding to which it could belong is it-self a problem, for we cannot form the most distant conception of the possibility of an understanding which should cognize an object, not discursively by means of categories, but intuitively in a non-sensuous intuition. Our understanding attains in this way a sort of negative extension. That is to say, it is not limited by, but rather limits, sensibility, by giving the name of noumena to things, not considered as phenomena, but as things in themselves. But it at the same time prescribes limits to itself, for it confesses itself unable to cognize these by means of the categories, and hence is compelled to cogitate them merely as an unknown something.

I find, however, in the writings of modern authors, an entirely different use of the expressions, *mundus sensibilis* and *intelligibilis*,* which quite departs from the meaning of the ancients —an acceptation in which, indeed, there is to be found no difficulty, but which at the same time depends on mere verbal quibbling. According to this meaning, some have chosen to call the complex of phenomena, in so far as it is intuited, *mundus sensibilis,* but in so far as the connection thereof is cogitated according to general laws of thought, *mundus intelligibilis.* Astronomy, in so far as we can mean by the word the mere observation of the starry heaven, may represent the former; a system of astronomy, such as the Copernican or Newtonian, the latter. But such twisting of words is a mere sophistical subterfuge, to avoid a difficult question, by modifying its meaning to suit our own convenience. To be sure, understanding and reason are employed in the cognition of phenomena; but the question is, whether these can be applied, when the object is not a phenomenon—and in this sense we regard it if it is cogitated as giving to the understanding alone, and not to the senses. The question therefore is, whether over and above the empirical use of the understanding, a transcendental use is possible, which applies to the noumenon as an object. The question we have answered in the negative.

When therefore we say, the senses represent objects *as they appear*, the understanding *as they are,* the latter statement must not be understood in a transcendental, but only in an empirical signification, that is, as they must be represented in the complete connection of phenomena, and not according to what they may be, apart from their relation to possible experience, consequently not as objects of the pure understanding. For this must ever remain unknown to us. Nay, it is also quite unknown to us, whether any such transcendental or extraordinary cognition is possible under any circumstances, at least, whether it is possible by means of our categories. *Understanding* and *sensibility,* with us, can determine objects only *in conjunction.* If we sepa-

* We must not translate this expression by *intellectual*, as is commonly done in German works; for it is *cognitions* alone that are intellectual or sensuous. Objects of the one or the other mode of intuition ought to be called, however harshly it may sound, *intelligible* or *sensible.*

rate them, we have intuitions without conceptions, or conceptions without intuitions; in both cases, representations, which we cannot apply to any determinate object.

If, after all our inquiries and explanations, any one still hesitates to abandon the mere transcendental use of the categories, let him attempt to construct with them a synthetical proposition. It would, of course, be unnecessary for this purpose to construct an analytical proposition, for that does not extend the sphere of the understanding, but, being concerned only about what is cogitated in the conception itself, it leaves it quite undecided whether the conception has any relation to objects, or merely indicates the unity of thought—complete abstraction being made of the modi in which an object may be given: in such a proposition, it is sufficient for the understanding to know what lies in the conception—to what it applies, is to it indifferent. The attempt must therefore be made with a synthetical and so-called transcendental principle, for example, Everything that exists exists as substance, or, Everything that is contingent exists as an effect of some other thing, viz., of its cause. Now I ask, whence can the understanding draw these synthetical propositions, when the conceptions contained therein do not relate to possible experience but to things in themselves (noumena)? Where is to be found the *third term,* which is always requisite in a synthetical proposition, which may connect in the same proposition conceptions which have no logical (analytical) connection with each other? The proposition never will be demonstrated; nay, more, the possibility of any such pure assertion never can be shown, without making reference to the empirical use of the understanding, and thus, *ipso facto,* completely renouncing pure and non-sensuous judgment. Thus the conception of pure and merely intelligible objects is completely void of all principles of its application, because we cannot imagine any mode in which they might be given, and the problematical thought which leaves a place open for them serves only, like a void space, to limit the use of empirical principles, without containing at the same time any other object of cognition beyond their sphere.

APPENDIX

Of the Equivocal Nature or Amphiboly of the Conceptions of Reflection from the Confusion of the Transcendental with the Empirical Use of the Understanding

Reflection (*reflexio*) is not occupied about objects themselves, for the purpose of directly obtaining conceptions of them, but is that state of the mind in which we set ourselves to discover the subjective conditions under which we obtain conceptions. It is the consciousness of the relation of given representations to the different sources or faculties of cognition, by which alone their relation to each other can be rightly determined. The first question which occurs in considering our representations is, to what faculty or cognition do they belong? To the understanding or to the senses? Many judgments are admitted to be true from mere habit or inclination; but, because reflection neither precedes nor follows, it is held to be a judgment that has its origin in the understanding. All judgments do not require *examination*, that is, investigation into the grounds of their truth. For, when they are immediately certain (for example, Between two points there can be only one straight line), no better or less mediate test of their truth can be found than that which they themselves contain and express. But all judgment, nay, all comparisons require *reflection*, that is, a distinction of the faculty of cognition to which the given conceptions belong. The act whereby I compare my representations with the faculty of cognition which originates them, and whereby I distinguish whether they are compared with each other as belonging to the pure understanding or to sensuous intuition, I term *transcendental reflection*. Now, the relations in which conceptions can stand to each other are those of *identity* and *difference*, *agreement* and *opposition*, of the *internal* and *external*, finally, of the *determinable* and the *determining* (matter and form). The proper determination of these relations rests on the question, to what faculty of cognition they *subjectively* belong, whether to sensibility or understanding? For, on the manner in which we solve this question depends the manner in which we must cogitate these relations.

Before constructing any objective judgment, we compare the conceptions that are to be placed in the judgment, and observe whether there exists *identity* (of many representations in one conception), if a *general* judgment is to be constructed, or *difference*, of a *particular;* whether there is *agreement* when *affirmative*, and *opposition* when *negative* judgments are to be constructed, and so on. For this reason we ought to call these conceptions, conceptions of comparison (*conceptus comparationis*). But as, when the question is not as to the logical form, but as to the content of conceptions, that is to say, whether the things themselves are identical or different, in agreement or opposition, and so on, the things can have a twofold relation to our faculty of cognition, to wit, a relation either to sensibility or to the understanding, and as on this relation depends their relation to each other, transcendental reflection, that is, the relation of given representations to one or the other faculty of cognition, can alone determine this latter relation. Thus we shall not be able to discover whether the things are identical or different, in agreement or opposition, etc., from the mere conception of the things by means of comparison (*comparatio*), but only by distinguishing the mode of cognition to which they belong, in other words, by means of transcendental reflection. We may, therefore with justice say, that *logical reflection* is mere comparison, for in it no account is taken of the faculty of cognition to which the given conceptions belong, and they are consequently, as far as regards their origin, to be treated as homogeneous; while *transcendental reflection* (which applies to the objects themselves) contains the ground of possibility of objective comparison of representations with each other, and is therefore very different from the former, because the faculties of cognition to which they belong are not even the same. Transcendental reflection is a duty which no one can neglect who wishes to establish an *à priori* judgment upon things. We shall now proceed to fulfil this duty, and thereby throw not a little light on the question as to the determination of the proper business of the understanding.

1. *Identity and Difference.*—When an object is presented to us several times, but always with the same internal determinations (*qualitas et quantitas*), it, if an object of pure understanding, is always the same, not several things, but only one thing (*numerica identitas*) ; but if a phenomenon, we do not concern ourselves with comparing the conception of the thing with the conception of some other, but, although they may be

in this respect perfectly the same, the difference of place at the same time is a sufficient ground for asserting the *numerical difference* of these objects (of sense). Thus, in the case of two drops of water, we may make complete abstraction of all internal difference (quality and quantity), and, the fact that they are intuited at the same time in different places, is sufficient to justify us in holding them to be numerically different. Leibnitz regarded phenomena as things in themselves, consequently as *intelligibilia*, that is, objects of pure understanding (although on account of the confused nature of their representations, he gave them the name of phenomena), and in this case his principle of the indiscernible (*principium identatis indiscernibilium*) is not to be impugned. But, as phenomena are objects of sensibility, and, as the understanding, in respect of them, must be employed empirically and not purely or transcendentally, plurality and numerical difference are given by space itself as the condition of external phenomena. For one part of space, although it may be perfectly similar and equal to another part, is still without it, and for this reason alone is different from the latter, which is added to it in order to make up a greater space. It follows that this must hold good of all things that are in the different parts of space at the same time, however similar and equal one may be to another.

2. *Agreement and Opposition.*—When reality is represented by the pure understanding (*realitas noumenon*), opposition between realities is incogitable—such a relation, that is, that when these realities are connected in one subject, they annihilate the effects of each other, and may be represented in the formula $3 - 3 = 0$. On the other hand, the real in the phenomenon (*realitas phenomenon*) may very well be in mutual opposition, and, when united in the same subject, the one may completely or in part annihilate the effect or *consequence of the other;* as in the case of two moving forces in the same straight line drawing or impelling a point in opposite directions, or in the case of a pleasure counterbalancing a certain amount of pain.

3. *The Internal and External.*—In an object of the pure understanding only that is internal which has no relation (as regards its existence) to anything different from itself. On the other hand, the internal determinations of a *substantia phenomenon* in space are nothing but relations, and it is itself nothing more than a complex of mere relations. Substance in space

we are cognizant of only through forces operative in it, either drawing others towards itself (attraction), or preventing others from forcing into itself (repulsion and impenetrability). We know no other properties that make up the conception of substance phenomenal in space, and which we term matter. On the other hand, as an object of the pure understanding, every substance must have internal determinations and forces. But what other internal attributes of such an object can I think than those which my internal sense presents to me?—That, to wit, which is either itself *thought*, or something analogous to it. Hence Leibnitz, who looked upon things as noumena, after denying them everything like external relation, and therefore also *composition* or combination, declared that all substances, even the component parts of matter, were simple substances with powers of representation, in one word, *monads*.

4. *Matter and Form.*—These two conceptions lie at the foundation of all other reflection, so inseparably are they connected with every mode of exercising the understanding. The former denotes the determinable in general, the second its determination, both in a transcendental sense, abstraction being made of every difference in that which is given, and of the mode in which it is determined. Logicians formerly termed the universal, matter, the specific difference of this or that part of the universal, form. In a judgment one may call the given conceptions logical matter (for the judgment) the relation of these to each other (by means of the copula), the form of the judgment. In an object, the composite parts thereof (*essentialia*) are the matter; the mode in which they are connected in the object, the form. In respect to things in general, unlimited reality was regarded as the matter of all possibility, the limitation thereof (negation) as the form, by which one thing is distinguished from another according to transcendental conceptions. The understanding demands that something be given (at least in the conception), in order to be able to determine it in a certain manner. Hence, in a conception of the pure understanding, the matter precedes the form, and for this reason Leibnitz first assumed the existence of things (monads) and of an internal power of representation in them, in order to found upon this their external relation and the community of their state (that is, of their representations). Hence, with him, space and time were possible—the former through the relation of substances,

the latter through the connection of their determinations with each other, as causes and effects. And so would it really be, if the pure understanding were capable of an immediate application to objects, and if space and time were determinations of things in themselves. But being merely sensuous intuitions, in which we determine all objects solely as phenomena, the form of intuition (as a subjective property of sensibility) must antecede all matter (sensations), consequently space and time must antecede all phenomena and all data of experience, and rather make experience itself possible. But the intellectual philosopher could not endure that the form should precede the things themselves, and determine their possibility; an objection perfectly correct, if we assume that we intuite things as they are although with confused representation. But as sensuous intuition is a peculiar subjective condition, which is *à priori* at the foundation of all perception, and the form of which is primitive, the form must be given per se, and so far from matter (or the things themselves which appear) lying at the foundation of experience (as we must conclude, if we judge by mere conceptions), the very possibility of itself presupposes, on the contrary, a given formal intuition (space and time).

Remark on the Amphiboly of the Conceptions of Reflection

Let me be allowed to term the position which we assign to a conception either in the sensibility or in the pure understanding, the *transcendental place*. In this manner, the appointment of the position which must be taken by each conception according to the difference in its use, and the directions for determining this place to all conceptions according to rules, would be a *transcendental topic*, a doctrine which would thoroughly shield us from the surreptitious devices of the pure understanding and the delusions which thence arise, as it would always distinguish to what faculty of cognition each conception properly belonged. Every conception, every title, under which many cognitions rank together, may be called a *logical place*. Upon this is based the *logical topic* of Aristotle, of which teachers and rhetoricians could avail themselves, in order, under certain titles of thought, to observe what would best suit the matter they had to treat, and thus enable themselves to quibble and talk with fluency and an appearance of profundity.

Transcendental topic, on the contrary, contains nothing more than the above-mentioned four titles of all comparison and distinction, which differ from categories in this respect, that they do not represent the object according to that which constitutes its conception (quantity, reality), but set forth merely the comparison of representations, which precedes our conceptions of things. But this comparison requires a previous reflection, that is, a determination of the place to which the representations of the things which are compared belong, whether, to wit, they are cogitated by the pure understanding or given by sensibility.

Conceptions may be logically compared without the trouble of inquiring to what faculty their objects belong, whether as noumena, to the understanding, or as phenomena to sensibility. If, however, we wish to employ these conceptions in respect of objects, previous transcendental reflection is necessary. Without this reflection I should make a very unsafe use of these conceptions, and construct pretended synthetical propositions which critical reason cannot acknowledge, and which are based solely upon a transcendental amphiboly, that is, upon a substitution of an object of pure understanding for a phenomenon.

For want of this doctrine of transcendental topic, and consequently deceived by the amphiboly of the conceptions of reflection, the celebrated Leibnitz constructed an *intellectual system of the world*, or rather, believed himself conpetent to cognize the internal nature of things, by comparing all objects merely with the understanding and the abstract formal conceptions of thought. Our table of the conceptions of reflection gives us the unexpected advantage of being able to exhibit the distinctive peculiarities of his system in all its parts, and at the same time of exposing the fundamental principle of this peculiar mode of thought, which rested upon nought but a misconception. He compared all things with each other merely by means of conceptions, and naturally found no other differences than those by which the understanding distinguishes its pure conceptions one from another. The conditions of sensuous intuition, which contain in themselves their own means of distinction, he did not look upon as primitive, because sensibility was to him but a confused mode of representation, and not any particular source of representations. A phenomenon was for him the representation of the thing in itself, although distinguished from cognition by the understanding only in respect of the logical form—the former with its usual want of analysis containing, according to him, a certain mixture of collateral representations in its conception of a thing, which it is the duty of the understanding to separate and distinguish. In one word, Leibnitz *intellectualized* phenomena, just as Locke, in his system of *noogony* (if I may be allowed to make use of such expressions) *sensualized* the conceptions of the understanding, that it to say, declared them to be nothing more than empirical or abstract conceptions of reflection. Instead of seeking in the understanding and sensibility two different sources of representations, which, however, can present us with objective judgments of things only in *conjunction*, each of these great men recognized but one of these faculties, which, in their opinion, applied immediately to things in themselves, the other having no duty but that of confusing or arranging the representations of the former.

Accordingly, the objects of sense were compared by Leibnitz as things in general merely in the understanding.

1st. He compares them in regard to their identity or difference—as judged by the understanding. As, therefore, he considered merely the conceptions of objects, and not their position in intuition, in which alone objects can be given, and left quite out of sight the transcendental *locale* of these conceptions—whether, that is, their object ought to be classed among phenomena, or among things in themselves, it was to be expected that he should extend the application of the principle of indiscernibles, which is valid solely of conceptions of things in general, tc objects of sense (*mundus phœnomenon*), and that he should believe that he had thereby contributed in no small degree to extend our knowledge of nature. In truth, if I cognize in all its inner determinations a drop of water as a thing in itself, I cannot look upon one drop as different from another, if the conception of the one is completely identical with that of the other. But if it is a phenomenon in space, it has a place not merely in the understanding (among conceptions), but also in sensuous external intuition (in space), and in this case, the physical *locale* is a matter of indifference in regard to the internal determination of things, and one place, *B*, may contain a thing which is perfectly similar and equal to another in a place, *A*, just as well as if the two things were in every respect different from each other. Difference of place without any other conditions, makes the plurality and distinction of objects as phenomena, not only possible in itself, but even necessary. Consequently, the above so-called law is not a law of nature. It is merely an analytical rule for the comparison of things by means of mere conceptions.

2d. The principle, " Realities (as simple affirmations) never logically contradict each other," is a proposition perfectly true respecting the relation of conceptions, but, whether as regards nature, or things in themselves (of which we have not the slightest conception), is without any the least meaning. For real opposition, in which A — B is = o, exists everywhere, an opposition, that is, in which one reality united with another in the same subject annihilates the effects of the other—a fact which is constantly brought before our eyes by the different antagonistic actions and operations in nature, which nevertheless, as depending on real forces, must be called *realitátes phenomena*. General mechanics can even present us with the empirical condition of this opposition in an *à priori* rule, as it directs its attention to the opposition in the direction of forces—a condition of which the transcendental conception of reality can tell us nothing. Although M. Leibnitz did not announce this proposition with precisely the pomp of a new principle, he yet employed it for the establishment of new propositions, and his followers introduced it into their Leibnitz-Wolfian system of philosophy. According to this principle, for example, all evils are but consequences of the limited nature of created beings, that is, negations, because these are the only opposite of reality. (In the mere conception of a thing in general this is really the case, but not in things as phenomena.) In like manner, the upholders of this system deem it not only possible, but natural also, to connect and unite all reality in one being, because they acknowledge no other sort of opposition than that of contradiction (by which the conception itself of a thing is annihilated), and find themselves unable to conceive an opposition of reciprocal destruction, so to speak, in which one real cause destroys the effect of another, and the conditions of whose representation we meet with only in sensibility.

3d. The Leibnitzian Monadology has really no better foundation than on this philosopher's mode of falsely representing the difference of the internal and external solely in relation to the understanding. Substances, in general, must have something inward, which is therefore free from external relations, consequently from that of composition also. The *simple*—that which can be represented by a unit—is therefore the foundation of that which is internal in things in themselves. The internal state of substances cannot therefore consist in place, shape, contact, or motion, determinations which are all external relations, and we can ascribe to them no other than that whereby we internally determine our faculty of sense itself, that is to say, the state of representation. Thus, then, were constructed the monads, which were to form the elements of the universe, the active force of which consists in representation, the effects of this force being thus entirely confined to themselves.

For the same reason, his view of the possible community of substances could not represent it but as a *predetermined harmony*, and by no means as a physical influence. For inasmuch as everything is occupied only internally, that is, with its own representations, the state of the representations of one substance could not stand in active and living connection with that of another, but some third cause operating on all without exception was necessary to make the different states correspond with one another. And this did not happen by means of assistance applied in each particular case (*systema assistentiæ*), but through the unity of the idea of a cause occupied and connected with all substances, in which they necessarily receive, according to the Leibnitzian school, their existence and permanence, consequently also reciprocal correspondence, according to universal laws.

4th. This philosopher's celebrated *doctrine of space and time*, in which he intellectualized these forms of sensibility, originated in the same delusion of transcendental reflection. If I attempt to represent by the mere understanding, the external relations of things, I can do so only by employing the conception of their reciprocal action, and if I wish to connect one state of the same thing with another state, I must avail myself of the notion of the order of cause and effect. And thus Leibnitz regarded space as a certain order in the community of substances, and time as the dynamical sequence of their states. That which space and time possess proper to themselves and independent of things, he ascribed to a necessary *confusion* in our conceptions of them, whereby that which is a mere form of dynamical relations is held to be a self-existent intuition, antecedent even to things themselves. Thus space and time were the intelligible form of the connection of things (substances and their states) in themselves. But things were intelligible substances (*substantiæ noumena*). At the same time, he made these conceptions valid of phenomena, because he did not allow to sensibility a peculiar mode of intuition, but sought all, even the empirical representation of objects, in the understanding, and left to sense nought but the despicable task of confusing and disarranging the representations of the former.

But even if we could frame any synthetical proposition concerning things in themselves by means of the pure understanding (which is impossible), it could not apply to phenomena, which do not represent things in themselves. In such a case I should be obliged in transcendental reflection to compare my conceptions only under the conditions of sensibility, and so space and time would not be determinations of things in themselves, but of phenomena. What things may be in themselves, I know not, and need not know because a thing is never presented to me otherwise than as a phenomenon.

I must adopt the same mode of procedure with the other conceptions of reflection. Matter is *substantia phænomenon*. That in it which is internal I seek to discover in all parts of space which it occupies, and in all the functions and operations it performs, and which are indeed never anything but phenomena of the external sense. I cannot therefore find anything that is absolutely, but only what is comparatively internal, and which itself consists of external relations. The absolutely internal in matter, and as it should be according to the pure understanding, is a mere chimera, for matter is not an object for the pure understanding. But the transcendental object, which is the foundation of the phenomenon which we call matter, is a mere *nescio quid*, the nature of which we could not understand, even though some one were found able to tell us. For we can understand nothing that does not bring with it something in intuition corresponding to the expressions employed. If by the complaint of being *unable to perceive the internal nature of things*, it is meant that we do not comprehend by the pure understanding what the things which appear to us may be in themselves, it is a silly and unreasonable complaint; for those who talk thus really desire that we should be able to cognize, consequently to intuite things without senses, and therefore wish that we possessed a faculty of cognition perfectly different from the human faculty, not merely in degree, but even as regards intuition and the mode thereof, so that thus we should not be men, but belong to a class of beings, the possibility of whose existence, much less their nature and constitution, we have no means of cognizing. By observation and analysis of phenomena we penetrate into the interior of nature, and no one can say what progress this knowledge may make in time. But those transcendental questions which pass beyond the limits of nature we could never answer, even although all nature were laid open to us, because we have not the power of observing our own mind with any other intuition than that of our internal sense. For herein lies the mystery of the origin and source of our faculty of sensibility. Its application to an object, and the transcendental ground of this unity of subjective and objective, lie too deeply concealed for us, who cognize ourselves only through the internal sense, consequently as phenomena, to be able to discover in our existence anything but phenomena, the non-sensuous cause of which we at the same time earnestly desire to penetrate to.

The great utility of this critique of conclusions arrived at by the processes of mere reflection, consists in its clear demonstration of the nullity of all conclusions respecting objects which are compared with each other in the understanding alone, while it at the same time confirms what we particularly insisted on, namely, that, although phenomena are not included as things in themselves among the objects of the pure understanding, they are nevertheless the only things by which our cognition can possess objective reality, that is to say, which give us intuitions to correspond with our conceptions.

When we reflect in a purely logical manner, we do nothing more than compare conceptions in our understanding, to discover whether both have the same content, whether they are self-contradictory or not, whether anything is contained in either conception, which of the two is given, and which is merely a mode of thinking that given. But if I apply these conceptions to an object in general (in the transcendental sense), without first determining whether it is an object of sensuous or intellectual intuition, certain limitations present themselves, which forbid us to pass beyond the conceptions, and render all empirical use of them impossible. And thus these limitations prove that the representation of an object as a thing in general is not only *insufficient,* but, without sensuous determination and independently of empirical conditions, *self-contradictory;* that we must therefore make abstraction of all objects, as in logic, or, admitting them, must think them under conditions of sensuous intuition; that, consequently, the intelligible requires an altogether peculiar intuition, which we do not possess, and in the absence of which it is for us nothing; while, on the other hand, phenomena cannot be objects in themselves. For, when I merely think things in general, the difference in their external relations cannot constitute a difference in the things themselves; on the contrary, the former presupposes the latter, and if the conception of one of two things is not internally different from that of the other, I am merely thinking the same thing in different relations. Further, by the addition of one affirmation (reality) to the other, the positive therein is really augmented, and nothing is abstracted or withdrawn from it; hence the real in things cannot be in contradiction with or opposition to itself —and so on.

The true use of the conceptions of reflection in the employment of the understanding, has, as we have shown, been so misconceived by Leibnitz, one of the most acute philosophers of either ancient or modern times, that he has been misled into the construction of a baseless system of intellectual cognition, which professes to determine its objects without the intervention of the senses. For this reason, the exposition of the cause of the amphiboly of these conceptions, as the origin of these false principles, is of great utility in determining with certainty the proper limits of the understanding.

It is right to say, whatever is affirmed or denied of the whole of a conception can be affirmed or denied of any part of it (*dictum de omni et nullo*); but it would be absurd so to alter this logical proposition, as to say, whatever is not contained in a general conception, is likewise not contained in the particular conceptions which rank under it; for the latter are particular conceptions, for the very reason that their content is greater than that which is cogitated in the general conception. And yet the whole intellectual system of Leibnitz is based upon this false principle, and with it must necessarily fall to the ground, together with all the ambiguous principles in reference to the employment of the understanding which have thence originated.

Leibnitz's principle of the identity of indiscernibles or indistinguishables is really based on the presupposition, that, if in the conception of a thing a certain distinction is not to be found, it is also not to be met with in things themselves; that, consequently, all things are completely identical (*numero eadem*) which are not distinguishable from each other (as to quality or quantity) in our conceptions of them. But, as in the mere conception of anything abstraction has been made of many necessary conditions of intuition, that of which abstraction has been made is rashly held to be non-existent, and nothing is attributed to the thing but what is contained in its conception.

The conception of a cubic foot of space, however I may think it, is in itself completely identical. But two cubic feet in space are nevertheless distinct from each other from the sole fact of their being in different places (they are *numero diversa*); and these places are conditions of intuition, wherein the object of this conception is given, and which do not belong to the conception, but to the faculty of sensibility. In like manner, there is in the conception of a thing no contradiction when a negative is not connected with an affirmative; and merely affirmative conceptions cannot, in conjunction, produce any negation. But in sensuous intuition, wherein reality (take for example, motion) is given, we find conditions (opposite directions)—of which abstraction has been made in the conception of motion in general—which render possible a contradiction or opposition (not indeed of a logical kind)—and which from pure positives produce zero $= o$. We are therefore not justified in saying, that all reality is in perfect agreement and harmony, because no contradiction is discoverable among its conceptions.* According to mere conceptions, that which is internal is the substratum of all relations or external determinations. When, therefore, I abstract all conditions of intuition, and confine myself solely to the conception of a thing in general, I can make abstraction of all external relations, and there must neverthe-

---

* If anyone wishes here to have recourse to the usual subterfuge, and to say, that at least *realitates noumena* cannot be in opposition to each other, it will be requisite for him to adduce an example of this pure and non-sensuous reality, that it may be understood whether the notion represents something or nothing. But an example cannot be found except in experience, which never presents to us anything more than *phenomena*, and thus the proposition means nothing more than the conception which contains only affirmatives, does not contain any negative—a proposition nobody ever doubted.

less remain a conception of that which indicates no relation, but merely internal determinations. Now it seems to follow, that in everything (substance) there is something which is absolutely internal, and which antecedes all external determinations, inasmuch as it renders them possible; and that therefore this substratum is something which does not contain any external relations, and is consequently simple (for corporeal things are never anything but relations, at least of their parts external to each other); and inasmuch as we know of no other absolutely internal determinations than those of the internal sense, this substratum is not only simple, but also, analogously with our internal sense, determined through *representations*, that is to say, all things are properly *monads*, or simple beings endowed with the power of representation. Now all this would be perfectly correct, if the conception of a thing were the only necessary condition of the presentation of objects of external intuition. It is, on the contrary, manifest that a permanent phenomenon in space (impenetrable extension) can contain mere relations, and nothing that is absolutely internal, and yet be the primary substratum of all external perception. By mere conceptions I cannot think anything external, without, at the same time, thinking something internal, for the reason that conceptions of relations presuppose given things, and without these are impossible. But, as in intuition there is something (that is, space, which, with all it contains, consists of purely formal, or, indeed, real relations) which is not found in the mere conception of a thing in general, and this presents to us the substratum which could not be cognized through conceptions alone, I cannot say: because a thing cannot be represented *by mere conceptions* without something absolutely internal, there is also, in the things themselves which are contained under these conceptions, and in *their intuition* nothing external to which something absolutely internal does not serve as the foundation. For, when we have made abstraction of all the conditions of intuition, there certainly remains in the mere conception nothing but the internal in general, through which alone the external is possible. But this necessity, which is grounded upon abstraction alone, does not obtain in the case of things themselves, in so far as they are given in intuition with such determinations as express mere relations, without having anything internal as their foundation; for they are not things in themselves, but only phenomena. What we cognize in matter is nothing but relations (what we call its internal determinations are but comparatively internal). But there are some self-subsistent and permanent, through which a determined object is given. That I, when abstraction is made of these relations, have nothing more to think, does not destroy the conception of a thing as phenomenon, nor the conception of an object *in abstracto*, but it does away with the possibility of an object that is determinable according to mere conceptions, that is, of a noumenon. It is certainly startling to hear that a thing consists solely of relations; but this thing is simply a phenomenon, and cannot be cogitated by means of the mere categories: it does itself consist in the mere relation of something in general to the senses. In the same way, we cannot cogitate relations of things *in abstracto*, if we commence with conceptions alone, in any other manner than that one is the cause of determinations in the other; for that is itself the conception of the understanding or category of relation. But, as in this case we make abstraction of all intuition, we lose altogether the mode in which the manifold determines to each of its parts its place, that is, the form of sensibility (space); and yet this mode antecedes all empirical causality.

If by intelligible objects we understand things which can be thought by means of the pure categories, without the need of the schemata of sensibility, such objects are impossible. For the condition of the objective use of all our conceptions of understanding is the mode of our sensuous intuition, whereby objects are given; and, if we make abstraction of the latter, the former can have no relation to an object. And even if we should suppose a different kind of intuition from our own, still our functions of thought would have no use or signification in respect thereof. But if we understand by the term, objects of a non-sensuous intuition, in respect of which our categories are not valid, and of which we can accordingly have no knowledge (neither intuition nor conception), in this merely negative sense noumena must be admitted. For this is no more than saying that our mode of intuition is not applicable to all things, but only to objects of our senses, that consequently its objective validity is limited, and that room is therefore left for another kind of intuition, and thus also for things that may be objects of it. But in this sense the conception of a noumenon is problematical, that is to say, it is the notion of a thing of which we can neither say that it is possible, nor that it is impossible, inasmuch as we do not know of any mode of intuition besides the sensuous, or of any other sort of conceptions than the categories —a mode of intuition and a kind of conception neither of which is applicable to a non-sensuous object. We are on this account incompetent to extend the sphere of our objects of thought beyond the conditions of our sensibility, and to assume the existence of objects of pure thought, that is, of noumena, inasmuch as these have no true positive signification. For it must be confessed of the categories, that they are not of themselves sufficient for the cognition of things in themselves, and without the data of sensibility are mere subjective forms of the unity of the understanding. Thought is certainly not a product of the senses, and in so far is not limited by them, but it does not therefore follow that it may be employed purely and without the intervention of sensibility, for it would then be without reference to an object. And we cannot call a noumenon an object of pure thought; for the representation thereof is but the problematical conception of an object for a perfectly different intuition and a perfectly different understanding from ours, both of which are consequently themselves problematical. The conception of a noumenon is therefore not the conception of an object, but merely a problematical conception inseparably connected with the limitation of our sensibility. That is to say, this conception contains the answer to the question—Are there objects quite unconnected with, and independent of, our intuition?—a question to which only an indeterminate answer can be given. That answer is: Inasmuch as sensuous intuition does not apply to all things without distinction, there remains room for other and different objects. The existence of these problematical objects is therefore not absolutely denied, in the absence of a determinate conception of them, but, as no category is valid in respect of them, neither must they be admitted as objects for our understanding.

Understanding accordingly limits sensibility, without at the same time enlarging its own field. While, moreover, it forbids sensibility to apply its forms and modes to things in themselves and restricts it to the sphere of phenomena, it cogitates an object in itself, only, however, as a transcendental object, which is the cause of a phenomenon (consequently not itself a phenomenon), and which cannot be thought either as a quantity or as reality, or as substance (because these conceptions always require sensuous forms in which to determine an object)—an object, therefore, of which we are quite unable to say whether it can be met with in ourselves or out of us, whether it would be annihilated together with sensibility, or, if this were taken away, would continue to exist. If we wish to call this object a noumenon, because the representation of it is non-sensuous, we are at liberty to do so. But as we can apply to it none of the conceptions of our understanding, the representation is for us quite void, and is available only for the indication of the limits of our sensuous intuition, thereby leaving at the same time an empty space, which we are competent to fill by the aid neither of possible experience, nor of the pure understanding.

The critique of the pure understanding, accordingly, does not permit us to create for ourselves a new field of objects beyond those which are presented to us as phenomena, and to stray into intelligible worlds; nay, it does not even allow us to endeavor to form so much as a conception of them. The specious error which leads to this—and which is a perfectly excusable one—lies in the fact that the employment of the understanding, contrary to its proper purpose and destination, is made transcendental, and objects, that is, possible intuitions, are made to regulate themselves according to conceptions, instead of the conceptions arranging themselves according to the intuitions, on which alone their own objective validity rests. Now the reason of this again is, that apperception, and with it, thought, antecedes all possible determinate arrangement of representations. Accordingly we think something in general, and determine it on the one hand sensuously, but, on the other, distinguish the general and *in abstracto* represented object from this particular mode of intuiting it. In this case there remains a mode of determining the object by mere thought, which is really but a logical form without content, which, however, seems to us to be a mode of the existence of the object in itself (noumenon), without regard to intuition which is limited to our senses.

Before ending this transcendental analytic, we must make an addition, which, although in itself of no particular importance, seems to be necessary to the completeness of the system. The highest conception, with which a trascendental philosophy commonly begins, is the division into possible and impossible. But as all division presupposes a divided conception, a still higher one must exist, and this is the conception of an object in general—problematically understood, and without its being decided, whether it is something or nothing. As the categories are the only conceptions, which apply to objects in general, the distinguishing of an object, whether it is something or nothing, must proceed according to the order and direction of the categories.

1. To the categories of quantity, that is, the conceptions of all, many, and one, the conception which annihilates all, that is, the conception of *none* is opposed. And thus the object of a conception, to which no intuition can be found to correspond, is = nothing. That is, it is a conception without an object (*ens rationis*), like noumena, which cannot be considered possible in the sphere of reality, though they must not therefore be held to be impossible—or like certain new fundamental forces in matter, the existence of which is cogitable without contradiction, though, as examples from experience are not forthcoming, they must not be regarded as possible.

2. Reality is *something;* negation is *nothing*, that is, a conception of the absence of an object, as cold, a shadow (*nihil privativum*).

3. The mere form of intuition, without substance, is in itself no object, but the merely formal condition of an object (as phenomenon), as pure space and pure time. These are certainly something, as forms of intuition, but are not themselves objects which are intuited (*ens imaginarium*).

4. The object of conception which is self-contradictory, is nothing, because the conception is nothing—is impossible, as a figure composed of two straight lines (*nihil negativum*).

The table of this division of the conception of *nothing* (the corresponding division of the conception of *something* does not require special description), must therefore be arranged a follows:

NOTHING.

As

I.

Empty conception without object.

ens rationis.

II.

Empty object of a conception,
nihil privativum.

III.

Empty intuition without object,
ens imaginarium.

IV.

Empty object without conception,
nihil negativum.

We see that the *ens rationis* is distinguished from the *nihil negativum* or pure nothing by the consideration, that the former must not be reckoned among possibilities, because it is a mere fiction—though not self-contradictory, while the latter is completely opposed to all possibility, inasmuch as the conception annihilates itself. Both, however, are empty conceptions. On the other hand, the *nihil privativum* and *ens imaginarium* are empty *data* for conceptions. If light be not given to the senses, we cannot represent to ourselves darkness, and if extended objects are not perceived, we cannot represent space. Neither the negation, nor the mere form of intuition can, without something real, be an object.

SECOND DIVISION

TRANSCENDENTAL DIALECTIC

I. Of Transcendental Illusory Appearance

We termed Dialectic in general a logic of appearance.* This does not signify a doctrine of *probability;* † for probability is truth, only cognized upon insufficient grounds, and though the information it gives us is imperfect, it is not therefore deceitful. Hence it must not be separated from the analytical part of logic. Still less must *phenomenon* ‡ and *appearance* be held to be identical. For truth or illusory appearance does not reside in the object, in so far as it is intuited, but in the judgment upon the object, in so far as it is thought. It is therefore quite correct to say that the senses do not err, not because they always judge correctly, but because *they do not* judge at all. Hence truth and error, consequently also, illusory appearance as the

---

* Schein.   † Wahrscheinlichkeit.   ‡ Erscheinung.

cause of error, are only to be found in a judgment, that is, in the relation of an object to our understanding. In a cognition, which completely harmonizes with the laws of the understanding, no error can exist. In a representation of the senses—as not containing any judgment—there is also no error. But no power of nature can of itself deviate from its own laws. Hence neither the understanding *per se* (without the influence of another cause), nor the senses *per se*, would fall into error; the former could not, because, if it acts only according to its own laws, the effect (the judgment) must necessarily accord with these laws. But in accordance with the laws of the understanding consists the formal element in all truth. In the senses there is no judgment—neither a true nor a false one. But, as we have no source of cognition besides these two, it follows, that error is caused solely by the unobserved influence of the sensibility upon the understanding. And thus it happens that the subjective grounds of a judgment blend and are confounded with the objective, and cause them to deviate from their proper determination,* just as a body in motion would always of itself proceed in a straight line, but if another impetus gives to it a different direction, it will then start off into a curvilinear line of motion. To distinguish the peculiar action of the understanding from the power which mingles with it, it is necessary to consider an erroneous judgment as the diagonal between two forces, that determine the judgment in two different directions, which, as it were, form an angle,.and to resolve this composite operation into the simple ones of the understanding and the sensibility. In pure *à priori* judgments this must be done by means of transcendental reflection, whereby, as has been already shown, each representation has its place appointed in the corresponding faculty of cognition, and consequently the influence of the one faculty upon the other is made apparent.

It is not at present our business to treat of empirical illusory appearance (for example, optical illusion), which occurs in the empirical application of otherwise correct rules of the understanding, and in which the judgment is misled by the influence of imagination. Our purpose is to speak of *transcendental illusory appearance*, which influences principles—that are not even

* Sensibility, subjected to the understanding, as the object upon which the understanding employs its functions, is the source of real cognitions. But, in so far as it exercises an influence upon the action of the understanding, and determines it to judgment, sensibility is itself the cause of error.

applied to experience, for in this case we should possess a sure
test of their correctness—but which leads us, in disregard of
all the warnings of criticism, completely beyond the empirical
employment of the categories, and deludes us with the chimera
of an extension of the sphere of the *pure understanding*. We
shall term those principles, the application of which is confined
entirely within the limits of possible experience, *immanent;*
those, on the other hand, which transgress these limits, we shall
call *transcendent* principles. But by these latter I do not understand principles of the *transcendental* use or misuse of the categories, which is in reality a mere fault of the judgment when not
under due restraint from criticism, and therefore not paying
sufficient attention to the limits of the sphere in which the pure
understanding is allowed to exercise its functions; but real
principles which exhort us to break down all those barriers, and
to lay claim to a perfectly new field of cognition, which recogni-
nizes no line of demarcation. Thus *transcendental* and *transcendent* are not identical terms. The principles of the pure understanding, which we have already propounded, ought to be of
empirical and not of transcendental use, that is, they are not
applicable to any object beyond the sphere of experience. A
principle which removes these limits, nay, which authorizes us
to overstep them, is called *transcendent*. If our criticism can
succeed in exposing the illusion in these pretended principles,
those which are limited in their employment to the sphere of
experience, may be called, in opposition to the others, *immanent*
principles of the pure understanding.

Logical illusion, which consists merely in the imitation of the
form of reason (the illusion in sophistical syllogisms), arises
entirely from a want of due attention to logical rules. So soon
as the attention is awakened to the case before us, this illusion
totally disappears. Transcendental illusion, on the contrary,
does not cease to exist, even after it has been exposed, and its
nothingness clearly perceived by means of transcendental criticism.—Take, for example, the illusion in the proposition, " The
world must have a beginning in time."—The cause of this is as
follows. In our reason, subjectively considered as a faculty of
human cognition, there exist fundamental rules and maxims of
its exercise, which have completely the appearance of objective
principles. Now from this cause it happens, that the subjective
necessity of a certain connection of our conceptions, is regarded

as an objective necessity of the determination of things in themselves. This illusion it is impossible to avoid, just as we cannot avoid perceiving that the sea appears to be higher at a distance than it is near the shore, because we see the former by means of higher rays than the latter, or, which is a still stronger case, as even the astronomer cannot prevent himself from seeing the moon larger at its rising than some time afterwards, although he is not deceived by this illusion.

Transcendental dialectic will therefore content itself with exposing the illusory appearance in transcendental judgments, and guarding us against it; but to make it, as in the case of logical illusion, entirely disappear and cease to be illusion, is utterly beyond its power. For we have here to do with a *natural* and unavoidable illusion, which rests upon subjective principles, and imposes these upon us as objective, while logical dialectic, in the detection of sophisms, has to do merely with an error in the logical consequence of the propositions, or with an artificially constructed illusion, in imitation of the natural error. There is therefore a natural and unavoidable dialectic of pure reason—not that in which the bungler, from want of the requisite knowledge, involves himself, nor that which the sophist devises for the purpose of misleading, but that which is an inseparable adjunct of human reason, and which, even after its illusion have been exposed, does not cease to deceive, and continually to lead reason into momentary errors, which it becomes necessary continually to remove.

II. Of Pure Reason as the Seat of the Transcendental Illusory Appearance

A.—*Of Reason in General*

All our knowledge begins with sense, proceeds thence to understanding, and ends with reason, beyond which nothing higher can be discovered in the human mind for elaborating the matter of intuition and subjecting it to the highest unity of thought. At this stage of our inquiry it is my duty to give an explanation of this, the highest faculty of cognition, and I confess I find myself here in some difficulty. Of reason, as of the understanding, there is a merely formal, that is, logical use, in which it makes abstraction of all content of cognition; but there is also a real use, inasmuch as it contains in itself the source of certain conceptions and principles, which it does not borrow either from the senses or the understanding. The former faculty has been long defined by logicians as the faculty of mediate conclusion in contradistinction to immediate conclusions (*consequentiæ immediatæ*); but the nature of the latter, which itself generates conceptions, is not to be understood from this definition. Now as a division of reason into a logical and a transcendental faculty presents itself here, it becomes necessary to seek for a higher conception of this source of cognition which shall comprehend both conceptions. In this we may expect, according to the analogy of the conceptions of the understanding, that the logical conception will give us the key to the transcendental, and that the table of the functions of the former will present us with the clue to the conceptions of reason.

In the former part of our transcendental logic, we defined the understanding to be the faculty of rules; reason may be distinguished from understanding as the *faculty of principles*.

The term *principle* is ambiguous, and commonly signifies merely a cognition that may be employed as a principle; although it is not in itself, and as regards its proper origin, entitled to the distinction. Every general proposition, even if derived from experience by the process of induction, may serve as the major in a syllogism; but it is not for that reason a principle. Mathematical axioms (for example, there can be only one straight line between two points) are general *à priori* cognitions, and are therefore rightly denominated principles, relatively to the cases which can be subsumed under them. But I cannot for this reason say that I cognize this property of a straight line from principles—I cognize it only in pure intuition.

Cognition from principles, then, is that cognition in which I cognize the particular in the general by means of conceptions. Thus every syllogism is a form of the deduction of a cognition from a principle. For the major always gives a conception, through which everything that is subsumed under the condition thereof, is cognized according to a principle. Now as every general cognition may serve as the major in a syllogism, and the understanding presents us with such general *à priori* propositions, they may be termed principles, in respect of their possible use.

But if we consider these principles of the pure understanding in relation to their origin, we shall find them to be anything rather than cognitions from conceptions. For they would not even be possible *à priori,* if we could not rely on the assistance of pure intuition (in mathematics), or on that of the conditions of a possible experience. That everything that happens has a cause, cannot be concluded from the general conception of that which happens; on the contrary the principle of causality instructs us as to the mode of obtaining from that which happens a determinate empirical conception.

Synthetical cognitions from conceptions the understanding cannot supply, and they alone are entitled to be called principles. At the same time, all general propositions may be termed comparative principles.

It has been a long-cherished wish—that (who knows how late) may one day be happily accomplished—that the principles of the endless variety of civil laws should be investigated and exposed; for in this way alone can we find the secret of simplifying legislation. But in this case, laws are nothing more than limitations of our freedom upon conditions under which it subsists in perfect harmony with itself; they consequently have for their object that which is completely our own work, and of which we ourselves may be the cause by means of these conceptions. But how objects as things in themselves—how the nature of things is subordinated to principles and is to be determined according to conceptions, is a question which it seems well nigh impossible to answer. Be this however as it may—for on this point our investigation is yet to be made—it is at least manifest from what we have said, that cognition from principles is something very different from cognition by means of the understanding, which may indeed precede other cognitions in the form of a principle, but in itself—in so far as it is synthetical—is neither based upon mere thought, nor contains a general proposition drawn from conceptions alone.

The understanding may be a faculty for the production of unity of phenomena by virtue of rules; the reason is a faculty for the production of unity of rules (of the understanding) under principles. Reason, therefore, never applies directly to experience, or to any sensuous object; its object is, on the contrary, the understanding, to the manifold cognition of which it gives a unity *à priori* by means of conceptions—a unity which may be called rational unity, and which is of a nature very different from that of the unity produced by the understanding.

The above is the general conception of the faculty of reason, in so far as it has been possible to make it comprehensible in the absence of examples. These will be given in the sequel.

B.—*Of the Logical use of Reason*

A distinction is commonly made between that which is immediately cognized and that which is inferred or concluded. That in a figure which is bounded by three straight lines, there are three angles, is an immediate cognition; but that these angles are together equal to two right angles, is an inference or conclusion. Now, as we are constantly employing this mode of thought, and have thus become quite accustomed to it, we no longer remark the above distinction, and, as in the case of the so-called deceptions of sense, consider as immediately perceived, what has really been inferred. In every reasoning or syllogism, there is a fundamental proposition, afterwards a second drawn from it, and finally the conclusion, which connects the truth in the first with the truth in the second—and that infallibly. If the judgment concluded is so contained in the first proposition, that it can be deduced from it without the mediation of a third notion, the conclusion is called immediate (*consequentia immediata*): I prefer the term conclusion of the understanding. But if, in addition to the fundamental cognition, a second judgment is necessary for the production of the conclusion, it is called a conclusion of the reason. In the proposition, *All men are mortal,* are contained the propositions, *Some men are mortal, Nothing that is not mortal is a man,* and these are therefore immediate conclusions from the first. On the other hand, the proposition, *All the learned are mortal,* is not contained in the main proposition (for the conception of a learned man does not occur in it), and it can be deduced from the main proposition only by means of a mediating judgment.

In every syllogism I first cogitate a *rule* (*the major*) by means of the *understanding.* In the next place I *subsume* a cognition under the condition of the rule (and this is the *minor*) by means of the *judgment.* And finally I *determine* my cognition by means of the predicate of the rule (this is the *conclusio*), consequently, I determine it *à priori* by means of the *reason.* The relations, therefore, which the major proposition, as the rule, represents between a cognition and its condition, constitute the different kinds of syllogisms. These are just threefold —analogously with all judgments, in so far as they differ in the mode of expressing the relation of a cognition in the understanding—namely, *categorical, hypothetical and disjunctive.*

When, as often happens, the conclusion is a judgment which may follow from other given judgments, through which a perfectly different object is cogitated, I endeavor to discover in the understanding whether the assertion in this conclusion does not stand under certain conditions according to a general rule. If I find such a condition, and if the object mentioned in the conclusion can be subsumed under the given condition, then this conclusion follows from a rule which is also valid for other objects of cognition. From this we see that reason endeavors to subject the great variety of the cognitions of the understanding to the smallest possible number of principles (general conditions), and thus to produce in it the highest unity.

C.—*Of the pure use of Reason*

Can we isolate reason, and, if so, is it in this case a peculiar source of conceptions and judgments which spring from it alone, and through which it can be applied to objects; or is it merely a subordinate faculty, whose duty it is to give a certain form to given cognitions—a form which is called logical, and through which the cognitions of the understanding are subordinated to each other, and lower rules to higher (those, to wit, whose condition comprises in its sphere the condition of the others), in so far as this can be done by comparison? This is the question which we have at present to answer. Manifold variety of rules and unity of principles is a requirement of reason, for the purpose of bringing the understanding into complete accordance with itself, just as understanding subjects the manifold content of intuition to conceptions, and thereby introduces connection into it. But this principle prescribes no law to objects, and does not contain any ground of the possibility of cognizing, or of determining them as such, but is merely a subjective law for the proper arrangement of the content of the understanding. The purpose of this law is, by a comparison of the conceptions of the understanding, to reduce them to the smallest possible number, although, at the same time, it does not justify us in demanding from objects themselves such an uni-

formity as might contribute to the convenience and the enlargement of the sphere of the understanding, or in expecting that it
will itself thus receive from them objective validity. In one
word, the question is, does reason in itself, that is, does pure reason contain *à priori* synthetical principles and rules, and what
are those principles?

The formal and logical procedure of reason in syllogisms
gives us sufficient information in regard to the ground on which
the transcendental principle of reason in its pure synthetical
cognition will rest.

1. Reason, as observed in the syllogistic process, is not applicable to intuitions, for the purpose of subjecting them to rules
—for this is the province of the understanding with its categories—but to conceptions and judgments. If pure reason does
apply to objects and the intuition of them, it does so not immediately, but mediately—through the understanding and its
judgments, which have a direct relation to the senses and their
intuition, for the purpose of determining their objects. The
unity of reason is therefore not the unity of a possible experience, but is essentially different from this unity, which is that of
the understanding. That everything which happens has a cause,
is not a principle cognized and prescribed by reason. This principle makes the unity of experience possible and borrows nothing from reason, which, without a reference to possible experience, could never have produced by means of mere conceptions
any such synthetical unity.

2. Reason, in its logical use, endeavors to discover the general condition of its judgment (the conclusion), and a syllogism is itself nothing but a judgment by means of the subsumption of its condition under a general rule (the major). Now as
this rule may itself be subjected to the same process of reason,
and thus the condition of the condition be sought (by means of
a prosyllogism) as long as the process can be continued, it is
very manifest that the peculiar principle of reason in its logical
use is—to find for the conditioned cognition of the understanding the unconditioned whereby the unity of the former is completed.

But this logical maxim cannot be a principle of *pure reason,*
unless we admit that, if the conditioned is given, the whole
series of conditions subordinated to one another—a series which

is consequently itself unconditioned—is also given, that is, contained in the object and its connection.

But this principle of pure reason is evidently *synthetical;* for analytically, the conditioned certainly relates to some condition, but not to the unconditioned. From this principle also there must originate different synthetical propositions, of which the pure understanding is perfectly ignorant, for it has to do only with objects of a possible experience, the cognition and synthesis of which is always conditioned. The unconditioned, if it does really exist, must be especially considered in regard to the determinations which distinguish it from whatever is conditioned, and will thus afford us material for many *à priori* synthetical propositions.

The principles resulting from this highest principle of pure reason will, however, be *transcendent* in relation to phenomena, that is to say, it will be impossible to make any adequate empirical use of this principle. It is therefore completely different from all principles of the understanding, the use made of which is entirely *immanent,* their object and purpose being merely the possibility of experience. Now our duty in the transcendental dialectic is as follows. To discover whether the principle, that the series of conditions (in the synthesis of phenomena, or of thought in general) extends to the unconditioned, is objectively true, or not; what consequences result therefrom affecting the empirical use of the understanding, or rather whether there exists any such objectively valid proposition of reason, and whether it is not, on the contrary, a merely logical precept which directs us to ascend perpetually to still higher conditions, to approach completeness in the series of them, and thus to introduce into our cognition the highest possible unity of reason. We must ascertain, I say, whether this requirement of reason has not been regarded, by a misunderstanding, as a transcendental principle of pure reason, which postulates a thorough completeness in the series of conditions in objects themselves. We must show, moreover, the misconceptions and illusions that intrude into syllogisms, the major proposition of which pure reason has supplied—a proposition which has perhaps more of the character of a *petitio* than of a *postulatum*—and that proceed from experience upwards to its conditions. The solution of these problems is our task in transcendental dialectic, which we are about to expose even at its source, that lies deep in human reason. We shall divide it into two parts, the first of which will treat of the *transcendent conceptions* of pure reason, the second of transcendent and *dialectical syllogisms*.

BOOK I

Of the Conceptions of Pure Reason

The conceptions of pure reason—we do not here speak of the possibility of them—are not obtained by reflection, but by inference or conclusion. The conceptions of understanding are also cogitated *à priori* antecedently to experience, and render it possible; but they contain nothing but the unity of reflection upon phenomena, in so far as these must necessarily belong to a possible empirical consciousness. Through them alone are cognition and the determination of an object possible. It is from them, accordingly, that we receive material for reasoning, and antecedently to them we possess no *à priori* conceptions of objects from which they might be deduced. On the other hand, the sole basis of their objective reality consists in the necessity imposed on them, as containing the intellectual form of all experience, of restricting their application and influence to the sphere of experience.

But the term, *conception of reason* or rational conception, itself indicates that it does not confine itself within the limits of experience, because its object-matter is a cognition, of which every empirical cognition is but a part—nay, the whole of possible experience may be itself but a part of it—a cognition to which no actual experience ever fully attains, although it does always pertain to it. The aim of rational conceptions is the *comprehension*, as that of the conceptions of understanding is the *understanding* of perceptions. If they contain the unconditioned, they relate to that to which all experience is subordinate, but which is never itself an object of experience—that towards which reason tends in all its conclusions from experience, and by the standard of which it estimates the degree of their empirical use, but which is never itself an element in an empirical synthesis. If, notwithstanding, such conceptions possess objective validity, they may be called *conceptus ratiocinati* (conceptions legitimately concluded); in cases where they do not, they have been admitted on account of having the appearance of being correctly concluded, and may be called *conceptus ratio-cinantes* (sophistical conceptions).   But as this can only be sufficiently demonstrated in that part of our treatise which relates to the dialectical conclusions of reason, we shall omit any consideration of it in this place.   As we called the pure conceptions of the understanding categories, we shall also distinguish those of pure reason by a new name, and call them transcendental ideas.   These terms, however, we must in the first place explain and justify.

Sec. I.—Of Ideas in General.

Spite of the great wealth of words which European languages possess, the thinker finds himself often at a loss for an expression exactly suited to his conception, for want of which he is unable to make himself intelligible either to others or to himself.   To coin new words is a pretension to legislation in language which is seldom successful; and, before recourse is taken to so desperate an expedient, it is advisable to examine the dead and learned languages, with the hope and the probability that we may there meet with some adequate expression of the notion we have in our minds.   In this case, even if the original meaning of the word has become somewhat uncertain, from carelessness or want of caution on the part of the authors of it, it is always better to adhere to and confirm its proper meaning—even although it may be doubtful whether it was formerly used in exactly this sense—than to make our labor vain by want of sufficient care to render ourselves intelligible.

For this reason, when it happens that there exists only a single word to express a certain conception, and this word, in its usual acceptation, is thoroughly adequate to the conception, the accurate distinction of which from related conceptions is of great importance, we ought not to employ the expression improvidently, or, for the sake of variety and elegance of style, use it as a synonym for other cognate words.   It is our duty, on the contrary, carefully to preserve its peculiar signification, as otherwise it easily happens that when the attention of the reader is no longer particularly attracted to the expression, and it is lost amid the multitude of other words of very different import, the thought which it conveyed, and which it alone conveyed, is lost with it.

Plato employed the expression *Idea* in a way that plainly showed he meant by it something which is never derived from the senses, but which far transcends even the conceptions of the understanding, (with which Aristotle occupied himself,) inasmuch as in experience nothing perfectly corresponding to them could be found. Ideas are, according to him, archetypes of things themselves, and not merely keys to possible experiences, like the categories. In his view they flow from the highest reason, by which they have been imparted to human reason, which, however, exists no longer in its original state, but is obliged with great labor to recall by reminiscence—which is called philosophy—the old but now sadly obscured ideas. I will not here enter upon any literary investigation of the sense which this sublime philosopher attached to this expression. I shall content myself with remarking that it is nothing unusual, in common conversation as well as in written works, by comparing the thoughts which an author has delivered upon a subject, to understand him better than he understood himself—inasmuch as he may not have sufficiently determined his conception, and thus have sometimes spoken, nay even thought, in opposition to his own opinions.

Plato perceived very clearly that our faculty of cognition has the feeling of a much higher vocation than that of merely spelling out phenomena according to synthetical unity, for the purpose of being able to read them as experience, and that our reason naturally raises itself to cognitions far too elevated to admit of the possibility of an object given by experience corresponding to them—cognitions which are nevertheless real, and are not mere phantoms of the brain.

This philosopher found his ideas especially in all that is practical,* that is, which rests upon freedom, which in its turn ranks under cognitions that are the peculiar product of reason. He who would derive from experience the conceptions of virtue, who would make (as many have really done) that, which at best can but serve as an imperfectly illustrative example, a model for the formation of a perfectly adequate idea on the sub-

---

* He certainly extended the application of his conception to the speculative cognitions also, provided they were given pure and completely *à priori*, nay, even to mathematics, although this science cannot possess an object otherwhere than in *possible* experience. I cannot follow him in this, and as little can I follow him in his mystical deduction of these ideas, or in his hypostatization of them; although, in truth, the elevated and exaggerated language which he employed in describing them is quite capable of an interpretation more subdued and more in accordance with fact and the nature of things.

ject, would in fact transform virtue into a nonentity changeable according to time and circumstance, and utterly incapable
of being employed as a rule. On the contrary, everyone is
conscious that, when any one is held up to him as a model of
virtue, he compares this so-called model with the true original
which he possesses in his own mind, and values him according
to this standard. But this standard is the idea of virtue, in relation to which all possible objects of experience are indeed serviceable as examples—proofs of the practicability in a certain
degree of that which the conception of virtue demands—but
certainly not as archetypes. That the actions of man will never
be in perfect accordance with all the requirements of the pure
ideas of reason, does not prove the thought to be chimerical.
For only through this idea are all judgments as to moral merit
or demerit possible; it consequently lies at the foundation of
every approach to moral perfection, however far removed from
it the obstacles in human nature—indeterminable as to degree
—may keep us.

The Platonic Republic has become proverbial as an example
—and a striking one—of imaginary perfection, such as can exist
only in the brain of the idle thinker; and Brucker ridicules the
philosopher for maintaining that a prince can never govern well,
unless he is participant in *the ideas*. But we should do better to
follow up this thought, and, where this admirable thinker leaves
us without assistance, employ new efforts to place it in clearer
light, rather than carelessly fling it aside as useless, under the
very miserable and pernicious pretext of impracticability. A
constitution of *the greatest possible human freedom* according
to laws, by which the *liberty of every individual can consist with
the liberty of every other* (not of the greatest possible happiness, for this follows necessarily from the former), is, to say
the least, a necessary idea, which must be placed at the foundation not only of the first plan of the constitution of a state, but
of all its laws. And in this it is not necessary at the outset to
take account of the obstacles which lie in our way—obstacles
which perhaps do not necessarily arise from the character of
human nature, but rather from the previous neglect of true ideas
in legislation. For there is nothing more pernicious and more
unworthy of a philosopher than the vulgar appeal to a so-
called adverse experience, which indeed would not have existed
if those institutions had been established at the proper time and

in accordance with ideas; while instead of this, conceptions, crude for the very reason that they have been drawn from experience, have marred and frustrated all our better views and intentions. The more legislation and government are in harmony with this idea, the more rare do punishments become, and thus it is quite reasonable to maintain, as Plato did, that in a perfect state no punishments at all would be necessary. Now although a perfect state may never exist, the idea is not on that account the less just, which holds up this *Maximum* as the archetype or standard of a constitution, in order to bring legislative government always nearer and nearer to the greatest possible perfection. For at what precise degree human nature must stop in its progress, and how wide must be the chasm which must necessarily exist between the idea and its realization, are problems which no one can or ought to determine—and for this reason, that it is the destination of freedom to overstep all assigned limits between itself and the idea.

But not only in that wherein human reason is a real causal agent and where ideas are operative causes (of actions and their objects), that is to say, in the region of ethics, but also in regard to nature herself, Plato saw clear proofs of an origin from ideas. A plant, an animal, the regular order of nature—probably also the disposition of the whole universe—give manifest evidence that they are possible only by means of and according to ideas; that, indeed, no one creature, under the individual conditions of its existence, perfectly harmonizes with the idea of the most perfect of its kind—just as little as man with the idea of humanity, which nevertheless he bears in his soul as the archetypal standard of his actions; that, notwithstanding, these ideas are in the highest sense individually, unchangeably and completely determined, and are the original causes of things; and that the totality of connected objects in the universe is alone fully adequate to that idea. Setting aside the exaggerations of expression in the writings of this philosopher, the mental power exhibited in this ascent from the ectypal mode of regarding the physical world to the architectonic connection thereof according to ends, that is, ideas, is an effort which deserves imitation and claims respect. But as regards the principles of ethics, of legislation and of religion, spheres in which ideas alone render experience possible, although they never attain to full expression therein, he has vindicated for himself

a position of peculiar merit, which is not appreciated only because it is judged by the very empirical rules, the validity of
which as principles is destroyed by ideas. For as regards
nature, experience presents us with rules and is the source of
truth, but in relation to ethical laws experience is the parent of
illusion, and it is in the highest degree reprehensible to limit or
to deduce the laws which dictate what I *ought to do*, from what
is done.

We must, however, omit the consideration of these important
subjects, the development of which is in reality the peculiar duty
and dignity of philosophy, and confine ourselves for the present
to the more humble but not less useful task of preparing a firm
foundation for those majestic edifices of moral science. For
this foundation has been hitherto insecure from the many sub-
terranean passages which reason in its confident but vain search
for treasures has made in all directions. Our present duty is to
make ourselves perfectly acquainted with the transcendental
use made of pure reason, its principles and ideas, that we may
be able properly to determine and value its influence and real
worth. But before bringing these introductory remarks to a
close, I beg those who really have philosophy at heart—and
their number is but small—if they shall find themselves convinced by the considerations following as well as by those above,
to exert themselves to preserve to the expression *idea* its original signification, and to take care that it be not lost among
those other expressions by which all sorts of representations are
loosely designated—that the interests of science may not thereby suffer. We are in no want of words to denominate adequately every mode of representation, without the necessity of
encroaching upon terms which are proper to others. The following is a graduated list of them. The genus is *representation*
in general (*representatio*). Under it stands representation with
consciousness (*perceptio*). A *perception* which relates solely
to the subject as a modification of its state, is a *sensation* (*sensatio*), an objective perception is a *cognition* (*cognitio*). A
cognition is either an *intuition* or a *conception* (*intuitus vel conceptus*). The former has an immediate relation to the object
and is singular and individual; the latter has but a mediate
relation, by means of a characteristic mark which may be common to several things. A conception is either *empirical* or *pure*.
A pure conception, in so far as it has its origin in the under-

standing alone, and is not the conception of a pure sensuous image, is called *notio*. A conception formed from notions, which transcends the possibility of experience, is an *idea,* or a conception of reason. To one who has accustomed himself to these distinctions, it must be quite intolerable to hear the representation of the color red called an idea. It ought not even to be called a notion or conception of understanding.

Sec. II.—Of Transcendental Ideas

Transcendental analytic showed us how the mere logical form of our cognition can contain the origin of pure conceptions *à priori*, conceptions which represent objects antecedently to all experience, or rather, indicate the synthetical unity which alone renders possible an empirical cognition of objects. The form of judgments—converted into a conception of the synthesis of intuitions—produced the categories, which direct the employment of the understanding in experience. This consideration warrants us to expect that the form of syllogisms, when applied to synthetical unity of intuitions, following the rule of the categories, will contain the origin of particular *à priori* conceptions, which we may call pure conceptions of reason or transcendental ideas, and which will determine the use of the understanding in the totality of experience according to principles.

The function of reason in arguments consists in the universality of a cognition according to conceptions, and the syllogism itself is a judgment which is determined *à priori* in the whole extent of its condition. The proposition, "Caius is mortal," is one which may be obtained from experience by the aid of the understanding alone; but my wish is to find a conception, which contains the condition under which the predicate of this judgment is given—in this case, the conception of *man*—and after subsuming under this condition, taken in its whole extent (all men are mortal), I determine according to it the cognition of the object thought, and say, "Caius is mortal."

Hence, in the conclusion of a syllogism we restrict a predicate to a certain object, after having thought it in the major in its whole extent under a certain condition. This complete quantity of the extent in relation to such a condition is called *universality (universalitas)*. To this corresponds *totality (universitas)* of conditions in the synthesis of intuitions. The transcendental conception of reason is therefore nothing else than the conception of the *totality of the conditions* of a given condition. Now as the *unconditioned* alone renders possible totality of conditions, and, conversely, the totality of conditions is itself always unconditioned; a pure rational conception in general can be defined and explained by means of the conception of the unconditioned, in so far as it contains a basis for the synthesis of the conditioned.

To the number of modes of relation which the understanding cogitates by means of the categories, the number of pure rational conceptions will correspond. We must therefore seek for, first, an *unconditioned* of the *categorical* synthesis in a *subject;* secondly, of the *hypothetical* synthesis of the members of a *series;* thirdly, of the *disjunctive* synthesis of parts in a *system.*

There are exactly the same number of modes of syllogisms, each of which proceeds through prosyllogisms to the unconditioned—one to the subject which cannot be employed as a predicate, another to the presupposition which supposes nothing higher than itself, and the third to an aggregate of the members of the complete division of a conception. Hence the pure rational conceptions of totality in the synthesis of conditions have a necessary foundation in the nature of human reason—at least as modes of elevating the unity of the understanding to the unconditioned. They may have no valid application, corresponding to their transcendental employment, *in concreto,* and be thus of no greater utility than to direct the understanding how, while extending them as widely as possible, to maintain its exercise and application in perfect consistence and harmony.

But, while speaking here of the totality of conditions and of the unconditioned as the common title of all conceptions of reason, we again light upon an expression, which we find it impossible to dispense with, and which nevertheless, owing to the ambiguity attaching to it from long abuse, we cannot employ with safety. The word *absolute* is one of the few words which, in its original signification, was perfectly adequate to the conception it was intended to convey—a conception which no other word in the same language exactly suits, and the loss—or, which is the same thing, the incautious and loose employment —of which must be followed by the loss of the conception itself. And, as it is a conception which occupies much of the attention of reason, its loss would be greatly to the detriment of all transcendental philosophy. The word *absolute* is at present frequently used to denote that something can be predicated of a thing considered *in itself* and intrinsically. In this sense *absolutely possible* would signify that which is possible in itself (*interne*)—which is, in fact, the *least* that one can predicate of an object. On the other hand, it is sometimes employed to indicate that a thing is valid in all respects—for example, absolute sovereignty. *Absolutely possible* would in this sense signify that which is *possible in all relations* and in every respect; and this is the most that can be predicated of the possibility of a thing. Now these significations do in truth frequently coincide. Thus, for example, that which is intrinsically impossible, is also impossible in all relations, that is, absolutely impossible. But in most cases they differ from each other *toto cælo,* and I can by no means conclude that, because a thing is in itself possible, it is also possible in all relations, and therefore absolutely. Nay, more, I shall in the sequel show, that absolute necessity does not by any means depend on internal necessity, and that therefore it must not be considered as synonymous with it. Of an opposite which is intrinsically impossible, we may affirm that it is in all respects impossible, and that consequently the thing itself, of which this is the opposite, is absolutely necessary; but I cannot reason conversely and say, the opposite of that which is absolutely necessary is intrinsically impossible, that is, that the *absolute* necessity of things is an *internal* necessity. For this internal necessity is in certain cases a mere empty word with which the least conception cannot be connected, while the conception of the necessity of a thing in all relations possesses very peculiar determinations. Now as the loss of a conception of great utility in speculative science cannot be a matter of indifference to the philosopher, I trust that the proper determination and careful preservation of the expression on which the conception depends will likewise be not indifferent to him.

In this enlarged signification then shall I employ the word *absolute,* in opposition to that which is valid only in some particular respect; for the latter is restricted by conditions, the former is valid without any restriction whatever.

Now the transcendental conception of reason has for its object nothing else than absolute totality in the synthesis of conditions, and does not rest satisfied till it has attained to the absolutely, that is, in all respects and relations, unconditioned. For pure reason leaves to the understanding everything that immediately relates to the object of intuition or rather to their synthesis in imagination. The former restricts itself to the absolute totality in the employment of the conceptions of the understanding, and aims at carrying out the synthetical unity which is cogitated in the category, even to the unconditioned. This unity may hence be called the *rational unity* * of phenomena, as the other, which the category expresses, may be termed the *unity of the understanding*.* Reason, therefore, has an immediate relation to the use of the understanding, not indeed in so far as the latter contains the ground of possible experience (for the conception of the absolute totality of conditions is not a conception that can be employed in experience, because no experience is unconditioned), but solely for the purpose of directing it to a certain unity, of which the understanding has no conception, and the aim of which is to collect into an *absolute whole* all acts of the understanding. Hence the objective employment of the pure conceptions of reason is always *transcendent*, while that of the pure conceptions of the understanding must, according to their nature, be always *immanent*, inasmuch as they are limited to possible experience.

I understand by idea a necessary conception of reason, to which no corresponding object can be discovered in the world of sense. Accordingly, the pure conceptions of reason at present under consideration are *transcendental ideas*. They are conceptions of pure reason, for they regard all empirical cognition as determined by means of an absolute totality of conditions. They are not mere fictions, but natural and necessary products of reason, and have hence a necessary relation to the whole sphere of the exercise of the understanding. And finally, they are transcendent, and overstep the limits of all experience, in which, consequently, no object can ever be presented that would be perfectly adequate to a transcendental idea. When we use the word *idea*, we say, as regards its object (an object of the pure understanding), a great deal, but, as regards its subject (that is, in respect of its reality under conditions of experience), exceedingly little, because the idea, as the conception of a maximum, can never be completely and adequately presented *in concreto*. Now, as in the merely specu-

* Vernunfteinheit, Verstandeseinheit.

lative employment of reason the latter is properly the sole aim, and as in this case the approximation to a conception, which is never attained in practice, is the same thing as if the conception were non-existent—it is commonly said of a conception of this kind, *it is only an idea.* So we might very well say, the absolute totality of all phenomena is only an idea, for as we never can present an adequate representation of it, it remains for us a *problem* incapable of solution. On the other hand, as in the practical use of the understanding we have only to do with action and practice according to rules, an idea of pure reason can always be given really *in concreto*, although only partially, nay, it is the indispensable condition of all practical employment of reason. The practice or execution of the idea is always limited and defective, but nevertheless within indeterminable boundaries, consequently always under the influence of the conception of an absolute perfection. And thus the practical idea is always in the highest degree fruitful, and in relation to real actions indispensably necessary. In the idea, pure reason possesses even causality and the power of producing that which its conception contains. Hence we cannot say of wisdom, in a disparaging way, *it is only an idea.* For, for the very reason that it is the idea of the necessary unity of all possible aims, it must be for all practical exertions and endeavors the primitive condition and rule—a rule which, if not constitutive, is at least limitative.

Now, although we must say of the transcendental conceptions of reason, *they are only ideas,* we must not, on this account, look upon them as superfluous and nugatory. For, although no object can be determined by them, they can be of great utility, unobserved and at the basis of the edifice of the understanding, as the canon for its extended and self-consistent exercise—a canon which, indeed, does not enable it to cognize more in an object than it would cognize by the help of its own conceptions, but which guides it more securely in its cognition. Not to mention that they perhaps render possible a transition from our conceptions of nature and the non-ego to the practical conceptions, and thus produce for even ethical ideas keeping, so to speak, and connection with the speculative cognitions of reason. The explication of all this must be looked for in the sequel.

But setting aside, in conformity with our original purpose, the consideration of the practical ideas, we proceed to contem-

plate reason in its speculative use alone, nay, in a still more restricted sphere, to wit, in the transcendental use; and here must
strike into the same path which we followed in our deduction
of the categories. That is to say, we shall consider the logical
form of the cognition of reason, that we may see whether reason
may not be thereby a source of conceptions which enable us to
regard objects in themselves as determined synthetically *à
priori,* in relation to one or other of the functions of reason.

Reason, considered as the faculty of a certain logical form
of cognition, is the faculty of conclusion, that is, of mediate
judgment—by means of the subsumption of the condition of a
possible judgment under the condition of a given judgment.
The given judgment is the general rule (major). The subsumption of the condition of another possible judgment under
the condition of the rule is the minor. The actual judgment,
which enounces the assertion of the rule in the subsumed case,
is the conclusion (*conclusio*). The rule predicates something
generally under a certain condition. The condition of the rule
is satisfied in some particular case. It follows, that what was
valid in general under that condition must also be considered as
valid in the particular case which satisfies this condition. It is
very plain that reason attains to a cognition, by means of acts
of the understanding which constitute a series of conditions.
When I arrive at the proposition, " All bodies are changeable,"
by beginning with the more remote cognition, (in which the
conception of body does not appear, but which nevertheless
contains the condition of that conception), " All [that is] compound is changeable," by proceeding from this to a less remote
cognition, which stands under the condition of the former,
" Bodies are compound," and hence to a third, which at length
connects for me the remote cognition (changeable) with the one
before me, " Consequently, bodies are changeable "—I have
arrived at a cognition (conclusion) through a series of conditions (premises). Now every series, whose exponent (of the
categorical or hypothetical judgment) is given, can be continued; consequently the same procedure of reason conducts us
to the *ratiocinatio polysyllogistica,* which is a series of syllogisms, that can be continued either on the side of the conditions (*per prosyllogismos*) or of the conditioned (*per episyl-
logismos*) to an indefinite extent.

But we very soon perceive that the chain or series of prosyllogisms, that is, of deduced cognitions on the side of the grounds or conditions of a given cognition, in other words, the *ascending series* of syllogisms must have a very different relation to the faculty of reason from that of the *descending series,* that is, the progressive procedure of reason on the side of the conditioned by means of episyllogisms. For, as in the former case the cognition (*conclusio*) is given only as conditioned, reason can attain to this cognition only under the pre-supposition that all the members of the series on the side of the conditions are given (totality in the series of premises), because only under this supposition is the judgment we may be considering possible *à priori;* while on the side of the conditioned or the inferences, only an incomplete and *becoming,* and not a pre-supposed or given series, consequently only a potential progression, is cogitated. Hence, when a cognition is contemplated as conditioned, reason is compelled to consider the series of conditions in an ascending line as completed and given in their totality. But if the very same cognition is considered at the same time as the condition of other cognitions, which together constitute a series of inferences or consequences in a descending line, reason may preserve a perfect indifference, as to how far this progression may extend *a parte posteriori,* and whether the totality of this series is possible, because it stands in no need of such a series for the purpose of arriving at the conclusion before it, inasmuch as this conclusion is sufficiently guaranteed and determined on grounds *a parte priori.* It may be the case, that upon the side of the conditions the series of premises has a *first* or highest condition, or it may not possess this, and so be *a parte priori* unlimited; but it must nevertheless contain totality of conditions, even admitting that we never could succeed in completely apprehending it; and the whole series must be unconditionally true, if the conditioned, which is considered as an inference resulting from it, is to be held as true. This is a requirement of reason, which announces its cognition as determined *à priori* and as necessary, either in itself—and in this case it needs no grounds to rest upon—or, if it is deduced, as a member of a series of grounds, which is itself unconditionally true.

Sec. III.—System of Transcendental Ideas

We are not at present engaged with a logical dialectic which makes complete abstraction of the content of cognition, and aims only at unveiling the illusory appearance in the form of syllogisms. Our subject is transcendental dialectic, which must contain, completely *à priori*, the origin of certain cognitions drawn from pure reason, and the origin of certain deduced conceptions, the object of which cannot be given empirically, and which therefore lie beyond the sphere of the faculty of understanding. We have observed, from the natural relation which the transcendental use of our cognition, in syllogisms as well as in judgments, must have to the logical, that there are three kinds of dialectical arguments, corresponding to the three modes of conclusion, by which reason attains to cognitions on principles; and that in all it is the business of reason, to ascend from the conditioned synthesis, beyond which the understanding never proceeds, to the unconditioned which the understanding never can reach.

Now the most general relations which can exist in our representations are, 1st, the relation to the subject; 2d, the relation to objects, either as phenomena, or as objects of thought in general. If we connect this subdivision with the main division, all the relations of our representations, of which we can form either a conception or an idea, are threefold: 1. The relation to the subject; 2. The relation to the manifold of the object as a phenomenon; 3. The relation to all things in general.

Now all pure conceptions have to do in general with the synthetical unity of representations; conceptions of pure reason (transcendental ideas) on the other hand, with the unconditional synthetical unity of all conditions. It follows that all transcendental ideas arrange themselves in three classes, the *first* of which contains the absolute (unconditioned) *unity of the thinking subject,* the *second* the absolute *unity of the series of the conditions* of a phenomenon, the *third* the absolute *unity of the condition of all objects of thought* in general.

The thinking subject is the object-matter of *Psychology;* the sum total of all phenomena (the world) is the object-matter of *Cosmology;* and the thing which contains the highest condition of the possibility of all that is cogitable (the being of all beings) is the object-matter of all *Theology.* Thus pure reason presents us with the idea of a transcendental doctrine of the soul (*psychologia rationalis*), of a transcendental science of the world (*cosmologia rationalis*), and finally of a transcendental doctrine of God (*theologia transcendentalis*). Understanding cannot originate even the outline of any of these sciences, even when connected with the highest logical use of reason, that is, all cogitable syllogisms—for the purpose of proceeding from one object (phenomenon) to all others, even to the utmost limits of the empirical synthesis. They are, on the contrary, pure and genuine products, or problems, of pure reason.

What modi of the pure conceptions of reason these transcendental ideas are, will be fully exposed in the following chapter. They follow the guiding thread of the categories. For pure reason never relates immediately to objects, but to the conceptions of these contained in the understanding. In like manner, it will be made manifest in the detailed explanation of these ideas—how reason, merely through the synthetical use of the same function which it employs in a categorical syllogism, necessarily attains to the conception of the absolute unity of the *thinking subject*—how the logical procedure in hypothetical ideas necessarily produces the idea of the absolutely unconditioned *in a series* of given conditions, and finally—how the mere form of the disjunctive syllogism involves the highest conception of a *being of all beings:* a thought which at first sight seems in the highest degree paradoxical.

An *objective deduction,* such as we were able to present in the case of the categories, is impossible as regards these transcendental ideas. For they have, in truth, no relation to any object, in experience, for the very reason that they are only ideas. But a subjective deduction of them from the nature of our reason is possible, and has been given in the present chapter.

It is easy to perceive that the sole aim of pure reason is, the absolute totality of the synthesis *on the side of the conditions,* and that it does not concern itself with the absolute completeness *on the part of the conditioned.* For of the former alone does she stand in need, in order to prepose the whole series of conditions, and thus present them to the understanding *à priori.* But if we once have a completely (and unconditionally) given condition, there is no further necessity, in proceeding with the series, for a conception of reason; for the understanding takes of itself every step downward, from the condition to the conditioned. Thus the transcendental ideas are available only for *ascending* in the series of conditions, till we reach the unconditioned, that is, principles. As regards *descending* to the conditioned, on the other hand, we find that there is a widely extensive logical use which reason makes of the laws of the understanding, but that a transcendental use thereof is impossible; and, that when we form an idea of the absolute totality of such a synthesis, for example, of the whole series of all *future* changes in the world, this idea is a mere *ens rationis,* an arbitrary fiction of thought, and not a necessary presupposition of reason. For the possibility of the conditioned presupposes the totality of its conditions, but not of its consequences. Consequently, this conception is not a transcendental idea—and it is with these alone that we are at present occupied.

Finally, it is obvious, that there exists among the transcendental ideas of a certain connection and unity, and that pure reason, by means of them, collects all its cognitions into one system. From the cognition of self to the cognition of the world, and through these to the supreme being, the progression is so natural, that it seems to resemble the logical march of reason from the premises to the conclusion.* Now whether there lies unobserved at the foundation of these ideas an analogy of the same kind as exists between the logical and transcendental procedure of reason, is another of those questions, the answer to which we must not expect till we arrive at a more advanced stage in our inquiries. In this cursory and preliminary view, we have, meanwhile, reached our aim. For we have dispelled the ambiguity which attached to the transcendental conceptions of reason, from their being commonly mixed up

---

* The science of Metaphysics has for the proper object of its inquiries only three grand ideas: God, Freedom, and Immortality, and it aims at showing that the second conception, conjoined with the first, must lead to the third, as a necessary conclusion. All the other subjects with which it occupies itself are merely means for the attainment and realization of these ideas. It does not require these ideas for the construction of a science of nature, but, on the contrary, for the purpose of passing beyond the sphere of nature. A complete insight into and comprehension of them would render *Theology, Ethics,* and through the conjunction of both, *Religion,* solely dependent on the speculative faculty of reason. In a systematic representation of these ideas the above-mentioned arrangement—the *synthetical* one—would be the most suitable; but in the investigation which must necessarily precede it, the *analytical,* which reverses this arrangement, would be better adapted to our purpose, as in it we should proceed from that which experience immediately presents to us—psychology, to cosmology, and thence to theology.

with other conceptions in the systems of philosophers, and not properly distinguished from the conceptions of the understanding; we have exposed their origin, and thereby at the same time their determinate number, and presented them in a systematic connection, and have thus marked out and inclosed a definite sphere of pure reason.

BOOK II

OF THE DIALECTICAL PROCEDURE OF PURE REASON

It may be said that the object of a merely transcendental idea is something of which we have no conception, although the idea may be a necessary product of reason according to its original laws. For, in fact, a conception of an object that is adequate to the idea given by reason, is impossible. For such an object must be capable of being presented and intuited in a possible experience. But we should express our meaning better, and with less risk of being misunderstood, if we said that, we can have no knowledge of an object, which perfectly corresponds to an idea, although we may possess a problematical conception thereof.

Now the transcendental (subjective) reality at least of the pure conceptions of reason rests upon the fact that we are led to such ideas by a necessary procedure of reason. There must therefore be syllogisms which contain no empirical premises, and by means of which we conclude from something that we do know, to something of which we do not even possess a conception, to which we, nevertheless, by an unavoidable illusion, ascribe objective reality. Such arguments are, as regards their result, rather to be termed sophisms than syllogisms, although indeed, as regards their origin, they are very well entitled to the latter name, inasmuch as they are not fictions or accidental products of reason, but are necessitated by its very nature. They are sophisms, not of men, but of pure reason herself, from which the wisest cannot free himself. After long labor he may be able to guard against the error, but he can never be thoroughly rid of the illusion which continually mocks and misleads him.

Of these dialectical arguments there are three kinds, corresponding to the number of the ideas, which their conclusions present. In the argument or syllogism of the *first class,* I conclude, from the transcendental conception of the subject which contains no manifold, the absolute unity of the subject itself, of which I cannot in this manner attain to a conception. This dialectical argument I shall call the Transcendental *Paralogism.* The *second class* of sophistical arguments is occupied with the transcendental conception of the absolute totality of the series of conditions for a given phenomenon, and I conclude, from the fact that I have always a self-contradictory conception of the unconditioned synthetical unity of the series upon one side, the truth of the opposite unity, of which I have nevertheless no conception. The condition of reason in these dialectical arguments, I shall term the *Antinomy* of pure reason. Finally, according to the third kind of sophistical argument, I conclude, from the totality of the conditions of thinking objects in general, in so far as they can be given, the absolute synthetical unity of all conditions of the possibility of things in general; that is, from things which I do not know in their mere transcendental conception, I conclude a being of all beings which I know still less by means of a transcendental conception, and of whose unconditioned necessity I can form no conception whatever. This dialectical argument I shall call the *Ideal* of pure reason.

Chapter I

Of the Paralogisms of Pure Reason

The logical paralogism consists in the falsity of an argument in respect of its form, be the content what it may. But a transcendental paralogism has a transcendental foundation, and concludes falsely, while the form is correct and unexceptionable. In this manner the paralogism has its foundation in the nature of human reason, and is the parent of an unavoidable, though not insoluble, mental illusion.

We now come to a conception, which was not inserted in the general list of transcendental conceptions, and yet must be reckoned with them, but at the same time without in the least altering, or indicating a deficiency in that table. This is the conception, or, if the term is preferred, the judgment, *I think.* But it is readily perceived that this thought is as it were the vehicle of all conceptions in general, and consequently of transcendental conceptions also, and that it is therefore regarded as a transcendental conception, although it can have no peculiar claim to be so ranked, inasmuch as its only use is to indicate that all thought is accompanied by consciousness. At the same time, pure as this conception is from all empirical content (impressions of the senses), it enables us to distinguish two different kinds of objects. *I,* as thinking, am an object of the internal sense, and am called soul. That which is an object of the external senses is called body. Thus the expression, I, as a thinking being, designates the object-matter of psychology, which may be called the rational doctrine of the soul, inasmuch as in this science I desire to know nothing of the soul but what, independently of all experience (which determines me *in concreto*), may be concluded from this conception *I,* in so far as it appears in all thought.

Now, the *rational* doctrine of the soul is really an undertaking of this kind. For if the smallest empirical element of thought, if any particular perception of my internal state, were to be introduced among the grounds of cognition of this science, it would not be a rational, but an *empirical* doctrine of the soul. We have thus before us a pretended science, raised upon the single proposition, *I think,* whose foundation or want of foundation we may very properly, and agreeably with the nature of a transcendental philosophy, here examine. It ought not to be objected that in this proposition, which expresses the perception of one's self, an internal experience is asserted, and that consequently the rational doctrine of the soul which is founded upon it, is not pure, but partly founded upon an empirical principle. For this internal perception is nothing more than the mere apperception, *I think,* which in fact renders all transcendental conceptions possible, in which we say, I think substance, cause, etc. For internal experience in general and its possibility, or perception in general, and its relation to other perceptions, unless some particular distinction or determination thereof is empirically given, cannot be regarded as empirical cognition, but as cognition of the empirical, and belongs to the investigation of the possibility of every experience, which is certainly transcendental. The smallest object of experience (for example, only pleasure or pain), that should be included in the general representation of self-consciousness, would immediately change the rational into an empirical psychology.

I think is therefore the only text of rational psychology, from which it must develop its whole system. It is manifest that this thought, when applied to an object (myself), can contain nothing but transcendental predicates thereof; because the least empirical predicate would destroy the purity of the science and its independence of all experience.

But we shall have to follow here the guidance of the categories—only, as in the present case a thing, I, as thinking being, is at first given, we shall—not indeed change the order of the categories as it stands in the table—but begin at the category of substance, by which a thing in itself is represented, and proceed backwards through the series. The topic of the rational doctrine of the soul, from which everything else it may contain must be deduced, is accordingly as follows:

I

The soul is SUBSTANCE.

II

As regards its quality, it is SIMPLE.

III

As regards the different times in which it exists, it is numerically identical, that is UNITY, not Plurality.

IV

It is in relation to *possible* objects in space.*

From these elements originate all the conceptions of pure psychology, by combination alone, without the aid of any other principle. This substance, merely as an object of the internal sense, gives the conception of *Immateriality;* as simple substance, that of *Incorruptibility;* its identity, as intellectual substance, gives the conception of *Personality;* all these three together, *Spirituality.* Its relation to objects in space gives us the conception of connection (*commercium*) with bodies. Thus it represents thinking substance as the principle of life in matter, that is, as a soul (*anima*), and as the ground of *Animality;* and

---

* The reader, who may not so easily perceive the psychological sense of these expressions—taken here in their transcendental abstraction, and cannot guess why the latter attribute of the soul belongs to the category of *existence*, will find the expressions sufficiently explained and justified in the sequel. I have, moreover, to apologize for the Latin terms which have been employed, instead of their German synonyms, contrary to the rules of correct writing. But I judged it better to sacrifice elegance of language to perspicuity of exposition.

this, limited and determined by the conception of spirituality, gives us that of *Immortality*.

Now to these conceptions relate four paralogisms of a transcendental psychology, which is falsely held to be a science of pure reason, touching the nature of our thinking being. We can, however, lay at the foundation of this science nothing but the simple and in itself perfectly contentless representation *I,* which cannot even be called a conception, but merely a consciousness which accompanies all conceptions. By this I, or He, or It, who or which thinks, nothing more is represented than a transcendental subject of thought = x, which is cognized only by means of the thoughts that are its predicates, and of which, apart from these, we cannot form the least conception. Hence we are obliged to go round this representation in a perpetual circle, inasmuch as we must always employ it, in order to frame any judgment respecting it. And this inconvenience we find it impossible to rid ourselves of, because consciousness in itself is not so much a representation distinguishing a particular object, as a form of representation in general, in so far as it may be termed cognition; for in and by cognition alone do I think anything.

It must, however, appear extraordinary at first sight that the condition, under which I think, and which is consequently a property of my subject, should be held to be likewise valid for every existence which thinks, and that we can presume to base upon a seemingly empirical proposition a judgment which is apodictic and universal, to wit, that everything which thinks is constituted as the voice of my consciousness declares it to be, that is, as a self-conscious being. The cause of this belief is to be found in the fact, that we necessarily attribute to things *à priori* all the properties which constitute conditions under which alone we can cogitate them. Now I cannot obtain the least representation of a thinking being by means of external experience, but solely through self-consciousness. Such objects are consequently nothing more than the transference of this consciousness of mine to other things which can only thus be represented as thinking beings. The proposition, *I think*, is, in the present case, understood in a problematical sense, not in so far as it contains a perception of an existence (like the Cartesian " Cogito, ergo sum "), but in regard to its mere possibility—for the purpose of discovering, what properties may be inferred from so simple a proposition and predicated of the subject of it.

If at the foundation of our pure rational cognition of thinking beings there lay more than the mere *Cogito*—if we could likewise call in aid observations on the play of our thoughts, and the thence derived natural laws of the thinking self, there would arise an empirical psychology which would be a kind of physiology of the internal sense, and might possibly be capable of explaining the phenomena of that sense. But it could never be available for discovering those properties which do not belong to possible experience (such as the quality of simplicity), nor could it make any apodictic enunciation on the nature of thinking beings:—it would therefore not be a rational psychology.

Now, as the proposition *I think* (in the problematical sense) contains the form of every judgment in general, and is the constant accompaniment of all the categories; it is manifest, that conclusions are drawn from it only by a transcendental employment of the understanding. This use of the understanding excludes all empirical elements; and we cannot, as has been shown above, have any favorable conception beforehand of its procedure. We shall therefore follow with a critical eye this proposition through all the predicaments of pure psychology; but we shall, for brevity's sake, allow this examination to proceed in an uninterrupted connection.

Before entering on this task, however, the following general remark may help to quicken our attention to this mode of argument. It is not merely through my thinking that I cognize an object, but only through my determining a given intuition in relation to the unity of consciousness in which all thinking consists. It follows that I cognize myself, not through my being conscious of myself as thinking, but only when I am conscious of the intuition of myself as determined in relation to the function of thought. All the modi of self-consciousness in thought are hence not conceptions of objects (conceptions of the understanding—categories); they are mere logical functions, which do not present to thought an object to be cognized, and cannot therefore present my Self as an object. Not the consciousness of the *determining*, but only that of the *determinable* self, that is, of my internal intuition (in so far as the manifold contained in it can be connected conformably with the general condition of the unity of apperception in thought), is the object.

1. In all judgments I am the *determining* subject of that relation which constitutes a judgment. But that the I which thinks, must be considered as in thought always a *subject*, and as a thing which cannot be a predicate to thought, is an apodictic and *identical* proposition. But this proposition does not signify that I, as an object, am, for myself, a *self-subsistent being* or *substance*. This latter statement—an ambitious one —requires to be supported by data which are not to be discovered in thought; and are perhaps (in so far as I consider the thinking self merely *as such*) not to be discovered in the thinking self at all.

2. That the *I* or *Ego* of apperception, and consequently in all thought, is *singular* or simple, and cannot be resolved into a plurality of subjects, and therefore indicates a logically simple subject—this is self-evident from the very conception of an Ego, and is consequently an analytical proposition. But this is not tantamount to declaring that the thinking Ego is a simple *substance*—for this would be a synthetical proposition. The conception of substance always relates to intuitions, which with me cannot be other than sensuous, and which consequently lie completely out of the sphere of the understanding and its thought: but to this sphere belongs the affirmation that the Ego is simple in thought. It would indeed be surprising, if the conception of substance, which in other cases requires so much labor to distinguish from the other elements presented by intuition—so much trouble too, to discover whether it can be simple (as in the case of the parts of matter), should be presented immediately to me, as if by revelation, in the poorest mental representation of all.

3. The proposition of the identity of my Self amid all the manifold representations of which I am conscious, is likewise a proposition lying in the conceptions themselves, and is consequently analytical. But this identity of the subject, of which I am conscious in all its representations, does not relate to or concern the intuition of the subject, by which it is given as an object. This proposition cannot therefore enounce the identity of the person, by which is understood the consciousness of the identity of its own substance as a thinking being in all change and variation of circumstances. To prove this, we should re-

quire not a mere analysis of the proposition, but synthetical judgments based upon a given intuition.

4. I distinguish my own existence, as that of a thinking being, from that of other things external to me—among which my body also is reckoned. This is also an analytical proposition, for *other* things are exactly those which I think as different or *distinguished* from myself. But whether this consciousness of myself is possible *without* things external to me; and whether therefore I can exist merely as a thinking being (without being man)—cannot be known or inferred from this proposition.

Thus we have gained nothing as regards the cognition of myself as object, by the analysis of the consciousness of my Self in thought. The logical exposition of thought in general is mistaken for a metaphysical determination of the object.

Our Critique would be an investigation utterly superfluous, if there existed a possibility of proving *à priori*, that all thinking beings are in themselves simple substances, as such, therefore, possess the inseparable attribute of personality, and are conscious of their existence apart from and unconnected with matter. For we should thus have taken a step beyond the world of sense, and have penetrated into the sphere of *noumena;* and in this case the right could not be denied us of extending our knowledge in this sphere, of establishing ourselves, and, under a favoring star, appropriating to ourselves possessions in it. For the proposition, "Every thinking being, as such, is simple substance," is an *à priori* synthetical proposition; because in the first place it goes beyond the conception which is the subject of it, and adds to the mere notion of a thinking being the *mode of its existence,* and in the second place annexes a predicate (that of simplicity) to the latter conception—a predicate which it could not have discovered in the sphere of experience. It would follow that *à priori* synthetical propositions are possible and legitimate, not only, as we have maintained, in relation to objects of possible experience, and as principles of the possibility of this experience itself, but are applicable to things as things in themselves—an inference which makes an end of the whole of this Critique, and obliges us to fall back on the old mode of metaphysical procedure. But indeed the danger is not so great, if we look a little closer into the question.

There lurks in the procedure of rational psychology a paralogism, which is represented in the following syllogism:

That which cannot be cogitated otherwise than as subject, does not exist otherwise than as subject, and is therefore substance.

A thinking being, considered merely as such, cannot be cogitated otherwise than as subject.

Therefore it exists also as such, that is, as substance.

In the major we speak of a being that can be cogitated generally and in every relation, consequently as it may be given in intuition. But in the minor we speak of the same being only in so far as it regards itself as subject, relatively to thought and the unity of consciousness, but not in relation to intuition, by which it is presented as an object to thought. Thus the conclusion is here arrived at by a *Sophisma figuræ dictionis.**

That this famous argument is a mere paralogism, will be plain to anyone who will consider the general remark which precedes our exposition of the principles of the pure understanding, and the section on noumena. For it was there proved that the conception of a thing, which can exist *per se*—only as a subject and never as a predicate, possesses no objective reality; that is to say, we can never know, whether there exists any object to correspond to the conception; consequently, the conception is nothing more than a conception, and from it we derive no proper knowledge. If this conception is to indicate by the term *substance,* an object that can be given, if it is to become a cognition; we must have at the foundation of the cognition a permanent intuition, as the indispensable condition of its objective reality. For through intuition alone can an object be given. But in internal intuition there is nothing permanent, for the Ego is but the consciousness of my thought. If, then, we appeal merely to thought, we cannot discover the necessary condition of the application of the conception of substance—that is, of a subject existing *per se*—to the subject as a thinking being. And thus the conception of the simple nature of substance, which is connected with the objective reality of

---

* *Thought* is taken in the two premisses in two totally different senses. In the major it is considered as relating and applying to objects in general, consequently to objects of intuition also. In the minor, we understand it as relating merely to self-consciousness. In this sense, we do not cogitate an object, but merely the relation to the self-consciousness of the subject, as the form of thought. In the former premise we speak of things which cannot be cogitated otherwise than as subjects. In the second, we do not speak of *things,* but of *thought* (all objects being abtracted), in which the Ego is always the subject of consciousness. Hence the conclusion cannot be, " I cannot exist otherwise than as subject;" but only " I can, in cogitating my existence, employ my Ego only as the subject of the judgment." But this is an identical proposition, and throws no light on the mode of my existence.

this conception, is shown to be also invalid, and to be, in fact, nothing more than the logical qualitative unity of self-consciousness in thought; while we remain perfectly ignorant, whether the subject is composite or not.

Refutation of the Argument of Mendelssohn for the Substantiality or Permanence of the Soul

This acute philosopher easily perceived the insufficiency of the common argument which attempts to prove that the soul—it being granted that it is a simple being—cannot perish by *dissolution* or *decomposition;* he saw it is not impossible for it to cease to be by *extinction,* or *disappearance.** He endeavored to prove in his *Phædo,* that the soul cannot be annihilated, by showing that a simple being cannot cease to exist. Inasmuch as, he said, a simple existence cannot diminish, nor gradually lose portions of its being, and thus be by degrees reduced to nothing (for it possesses no parts, and therefore no multiplicity), between the moment in which it is, and the moment in which it is not, no time can be discovered—which is impossible. But this philosopher did not consider, that, granting the soul to possess this simple nature, which contains no parts external to each other, and consequently no extensive quantity, we cannot refuse to it, any less than to any other being, intensive quantity, that is, a degree of reality in regard to all its faculties, nay, to all that constitutes its existence. But this degree of reality can become less and less through an infinite series of smaller degrees. It follows, therefore, that this supposed substance—this thing, the permanence of which is not assured in any other way, may, if not by decomposition, by gradual loss (*remissio*) of its powers (consequently by elanguescence, if I may employ this expression), be changed into nothing. For consciousness itself has always a degree, which may be lessened.† Consequently the faculty of being conscious

---

* Verschwinden.

† Clearness is not, as logicians maintain, the consciousness of a representation. For a certain degree of consciousness, which may not, however, be sufficient for recollection, is to be met with in many dim representations. For without any consciousness at all, we should not be able to recognize any difference in the obscure representations we connect; as we really can do with many conceptions, such as those of right and justice, and those of the musician, who strikes at once several notes in improvising a piece of music. But a representation is clear, in which our consciousness is sufficient for the *consciousness of the difference* of this representation from others. If we are only conscious that there is a difference, but are not conscious of the difference—that is, what the difference is—the representation must be termed obscure. There is, consequently, an infinite series of degrees of consciousness down to its entire disappearance.

may be diminished; and so with all other faculties. The permanence of the soul, therefore, as an object of the internal sense, remains undemonstrated, nay, even indemonstrable. Its permanence in life is evident, *per se,* inasmuch as the thinking being (as man) is to itself, at the same time, an object of the external senses. But this does not authorize the rational psychologist to affirm, from mere conceptions, its permanence beyond life.*

If, now, we take the above propositions—as they must be accepted as valid for all thinking beings in the system of rational psychology—in synthetical connection, and proceed, from the category of relation, with the proposition, "All thinking beings are, as such, substances," backwards through the series, till the circle is completed; we come at last to their existence, of which, in this system of rational psychology, substances are held to be conscious, independently of external things; nay, it is asserted that, in relation to the permanence which is a necessary characteristic of substance, they can of themselves determine external things. It follows that *Idealism*—at least

* There are some who think they have done enough to establish a new possibility in the mode of the existence of souls, when they have shown that there is no contradiction in their hypotheses on this subject. Such are those who affirm the possibility of thought—of which they have no other knowledge than what they derive from its use in connecting empirical intuitions presented in this our human life—after this life has ceased. But it is very easy to embarrass them by the introduction of counter-possibilities, which rest upon quite as good a foundation. Such, for example, is the possibility of the division of a *simple substance* into several substances; and conversely, of the coalition of several into one simple substance. For, although divisibility presupposes composition, it does not necessarily require a composition of substances, but only of the degrees (of the several faculties) of one and the same substance. Now we can cogitate all the powers and faculties of the soul—even that of consciousness—as diminished by one-half, the substance still remaining. In the same way we can represent to ourselves without contradiction this obliterated half as preserved, not in the soul, but without it; and we can believe that, as in this case everything that is real in the soul, and has a degree—consequently its entire existence—has been halved, a particular substance would arise out of the soul. For the multiplicity, which has been divided, formerly existed, but not as a multiplicity of substances, but of every reality as the quantum of existence in it; and the unity of substance was merely a mode of existence, which by this division alone has been transformed into a plurality of subsistence. In the same manner several simple substances might coalesce into one, without anything being lost except the plurality of subsistence, inasmuch as the one substance would contain the degree of reality of all the former substances. Perhaps, indeed, the simple substances, which appear under the form of matter, might (not indeed by a mechanical or chemical influence upon each other, but by an unknown influence, of which the former would be but the phenomenal appearance), by means of such a *dynamical* division of the parent-souls, as *intensive quantities,* produce other souls, while the former repaired the loss thus sustained with new matter of the same sort. I am far from allowing any value to such chimeras; and the principles of our analytic have clearly proved that no other than an empirical use of the categories—that of substance, for example—is possible. But if the rationalist is bold enough to construct, on the mere authority of the faculty of thought —without any intuition, whereby an object is given—a self-subsistent being, merely because the unity of apperception in thought cannot allow him to believe in a composite being, instead of declaring, as he ought to do, that he is unable to explain the possibility of a thinking nature; what ought to hinder the *materialist,* with as complete an independence of experience, to employ the principle of the rationalist in a directly opposite manner—still preserving the formal unity required by his opponent?

problematical Idealism, is perfectly unavoidable in this rationalistic system. And, if the existence of outward things is not held to be requisite to the determination of the existence of a substance in time; the existence of these outward things at all, is a gratuitous assumption which remains without the possibility of a proof.

But if we proceed *analytically*—the " I think " as a proposition containing in itself an existence as given, consequently modality being the principle—and dissect this proposition, in order to ascertain its content, and discover whether and how this Ego determines its existence in time and space without the aid of anything external; the propositions of rationalistic psychology would not begin with the conception of a thinking being, but with a reality, and the properties of a thinking being in general would be deduced from the mode in which this reality is cogitated, after everything empirical had been abstracted: as is shown in the following table:

I
I think,

II   III
as Subject,   *as simple Subject,*

IV
as identical Subject,
in every state of my thought.

Now, inasmuch as it is not determined in this second proposition, whether I can exist and be cogitated only as subject, and not also as a predicate of another being, the conception of a subject is here taken in a merely logical sense; and it remains undetermined, whether substance is to be cogitated under the conception or not. But in the third proposition, the absolute unity of apperception—the simple *Ego* in the representation to which all connection and separation which constitute thought, relate, is of itself important; even although it presents us with no information about the constitution or subsistence of the subject. Apperception is something real, and the simplicity of its nature is given in the very fact of its possibilty. Now in space there is nothing real that is at the same time simple; for points, which are the only simple things in space, are merely limits, but not constituent parts of space. From this follows the impossibility of a definition on the basis of materialism of the constitution of my *Ego* as a merely thinking subject. But, because my existence is considered in the first proposition as given, for it does not mean, "Every thinking being exists" (for this would be predicating of them absolute necessity), but only, "*I exist* thinking"; the proposition is quite empirical, **and** contains the determinability of my existence merely in relation to my representations in time. But as I require for this purpose something that is permanent, such as is not given in internal intuition; the mode of my existence, whether as substance or as accident, cannot be determined by means of this simple self-consciousness. Thus, if materialism is inadequate to explain the mode in which I exist, spiritualism is likewise as insufficient; and the conclusion is, that we are utterly unable to attain to any knowledge of the constitution of the soul, in so far as relates to the possibility of its existence apart from external objects.

And, indeed, how should it be possible, merely by the aid of the unity of consciousness—which we cognize only for the reason that it is indispensable to the possibility of experience— to pass the bounds of experience (our existence in this life); and to extend our cognition to the nature of all thinking beings by means of the empirical—but in relation to every sort of intuition, perfectly undetermined—proposition, "I think?"

There does not then exist any rational psychology as a *doctrine* furnishing any addition to our knowledge of ourselves. It is nothing more than a *discipline*, which sets impassable limits to speculative reason in this region of thought, to prevent it, on the one hand, from throwing itself into the arms of a soulless materialism, and, on the other, from losing itself in the mazes of a baseless spiritualism. It teaches us to consider this refusal of our reason to give any satisfactory answer to questions which reach beyond the limits of this our human life, as a hint to abandon fruitless speculation; and to direct, to a practical use, our knowledge of ourselves—which, although applicable only to objects of experience, receives its principles from a higher source, and regulates its procedure as if our destiny reached far beyond the boundaries of experience and life.

From all this it is evident that rational psychology has its

origin in a mere misunderstanding. The unity of consciousness, which lies at the basis of the categories, is considered to
be an intuition of the subject as an object; and the category
of substance is applied to the intuition. But this unity is nothing more than the unity in *thought,* by which no object is given;
to which therefore the category of substance—which always
presupposes a given intuition—cannot be applied. Consequently, the subject cannot be cognized. The subject of the categories cannot, therefore, for the very reason that it cogitates
these, frame any conception of itself as an object of the categories; for, to cogitate these, it must lay at the foundation
its own pure self-consciousness—the very thing that it wishes
to explain and describe. In like manner, the subject, in which
the representation of time has its basis, cannot determine, for
this very reason, its own existence in time. Now, if the latter
is impossible, the former, as an attempt to determine itself by
means of the categories as a thinking being in general, is no
less so.*

Thus, then, appears the vanity of the hope of establishing a
cognition which is to extend its rule beyond the limits of experience—a cognition which is one of the highest interests of
humanity; and thus is proved the futility of the attempt of
speculative philosophy in this region of thought. But, in this
interest of thought, the severity of criticism has rendered to
reason a not unimportant service, by the demonstration of the
impossibility of making any dogmatical affirmation concerning
an object of experience beyond the boundaries of experience.

---

* The " I think " is, as has been already stated, an empirical proposition,
and contains the expression, " I exist."
But I cannot say " Everything, which
thinks, exists;" for in this case the
property of thought would constitute
all beings possessing it, necessary beings. Hence my existence cannot be
considered as an inference from the
proposition, " I think," as Descartes
maintained—because in this case the
major premise, " Everything, which
thinks, exists," must precede—but the
two propositions are identical. The
proposition " I think " expresses an undetermined empirical tuition, that is,
perception (proving consequently that
sensation, which must belong to sensibility, lies at the foundation of this
proposition); but it precedes experience,
whose province it is to determine an
object of perception by means of the
categories in relation to time; and existence in this proposition is not a
category, as it does not apply to an
undetermined given object, but only to
one of which we have a conception, and
about which we wish to know whether
it does or does not exist, out of, and
apart from this conception. An undetermined perception signifies here merely something real that has been given,
only, however, to thought in general—
but not as a phenomenon, nor as a thing
in itself (noumenon), but only as something that really exists, and is designated as such in the proposition, " I
think." For it must be remarked that,
when I call the proposition, " I think,"
an empirical proposition, I do not
thereby mean that the *Ego* in the proposition is an empirical representation; on
the contrary, it is purely intellectual,
because it belongs to thought in general.
But without some empirical representation, which presents to the mind material for thought, the mental act, " I
think," would not take place; and the
empirical is only the condition of the
application or employment of the pure
intellectual faculty.

She has thus fortified reason against all affirmations of the contrary. Now, this can be accomplished in only two ways. Either our proposition must be proved apodictically; or, if this is unsuccessful, the sources of this inability must be sought for, and if these are discovered to exist in the natural and necessary limitation of our reason, our opponents must submit to the same law of renunciation, and refrain from advancing claims to dogmatic assertion.

But the right, say rather the necessity to admit a future life, upon principles of the practical conjoined with the speculative use of reason, has lost nothing by this renunciation; for the merely speculative proof has never had any influence upon the common reason of men. It stands upon the point of a hair, so that even the schools have been able to preserve it from falling only by incessantly discussing it and spinning it like a top; and even in their eyes it has never been able to present any safe foundation for the erection of a theory. The proofs which have been current among men, preserve their value undiminished; nay, rather gain in clearness and unsophisticated power, by the rejection of the dogmatical assumptions of speculative reason. For reason is thus confined within her own peculiar province— the arrangement of ends or aims, which is at the same time the arrangement of nature; and, as a practical faculty, without limiting itself to the latter, it is justified in extending the former, and with it our own existence, beyond the boundaries of experience and life. If we turn our attention to the *analogy of the nature* of living beings in this world, in the consideration of which reason is obliged to accept as a principle, that no organ, no faculty, no appetite is useless, and that nothing is superfluous, nothing disproportionate to its use, nothing unsuited to its end; but that, on the contrary, everything is perfectly conformed to its destination in life—we shall find that man, who alone is the final end and aim of this order, is still the only animal that seems to be accepted from it. For his natural gifts, not merely as regards the talents and motives that may incite him to employ them—but especially the moral law in him, stretch so far beyond all mere earthly utility and advantage, that he feels himself bound to prize the mere consciousness of probity, apart from all advantageous consequences—even the shadowy gift of posthumous fame—above everything; and he is conscious of an inward call to constitute himself, by his conduct in this world—without regard to mere sublinary interests —the citizen of a better. This mighty, irresistible proof—accompanied by an ever-increasing knowledge of the conformability to a purpose in everything we see around us, by the conviction of the boundless immensity of creation, by the consciousness of a certain illimitableness in the possible extension of our knowledge, and by a desire commensurate therewith— remains to humanity, even after the theoretical cognition of ourselves has failed to establish the necessity of an existence after death.

Conclusion of the Solution of the Psychological Paralogism

The dialectical illusion in rational psychology arises from our confounding an idea of reason (of a pure intelligence) with the conception—in every respect undetermined—of a thinking being in general. I cogitate myself in behalf of a possible experience, at the same time making abstraction of all actual experience; and infer therefrom that I can be conscious of myself apart from experience and its empirical conditions. I consequently confound the possible *abstraction* of my empirically determined existence with the supposed consciousness of a possible *separate* existence of my thinking self; and I believe that I cognize what is substantial in myself as a transcendental subject, when I have nothing more in thought than the unity of consciousness, which lies at the basis of all determination of cognition.

The task of explaining the community of the soul with the body does not properly belong to the psychology of which we are here speaking; because it proposes to prove the personality of the soul apart from this communion (after death), and is therefore *transcendent* in the proper sense of the word, although occupying itself with an object of experience—only in so far, however, as it ceases to be an object of experience. But a sufficient answer may be found to the question in our system. The difficulty which lies in the execution of this task consists, as is well known, in the presupposed heterogeneity of the object of the internal sense (the soul) and the objects of the external senses; inasmuch as the formal condition of the intuition of the one is time, and of that of the other space also. But if we consider that both kinds of objects do not differ internally, but only in so far as the one *appears* externally to the other—consequently, that what lies at the basis of phenomena, as a thing in itself, may not be heterogeneous; this difficulty disappears. There then remains no other difficulty than is to be found in the question—how a community of substances is possible; a question which lies out of the region of psychology, and which the reader, after what in our Analytic has been said of primitive forces and faculties, will easily judge to be also beyond the region of human cognition.

General Remark.—On the Transition from Rational Psychology to Cosmology

The proposition " I think," or " I exist thinking," is an empirical proposition. But such a proposition must be based on empirical intuition, and the object cogitated as a phenomenon; and thus our theory appears to maintain that the soul, even in thought, is merely a phenomenon; and in this way our consciousness itself, in fact, abuts upon nothing.

Thought, *per se*, is merely the purely spontaneous logical function which operates to connect the manifold of a possible intuition; and it does not represent the subject of consciousness as a phenomenon—for this reason alone, that it pays no attention to the question whether the mode of intuiting it is sensuous or intellectual. I therefore do not represent myself in thought either as I am, or as I appear to myself; I merely cogitate myself as an object in general, of the mode of intuiting which I make abstraction. When I represent myself as the *subject* of thought, or as the *ground* of thought, these modes of representation are not related to the categories of substance or of cause; for these are functions of thought applicable only to our sensuous intuition. The application of these categories to the *Ego* would, however, be necessary, if I wished to make myself an object of knowledge. But I wish to be conscious of myself only as thinking; in what mode my Self is given in intuition, I do not consider, and it may be that I, who think, am a phenomenon—although not in so far as I am a thinking being; but in the consciousness of myself in mere thought I am a being, though this consciousness does not present to me any property of this being as material for thought.

But the proposition " I think," in so far as it declares, "*I exist* thinking," is not the mere representation of a logical function. It determines the subject (which is in this case an object also) in relation to existence; and it cannot be given without the aid of the internal sense, whose intuition presents to us an object, not as a thing in itself, but always as a phenomenon. In this proposition there is therefore something more to be found than the mere spontaneity of thought; there is also the receptivity of intuition, that is, my thought of myself applied to the empirical intuition of myself. Now, in this intuition the thinking self must seek the conditions of the employment of its logical functions as categories of substance, cause, and so forth; not merely for the purpose of distinguishing itself as an object in itself by means of the representation *I*, but also for the purpose of determining the mode of its existence, that is, of cognizing itself as noumenon. But this is impossible, for the internal empirical intuition is sensuous, and presents us with nothing but phenomenal data, which do not assist the object of pure consciousness in its attempt to cognize itself as a separate existence, but are useful only as contributions to experience.

But, let it be granted that we could discover, not in experience, but in certain firmly established *à priori* laws of the use of pure reason—laws relating to our existence, authority to consider ourselves as legislating *à priori* in relation to our own existence and as determining this existence; we should, on this supposition, find ourselves possessed of a spontaneity, by which our actual existence would be determinable, without the aid of the conditions of empirical intuition. We should also become aware, that in the consciousness of our existence there was an *à priori* content, which would serve to determine our own existence—an existence only sensuously determinable—relatively, however, to a certain internal faculty in relation to an intelligible world.

But this would not give the least help to the attempts of rational psychology. For this wonderful faculty, which the consciousness of the moral law in me reveals, would present me with a principle of the determination of my own existence which is purely intellectual—but by what predicates? By none other than those which are given in sensuous intuition. Thus I should find myself in the same position in rational psychology which I formerly occupied, that is to say, I should find myself still in need of sensuous intuitions, in order to give significance to my conceptions of substance and cause, by means of which alone I can possess a knowledge of myself: but these intuitions can never raise me above the sphere of experience. I should be justified, however, in applying these conceptions, in regard to their practical use, which is always directed to objects of experience—in conformity with their analogical significance when employed theoretically—to freedom and its subject. At the same time, I should understand by them merely the logical functions of subject and predicate, of principle and consequence, in conformity with which all actions are so determined, that they are capable of being explained along with the laws of nature, conformably to the categories of substance and cause, although they originate from a very different principle. We have made these observations for the purpose of guarding against misunderstanding, to which the doctrine of our intuition of self as a phenomenon is exposed. We shall have occasion to perceive their utility in the sequel.

CHAPTER II

The Antinomy of Pure Reason

We showed in the introduction to this part of our work, that all transcendental illusion of pure reason arose from dialectical arguments, the schema of which logic gives us in its three formal species of syllogisms—just as the categories find their logical schema in the four functions of all judgments. The first kind of these sophistical arguments related to the unconditioned unity of the *subjective* conditions of all representations in general (of the subject or soul), in correspondence with the *categorical* syllogisms, the major of which, as the principle, enounces the relation of a predicate to a subject. The second kind of dialectical argument will therefore be concerned, following the analogy with *hypothetical* syllogisms, with the unconditioned unity of the objective conditions in the phenomenon; and, in this way, the theme of the third kind to be treated of in the following chapter, will be the unconditioned unity of the objective conditions of the possibility of objects in general.

But it is worthy of remark, that the transcendental paralogism produced in the mind only a one-sided illusion, in regard to the idea of the subject of our thought; and the conceptions of reason gave no ground to maintain the contrary proposition. The advantage is completely on the side of Pneumatism; although this theory itself passes into naught, in the crucible of pure reason.

Very different is the case, when we apply reason to the *objective synthesis* of phenomena. Here, certainly, reason establishes, with much plausibility, its principle of unconditioned unity; but it very soon falls into such contradictions, that it is compelled, in relation to cosmology, to renounce its pretensions.

For here a new phenomenon of human reason meets us— a perfectly natural antithetic, which does not require to be sought for by subtle sophistry, but into which reason of itself unavoidably falls. It is thereby preserved, to be sure, from the slumber of a fancied conviction—which a merely one-sided illusion produces; but it is at the same time compelled, either, on the one hand, to abandon itself to a despairing scepticism, or, on the other, to assume a dogmatical confidence and obstinate persistence in certain assertions, without granting a fair hearing to the other side of the question. Either is the death of a sound philosophy, although the former might perhaps deserve the title of the Euthanasia of pure reason.

Before entering this region of discord and confusion, which the conflict of the laws of pure reason (antinomy) produces, we shall present the reader with some considerations, in explanation and justification of the method we intend to follow in our treatment of this subject. I term all transcendental ideas, in so far as they relate to the absolute totality in the synthesis of phenomena, *cosmical conceptions;* partly on account of this unconditioned totality, on which the conception of the world-whole is based—a conception which is itself an idea—partly because they relate solely to the synthesis of phenomena—the empirical synthesis; while, on the other hand, the absolute totality in the synthesis of the conditions of all possible things gives rise to an ideal of pure reason, which is quite distinct from the cosmical conception, although it stands in relation with it. Hence, as the paralogisms of pure reason laid the foundation for a dialectical psychology, the antinomy of pure reason will present us with the transcendental principles of a pretended pure (rational) cosmology—not, however, to declare it valid and to appropriate it, but—as the very term of a conflict of reason sufficiently indicates, to present it as an idea which cannot be reconciled with phenomena and experience.

Sec. I.—System of Cosmological Ideas

That we may be able to enumerate with systematic precision these ideas according to a principle, we must remark, *in the first place,* that it is from the understanding alone that pure and transcendental conceptions take their origin; that the reason does not properly give birth to any conception, but only frees the conception of the understanding from the unavoidable limitation of a possible experience, and thus endeavors to raise it above the empirical, though it must still be in connection with it. This happens from the fact, that for a given conditioned, reason demands absolute totality on the side of the conditions (to which the understanding submits all phenomena), and thus makes of the category a transcendental idea. This it does that it may be able to give absolute completeness to the empirical synthesis, by continuing it to the unconditioned (which is not to be found in experience, but only in the idea). Reason requires this according to the principle, *If the conditioned is given, the whole of the conditions, and consequently the absolutely unconditioned, is also given,* whereby alone the former was possible. *First,* then, the transcendental ideas are properly nothing but categories elevated to the unconditioned; and they may be arranged in a table according to the titles of the latter. But, *secondly,* all the categories are not available for this purpose, but only those in which the synthesis constitutes a series—of conditions subordinated to, not co-ordinated with, each other. Absolute totality is required of reason only in so far as concerns the ascending series of the conditions of a conditioned; not, consequently, when the question relates to the descending series of consequences, or to the aggregate of the co-ordinated conditions of these consequences. For, in relation to a given conditioned, conditions are presupposed and considered to be given along with it. On the other hand, as the consequences do not render possible their conditions, but rather presuppose them—in the consideration of the procession of consequences (or in the descent from the given condition to the conditioned), we may be quite unconcerned whether the series ceases or not; and their totality is not a necessary demand of reason.

Thus we cogitate—and necessarily—a given time completely elapsed up to a given moment, although that time is not determinable by us. But as regards time future, which is not the condition of arriving at the present, in order to conceive it; it is quite indifferent whether we consider future time as ceasing at some point, or as prolonging itself to infinity. Take, for example, the series *m, n, o*, in which *n* is given as conditioned in relation to *m*, but at the same time as the condition of *o*, and let the series proceed upwards from the conditioned *n* to *m* (*l, k, i*, etc.), and also downwards from the condition *n* to the conditioned *o* (*p, q, r*, etc.)—I must presuppose the former series, to be able to consider *n* as given, and *n* is according to reason (the totality of conditions) possible only by means of that series. But its possibility does not rest on the following series *o, p, q, r*, which for this reason cannot be regarded as given, but only as capable of being given (*dabilis*).

I shall term the synthesis of the series on the side of the conditions—from that nearest to the given phenomenon up to the more remote—*regressive;* that which proceeds on the side of the conditioned, from the immediate consequence to the more remote, I shall call the *progressive* synthesis. The former proceeds *in antecedentia*, the latter *in consequentia*. The cosmological ideas are therefore occupied with the totality of the regressive synthesis, and proceed *in antecedentia*, not *in consequentia*. When the latter takes place, it is an arbitrary and not a necessary problem of pure reason; for we require, for the complete understanding of what is given in a phenomenon, not the consequences which succeed, but the grounds or principles which precede.

In order to construct the table of ideas in correspondence with the table of categories, we take first the two primitive *quanta* of all our intuition, time and space. Time is in itself a series (and the formal condition of all series), and hence, in relation to a given present, we must distinguish *à priori* in it the *antecedentia* as conditions, time past) from the *consequentia* (time future). Consequently, the transcendental idea of the absolute totality of the series of the conditions of a given conditioned, relates merely to all past time. According to the idea of reason, the whole past time, as the condition of the given moment, is necessarily cogitated as given. But as regards space there exists in it no distinction between *progressus* and *regressus;* for it is an *aggregate* and not a series—its parts existing together at the same time. I can consider a given point

of time in relation to past time only as conditioned, because
this given moment comes into existence only through the past
time—or rather through the passing of the preceding time. But
as the parts of space are not subordinated, but co-ordinated to
each other, one part cannot be the condition of the possibility
of the other; and space is not in itself, like time, a series. But
the synthesis of the manifold parts of space—(the syntheses
whereby we apprehend space)—is nevertheless successive; it
takes place, therefore, in time, and contains a series. And as
in this series of aggregated spaces (for example, the feet in
a rood), beginning with a given portion of space, those which
continue to be annexed form the *condition of the limits* of the
former—the measurement of a space must also be regarded as
a synthesis of the series of the conditions of a given conditioned. It differs, however, in this respect from that of time,
that the side of the conditioned is not in itself distinguishable
from the side of the condition; and, consequently, *regressus*
and *progressus* in space seem to be identical. But, inasmuch
as one part of space is not given, but only limited, by and
through another, we must also consider every limited space as
conditioned, in so far as it presupposes some other space as
the condition of its limitation, and so on. As regards limitation, therefore, our procedure in space is also a *regressus,* and
the transcendental idea of the absolute totality of the synthesis
in a series of conditions applies to space also; and I am entitled
to demand the absolute totality of the phenomenal synthesis in
space as well as in time. Whether my demand can be satisfied,
is a question to be answered in the sequel.

Secondly, the real in space—that is, matter, is conditioned.
Its internal conditions are its parts, and the parts of parts its
remote conditions; so that in this case we find a regressive
synthesis, the absolute totality of which is a demand of reason.
But this cannot be obtained otherwise than by a complete division of parts, whereby the real in matter becomes either nothing or that which is not matter, that is to say, the simple.* Consequently we find here also a series of conditions and a progress
to be unconditioned.

Thirdly, as regards the categories of a real relation between
phenomena, the category *of substance* and its accidents is not
suitable for the formation of a transcendental idea; that is to

* Das Einfache.

say, reason has no ground, in regard to it, to proceed regressively with conditions. For accidents (in so far as they inhere in a substance) are co-ordinated with each other, and do not constitute a series. And, in relation to substance, they are not properly subordinated to it, but are the mode of existence of the substance itself. The conception of the *substantial* might nevertheless seem to be an idea of the transcendental reason. But, as this signifies nothing more than the conception of an object in general, which subsists in so far as we cogitate in it merely a transcendental subject without any predicates; and as the question here is of an unconditioned in the series of phenomena—it is clear that the substantial can form no member thereof. The same holds good of substances in community, which are mere aggregates, and do not form a series. For they are not subordinated to each other as conditions of the possibility of each other; which, however, may be affirmed of spaces, the limits of which are never determined in themselves, but always by some other space. It is, therefore, only in the category of *causality*, that we can find a series of causes to a given effect, and in which we ascend from the latter, as the conditioned, to the former as the conditions, and thus answer the question of reason.

Fourthly, the conceptions of the *possible,* the *actual,* and the *necessary* do not conduct us to any series—excepting only in so far as the contingent in existence must always be regarded as conditioned, and as indicating, according to a law of the understanding, a condition, under which it is necessary to rise to a higher, till in the totality of the series, reason arrives at unconditioned *necessity.*

There are, accordingly, only four cosmological ideas, corresponding with the four titles of the categories. For we can select only such as necessarily furnish us with a series in the synthesis of the manifold.

I

The absolute Completeness
of the
COMPOSITION
of the given totality of all phenomena.

II

The absolute Completeness
of the
DIVISION
*of a given totality
in a phenomenon.*

III

The absolute Completeness
of the
ORIGINATION
of a phenomenon.

IV

The absolute Completeness
of the DEPENDENCE *of the* EXISTENCE
of what is changeable in a phenomenon.

We must here remark, in the first place, that the idea of absolute totality relates to nothing but the exposition of *phenomena,* and therefore not to the pure conception of a totality of things. Phenomena are here, therefore, regarded as given, and reason requires the absolute completeness of the conditions of their possibility, in so far as these conditions constitute a series—consequently an absolutely (that is, in every respect) complete synthesis, whereby a phenomenon can be explained according to the laws of the understanding.

Secondly, it is properly the unconditioned alone, that reason seeks in this serially and regressively conducted synthesis of conditions. It wishes, to speak in another way, to attain to completeness in the series of premises, so as to render it unnecessary to presuppose others. This *unconditioned* is always contained in the *absolute totality of the series,* when we endeavor to form a representation of it in thought. But this absolutely complete synthesis is itself but an idea; for it is impossible, at least beforehand, to know whether any such synthesis is possible in the case of phenomena. When we represent all existence in thought by means of pure conceptions of the understanding, without any conditions of sensuous intuition, we may say with justice that for a given conditioned the whole series of conditions subordinated to each other is also given; for the former is only given through the latter. But we find in the case of phenomena a particular limitation of the mode in which conditions are given, that is, through the successive synthesis of the manifold of intuition, which must be complete in the regress. Now whether this completeness is sensuously possible, is a problem. But the idea of it lies in the reason—be it possible or impossible to connect with the idea adequate empirical conceptions. Therefore, as in the absolute totality of the regressive synthesis of the manifold in a phenomenon (following the guidance of the categories, which represent it as a series of conditions to a given conditioned) the unconditioned is necessarily contained—it being still left unascertained whether and how this totality exists; reason sets out from the idea of totality, although its proper and final aim is the *unconditioned*—of the whole series, or of a part thereof.

This unconditioned may be cogitated—either as existing only in the entire series, all the members of which therefore would be without exception conditioned and only the totality absolutely unconditioned—and in this case the *regressus* is called infinite; or the absolutely unconditioned is only a part of the series, to which the other members are subordinated, but which is not itself submitted to any other condition.* In the former case the series is *a parte priori* unlimited (without beginning), that is, infinite, and nevertheless completely given. But the regress in it is never completed, and can only be called *potentially* infinite. In the second case there exists a first in the series. This first is called, in relation to past time, the *beginning of the world;* in relation to space, the *limit of the world;* in relation to the parts of a given limited whole, the *simple;* in relation to causes, absolute *spontaneity* (liberty); and in relation to the existence of changeable things, absolute *physical necessity.*

We possess two expressions, *world* and *nature,* which are generally interchanged. The first denotes the mathematical total of all phenomena and the totality of their synthesis—in its progress by means of composition, as well as by division. And the world is termed nature,† when it is regarded as a dynamical whole—when our attention is not directed to the aggregation in space and time, for the purpose of cogitating it as a quantity,

---

* The absolute totality of the series of conditions to a given conditioned is always unconditioned; because beyond it there exist no other conditions, on which it might depend. But the absolute totality of such a series is only an idea, or rather a problematical conception, the possibility of which must be investigated—particularly in relation to the mode in which the unconditioned, as the transcendental idea which is the real subject of inquiry, may be contained therein.

† Nature, understood *adjectivè (for-* *maliter),* signifies the complex of the determinations of a thing, connected according to an internal principle of causality. On the other hand, we understand by nature, *substantive (materialiter),* the sum-total of phenomena, in so far as they, by virtue of an internal principle of causality, are connected with each other throughout. In the former sense we speak of the nature of liquid matter, of fire, etc., and employ the word only *adjectivè;* while, if speaking of the objects of nature, we have in our minds the idea of a subsisting whole.

but to the unity in the *existence* of phenomena. In this case the condition of that which happens is called a cause; the unconditioned causality of the cause in a phenomenon is termed liberty; the conditioned cause is called in a more limited sense a natural cause. The conditioned in existence is termed contingent, and the unconditioned necessary. The unconditioned necessity of phenomena may be called *natural necessity.*

The ideas which we are at present engaged in discussing I have called cosmological ideas; partly because by the term *world* is understood the entire content of all phenomena, and our ideas are directed solely to the unconditioned among phenomena; partly also, because *world,* in the transcendental sense, signifies the absolute totality of the content of existing things, and we are directing our attention only to the completeness of the synthesis—although, properly, only in regression. In regard to the fact that these ideas are all transcendent, and, although they do not transcend phenomena as regards their mode, but are concerned solely with the world of sense (and not with noumena), nevertheless carry their synthesis to a degree far above all possible experience—it still seems to me that we can, with perfect propriety, designate them *cosmical conceptions.* As regards the distinction between the mathematically and the dynamically unconditioned which is the aim of the regression of the synthesis, I should call the two former, in a more limited signification, cosmical conceptions, the remaining two *transcendent physical conceptions.* This distinction does not at present seem to be of particular importance, but we shall afterwards find it to be of some value.

Sec. II.—Antithetic of Pure Reason

Thetic is the term applied to every collection of dogmatical propositions. By antithetic I do not understand dogmatical assertions of the opposite, but the self-contradiction of seemingly dogmatical cognitions (*thesis cum antithesi*), in none of which we can discover any decided superiority. Antithetic is not therefore occupied with one-sided statements, but is engaged in considering the contradictory nature of the general cognitions of reason, and its causes. Transcendental antithetic is an investigation into the antinomy of pure reason, its causes and result. If we employ our reason not merely in the application of the principles of the understanding to objects of experience, but venture with it beyond these boundaries, there arise certain sophistical propositions or theorems. These assertions have the following peculiarities: They can find neither confirmation nor confutation in experience; and each is in itself not only self-consistent, but possesses conditions of its necessity in the very nature of reason—only that, unluckily, there exist just as valid and necessary grounds for maintaining the contrary proposition.

The questions which naturally arise in the consideration of this dialectic of pure reason, are, therefore: 1st. In what propositions is pure reason unavoidably subject to an antinomy? 2d. What are the causes of this antinomy? 3d. Whether and in what way can reason free itself from this self-contradiction?

A dialectical proposition or theorem of pure reason, must, according to what has been said, be distinguishable from all sophistical propositions, by the fact that it is not an answer to an arbitrary question, which may be raised at the mere pleasure of any person, but to one which human reason must necessarily encounter in its progress. In the second place, a dialectical proposition, with its opposite, does not carry the appearance of a merely artificial illusion, which disappears as soon as it is investigated, but a natural and unavoidable illusion, which, even when we are no longer deceived by it, continues to mock us, and, although rendered harmless, can never be completely removed.

This dialectical doctrine will not relate to the unity of understanding in empirical conceptions, but to the unity of reason in pure ideas. The conditions of this doctrine are—inasmuch as it must, as a synthesis according to rules, be conformable to the understanding, and at the same time as the absolute unity of the synthesis, to the reason—that, if it is adequate to the unity of reason, it is too great for the understanding, if according with the understanding, it is too small for the reason. Hence arises a mutual opposition, which cannot be avoided, do what we will.

These sophistical assertions of dialectic open, as it were, a battle-field, where that side obtains the victory which has been permitted to make the attack, and he is compelled to yield who has been unfortunately obliged to stand on the defensive. And hence, champions of ability, whether on the right or on the the wrong side, are certain to carry away the crown of victory, if they only take care to have the right to make the last attack, and are not obliged to sustain another onset from their opponent. We can easily believe that this arena has been often trampled by the feet of combatants, that many victories have been obtained on both sides, but that the last victory, decisive of the affair between the contending parties, was won by him who fought for the right, only if his adversary was forbidden to continue the tourney. As impartial umpires, we must lay aside entirely the consideration whether the combatants are fighting for the right or for the wrong side, for the true or for the false, and allow the combat to be first decided. Perhaps, after they have wearied more than injured each other, they will discover the nothingness of their cause of quarrel, and part good friends.

This method of watching, or rather of originating, a conflict of assertions, not for the purpose of finally deciding in favor of either side, but to discover whether the object of the struggle is not a mere illusion, which each strives in vain to reach, but which would be no gain even when reached—this procedure, I say, may be termed the *sceptical method.* It is thoroughly distinct from *scepticism*—the principle of a technical and scientific ignorance, which undermines the foundations of all knowledge, in order, if possible, to destroy our belief and confidence therein. For the sceptical method aims at certainty, by endeavoring to discover in a conflict of this kind, conducted honestly and intelligently on both sides, the point of misunderstanding; just as wise legislators derive, from the embarrassment of judges in lawsuits, information in regard to the defective and ill-defined parts of their statutes. The antinomy which reveals itself in the application of laws, is for our limited wisdom the best criterion of legislation. For the attention of reason, which in abstract speculation does not easily become conscious of its errors, is thus roused to the momenta in the determination of its principles.

But this sceptical method is essentially peculiar to transcendental philosophy, and can perhaps be dispensed with in every other field of investigation. In mathematics its use would be absurd; because in it no false assertions can long remain hidden, inasmuch as its demonstrations must always proceed under the guidance of pure intuition, and by means of an always evident synthesis. In experimental philosophy doubt and delay may be very useful; but no misunderstanding is possible, which cannot be easily removed; and in experience means of solving the difficulty and putting an end to the dissension must at last be found, whether soon or later. Moral philosophy can always exhibit its principles, with their practical consequences, *in concreto*—at least in possible experiences, and thus escape the mistakes and ambiguities of abstraction. But transcendental propositions, which lay claim to insight beyond the region of possible experience, cannot, on the one hand, exhibit their abstract synthesis in any *à priori* intuition, nor, on the other, expose a lurking error by the help of experience. Transcendental reason, therefore, presents us with no other criterion, than that of an attempt to reconcile such assertions, and for this purpose to permit a free and unrestrained conflict between them. And this we now proceed to arrange.*

First Conflict of the Transcendental Ideas

Thesis

The world has a beginning in time, and is also limited in regard to space.

PROOF

Granted, that the world has no beginning in time; up to every given moment of time, an eternity must have elapsed, and therewith passed away an infinite series of successive conditions or states of things in the world. Now the infinity of a series consists in the fact, that it never can be completed by means of a successive synthesis. It follows that an infinite series already elapsed is impossible, and that consequently a beginning of the world is a necessary condition of its existence. And this was the first thing to be proved.

As regards the second, let us

Antithesis

The world has no beginning, and no limits in space, but is, in relation both to time and space, infinite.

PROOF

For let it be granted, that it has a beginning. A beginning is an existence which is preceded by a time in which the thing does not exist. On the above supposition, it follows that there must have been a time in which the world did not exist, that is, a void time. But in a void time the origination of a thing is impossible; because no part of any such time contains a distinctive condition of being, in preference to that of non-being (whether the supposed thing originate of itself, or by means of some other cause). Consequently, many series of things may have a beginning in the world, but the world

* The antinomies stand in the order of the four transcendental ideas above detailed.

take the opposite for granted. In this case, the world must be an infinite given total of co-existent things. Now we cannot cogitate the dimensions of a quantity, which is not given within certain limits of an intuition,* in any other way than by means of the synthesis of its parts, and the total of such a quantity only by means of a completed synthesis, or the repeated addition of unity to itself. Accordingly, to cogitate the world, which fills all spaces, as a whole, the successive synthesis of the parts of an infinite world must be looked upon as completed, that is to say, an infinite time must be regarded as having elapsed in the enumeration of all co-existing things; which is impossible. For this reason an infinite aggregate of actual things cannot be considered as a given whole, consequently, not as a contemporaneously given whole. The world is consequently, as regards extension in space, *not infinite*, but enclosed in limits. And this was the second thing to be proved.

* We may consider an undetermined quantity as a whole, when it is enclosed within limits, although we cannot construct or ascertain its totality by measurement, that is, by the successive synthesis of its parts. For its limits of themselves determine its completeness as a whole.

itself cannot have a beginning, and is, therefore, in relation to past time, infinite.

As regards the second statement, let us first take the opposite for granted—that the world is finite and limited in space; it follows that it must exist in a void space, which is not limited. We should therefore meet not only with a relation of things *in space*, but also a relation of things *to space*. Now, as the world is an absolute whole, out of and beyond which no object of intuition, and consequently no correlate to which can be discovered, this relation of the world to a void space is merely a relation to *no object*. But such a relation, and consequently the limitation of the world by void space, is nothing. Consequently, the world, as regards space, is not limited, that is, it is infinite in regard to extension.*

* Space is merely the form of external intuition (formal intuition), and not a real object which can be externally perceived. Space, prior to all things which determine it (fill or limit it), or, rather, which present an *empirical intuition* conformable to it, is, under the title of absolute space, nothing but the mere possibility of external phenomena, in so far as they exist in themselves, or can annex themselves to given intuitions. Empirical intuition is therefore not a composition of phenomena and space (of perception and empty intuition). The one is not the correlate of the other in a synthesis, but they are vitally connected in the same empirical intuition, as matter and form. If we wish to set one of these two apart from the other—space from phenomena—there arise all sorts of empty determinations of external intuition, which are very far from being possible perceptions. For example, motion or rest of the world in an infinite empty space, or a determination of the mutual relation of both, cannot possibly be perceived, and is therefore merely the predicate of a notional entity.

Observations on the First Antinomy

ON THE THESIS

In bringing forward these conflicting arguments, I have not been on the search for sophisms, for the purpose of availing myself of special pleading, which takes advantage of the carelessness of the opposite party, appeals to a misunderstood statute, and erects its unrighteous claims upon an unfair interpretation. Both proofs originate fairly from the nature of the case, and the advantage presented by the mistakes of the dogmatists of both parties has been completely set aside.

The thesis might also have been unfairly demonstrated, by the introduction of an erroneous conception of the infinity of a given quantity. A quantity is infinite, if a greater than itself cannot possibly exist. The quantity is measured by the number of given units —which are taken as a standard—contained in it. Now no number can be the greatest, because one or more units can always be added. It follows that an infinite given quantity, consequently an infinite world (both as regards time and extension) is impossible. It is, therefore, limited in both respects. In this manner I might

ON THE ANTITHESIS

The proof in favor of the infinity of the cosmical succession and the cosmical content is based upon the consideration, that, in the opposite case, a void time and a void space must constitute the limits of the world. Now I am not unaware, that there are some ways of escaping this conclusion. It may, for example, be alleged, that a limit to the world, as regards both space and time, is quite possible, without at the same time holding the existence of an absolute time before the beginning of the world, or an absolute space extending beyond the actual world—which is impossible. I am quite well satisfied with the latter part of this opinion of the philosophers of the Leibnitzian school. Space is merely the form of external intuition, but not a real object which can itself be externally intuited; it is not a correlate of phenomena, it is the form of phenomena itself. Space, therefore, cannot be regarded as absolutely and in itself something determinative of the existence of things, because it is not itself an object, but only the form of possible objects. Consequently, things,

have conducted my proof; but the conception given in it does not agree with the true conception of an infinite whole. In this there is no representation of its quantity, it is not said how large it is; consequently its conception is not the conception of a *maximum*. We cogitate in it merely its relation to an arbitrarily assumed unit, in relation to which it is greater than any number. Now, just as the unit which is taken is greater or smaller, the infinite will be greater or smaller; but the infinity, which consists merely in the relation to this given unit, must remain always the same, although the absolute quantity of the whole is not thereby cognized.

The true (transcendental) conception of infinity is: that the successive synthesis of unity in the measurement of a given quantum can never be completed.* Hence it follows, without possibility of mistake, that an eternity of actual successive states up to a given (the present) moment cannot have elapsed, and that the world must therefore have a beginning.

In regard to the second part of the thesis, the difficulty as

as phenomena, determine space; that is to say, they render it possible that, of all the possible predicates of space (size and relation), certain may belong to reality. But we cannot affirm the converse, that space, as something self-subsistent, can determine real things in regard to size or shape, for it is in itself not a real thing. Space (filled or void)* may therefore be limited by phenomena, but phenomena cannot be limited by an empty space without them. This is true of time also. All this being granted, it is nevertheless indisputable, that we must assume these two nonentities, void space without and void time before the world, if we assume the existence of cosmical limits, relatively to space or time.

For, as regards the subterfuge adopted by those who endeavor to evade the consequence—that, if the world is limited as to space and time, the infinite void must determine the existence of actual things in regard to their dimensions — it arises solely from the fact that, instead of a *sensuous world*, an *intelligi-*

---

* The quantum in this sense contains a congeries of given units, which is greater than any number—and this is the mathematical conception of the infinite.

* It is evident that what is meant here is, that empty space, in so far as it is limited by phenomena—space, that is, *within* the world—does not at least contradict transcendental principles, and may therefore, as regards them, be admitted, although its possibility cannot on that account be affirmed.

to an infinite and yet elapsed series disappears; for the manifold of a world infinite in extension is contemporaneously given. But, in order to cogitate the total of this manifold, as we cannot have the aid of limits constituting by themselves this total in intuition, we are obliged to give some account of our conception, which in this case cannot proceed from the whole to the determined quantity of the parts, but must demonstrate the possibility of a whole by means of a successive synthesis of the parts. But as this synthesis must constitute a series that cannot be completed, it is impossible for us to cogitate prior to it, and consequently not by means of it, a totality. For the conception of totality itself is in the present case the representation of a completed synthesis of the parts; and this completion, and consequently its conception, is impossible.

ble world—of which nothing is known—is cogitated; instead of a real beginning (an existence, which is preceded by a period in which nothing exists) an existence which presupposes *no other condition* than that of time; and, instead of limits of extension, boundaries of the universe. But the question relates to the *mundus phenomenon*, and its quantity; and in this case we cannot make abstraction of the conditions of sensibility, without doing away with the essential reality of this world itself. The world of sense, if it is limited, must necessarily lie in the infinite void. If this, and with it space as the *à priori* condition of the possibility of phenomena, is left out of view, the whole world of sense disappears. In our problem is this alone considered as given. The *mundus intelligibilis* is nothing but the general conception of a world, in which abstraction has been made of all conditions of intuition, and in relation to which no synthetical proposition — either affirmative or negative—is possible.

SECOND CONFLICT OF THE TRANSCENDENTAL IDEAS

Thesis

Every composite substance in the world consists of simple parts; and there exists nothing that is not either itself simple, or composed of simple parts.

PROOF

For, grant that composite substances do not consist of simple parts; in this case, if all combination or composition were annihilated in thought, no composite part, and (as, by the supposition, there do not exist simple parts) no simple part would exist. Consequently, no substance; consequently, nothing would exist. Either, then, it is impossible to annihilate composition in thought; or, after such annihilation, there must remain something that subsists without composition, that is, something that is simple. But in the former case the composite could not itself consist of substances, because with substances composition is merely a contingent relation, apart from which they must still exist as self-subsistent beings. Now, as this case contradicts the supposition, the second must contain the truth—that the substantial composite in the world consists of simple parts.

It follows as an immediate inference, that the things in the world are all, without exception, simple beings—that composition is merely an external condition pertaining to them—and that, although we never can separate and isolate the elementary substances from the state of composition,

Antithesis

No composite thing in the world consists of simple parts; and there does not exist in the world any simple substance.

PROOF

Let it be supposed that a composite thing (as substance) consists of simple parts. Inasmuch as all external relation, consequently all composition of substances, is possible only in space; the space, occupied by that which is composite, must consist of the same number of parts as is contained in the composite. But space does not consist of simple parts, but of spaces. Therefore, every part of the composite must occupy a space. But the absolutely primary parts of what is composite are simple. It follows that what is simple occupies a space. Now, as everything real that occupies a space, contains a manifold the parts of which are external to each other, and is consequently composite—and a real composite, not of accidents (for these cannot exist external to each other apart from substance), but of substances—it follows that the simple must be a substantial composite, which is self-contradictory.

The second proposition of the antithesis—that there exists in the world nothing that is simple—is here equivalent to the following: The existence of the absolutely simple cannot be demonstrated from any experience or perception either external or internal; and the absolutely simple is a mere

reason must cogitate these as the primary subjects of all composition, and consequently, as prior thereto—and as simple substances.

idea, the objective reality of which cannot be demonstrated in any possible experience; it is consequently, in the exposition of phenomena, without application and object. For, let us take for granted that an object may be found in experience for this transcendental idea; the empirical intuition of such an object must then be recognized to contain absolutely no manifold with its parts external to each other, and connected into unity. Now, as we cannot reason from the non-consciousness of such a manifold to the impossibility of its existence in the intuition of an object, and as the proof of this impossibility is necessary for the establishment and proof of absolute simplicity; it follows, that this simplicity cannot be inferred from any perception whatever. As, therefore, an absolutely simple object cannot be given in any experience, and the world of sense must be considered as the sum-total of all possible experiences; nothing simple exists in the world.

This second proposition in the antithesis has a more extended aim than the first. The first merely banishes the simple from the intuition of the composite; while the second drives it entirely out of nature. Hence we were unable to demonstrate it from the conception of a given object of external intuition (of the composite), but we were obliged to prove it from the relation of a given object to a possible experience in general.

Observations on the Second Antinomy

ON THE THESIS

When I speak of a *whole*, which necessarily consists of simple parts, I understand thereby only a substantial whole, as the true composite; that is to say, I understand that contingent unity of the manifold which is given as perfectly isolated (at least in thought), placed in reciprocal connection, and thus constituted a unity. Space ought not to be called a *compositum* but a *totum*, for its parts are possible in the whole, and not the whole by means of the parts. It might perhaps be called a *compositum ideale*, but not a *compositum reale*. But this is of no importance. As space is not a composite of substances (and not even of real accidents), if I abstract all composition therein—nothing, not even a point, remains; for a point is possible only as the limit of a space—consequently of a composite. Space and time, therefore, do not consist of simple parts. That which belongs only to the condition or state of a substance, even although it possesses a quantity (motion or change, for example), likewise does not consist of simple parts. That is to say, a certain de-

ON THE ANTITHESIS

Against the assertion of the infinite subdivisibility of matter, whose ground of proof is purely mathematical, objections have been alleged by the Monadists. These objections lay themselves open, at first sight, to suspicion, from the fact that they do not recognize the clearest mathematical proofs as propositions relating to the constitution of space, in so far as it is really the formal condition of the possibility of all matter, but regard them merely as inferences from abstract but arbitrary conceptions, which cannot have any application to real things. Just as if it were possible to imagine another mode ot intuition than that given in the primitive intuition of space; and just as if its *à priori* determinations did not apply to everything, the existence of which is possible, from the fact alone of its filling space. If we listen to them, we shall find ourselves required to cogitate, in addition to the mathematical point, which is simple—not, however, a part, but a mere limit of space—physical points, which are indeed likewise simple, but possess the peculiar property, as parts of

gree of change does not originate from the addition of many simple changes. Our inference of the simple from the composite is valid only of self-subsisting things. But the accidents of a state are not self-subsistent. The proof, then, for the necessity of the simple, as the component part of all that is substantial and composite, may prove a failure, and the whole case of this thesis be lost, if we carry the proposition too far, and wish to make it valid of everything that is composite without distinction—as indeed has really now and then happened. Besides, I am here speaking only of the simple, in so far as it is necessarily given in the composite—the latter being capable of solution into the former as its component parts. The proper signification of the word *monas* (as employed by Leibnitz) ought to relate to the simple, given *immediately* as simple substance (for example, in consciousness), and not as an element of the composite. As an element, the term *atomus* * would be more appropriate. And as I wish

* A masculine formed by Kant, instead of the common neuter *atomon*, which is generally translated in the scholastic philosophy by the terms *inseparabile, indiscernibile, simplex.* Kant wished to have a term opposed to *monas,* and so hit upon this ἄπαξ λεγόμενον With Democritus ἄτομος, and with Cicero *atomus* is feminine.—*Note by Rosenkranz.*

space, of filling it merely by their aggregation. I shall not repeat here the common and clear refutations of this absurdity, which are to be found everywhere in numbers: every one knows that it is impossible to undermine the evidence of mathematics by mere discursive conceptions; I shall only remark, that, if in this case philosophy endeavors to gain an advantage over mathematics by sophistical artifices, it is because it forgets that the discussion relates solely to *phenomena* and their conditions. It is not sufficient to find the conception of the simple for the pure *conception* of the composite, but we must discover for the *intuition* of the composite (matter), the intuition of the simple. Now this, according to the laws of sensibility, and consequently in the case of objects of sense, is utterly impossible. In the case of a whole composed of substances, which is cogitated solely by the pure understanding, it may be necessary to be in possession of the simple before composition is possible. But this does not hold good of the *Totum substantiale phenomenon*, which, as an empirical intuition in space, possesses the necessary property of containing no simple part, for the very reason that no

to prove the existence of simple substances, only in relation to, and as the elements of, the composite, I might term the antithesis of the second Antinomy, transcendental *Atomistic*. But as this word has long been employed to designate a particular theory of corporeal phenomena (*moleculæ*), and thus presupposes a basis of empirical conceptions, I prefer calling it the dialectical principle of *Monadology*.

part of space is simple. Meanwhile, the Monadists have been subtle enough to escape from this difficulty, by presupposing intuition and the dynamical relation of substances as the condition of the possibility of space, instead of regarding space as the condition of the possibility of the objects of external intuition, that is, of bodies. Now we have a conception of bodies only as phenomena, and, as such, they necessarily presuppose space as the condition of all external phenomena. The evasion is therefore in vain; as, indeed, we have sufficiently shown in our Æsthetic. If bodies were *things in themselves*, the proof of the Monadists would be unexceptionable.

The second dialectical assertion possesses the peculiarity of having opposed to it a dogmatical proposition, which, among all such sophistical statements, is the only one that undertakes to prove in the case of an object of experience, that which is properly a transcendental idea—the absolute simplicity of substance. The proposition is, that the object of the internal sense, the thinking Ego, is an absolute simple substance. Without at present entering upon this subject— as it has been considered at length in a former chapter—I shall merely remark, that, if something is cogitated merely as an object, without the addition of any synthetical determination of its intuition—as happens in the case of the bare representation, *I*—it is certain that no manifold and no composition can be perceived in such a representation. As, moreover, the predicates whereby I cogitate this object are merely intuitions of the internal sense, there cannot be discovered in them anything to prove the existence of a manifold whose parts are external to each other, and consequently, nothing to prove the existence of real composition. Consciousness, therefore, is so constituted, that, inasmuch as the thinking subject is at the same time its own object, it cannot divide itself—although it can divide its inhering determinations. For every object in relation to itself is absolute unity. Nevertheless, if the subject is regarded *externally*, as an object of intuition, it must, in its character of phenomenon, possess the property of composition. And it must always be regarded in this manner, if we wish to know whether there is or is not contained in it a manifold whose parts are external to each other.

Third Conflict of Transcendental Ideas

Thesis	Antithesis
Causality according to the laws of nature is not the only causality operating to originate the phenomena of the world. A causality of freedom is also necessary to account fully for these phenomena.	There is no such thing as freedom, but everything in the world happens solely according to the laws of nature.

PROOF	PROOF
Let it be supposed, that there is no other kind of causality than that according to the laws of nature. Consequently, everything that happens presupposes a previous condition, which it follows with absolute certainty, in conformity with a rule. But this previous condition must itself be something that has happened (that has arisen in time, as it did not exist before), for, if it has always been in existence, its consequence or effect would not thus originate for the first time, but would likewise have always existed. The causality, therefore, of a cause, whereby something happens, is itself a thing that has *happened*. Now this again presupposes, in conformity with the law of nature, a previous condition and its causality, and this another anterior to the former, and so on. If, then, everything happens solely in accordance with the laws of nature, there cannot be any real first beginning of things, but only a subaltern or comparative beginning. There cannot, therefore, be a completeness of series on the side of the causes which originate the one from the other. But the law of nature is, that nothing can happen without a sufficient *à priori* determined cause. The proposition, therefore—if all	Granted, that there does exist *freedom* in the transcendental sense, as a peculiar kind of causality, operating to produce events in the world—a faculty, that is to say, of originating a state, and consequently a series of consequences from that state. In this case, not only the series originated by this spontaneity, but the determination of this spontaneity itself to the production of th' series, that is to say, the causality itself must have an absolute commencement, such, that nothing can precede to determine this action according to unvarying laws. But every beginning of action presupposes in the acting cause a state of inaction; and a dynamically primal beginning of action presupposes a state, which has no connection—as regards causality—with the preceding state of the cause,—which does not, that is, in any wise result from it. Transcendental freedom is therefore opposed to the natural law of cause and effect, and such a conjunction of successive states in effective causes is destructive of the possibility of unity in experience, and for that reason not to be found in experience—is consequently a mere fiction of thought. We have, therefore, nothing but

causality is possible only in accordance with the laws of nature—is, when stated in this unlimited and general manner, self-contradictory. It follows that this cannot be the only kind of causality.

From what has been said, it follows that a causality must be admitted, by means of which something happens, without its cause being determined according to the necessary laws by some other cause preceding. That is to say, there must exist an *absolute spontaneity* of cause, which of itself originates a series of phenomena which proceeds according to natural laws—consequently transcendental freedom, without which even in the course of nature the succession of phenomena on the side of causes is never complete.

nature, to which we must look for connection and order in cosmical events. Freedom—independence of the laws of nature—is certainly a deliverance from restraint, but it is also a relinquishing of the guidance of law and rule. For it cannot be alleged, that, instead of the laws of nature, laws of freedom may be introduced into the causality of the course of nature. For, if freedom were determined according to laws, it would be no longer freedom, but merely nature. Nature, therefore, and transcendental freedom are distinguishable as conformity to law and lawlessness. The former imposes upon understanding the difficulty of seeking the origin of events ever higher and higher in the series of causes, inasmuch as causality is always conditioned thereby; while it compensates this labor by the guarantee of a unity complete and in conformity with law. The latter on the contrary, holds out to the understanding the promise of a point of rest in the chain of causes, by conducting it to an unconditioned causality, which professes to have the power of spontaneous origination, but which, in its own utter blindness, deprives it of the guidance of rules, by which alone a completely connected experience is possible.

Observations on the Third Antinomy

ON THE THESIS

The transcendental idea of freedom is far from constituting the entire content of the psychological conception so termed, which is for the most part empirical. It merely pre-

ON THE ANTITHESIS

The assertor of the all-sufficiency of nature in regard to causality (transcendental *Physiocracy*), in opposition to the doctrine of freedom, would defend his view of the ques-

sents us with the conception of spontaneity of action, as the proper ground for imputing freedom to the cause of a certain class of objects. It is, however, the true stumbling-stone to philosophy, which meets with unconquerable difficulties in the way of its admitting this kind of unconditioned causality. That element in the question of the freedom of the will, which has for so long a time placed speculative reason in such perplexity, is properly only transcendental, and concerns the question, whether there must be held to exist a faculty of *spontaneous* origination of a series of successive things or states. How such a faculty is possible, is not a necessary inquiry; for in the case of natural causality itself, we are obliged to content ourselves with the *à priori* knowledge that such a causality must be presupposed, although we are quite incapable of comprehending how the being of one thing is possible through the being of another, but must for this information look entirely to experience. Now we have demonstrated this necessity of a free first beginning of a series of phenomena, only in so far as it is required for the comprehension of an origin of the world, all following states

tion somewhat in the following manner. He would say, in answer to the sophistical arguments of the opposite party: *If you do not accept a mathematical first, in relation to time, you have no need to seek a dynamical first, in regard to causality.* Who compelled you to imagine an absolutely primal condition of the world, and therewith an absolute beginning of the gradually progressing successions of phenomena—and, as some foundation for this fancy of yours, to set bounds to unlimited nature? Inasmuch as the substances in the world have always existed—at least the unity of experience renders such a supposition quite necessary—there is no difficulty in believing also, that the changes in the conditions of these substances have always existed; and, consequently, that a first beginning, mathematical or dynamical, is by no means required. The possibility of such an infinite derivation, without any initial member from which all the others result, is certainly quite incomprehensible. But if you are rash enough to deny the enigmatical secrets of nature for this reason, you will find yourselves obliged to deny also the existence of many fundamental properties of natural

being regarded as a succession according to laws of nature alone. But, as there has thus been proved the existence of a faculty which can of itself originate a series in time—although we are unable to explain how it can exist—we feel ourselves authorized to admit, even in the midst of the natural course of events, a beginning, as regards causality, of different successions of phenomena, and at the same time to attribute to all substances a faculty of free action. But we ought in this case not to allow ourselves to fall into a common misunderstanding, and to suppose that, because a successive series in the world can only have a comparatively first beginning—another state or condition of things always preceding—an absolutely first beginning of a series in the course of nature is impossible. For we are not speaking here of an absolutely first beginning in relation to time, but as regards causality alone. When, for example, I, completely of my own free will, and independently of the necessarily determinative influence of natural causes, rise from my chair, there commences with this event, including its material consequences *in infinitum,* an absolutely new series; although, in relation to

objects (such as fundamental forces), which you can just as little comprehend; and even the possibility of so simple a conception as that of change must present to you insuperable difficulties. For if experience did not teach you that it was real, you never could conceive *à priori* the possibility of this ceaseless sequence of being and non-being.

But if the existence of a transcendental faculty of freedom is granted—a faculty of originating changes in the world—this faculty must at least exist out of and apart from the world; although it is certainly a bold assumption, that, over and above the complete content of all possible intuitions, there still exists an object which cannot be presented in any possible perception. But, to attribute to substances in the world itself such a faculty, is quite inadmissible; for, in this case, the connection of phenomena reciprocally determining and determined according to general laws, which is termed nature, and along with it the criteria of empirical truth, which enable us to distinguish experience from mere visionary dreaming, would almost entirely disappear. In proximity with such a lawless faculty of freedom, a system of nature

time, this event is merely the continuation of a preceding series. For this resolution and act of mine do not form part of the succession of effects in nature, and are not mere continuations of it; on the contrary, the determining causes of nature cease to operate in reference to this event, which certainly *succeeds* the acts of nature, but does not *proceed* from them. For these reasons, the action of a free agent must be termed, in regard to causality, if not in relation to time, an absolutely primal beginning of a series of phenomena.

The justification of this need of reason to rest upon a free act as the first beginning of the series of natural causes, is evident from the fact, that all philosophers of antiquity (with the exception of the Epicurean school) felt themselves obliged, when constructing a theory of the motions of the universe, to accept a *prime mover*, that is, a freely acting cause, which spontaneously and prior to all other causes evolved this series of states. They always felt the need of going beyond mere nature, for the purpose of making a first beginning comprehensible.

is hardly cogitable; for the laws of the latter would be continually subject to the intrusive influences of the former, and the course of the phenomena, which would otherwise proceed regularly and uniformly, would become thereby confused and disconnected.

FOURTH CONFLICT OF THE TRANSCENDENTAL IDEAS

Thesis	Antithesis
There exists either in, or in connection with the world—either as a part of it, or as the cause of it—an absolutely necessary being.	An absolutely necessary being does not exist, either in the world or out of it—as its cause.

PROOF

The world of sense, as the sum-total of all phenomena, contains a series of changes. For, without such a series, the mental representation of the series of time itself, as the condition of the possibility of the sensuous world, could not be presented to us.* But every change stands under its condition, which precedes it in time and renders it necessary. Now the existence of a given condition presupposes a complete series of conditions up to the absolutely unconditioned, which alone is absolutely necessary. It follows that something that is absolutely necessary must exist, if change exists as its consequence. But this necessary thing itself belongs to the sensuous world. For suppose it to exist out of and apart from it, the series of cosmical changes would receive from it a beginning, and yet this necessary cause would not itself belong to the world of sense. But this is impossible. For, as the beginning of a series in time is determined only by that which precedes it in time, the supreme condition of the beginning of a series of changes must exist in the time in which this series itself did not exist; for a beginning supposes a time pre-

PROOF

Grant that either the world itself is necessary, or that there is contained in it a necessary existence. Two cases are possible. *First,* there must either be in the series of cosmical changes a beginning, which is unconditionally necessary and therefore uncaused —which is at variance with the dynamical law of the determination of all phenomena in time; or *secondly,* the series itself is without beginning, and although contingent and conditioned in all its parts, is nevertheless absolutely necessary and unconditioned as a whole—which is self-contradictory. For the existence of an aggregate cannot be necessary, if no single part of it possesses necessary existence.

Grant on the other hand, that an absolutely necessary cause exists out of and apart from the world. This cause, as the highest member in the series of the causes of cosmical changes, must originate or begin † the existence of the latter and their series. In this case it must also begin to act, and its causality would therefore belong to time, and consequently to the sum-total of phenomena, that is, to the world. It follows that

---

* *Objectively,* time, as the formal condition of the possibility of change, precedes all changes; but *subjectively,* and in consciousness, the representation of time, like every other, is given solely by *occasion* of perception.

† The word *begin* is taken in two senses. The first is active—the cause being regarded as beginning a series of conditions as its effect (*infit*). The second is passive—the causality in the cause itself beginning to operate (*fit*). I reason here from the first to the second.

ceding, in which the thing that begins to be was not in existence. The causality of the necessary cause of changes, and consequently the cause itself, must for these reasons belong to time —and to phenomena, time being possible only as the form of phenomena. Consequently, it cannot be cogitated as separated from the world of sense—the sumtotal of all phenomena. There is, therefore, contained in the world, something that is absolutely necessary—whether it be the whole cosmical series itself, or only a part of it.

the cause cannot be out of the world; which is contradictory to the hypothesis. Therefore, neither in the world, nor out of it (but in causal connection with it), does there exist any absolutely necessary being.

Observations on the Fourth Antinomy

ON THE THESIS

To demonstrate the existence of a necessary being, I cannot be permitted in this place to employ any other than the *cosmological* argument, which ascends from the conditioned in phenomena to the unconditioned in conception— the unconditioned being considered the necessary condition of the absolute totality of the series. The proof, from the mere idea of a supreme being, belongs to another principle of reason, and requires separate discussion.

The pure cosmological proof demonstrates the existence of a necessary being, but at the same time leaves it quite unsettled, whether this being is the world itself, or quite distinct from it. To establish the

ON THE ANTITHESIS

The difficulties which meet us, in our attempt to rise through the series of phenomena to the existence of an absolutely necessary supreme cause, must not originate from our inability to establish the truth of our mere conceptions of the necessary existence of a thing. That is to say, our objections must not be ontological, but must be directed against the causal connection with a series of phenomena of a condition which is itself unconditioned. In one word, they must be cosmological, and relate to empirical laws. We must show that the regress in the series of causes (in the world of sense) cannot conclude with an empirically unconditioned condition, and

truth of the latter view, principles are requisite, which are not cosmological, and do not proceed in the series of phenomena. We should require to introduce into our proof conceptions of contingent beings—regarded merely as objects of the understanding, and also a principle which enables us to connect these, by means of mere conceptions, with a necessary being. But the proper place for all such arguments is a *transcendent* philosophy, which has unhappily not yet been established.

But, if we begin our proof cosmologically, by laying at the foundation of it the series of phenomena, and the regress in it according to empirical laws of causality, we are not at liberty to break off from this mode of demonstration and to pass over to something which is not itself a member of the series. The condition must be taken in exactly the same signification as the relation of the conditioned to its condition in the series has been taken, for the series must conduct us in an unbroken regress to this supreme condition. But if this relation is sensuous, and belongs to the possible empirical employment of the understanding, the supreme condition or cause must close the regressive series according to

that the cosmological argument from the contingency of the cosmical state—a contingency alleged to arise from change—does not justify us in accepting a first cause, that is, a prime originator of the cosmical series.

The reader will observe in this antinomy a very remarkable contrast. The very same grounds of proof which established in the thesis the existence of a supreme being, demonstrated in the antithesis—and with equal strictness—the non-existence of such a being. We found, first, that *a necessary being exists,* because the whole time past contains the series of all conditions, and with it, therefore, the unconditioned (the necessary); secondly, that *there does not exist any necessary being,* for the same reason, that the whole time past contains the series of all conditions—which are themselves therefore, in the aggregate, conditioned. The cause of this seeming incongruity is as follows. We attend, in the first argument, solely to the *absolute totality* of the series of conditions, the one of which determines the other in time, and thus arrive at a necessary unconditioned. In the second, we consider, on the contrary, the *contingency* of everything that is deter-the laws of sensibility, and consequently must belong to the series of time. It follows that this necessary existence must be regarded as the highest member of the cosmical series.

Certain philosophers have, nevertheless, allowed themselves the liberty of making such a *saltus* (μετάβασις εἰς ἄλλο γένος). From the changes in the world they have concluded their empirical contingency, that is, their dependence on empirically determined causes, and they thus admitted an ascending series of empirical conditions: and in this they are quite right. But as they could not find in this series any primal beginning or any highest member, they passed suddenly from the empirical conception of contingency to the pure category, which presents us with a series—not sensuous, but intellectual — whose completeness does certainly rest upon the existence of an absolutely necessary cause. Nay, more, this intellectual series is not tied to any sensuous conditions; and is therefore free from the condition of time, which requires it spontaneously to begin its causality in time.—But such a procedure is perfectly inadmissible, as will be made plain from what follows.

mined in the *series of time*— for every event is preceded by a time, in which the condition itself must be determined as conditioned—and thus everything that is unconditioned or absolutely necessary disappears. In both, the mode of proof is quite in accordance with the common procedure of human reason, which often falls into discord with itself, from considering an object from two different points of view. Herr von Mairan regarded the controversy between two celebrated astronomers, which arose from a similar difficulty as to the choice of a proper standpoint, as a phenomenon of sufficient importance to warrant a separate treatise on the subject. The one concluded: *the moon revolves on its own axis,* because it constantly presents the same side to the earth; the other declared that *the moon does not revolve on its own axis,* for the same reason. Both conclusions were perfectly correct, according to the point of view from which the motions of the moon were considered.

In the pure sense of the categories, that is contingent, the contradictory opposite of which is possible. Now we cannot reason from empirical contingency to intellectual. The opposite of that which is changed—the opposite of its state—is actual at another time, and is therefore possible. Consequently, it is not the contradictory opposite of the former state. To be *that,* it is necessary that in the same time in which the preceding state existed, its opposite could have existed in its place; but such a cognition is not given us in the mere phenomenon of change. A body that was in motion $= A$, comes into a state of rest $= non\text{-}A$. Now it cannot be concluded from the fact that a state opposite to the state A follows it, that the contradictory opposite of A is possible; and that A is therefore contingent. To prove this, we should require to know that the state of rest could have existed in the very same time in which the motion took place. Now we know nothing more than that the state of rest was actual in the time that followed the state of motion; consequently, that it was also possible. But motion at one time, and rest at another time, are not contradictorily opposed to each other. It follows from what has been said

that the succession of opposite
determinations, that is,
change, does not demonstrate
the fact of contingency as represented in the conceptions of
the pure understanding; and
that it cannot, therefore, conduct us to the fact of the existence of a necessary being.
Change proves merely em-
pirical contingency, that is to
say, that the new state could
not have existed without a
cause, which belongs to the
preceding time. This cause—
even although it is regarded
as absolutely necessary—must
be presented to us in time, and
must belong to the series of
phenomena.

Sec. III.—Of the Interest of Reason in these Self-contra-dictions

We have thus completely before us the dialectical procedure
of the cosmological ideas. No possible experience can present
us with an object adequate to them in extent. Nay, more,
reason itself cannot cogitate them as according with the general
laws of experience. And yet they are not arbitrary fictions of
thought. On the contrary, reason, in its uninterrupted progress in the empirical synthesis, is necessarily conducted to them,
when it endeavors to free from all conditions and to comprehend
in its unconditioned totality, that which can only be determined
conditionally in accordance with the laws of experience. These
dialectical propositions are so many attempts to solve four natural and unavoidable problems of reason.—There are neither
more, nor can there be less, than this number, because there
are no other series of synthetical hypotheses, limiting *à priori*
the empirical synthesis.

The brilliant claims of reason striving to extend its dominion
beyond the limits of·experience, have been represented above
only in dry formulæ, which contain merely the grounds of its

pretensions. They have, besides, in conformity with the character of a transcendental philosophy, been freed from every empirical element; although the full splendor of the promises they hold out, and the anticipations they excite, manifest themselves only when in connection with empirical cognitions. In the application of them, however, and in the advancing enlargement of the employment of reason, while struggling to rise from the region of experience and to soar to those sublime ideas, philosophy discovers a value and a dignity, which, if it could but make good its assertions, would raise it far above all other departments of human knowledge—professing, as it does, to present a sure foundation for our highest hopes and the ultimate aims of all the exertions of reason. The questions: whether the world has a beginning and a limit to its extension in space; whether there exists anywhere, or perhaps, in my own thinking Self an indivisible and indestructible unity—or whether nothing but what is divisible and transitory exists; whether I am a free agent, or, like other beings, am bound in the chains of nature and fate; whether, finally, there is a supreme cause of the world, or all our thought and speculation must end with nature and the order of external things—are questions, for the solution of which the mathematician would willingly exchange his whole science; for in it there is no satisfaction for the highest aspirations and most ardent desires of humanity. Nay, it may even be said that the true value of mathematics—that pride of human reason—consists in this: that she guides reason to the knowledge of nature—in her greater, as well as in her less manifestations—in her beautiful order and regularity—guides her, moreover, to an insight into the wonderful unity of the moving forces in the operations of nature, far beyond the expectations of a philosophy building only on experience; and that she thus encourages philosophy to extend the province of reason beyond all experience, and at the same time provides it with the most excellent materials for supporting its investigations, in so far as their nature admits, by adequate and accordant intuitions.

Unfortunately for speculation—but perhaps fortunately for the practical interests of humanity—reason, in the midst of her highest anticipations, finds herself hemmed in by a press of opposite and contradictory conclusions, from which neither her honor nor her safety will permit her to draw back. Nor can

she regard these conflicting trains of reasoning with indifference as mere passages at arms, still less can she command
peace; for in the subject of the conflict she has a deep interest.
There is no other course left open to her, than to reflect with
herself upon the origin of this disunion in reason—whether it
may not arise from a mere misunderstanding. After such an
inquiry, arrogant claims would have to be given up on both
sides; but the sovereignty of reason over understanding and
sense would be based upon a sure foundation.

We shall at present defer this radical inquiry, and in the
meantime consider for a little—what side in the controversy
we should most willingly take, if we were obliged to become
partisans at all. As, in this case, we leave out of sight altogether the logical criterion of truth, and merely consult our
own interest in reference to the question, these considerations,
although inadequate to settle the question of right in either
party, will enable us to comprehend, how those who have taken
part in the struggle, adopt the one view rather than the other
—no special insight into the subject, however, having influenced
their choice. They will, at the same time, explain to us many
other things by the way—for example, the fiery zeal on the
one side and the cold maintenance of their cause on the other;
why the one party has met with the warmest approbations, and
the other has always been repulsed by irreconcilable prejudices.

There is one thing, however, that determines the proper point
of view, from which alone this preliminary inquiry can be instituted and carried on with the proper completeness—and that is
the comparison of the principles, from which both sides—thesis
and antithesis, proceed. My readers would remark in the propositions of the antithesis a complete uniformity in the mode of
thought and a perfect unity of principle. Its principle was that
of pure empiricism, not only in the explication of the phenomena
in the world, but also in the solution of the transcendental ideas,
even of that of the universe itself. The affirmations of the
thesis on the contrary, were based, in addition to the empirical
mode of explanation employed in the series of phenomena, on
intellectual propositions; and its principles were in so far not
simple. I shall term the thesis, in view of its essential characteristic, the *dogmatism* of pure reason.

On the side of dogmatism, or of the thesis, therefore, in the
determination of the cosmological ideas, we find:

1. A *practical interest*, which must be very dear to every right-thinking man. That the world has a beginning—that the nature of my thinking self is simple, and therefore indestructible—that I am a free agent, and raised above the compulsion of nature and her laws—and, finally, that the entire order of things, which form the world, is dependent upon a Supreme Being, from whom the whole receives unity and connection— these are so many foundation-stones of morality and religion. The antithesis deprives us of all these supports—or, at least, seems so to deprive us.

2. A *speculative interest* of reason manifests itself on this side. For, if we take the transcendental ideas and employ them in the manner which the thesis directs, we can exhibit completely *à priori* the entire chain of conditions, and understand the derivation of the conditioned—beginning from the unconditioned. This the antithesis does not do; and for this reason does not meet with so welcome a reception. For it can give no answer to our questions respecting the conditions of its synthesis—except such as must be supplemented by another question, and so on to infinity. According to it, we must rise from a given beginning to one still higher; every part conducts us to a still smaller one; every event is preceded by another event which is its cause; and the conditions of existence rest always upon other and still higher conditions, and find neither end nor basis in some self-subsistent thing as the primal being.

3. This side has also the advantage of *popularity;* and this constitutes no small part of its claim to favor. The common understanding does not find the least difficulty in the idea of the unconditioned beginning of all synthesis—accustomed, as it is, rather to follow out consequences, than to seek for a proper basis for cognition. In the conception of an absolute first, moreover—the possibility of which it does not inquire into —it is highly gratified to find a firmly-established point of departure for its attempts at theory; while in the restless and continuous ascent from the conditioned to the condition, always with one foot in the air, it can find no satisfaction.

On the side of the Antithesis, or *Empiricism* in the determination of the cosmological ideas:

1. We cannot discover any such practical interest arising from pure principles of reason, as morality and religion present. On the contrary, pure empiricism seems to empty them of all their

power and influence. If there does not exist a Supreme Being distinct from the world—if the world is without beginning, consequently without a Creator—if our wills are not free, and the soul is divisible and subject to corruption just like matter —the ideas and principles of morality lose all validity, and fall with the transcendental ideas which constituted their theoretical support.

2. But empiricism, in compensation, holds out to reason, in its speculative interests, certain important advantages, far exceeding any that the dogmatist can promise us. For, when employed by the empiricist, understanding is always upon its proper ground of investigation—the field of possible experience, the laws of which it can explore, and thus extend its cognition securely and with clear intelligence without being stopped by limits in any direction. Here can it and ought it to find and present to intuition its proper object—not only in itself, but in all its relations; or, if it employ conceptions, upon this ground it can always present the corresponding images in clear and unmistakable intuitions. It is quite unnecessary for it to renounce the guidance of nature, to attach itself to ideas, the objects of which it cannot know; because, as mere intellectual entities, they cannot be presented in any intuition. On the contrary, it is not even permitted to abandon its proper occupation, under the pretense that it has been brought to a conclusion (for it never can be), and to pass into the region of idealizing reason and transcendent conceptions, where it is not required to observe and explore the laws of nature, but merely to *think* and to *imagine*—secure from being contradicted by facts, because they have not been called as witnesses, but passed by, or perhaps subordinated to the so-called higher interests and considerations of pure reason.

Hence the empiricist will never allow himself to accept any epoch of nature for the first—the absolutely primal state; he will not believe that there can be limits to his outlook into her wide domains, nor pass from the objects of nature, which he can satisfactorily explain by means of observation and mathematical thought—which he can determine synthetically in intuition, to those which neither sense nor imagination can ever present *in concreto;* he will not concede the existence of a faculty in nature, operating independently of the laws of nature—a concession which would introduce uncertainty into the proced-

ture of the understanding, which is guided by necessary laws to the observation of phenomena; nor, finally, will he permit himself to seek a cause beyond nature, inasmuch as we know nothing but it, and from it alone receive an objective basis for all our conceptions and instruction in the unvarying laws of things.

In truth, if the empirical philosopher had no other purpose in the establishment of his antithesis, than to check the presumption of a reason which mistakes its true destination, which boasts of its insight and its knowledge, just where all insight and knowledge cease to exist, and regards that which is valid only in relation to a practical interest, as an advancement of the speculative interests of the mind (in order, when it is convenient for itself, to break the thread of our physical investigations, and, under pretense of extending our cognition, connect them with transcendental ideas, by means of which we really know only that we know nothing)—if, I say, the empiricist rested satisfied with this benefit, the principle advanced by him would be a maxim recommending moderation in the pretensions of reason and modesty in its affirmations, and at the same time would direct us to the right mode of extending the province of the understanding, by the help of the only true teacher, experience. In obedience to this advice, intellectual *hypotheses* and *faith* would not be called in aid of our practical interests; nor should we introduce them under the pompous titles of science and insight. For speculative *cognition* cannot find an objective basis any other where than in experience; and, when we overstep its limits, our synthesis, which requires ever new cognitions independent of experience, has no substratum of intuition upon which to build.

But if—as often happens—empiricism, in relation to ideas, becomes itself dogmatic, and boldly denies that which is above the sphere of its phenomenal cognition, it falls itself into the error of intemperance—an error which is here all the more reprehensible, as thereby the practical interest of reason receives an irreparable injury.

And this constitutes the opposition between Epicureanism * and Platonism.

* It is, however, still a matter of doubt whether Epicurus ever propounded these principles as directions for the objective employment of the understanding. If, indeed, they were nothing more than maxims for the speculative exercise of reason, he gives evidence therein of a more genuine philosophic

Both Epicurus and Plato assert more in their systems than they know. The former encourages and advances science— although to the prejudice of the practical; the latter presents us with excellent principles for the investigation of the practical, but, in relation to everything regarding which we can attain to speculative cognition, permits reason to append idealistic explanations of natural phenomena, to the great injury of physical investigation.

3. In regard to the third motive for the preliminary choice of a party in this war of assertions, it seems very extraordinary that empiricism should be utterly unpopular. We should be inclined to believe, that the common understanding would receive it with pleasure—promising as it does, to satisfy it without passing the bounds of experience and its connected order; while transcendental dogmatism obliges it to rise to conceptions, which far surpass the intelligence and ability of the most practised thinkers. But in this, in truth, is to be found its real motive. For the common understanding thus finds itself in a situation, where not even the most learned can have the advantage of it. If it understands little or nothing about these transcendental conceptions, no one can boast of understanding any more; and although it may not express itself in so scholastically correct a manner as others, it can busy itself with reasoning and arguments without end, wandering among mere ideas, about which one can always be very eloquent, because we know nothing about them; while, in the observation and investigation of nature, it would be forced to remain dumb and to confess its utter ignorance. Thus indolence and vanity form of themselves strong recommendations of these principles. Besides, although it is a hard thing for a philosopher to assume a principle, of which he can give to himself no reasonable account, and still more to employ conceptions, the objective reality of which cannot be established, nothing is more usual with the common un-

spirit than any of the philosophers of antiquity. That, in the explanation of phenomena, we must proceed as if the field of inquiry had neither limits in space nor commencement in time; that we must be satisfied with the teaching of experience in reference to the material of which the world is composed; that we must not look for any other mode of the origination of events than that which is determined by the unalterable laws of nature; and finally, that we must not employ the hypothesis of a

cause distinct from the world to account for a phenomenon or for the world itself—are principles for the extension of speculative philosophy, and the discovery of the true sources of the principles of morals, which, however little conformed to in the present day, are undoubtedly correct. At the same time, anyone desirous of *ignoring*, in mere speculation, these dogmatical propositions, need not for that reason be accused of *denying* them.

derstanding. It wants something, which will allow it to go to work with confidence. The difficulty of even comprehending a supposition, does not disquiet it, because—not knowing what comprehending means—it never even thinks of the supposition it may be adopting as a principle; and regards as known, that with which it has become familiar from constant use. And, at last, all speculative interests disappear before the practical interests which it holds dear; and it fancies that it understands and knows what its necessities and hopes incite it to assume or to believe. Thus the empiricism of transcendentally idealizing reason is robbed of all popularity; and, however prejudicial it may be to the highest practical principles, there is no fear that it will ever pass the limits of the schools, or acquire any favor or influence in society or with the multitude.

Human reason is by nature architectonic. That is to say, it regards all cognitions as parts of a possible system, and hence accepts only such principles, as at least do not incapacitate a cognition to which we may have attained from being placed along with others in a general system. But the propositions of the antithesis are of a character which renders the completion of an edifice of cognitions impossible. According to these, beyond one state or epoch of the world there is always to be found one more ancient; in every part always other parts themselves divisible; preceding every event another, the origin of which must itself be sought still higher; and everything in existence is conditioned, and still not dependent on an unconditioned and primal existence. As, therefore, the antithesis will not concede the existence of a first beginning which might be available as a foundation, a complete edifice of cognition, in the presence of such hypothesis, is utterly impossible. Thus the architectonic interest of reason, which requires a unity—not empirical, but à priori and rational, forms a natural recommendation for the assertions of the thesis in our antinomy.

But if anyone could free himself entirely from all considerations of interest, and weigh without partiality the assertions of reason, attending only to their content, irrespective of the consequences which follow from them; such a person, on the supposition that he knew no other way out of the confusion than to settle the truth of one or other of the conflicting doctrines, would live in a state of continual hesitation. To-day, he would feel convinced that the human will is free; to-morrow, considering the indissoluble chain of nature, he would look on freedom as a mere illusion, and declare *nature* to be all-in-all. But, if he were called to action, the play of the merely speculative reason would disappear like the shapes of a dream, and practical interest would dictate his choice of principles. But, as it well befits a reflective and inquiring being to devote certain periods of time to the examination of its own reason—to divest itself of all partiality, and frankly to communicate its observations for the judgment and opinion of others; so no one can be blamed for, much less prevented from placing both parties on their trial, with permission to defend themselves, free from intimidation, before a sworn jury of equal condition with themselves—the condition of weak and fallible men.

Sec. IV.—Of the necessity imposed upon Pure Reason of presenting a Solution of its Transcendental Problems

To avow an ability to solve all problems and to answer all questions, would be a profession certain to convict any philosopher of extravagant boasting and self-conceit, and at once to destroy the confidence that might otherwise have been reposed in him. There are, however, sciences so constituted, that every question arising within their sphere, must necessarily be capable of receiving an answer from the knowledge already possessed, for the answer must be received from the same sources whence the question arose. In such sciences it is not allowable to excuse ourselves on the plea of necessary and unavoidable ignorance; a solution is absolutely requisite. The rule of *right* and *wrong* must help us to the knowledge of what is right or wrong in all possible cases; otherwise, the idea of obligation or duty would be utterly null, for we cannot have any obligation to that *which we cannot know*. On the other hand, in our investigations of the phenomena of nature, much must remain uncertain, and many questions continue insoluble; because what we know of nature is far from being sufficient to explain all the phenomena that are presented to our observation. Now the question is: Whether there is in transcendental philosophy any question, relating to an object presented to pure reason, which is unanswerable by this reason; and whether we must regard the subject of the question as quite uncertain— so far as our knowledge extends, and must give it a place among those subjects, of which we have just so much conception as is sufficient to enable us to raise a question—faculty or materials failing us, however, when we attempt an answer.

Now I maintain, that among all speculative cognition, the peculiarity of transcendental philosophy is, that there is no question, relating to an object presented to pure reason, which is insoluble by this reason; and that the profession of unavoidable ignorance—the problem being alleged to be beyond the reach of our faculties—cannot free us from the obligation to present a complete and satisfactory answer. For the very conception, which enables us to raise the question, must give us the power of answering it; inasmuch as the object, as in the case of right and wrong, is not to be discovered out of the conception.

But, in transcendental philosophy, it is only the cosmological questions, to which we can demand a satisfactory answer in relation to the constitution of their object; and the philosopher is not permitted to avail himself of the pretext of necessary ignorance and impenetrable obscurity. These questions relate solely to the cosmological ideas. For the object must be given in experience, and the question relates to the adequateness of the object to an idea. If the object is transcendental, and therefore itself unknown; if the question, for example, is whether the object—the something, the phenomenon of which (internal—in ourselves) is thought—that is to say, the soul, is in itself a simple being; or whether there is a cause of all things, which is absolutely necessary—in such cases we are seeking for our idea an object, of which we may confess, that it is unknown to us, though we must not on that account assert that it is impossible.* The cosmological ideas alone possess the peculiarity, that we can presuppose the object of them and the empirical synthesis requisite for the conception of that object to be given; and the question, which arises from these ideas, relates merely to the progress of this synthesis, in so far as it must contain

* The question, what is the constitution of a transcendental object, is unanswerable—we are unable to say *what it is*, but we can perceive that the *question* itself *is nothing;* because it does not relate to any object that can be presented to us. For this reason, we must consider all the questions raised in transcendental psychology as answerable, and as really answered; for they relate to the transcendental subject of all internal phenomena, which is not itself phenomenon, and consequently not given as an object, in which, moreover, none of the categories—and it is to them that the question is properly directed—find any conditions of its application. Here, therefore, is a case where no answer is the only proper answer. For a question regarding the constitution of a something, which cannot be cogitated by any determined predicate—being completely beyond the sphere of objects and experience, is perfectly null and void.

absolute totality—which, however, is not empirical, as it cannot be given in any experience. Now, as the question here is solely in regard to a thing as the object of a possible experience, and not as a thing in itself, the answer to the transcendental cosmological question need not be sought out of the idea, for the question does not regard an object in itself. The question in relation to a possible experience, is not, what can be given in an experience *in concreto*—but, what is contained in the idea, to which the empirical synthesis must approximate. The question must therefore be capable of solution from the idea alone. For the idea is a creation of reason itself, which therefore cannot disclaim the obligation to answer or refer us to the unknown object.

It is not so extraordinary as it at first sight appears, that a science should demand and expect satisfactory answers to all the questions that may arise within its own sphere (*questiones domesticæ*), although, up to a certain time, these answers may not have been discovered. There are, in addition to transcendental philosophy, only two pure sciences of reason; the one with a speculative, the other with a practical content—*pure mathematics* and *pure ethics*. Has anyone ever heard it alleged that, from our complete and necessary ignorance of the conditions, it is *uncertain* what exact relation the diameter of a circle bears to the circle in rational or irrational numbers? By the former the sum cannot be given exactly, by the latter only approximately; and therefore we decide, that the impossibility of a solution of the question is evident. Lambert presented us with a demonstration of this. In the general principles of morals there can be nothing uncertain, for the propositions are either utterly without meaning, or must originate solely in our rational conceptions. On the other hand, there must be in physical science an infinite number of conjectures, which can never become certainties; because the phenomena of nature are not given as objects dependent on our conceptions. The key to the solution of such questions cannot therefore be found in our conceptions or in pure thought, but must lie without us, and for that reason is in many cases not to be discovered; and consequently a satisfactory explanation cannot be expected. The questions of transcendental analytic, which relate to the deduction of our pure cognition, are not to be regarded as of the same kind as those mentioned above; for we are not at present treating of the certainty of judgments in relation to the origin of our conceptions, but only of that certainty in relation to objects.

We cannot, therefore, escape the responsibility of at least a critical solution of the questions of reason, by complaints of the limited nature of our faculties, and the seemingly humble confession that it is beyond the power of our reason to decide, whether the world has existed from all eternity or had a beginning—whether it is infinitely extended, or enclosed within certain limits—whether anything in the world is simple, or whether everything must be capable of infinite divisibility—whether freedom can originate phenomena, or whether everything is absolutely dependent on the laws and order of nature—and, finally, whether there exists a being that is completely unconditioned and necessary, or whether the existence of everything is conditioned and consequently dependent on something external to itself, and therefore in its own nature contingent. For all these questions relate to an object, which can be given nowhere else than in thought. This object is the absolutely unconditioned totality of the synthesis of phenomena. If the conceptions in our minds do not assist us to some certain result in regard to these problems, we must not defend ourselves on the plea that the object itself remains hidden from and unknown to us. For no such thing or object can be given—it is not to be found out of the idea in our minds. We must seek the cause of our failure in our idea itself, which is an insoluble problem, and in regard to which we obstinately assume that there exists a real object corresponding and adequate to it. A clear explanation of the dialectic which lies in our conception, will very soon enable us to come to a satisfactory decision in regard to such a question.

The pretext, that we are unable to arrive at certainty in regard to these problems, may be met with this question, which requires at least a plain answer: From what source do the ideas originate, the solution of which involves you in such difficulties? Are you seeking for an explanation of certain phenomena; and do you expect these ideas to give you the principles or the rules of this explanation? Let it be granted that all nature was laid open before you; that nothing was hid from your senses and your consciousness. Still, you could not cognize *in concreto* the object of your ideas in any experience. For what is demanded, is, not only this full and complete intuition, but also a complete synthesis and the consciousness of its absolute totality; and this is not possible by means of any empirical cognition. It follows that your question—your idea is by no means necessary for the explanation of any phenomenon; and the idea cannot have been in any sense given by the object itself. For such an object can never be presented to us, because it cannot be given by any possible experience. Whatever perceptions you may attain to, you are still surrounded by *conditions*—in space, or in time, and you cannot discover anything unconditioned; nor can you decide whether this unconditioned is to be placed in an absolute beginning of the synthesis, or in an absolute totality of the series without beginning. A whole, in the empirical signification of the term, is always merely comparative. The absolute whole of quantity (the universe), of division, of derivation, of the condition of existence, with the question—whether it is to be produced by a finite or infinite synthesis, no possible experience can instruct us concerning. You will not, for example, be able to explain the phenomena of a body in the least degree better, whether you believe it to consist of simple, or of composite parts; for a simple phenomenon—and just as little an infinite series of composition—can never be presented to your perception. Phenomena require and admit of explanation only in so far as the conditions of that explanation are given in perception; but the sum-total of that which is given in phenomena, considered as an absolute whole, is itself a perception—and we cannot therefore seek for explanations of this whole beyond itself, in other pereceptions. The explanation of this whole is the proper object of the transcendental problems of pure reason.

Although, therefore, the solution of these problems is unattainable through experience, we must not permit ourselves to say, that it is uncertain how the object of our inquiries is constituted. For the object is in our own mind, and cannot be discovered in experience; and we have only to take care that our thoughts are consistent with each other, and to avoid falling into the amphiboly of regarding our idea as a representation of an object empirically given, and therefore to be cognized according to the laws of experience. A dogmatical solution is therefore not only unsatisfactory, but impossible. The critical solution, which may be a perfectly certain one, does not consider the question objectively, but proceeds by inquiring into the basis of the cognition upon which the question rests.

Sec. V.—Sceptical Exposition of the Cosmological Problems presented in the four Transcendental Ideas

We should be quite willing to desist from the demand of a dogmatical answer to our questions, if we understood beforehand that, be the answer what it may, it would only serve to increase our ignorance, to throw us from one incomprehensibility into another, from one obscurity into another still greater, and perhaps lead us into irreconcilable contradictions. If a dogmatical affirmative or negative answer is demanded, is it at all prudent, to set aside the probable grounds of a solution which lie before us, and to take into consideration, what advantage we shall gain, if the answer is to favor the one side or the other? If it happens that in both cases the answer is mere nonsense, we have in this an irresistible summons, to institute a critical investigation of the question, for the purpose of discovering whether it is based on a groundless presupposition, and relates to an idea, the falsity of which would be more easily exposed in its application and consequences, than in the mere representation of its content. This is the great utility of the sceptical mode of treating the questions addressed by pure reason to itself. By this method we easily rid ourselves of the confusions of dogmatism, and establish in its place a temperate criticism, which, as a genuine cathartic, will successfully remove the presumptuous notions of philosophy and their consequence—the vain pretension to universal science.

If, then, I could understand the nature of a cosmological idea, and perceive, before I entered on the discussion of the subject at all, that, whatever side of the question regarding the unconditioned of the regressive synthesis of phenomena it favored, it must either be *too great* or *too small* for every *conception of the understanding;*—I would be able to comprehend how the idea, which relates to an object of experience—an experience which must be adequate to and in accordance with a possible conception of the understanding—must be completely void and without significance, inasmuch as its object is inadequate, consider it as we may. And this is actually the case with all cosmological conceptions, which, for the reason above mentioned, involve reason, so long as it remains attached to them, in an unavoidable antinomy. For suppose:

First, that *the world has no beginning*—in this case it is too large for our conception; for this conception, which consists in a successive regress, cannot overtake the whole eternity that has elapsed. Grant that *it has a beginning*, it is then too small for the conception of the undertaking. For, as a beginning presupposes a time preceding, it cannot be unconditioned; and the law of the empirical employment of the understanding imposes the necessity of looking for a higher condition of time; and the world is, therefore, evidently too small for this law.

The same is the case with the double answer to the question regarding the extent, in space, of the world. For, if it is *infinite* and unlimited, it must be *too large* for every possible empirical conception. If it is *finite* and limited, we have a right to ask —what determines these limits? Void space is not a self-subsistent correlate of things, and cannot be a final condition—and still less an empirical condition, forming a part of a possible experience. For how can we have any experience or perception of an absolute void? But the absolute totality of the empirical synthesis requires that the unconditioned be an empirical conception. Consequently, a finite world is *too small* for our conception.

Secondly, if every phenomenon (matter) in space consists of an *infinite number of parts*, the regress of the division is always too great for our conception; and if the *division* of space must *cease* with some member of the division (the simple) it is too small for the idea of the unconditioned. For the member at which we have discontinued our division still admits a regress to many more parts contained in the object.

Thirdly, suppose that every event in the world happens in accordance with the laws of nature; the causality of a cause must itself be an event, and necessitates a regress to a still higher cause, and consequently the unceasing prolongation of the series of conditions *a parte priori*. Operative nature is therefore too large for every conception we can form in the synthesis of cosmical events.

If we admit the existence of *spontaneously* produced events, that is, of *free* agency, we are driven, in our search for sufficient reasons, on an unavoidable law of nature, and are compelled to appeal to the empirical law of causality, and we find that any such totality of connection in our synthesis is too small for our necessary empirical conception.

Fourthly, if we assume the existence of an *absolutely neces-*

sary being—whether it be the world or something in the world, or the cause of the world; we must place it in a time at an infinite distance from any given moment; for, otherwise, it must be dependent on some other and higher existence. Such an existence is, in this case, too large for our empirical conception, and unattainable by the continued regress of any synthesis.

But if we believe that everything in the world—be it condition or conditioned—is *contingent;* every given existence is too small for our conception. For in this case we are compelled to seek for some other existence upon which the former depends.

We have said that in all these cases the cosmological idea is either too great or too small for the empirical regress in a synthesis, and consequently for every possible conception of the understanding. Why did we not express ourselves in a manner exactly the reverse of this, and, instead of accusing the cosmological idea of overstepping or of falling short of its true aim—possible experience, say that, in the first case, the empirical conception is always too small for the idea, and in the second too great, and thus attach the blame of these contradictions to the empirical regress? The reason is this: Possible experience can alone give reality to our conceptions; without it a conception is merely an idea, without truth or relation to an object. Hence a possible empirical conception must be the standard by which we are to judge whether an idea is anything more than an idea and fiction of thought, or whether it relates to an object in the world. If we say of a thing that in relation to some other thing it is too large or too small, the former is considered as existing for the sake of the latter, and requiring to be adapted to it. Among the trivial subjects of discussion in the old schools of dialectics was this question: If a ball cannot pass through a hole, shall we say that ball is too large or the hole too small? In this case it is indifferent what expression we employ; for we do not know which exists for the sake of the other. On the other hand, we cannot say—the man is too long for his coat, but—the coat is too short for the man.

We are thus led to the well-founded suspicion, that the cosmological ideas, and all the conflicting sophistical assertions connected with them, are based upon a false and fictitious conception of the mode in which the object of these ideas is presented to us; and this suspicion will probably direct us how to expose the illusion that has so long led us astray from the truth.

Sec. VI.—Transcendental Idealism as the Key to the Solution of Pure Cosmological Dialectic

In the transcendental æsthetic, we proved, that everything intuited in space and time—all objects of a possible experience, are nothing but phenomena, that is, mere representations; and that these, as presented to us—as extended bodies, or as series of changes—have no self-subsistent existence apart from human thought. This doctrine I call *Transcendental Idealism.** The realist in the transcendental sense regards these modifications of our sensibility—these mere representations, as things subsisting in themselves.

It would be unjust to accuse us of holding the long-decried theory of empirical idealism, which, while admitting the reality of space, denies, or at least doubts, the existence of bodies extended in it, and thus leaves us without a sufficient criterion of reality and illusion. The supporters of this theory find no difficulty in admitting the reality of the phenomena of the internal sense in time; nay, they go the length of maintaining that this internal experience is of itself a sufficient proof of the real existence of its object as a thing in itself.

Transcendental idealism allows that the objects of external intuition—as intuited in space, and all changes in time—as represented by the internal sense, are real. For, as space is the form of that intuition which we call external, and without objects in space, no empirical representation could be given us; we can and ought to regard extended bodies in it as real. The case is the same with representations in time. But time and space, with all phenomena therein, are not in themselves *things*. They are nothing but representations, and cannot exist out of and apart from the mind. Nay, the sensuous internal intuition of the mind (as the object of consciousness), the determination of which is represented by the succession of different states in time, is not the real, proper self, as it exists in itself—not the transcendental subject, but only a phenomenon, which is presented to the sensibility of this, to us, unknown being. This

---

* I have elsewhere termed this theory *formal* idealism, to distinguish it from *material* idealism, which doubts or denies the existence of external things. To avoid ambiguity, it seems advisable in many cases to employ this term instead of that mentioned in the text.

internal phenomenon cannot be admitted to be a self-subsisting thing; for its condition is time, and time cannot be the condition of a thing in itself. But the empirical truth of phenomena in space and time is guaranteed beyond the possibility of doubt, and sufficiently distinguished from the illusion of dreams or fancy—although both have a proper and thorough connection in an experience according to empirical laws. The objects of experience then are not things in themselves,* but are given only in experience, and have no existence apart from and independently of experience. That there may be inhabitants in the moon, although no one has ever observed them, must certainly be admitted; but this assertion means only, that we may in the possible progress of experience discover them at some future time. For that, which stands in connection with a perception according to the laws of the progress of experience, is real. They are therefore really existent, if they stand in empirical connection with my actual or real consciousness, although they are not in themselves real, that is, apart from the progress of experience.

There is nothing actually given—we can be conscious of nothing as real, except a perception and the empirical progression from it to other possible perceptions. For phenomena, as mere representations, are real only in perception; and perception is, in fact, nothing but the reality of an empirical representation, that is, a phenomenon. To call a phenomenon a real thing prior to perception, means either, that we must meet with this phenomenon in the progress of experience, or it means nothing at all. For I can say only of a thing in itself that it exists without relation to the senses and experience. But we are speaking here merely of phenomena in space and time, both of which are determinations of sensibility, and not of things in themselves. It follows that phenomena are not things in themselves, but are mere representations, which, if not given in us —in perception, are non-existent.

The faculty of sensuous intuition is properly a receptivity— a capacity of being affected in a certain manner by representations, the relation of which to each other is a pure intuition of space and time—the pure forms of sensibility. These representations, in so far as they are connected and determinable in this relation (in space and time) according to laws of the unity

* Dinge an sich, Sachen an sich.

of experience, are called *objects*. The non-sensuous cause of
these representations is completely unknown to us, and hence
cannot be intuited as an object. For such an object could not
be represented either in space or in time; and without these
conditions intuition or representation is impossible. We may,
at the same time, term the non-sensuous cause of phenomena
the transcendental object—but merely as a mental correlate to
sensibility, considered as a receptivity. To this transcendental
object we may attribute the whole connection and extent of our
possible perceptions, and say that it is given and exists in itself
prior to all experience. But the phenomena, corresponding to
it, are not given as things in themselves, but in experience alone.
For they are mere representations, receiving from perceptions
alone significance and relation to a real object, under the condition that this or that perception—indicating an object—is in
complete connection with all others in accordance with the rules
of the unity of experience. Thus we can say: the things that
really existed in past time, are given in the transcendental object
of experience. But these are to me real objects, only in so far
as I can represent to my own mind, that a regressive series of
possible perceptions—following the indications of history, or
the footsteps of cause and effect—in accordance with empirical
laws—that, in one word, the course of the world conducts us to
an elapsed series of time as the condition of the present time.
This series in past time is represented as real, not in itself, but
only in connection with a possible experience. Thus, when I
say that certain events occurred in past time, I merely assert
the possibility of prolonging the chain of experience, from the
present perception, upwards to the conditions that determine
it according to time.

If I represent to myself all objects existing in all space and
time, I do not thereby place these in space and time prior to
all experience; on the contrary, such a representation is nothing more than the notion of a possible experience, in its absolute
completeness. In experience alone are those objects, which are
nothing but representations, given. But, when I say, they existed prior to my experience; this means only that I must begin
with the perception present to me, and follow the track indicated, until I discover them in some part or region of experience. The cause of the empirical condition of this progression
—and consequently at what member therein I must stop, and

at what point in the regress I am to find this member—is transcendental, and hence necessarily incognizable. But with this we have not to do; our concern is only with the law of progression in experience, in which objects, that is, phenomena, are given. It is a matter of indifference, whether I say—I may in the progress of experience discover stars, at a hundred times greater distance than the most distant of those now visible, or —stars at this distance may be met in space, although no one has, or ever will discover them. For, if they are given as things in themselves, without any relation to possible experience; they are for me non-existent, consequently, are not objects, for they are not contained in the regressive series of experience. But, if these phenomena must be employed in the construction or support of the cosmological idea of an absolute whole—and, when we are discussing a question that oversteps the limits of possible experience; the proper distinction of the different theories of the reality of sensuous objects is of great importance, in order to avoid the illusion which must necessarily arise from the misinterpretation of our empirical conceptions.

Sec. VII.—Critical Solution of the Cosmological Problem

The antinomy of pure reason is based upon the following dialectical argument: If that which is conditioned is given, the whole series of its conditions is also given; but sensuous objects are given as conditioned; consequently. . . . This syllogism, the major of which seems so natural and evident, introduces as many cosmological ideas as there are different kinds of conditions in the synthesis of phenomena, in so far as these conditions constitute a series. These ideas require absolute totality in the series, and thus place reason in inextricable embarrassment. Before proceeding to expose the fallacy in this dialectical argument, it will be necessary to have a correct understanding of certain conceptions that appear in it.

In the first place, the following proposition is evident, and indubitably certain: If the conditioned is given, a regress in the series of all its conditions is thereby imperatively *required*. For the very conception of a conditioned, is a conception of something related to a condition, and, if this condition is itself conditioned, to another condition—and so on through all the members of the series. This proposition is, therefore, analytical, and has nothing to fear from transcendental criticism. It is a logical postulate of reason: to pursue, as far as possible, the connection of a conception with its conditions.

If, in the second place, both the conditioned and the condition are things in themselves, and if the former is given, not only is the regress to the latter requisite, but the latter is really *given with* the former. Now, as this is true of all the members of the series, the entire series of conditions, and with them the unconditioned is at the same time given in the very fact of the conditioned, the existence of which is possible only in and through that series, being given. In this case, the synthesis of the conditioned with its condition, is a synthesis of the understanding merely, which represents things *as they are,* without regarding whether and how we can cognize them. But if I have to do with phenomena, which, in their character of mere representations, are not given, if I do not attain to a cognition of them (in other words, to themselves, for they are nothing more than empirical cognitions), I am not entitled to say: If the conditioned is given, all its conditions (as phenomena) are also given. I cannot, therefore, from the fact of a conditioned being given, infer the absolute totality of the series of its conditions. For phenomena are nothing but an empirical synthesis in apprehension or perception, and are therefore given only in it. Now, in speaking of phenomena, it does not follow, that, if the conditioned is given, the synthesis which constitutes its empirical condition is also thereby given and presupposed; such a synthesis can be established only by an actual regress in the series of conditions. But we are entitled to say in this case: that a *regress* to the conditions of a conditioned, in other words, that a continuous empirical synthesis is enjoined; that, if the conditions are not *given,* they are at least *required;* and that we are certain to discover the conditions in this regress.

We can now see that the major in the above cosmological syllogism, takes the conditioned in the transcendental signification which it has in the pure category, while the minor speaks of it in the empirical signification which it has in the category as applied to phenomena. There is, therefore, a dialectical fallacy in the syllogism—a *sophisma figuræ dictionis.* But this fallacy is not a consciously devised one, but a perfectly natural illusion of the common reason of man. For, when a thing is given as conditioned, we presuppose in the major its conditions and their series, unperceived, as it were, and unseen; because this is nothing more than the logical requirement of complete and satisfactory premises for a given conclusion. In this case, time is altogether left out in the connection of the conditioned with the condition; they are supposed to be given in themselves, and *contemporaneously*. It is, moreover, just as natural to regard phenomena (in the minor) as things in themselves and as objects presented to the pure understanding, as in the major, in which complete abstraction was made of all conditions of intuition. But it is under these conditions alone that objects are given. Now we overlooked a remarkable distinction between the conceptions. The synthesis of the conditioned with its condition, and the complete series of the latter (in the major) are not limited by time, and do not contain the conception of succession. On the contrary, the empirical synthesis, and the series of conditions in the phenomenal world—subsumed in the minor—are necessarily successive, and given in time alone. It follows that I cannot presuppose in the minor, as I did in the major, the absolute *totality* of the synthesis and of the series therein represented; for in the major all the members of the series are given as things in themselves—without any limitations or conditions of time, while in the minor they are possible only in and through a successive regress, which cannot exist, except it be actually carried into execution in the world of phenomena.

After this proof of the viciousness of the argument commonly employed in maintaining cosmological assertions, both parties may now be justly dismissed, as advancing claims without grounds or title. But the process has not been ended, by convincing them that one or both were in the wrong, and had maintained an assertion which was without valid grounds of proof. Nothing seems to be clearer than that, if one maintains: the world has a beginning, and another: the world has no beginning, one of the two must be right. But it is likewise clear, that, if the evidence on both sides is equal, it is impossible to discover on what side the truth lies; and the controversy continues, although the parties have been recommended to peace before the tribunal of reason. There remains, then, no other means of settling the question than to convince the parties, who refute each other with such conclusiveness and ability, that they are disputing about nothing, and that a transcendental illusion has been mocking them with visions of reality where there is none. This mode of adjusting a dispute which cannot be decided upon its own merits, we shall now proceed to lay before our readers.

Zeno of Elea, a subtle dialectician, was severely reprimanded by Plato as a sophist, who, merely from the base motive of exhibiting his skill in discussion, maintained and subverted the same proposition by arguments as powerful and convincing on the one side as on the other. He maintained, for example, that God (who was probably nothing more, in his view, than the world) is neither finite nor infinite, neither in motion nor in rest, neither similar nor dissimilar to any other thing. It seemed to those philosophers who criticised his mode of discussion, that his purpose was to deny completely both of two self-contradictory propositions—which is absurd. But I cannot believe that there is any justice in this accusation. The first of these propositions I shall presently consider in a more detailed manner. With regard to the others, if by the word *God* he understood merely the *Universe,* his meaning must have been, that it cannot be permanently present in one place—that is, at rest, nor be capable of changing its place—that is, of moving, because all places are in the universe, and the universe itself is, therefore, in no place. Again, if the universe contains in itself everything that exists, it cannot be similar or dissimilar to any *other* thing, because there is, in fact, no *other* thing with which it can be compared. If two opposite judgments presuppose a contingent impossible, or arbitrary condition, both—in spite of their opposition (which is, however, not properly or really a contradiction)—fall away; because the condition, which insured the validity of both, has itself disappeared.

If we say: everybody has either a good or a bad smell, we have omitted a third possible judgment—it has no smell at all; and thus both conflicting statements may be false. If we say: it is either good-smelling or not good-smelling (*vel suaveolens vel non-suaveolens*), both judgments are contradictorily opposed; and the contradictory opposite of the former judgment —some bodies are not good-smelling—embraces also those bodies which have no smell at all. In the preceding pair of opposed judgments (*per disparata*), the contingent condition of the conception of body (smell) attached to both conflicting statements, instead of having been omitted in the latter, which is consequently not the contradictory opposite of the former.

If, accordingly, we say: the world is either infinite in extension, or it is not infinite (*non est infinitus*); and if the former proposition is false, its contradictory opposite—the world is not infinite, must be true. And thus I should deny the existence of an infinite, without, however, affirming the existence of a finite world. But if we construct our proposition thus—the world is either infinite or finite (non-infinite), both statements may be false. For, in this case, we consider the world as *per se* determined in regard to quantity, and while, in the one judgment, we deny its infinite and consequently, perhaps, its independent existence; in the other, we append to the world, regarded as a thing in itself, a certain determination—that of finitude; and the latter may be false as well as the former, if the world is not given as a *thing in itself*, and thus neither as finite nor as infinite in quantity. This kind of opposition I may be allowed to term *dialectical;* that of contradictories may be called *analytical opposition.* Thus then, of two dialectically opposed judgments both may be false, from the fact, that the one is not a mere contradictory of the other, but actually enounces more than is requisite for a full and complete contradiction.

When we regard the two propositions—the world is infinite in quantity, and, the world is finite in quantity, as contradictory opposites, we are assuming that the world—the complete series of phenomena—is a thing in itself. For it remains as a permanent quantity, whether I deny the infinite or the finite regress in the series of its phenomena. But if we dismiss this assumption—this transcendental illusion, and deny that it is a thing in itself, the contradictory opposition is metamorphosed into a merely dialectical one; and the world, as not existing in itself —independently of the regressive series of my representations, exists in like manner neither as a whole which is infinite nor as a whole which is finite in itself. The universe exists for me only in the empirical regress of the series of phenomena, and not *per se*. If, then, it is always conditioned, it is never given completely or as a whole; and it is, therefore, not an unconditioned whole, and does not exist as such, either with an infinite, or with a finite quantity.

What we have here said of the first cosmological idea—that of the absolute totality of quantity in phenomena, applies also to the others. The series of conditions is discoverable only in the regressive synthesis itself, and not in the phenomenon considered as a thing in itself—given prior to all regress. Hence I am compelled to say: the aggregate of parts in a given phenomenon is in itself neither finite nor infinite; and these parts are given only in the regressive synthesis of decomposition— a synthesis which is never given in absolute *completeness,* either as finite, or as infinite. The same is the case with the series of subordinated causes, or of the conditioned up to the unconditioned and necessary existence, which can never be regarded as in itself, and in its totality, either as finite or as infinite; because, as a series of subordinate representations, it subsists only in the dynamical regress, and cannot be regarded as existing previously to this regress, or as a self-subsistent series of things.

Thus the antinomy of pure reason in its cosmological ideas disappears. For the above demonstration has established the fact that it is merely the product of a dialectical and illusory opposition, which arises from the application of the idea of absolute totality—admissible only as a condition of things in themselves, to phenomena, which exist only in our representations, and—when constituting a series—in a successive regress. This antinomy of reason may, however, be really profitable to our speculative interests, not in the way of contributing any dogmatical addition, but as presenting to us another material support in our critical investigations. For it furnishes us with an indirect proof of the transcendental ideality of phenomena, if our minds were not completely satisfied with the direct proof set forth in the Transcendental Æsthetic. The proof would proceed in the following dilemma. If the world is a whole existing in itself, it must be either finite or infinite. But it is neither finite nor infinite—as has been shown, on the one side, by the thesis, on the other, by the antithesis. Therefore the world—the content of all phenomena—is not a whole existing in itself. It follows that phenomena are nothing, apart from our representations. And this is what we mean by transcendental ideality.

This remark is of some importance. It enables us to see that the proofs of the fourfold antinomy are not mere sophistries— are not fallacious, but grounded on the nature of reason, and valid—under the supposition that phenomena are things in themselves. The opposition of the judgments which follow make it evident that a fallacy lay in the initial supposition, and thus helps us to discover the true constitution of objects of sense. This transcendental dialectic does not favor scepticism, although it presents us with a triumphant demonstration of the advantages of the sceptical method, the great utility of which is apparent in the antinomy, where the arguments of reason were allowed to confront each other in undiminished force. And although the result of these conflicts of reason is not what we expected—although we have obtained no positive dogmatical addition to metaphysical science, we have still reaped a great advantage in the correction of our judgments on these subjects of thought.

Sec. VIII.—Regulative Principle of Pure Reason in relation to the Cosmological Ideas

The cosmological principle of totality could not give us any certain knowledge in regard to the *maximum* in the series of conditions in the world of sense, considered as a thing in itself. The actual regress in the series is the only means of approaching this maximum. This principle of pure reason, therefore, may still be considered as valid—not as an *axiom* enabling us to cogitate totality in the object as actual, but as a *problem* for the understanding, which requires it to institute and to continue, in conformity with the idea of totality in the mind, the regress in the series of the conditions of a given conditioned. For in the world of sense, that is, in space and time, every condition which we discover in our investigation of phenomena is itself conditioned; because sensuous objects are not things in themselves (in which case an absolutely unconditioned might be reached in the progress of cognition), but are merely empirical representations, the conditions of which must always be found in intuition. The principle of reason is therefore properly a mere rule—prescribing a regress in the series of conditions for given phenomena, and prohibiting any pause or rest on an absolutely unconditioned. It is, therefore, not a principle of the possibility of experience or of the empirical cognition of sensuous objects—consequently not a principle of the understanding; for every experience is confined within certain proper limits determined by the given intuition. Still less is it a *constitutive principle* of reason authorizing us to extend our conception of the sensuous world beyond all possible experience. It is merely a principle for the enlargement and extension of experience as far as is possible for human faculties. It forbids us to consider any empirical limits as absolute. It is, hence, a principle of reason, which, as a *rule,* dictates how we ought to proceed in our empirical regress, but is unable to *anticipate* or indicate prior to the empirical regress what is given in the object itself. I have termed it for this reason a *regulative* principle of reason; while the principle of the absolute totality of the series of conditions, as existing in itself and given in the object, is a constitutive cosmological principle. This distinction will at once demonstrate the falsehood of the constitutive principle, and prevent us from attributing (by a transcendental *subreptio*) objective reality to an idea, which is valid only as a rule.

In order to understand the proper meaning of this rule of pure reason, we must notice first, that it cannot tell us *what the object is,* but only *how the empirical regress is to be proceeded with* in order to attain to the complete conception of the object. If it gave us any information in respect to the former statement, it would be a constitutive principle—a principle impossible from the nature of pure reason. It will not therefore enable us to establish any such conclusions as—the series of conditions for a given conditioned is in itself finite, or, it is infinite. For, in this case, we should be cogitating in the mere idea of absolute totality, an object which is not and cannot be given in experience; inasmuch as we should be attributing a reality objective and independent of the empirical synthesis, to a series of phenomena. This idea of reason cannot then be regarded as valid—except as a rule for the regressive synthesis in the series of conditions, according to which we must proceed from the conditioned, through all intermediate and subordinate conditions, up to the unconditioned; although this goal is unattained and unattainable. For the absolutely unconditioned cannot be discovered in the sphere of experience.

We now proceed to determine clearly our notion of a synthesis which can never be complete. There are two terms commonly employed for this purpose. These terms are regarded as expressions of different and distinguishable notions, although the ground of the distinction has never been clearly exposed. The term employed by the mathematicians, is *progressus in infinitum.* The philosophers prefer the expression *progressus in indefinitum.* Without detaining the reader with an examination of the reasons for such a distinction, or with remarks on the right or wrong use of the terms, I shall endeavor clearly to determine these conceptions, so far as is necessary for the purpose of this Critique.

We may, with propriety, say of a straight line, that it may be produced to infinity. In this case the distinction between a *progressus in infinitum* and a *progressus in indefinitum* is a mere piece of subtlety. For, although when we say, produce a straight line—it is more correct to say *in indefinitum* than *in infinitum;* because the former means, produce it as far as you *please,* the second, you *must* not cease to produce it; the expression *in infinitum* is, when we are speaking of the *power* to do it, perfectly correct, for we can always make it longer if we please—on to infinity. And this remark holds good in all cases, when we speak of a *progressus,* that is, an advancement from the condition to the conditioned; this possible advancement always proceeds to infinity. We may proceed from a given pair in the descending line of generation from father to son, and cogitate a never-ending line of descendants from it. For in such a case reason does not demand absolute totality in the series, because it does not presuppose it as a condition and as given (*datum*), but merely as conditioned, and as capable of being given (*dabile*).

Very different is the case with the problem—how far the regress, which ascends from the given conditioned to the conditions, must extend; whether I can say—it is a *regress in infinitum,* or only *in indefinitum;* and whether, for example, setting out from the human beings at present alive in the world, I may ascend in the series of their ancestors, *in infinitum*—or whether all that can be said is, that so far as I have proceeded, I have discovered no empirical ground for considering the series limited, so that I am justified, and indeed, compelled to search for ancestors still further back, although I am not obliged by the idea of reason to presuppose them.

My answer to this question is: If the series is given in empirical intuition as a whole, the regress in the series of its internal conditions proceeds *in infinitum;* but, if only one member of the series is given, from which the regress is to proceed to absolute totality, the regress is possible only *in indefinitum.* For example, the division of a portion of matter given within certain limits—of a body, that is—proceeds *in infinitum.* For,

as the condition of this whole is its part, and the condition of
the part a part of the part, and so on, and as in this regress
of decomposition an unconditioned indivisible member of the
series of conditions is not to be found; there are no reasons or
grounds in experience for stopping in the division, but, on the
contrary, the more remote members of the division are actually
and empirically given prior to this division. That is to say, the
division proceeds to infinity. On the other hand, the series of
ancestors of any given human being is not given, in its absolute
totality, in any experience; and yet the regress proceeds from
every genealogical member of this series to one still higher,
and does not meet with any empirical limit presenting an absolutely unconditioned member of the series. But as the members of such a series are not contained in the empirical intuition
of the whole, prior to the regress, this regress does not proceed
to infinity, but only *in indefinitum*, that is, we are called upon
to discover other and higher members, which are themselves
always conditioned.

In neither case—the *regressus in infinitum*, nor the *regressus
in indefinitum*, is the series of conditions to be considered as
actually infinite in the object itself. This might be true of
things in themselves, but it cannot be asserted of phenomena,
which, as conditions of each other, are only given in the empirical regress itself. Hence, the question no longer is, What
is the quantity of this series of conditions in itself—is it finite
or infinite? for it is nothing in itself; but, How is the empirical
regress to be commenced, and how far ought we to proceed
with it? And here a signal distinction in the application of this
rule becomes apparent. If the whole is given empirically, it is
possible to recede in the series of its internal conditions *to infinity*. But if the whole is not given, and can only be given by
and through the empirical regress, I can only say—it is *possible
to infinity*, to proceed to still higher conditions in the series.
In the first case I am justified in asserting that more members
are empirically given in the object than I attain to in the regress
(of decomposition). In the second case, I am justified only in
saying, that I can always proceed further in the regress, because no member of the series is given as absolutely conditioned,
and thus a higher member is possible, and an inquiry with regard to it is necessary. In the one case it is necessary to *find*
other members of the series, in the other it is necessary to *in-*

quire for others, inasmuch as experience presents no absolute limitation of the regress. For, either you do not possess a perception which absolutely limits your empirical regress, and in this case the regress cannot be regarded as complete; or, you do possess such a limitative perception, in which case it is not a part of your series (for that which *limits* must be distinct from that which is *limited* by it), and it is incumbent on you to continue your regress up to this condition, and so on.

These remarks will be placed in their proper light by their application in the following section.

Sec. IX.—Of the Empirical Use of the Regulative Principle of Reason with Regard to the Cosmological Ideas

We have shown that no transcendental use can be made either of the conceptions of reason or of understanding. We have shown, likewise, that the demand of absolute totality in the series of conditions in the world of sense arises from a transcendental employment of reason, resting on the opinion that phenomena are to be regarded as things in themselves. It follows that we are not required to answer the question respecting the absolute quantity of a series—whether it is *in itself* limited or unlimited. We are only called upon to determine how far we must proceed in the empirical regress from condition to condition, in order to discover, in conformity with the rule of reason, a full and correct answer to the questions proposed by reason itself.

This principle of reason is hence valid only as a rule for the *extension* of a possible experience—its invalidity as a principle constitutive of phenomena in themselves having been sufficiently demonstrated. And thus, too, the antinomial conflict of reason with itself is completely put an end to; inasmuch as we have not only presented a critical solution of the fallacy lurking in the opposite statements of reason, but have shown the true meaning of the ideas which gave rise to these statements. The *dialectical* principle of reason has, therefore, been changed into a *doctrinal* principle. But in fact, if this principle, in the subjective signification which we have shown to be its only true sense, may be guaranteed as a principle of the unceasing extension of the employment of our understanding, its influence and value are just as great as if it were an axiom for the *à priori* determination of objects. For such an axiom could not exert a stronger influence on the extension and rectification of our knowledge, otherwise than by procuring for the principles of the understanding the most widely expanded employment in the field of experience.

I.—SOLUTION OF THE COSMOLOGICAL IDEA OF THE TOTALITY OF THE COMPOSITION OF PHENOMENA IN THE UNIVERSE

Here, as well as in the case of the other cosmological problems, the ground of the regulative principle of reason is the proposition, that in our empirical regress *no experience of an absolute limit*, and consequently no experience of a condition, which is itself *absolutely unconditioned*, is discoverable. And the truth of this proposition itself rests upon the consideration, that such an experience must represent to us phenomena as limited by nothing or the mere void, on which our continued regress by means of perception must abut—which is impossible.

Now this proposition, which declares that every condition attained in the empirical regress must itself be considered empirically conditioned, contains the rule *in terminis*, which requires me, to whatever extent I may have proceeded in the ascending series, always to look for some higher member in the series—whether this member is to become known to me through experience, or not.

Nothing further is necessary, then, for the solution of the first cosmological problem, than to decide whether, in the regress to the unconditioned quantity of the universe (as regards space and time), this never limited ascent ought to be called a *regressus in infinitum* or *in indefinitum*.

The general representation which we form in our minds of the series of all past states or conditions of the world, or of all the things which at present exist in it, is itself nothing more than a *possible* empirical regress, which is cogitated—although in an undetermined manner—in the mind, and which gives rise to the conception of a series of conditions for a given object.* Now I have a conception of the universe, but not an intuition—that is, not an intuition of it as a whole. Thus I cannot infer the magnitude of the regress from the quantity or magnitude of the world,

---

* The cosmical series can neither be greater nor smaller than the possible empirical regress, upon which its conception is based. And as this regress cannot be a determinate infinite regress, still less a determinate finite (absolutely limited), it is evident that we cannot regard the world as either finite or infinite, because the regress, which gives us the representation of the world, is neither finite nor infinite.

and determine the former by means of the latter; on the contrary, I must first of all form a conception of the quantity or magnitude of the world from the magnitude of the empirical regress. But of this regress I know nothing more, than that I ought to proceed from every given member of the series of conditions to one still higher. But the quantity of the universe is not thereby determined, and we cannot affirm that this regress proceeds *in infinitum*. Such an affirmation would *anticipate* the members of the series which have not yet been reached, and represent the number of them as beyond the grasp of any empirical synthesis; it would consequently *determine* the cosmical quantity prior to the regress (although only in a negative manner)—which is impossible. For the world is not given in its totality in any intuition: consequently, its quantity cannot be given prior to the regress. It follows that we are unable to make any declaration respecting the cosmical quantity in itself—not even that the regress in it is a regress *in infinitum;* we must only endeavor to attain to a conception of the quantity of the universe, in conformity with the rule which determines the empirical regress in it. But this rule merely requires us never to admit an absolute limit to our series—how far soever we may have proceeded in it, but always, on the contrary, to subordinate every phenomenon to some other as its condition, and consequently to proceed to this higher phenomenon. Such a regress is, therefore, the *regressus in indefinitum*, which, as not determining a quantity in the object, is clearly distinguishable from the *regressus in infinitum.*

It follows from what we have said that we are not justified in declaring the world to be infinite in space, or as regards past time. For this conception of an infinite given quantity is empirical; but we cannot apply the conception of an infinite quantity to the world as an object of the senses. I cannot say, the regress from a given perception to every thing limited either in space or time, proceeds *in infinitum*—for this presupposes an infinite cosmical quantity; neither can I say, it is *finite*—for an absolute limit is likewise impossible in experience. It follows that I am not entitled to make any assertion at all respecting the whole object of experience—the world of sense; I must limit my declarations to the rule, according to which experience or empirical knowledge is to be attained.

To the question, therefore, respecting the cosmical quantity, the first and negative answer is: The world has no beginning in time, and no absolute limit in space.

For, in the contrary case, it would be limited by a void time on the one hand, and by a void space on the other. Now, since the world, as a phenomenon, cannot be thus limited in itself—for a phenomenon is not a thing in itself; it must be possible for us to have a perception of this limitation by a void time and a void space. But such a perception—such an experience is impossible; because it has no content. Consequently, an absolute cosmical limit is empirically, and therefore absolutely, impossible.*

From this follows the *affirmative* answer: The regress in the series of phenomena—as a determination of the cosmical quantity, proceeds *in indefinitum.* This is equivalent to saying—the world of sense has no absolute quantity, but the empirical regress (through which alone the world of sense is presented to us on the side of its conditions) rests upon a rule, which requires it to proceed from every member of the series—as conditioned to one still more remote (whether through personal experience, or by means of history, or the chain of cause and effect), and not to cease at any point in this extension of the possible empirical employment of the understanding. And this is the proper and only use which reason can make of its principles.

The above rule does not prescribe an unceasing regress in one kind of phenomena. It does not, for example, forbid us, in our ascent from an individual human being through the line of his ancestors, to expect that we shall discover at some point of the regress a primeval pair, or to admit, in the series of heavenly bodies, a sun at the farthest possible distance from some centre. All that it demands is a perpetual progress from phenomena to phenomena, even although an actual perception is not presented by them (as in the case of our perceptions being so weak, as that we are unable to become conscious of them), since they, nevertheless, belong to possible experience.

Every beginning is in time, and all limits to extension are in space. But space and time are in the world of sense. Consequently phenomena *in the world* are conditionally limited, but

---

* The reader will remark that the proof presented above is very different from the dogmatical demonstration given in the antithesis of the first antinomy. In that demonstration, it was taken for granted that the world is a thing in itself—given in its totality prior to all regress, and a determined position in space and time was denied to it—if it was not considered as occupying all time and all space. Hence our conclusion differed from that given above; for we inferred in the antithesis the actual infinity of the world.

the world itself is not limited, either conditionally or unconditionally.

For this reason, and because neither the world nor the cosmical series of conditions to a given conditioned can be *completely given,* our conception of the cosmical quantity is given only in and through the regress and not prior to it—in a collective intuition. But the regress itself is really nothing more than the *determining* of the cosmical quantity, and cannot therefore give us any *determined* conception of it—still less a conception of a quantity which is, in relation to a certain standard, infinite. The regress does not, therefore, proceed to infinity (an infinity given), but only to an indefinite extent, for the purpose of presenting to us a quantity—realized only in and through the regress itself.

II.—SOLUTION OF THE COSMOLOGICAL IDEA OF THE TOTALITY OF THE DIVISION OF A WHOLE GIVEN IN INTUITION

When I divide a whole which is given in intuition, I proceed from a conditioned to its conditions. The divison of the parts of the whole (*subdivisio* or *decompositio*) is a regress in the series of these conditions. The absolute totality of this series would be actually attained and given to the mind, if the regress could arrive at *simple* parts. But if all the parts in a continuous decomposition are themselves divisible, the division, that is to say, the regress, proceeds from the conditioned to its conditions *in infinitum;* because the conditions (the parts) are themselves contained in the conditioned, and, as the latter is given in a limited intuition, the former are all given along with it. This regress cannot, therefore, be called a *regressus in indefinitum,* as happened in the case of the preceding cosmological idea, the regress in which proceeded from the conditioned to the conditions not given contemporaneously and along with it, but discoverable only through the empirical regress. We are not, however, entitled to affirm of a whole of this kind, which is divisible *in infinitum,* that *it consists of an infinite number of parts.* For, although all the parts are contained in the intuition of the whole, the *whole division* is not contained therein. The division is contained only in the progressing decomposition—in the regress itself, which is the condition of the possibility and actuality of the series. Now, as this regress is infinite, all the members (parts) to which it attains must be contained in the given whole as an *aggregate.* But the complete *series of division* is not contained therein. For this series, being infinite in succession and always incomplete, cannot represent an infinite number of members, and still less a composition of these members into a whole.

To apply this remark to space. Every limited part of space presented to intuition is a whole, the parts of which are always spaces—to whatever extent subdivided. Every limited space is hence divisible to infinity.

Let us again apply the remark to an external phenomenon enclosed in limits, that is a body. The divisibility of a body rests upon the divisibility of space, which is the condition of the possibility of the body as an extended whole. A body is consequently divisible to infinity, though it does not, for that reason, consist of an infinite number of parts.

It certainly seems that, as a body must be cogitated as substance in space, the law of divisibility would not be applicable to it as substance. For we may and ought to grant, in the case of space, that division or decomposition, to any extent, never can utterly annihilate composition (that is to say, the smallest part of space must still consist of spaces); otherwise space would entirely cease to exist—which is impossible. But, the assertion on the other hand, that when all composition in matter is annihilated in thought, nothing remains, does not seem to harmonize with the conception of substance, which must be properly the subject of all composition and must remain, even after the conjunction of its attributes in space—which constituted a body— is annihilated in thought. But this is not the case with substance in the phenomenal world, which is not a thing in itself cogitated by the pure category. Phenomenal substance is not an absolute subject; it is merely a permanent sensuous image, and nothing more than an intuition, in which the unconditioned is not to be found.

But, although this rule of progress to infinity is legitimate and applicable to the subdivision of a phenomenon, as a mere occupation or filling of space, it is not applicable to a whole consisting of a number of distinct parts and constituting a *quantum discretum*—that is to say, an organized body. It cannot be admitted that every part in an organized whole is itself organized, and that, in analyzing it to infinity, we must always meet with organized parts; although we may allow that the parts of the matter which we decompose *in infinitum* may be organized.

For the infinity of the division of a phenomenon in space rests altogether on the fact that the divisibility of a phenomenon is given only in and through this infinity, that is an undetermined number of parts is given, while the parts themselves are given and determined only in and through the subdivision; in a word, the infinity of the division necessarily presupposes that the whole is not already divided *in se*. Hence our division determines a number of parts in the whole—a number which extends just as far as the actual regress in the division; while, on the other hand, the very notion of a body organized to infinity represents the whole as already and in itself divided. We expect, therefore, to find in it a determinate, but, at the same time, infinite, number of parts—which is self-contradictory. For we should thus have a whole containing a series of members which could not be completed in any regress—which is infinite, and at the same time complete in an organized composite. Infinite divisibility is applicable only to a *quantum continuum,* and is based entirely on the infinite divisibility of space. But in a *quantum discretum* the multitude of parts or units is always determined, and hence always equal to some number. To what extent a body may be organized, experience alone can inform us; and although, so far as our experience of this or that body has extended, we may not have discovered any inorganic part, such parts must exist in possible experience. But how far the transcendental division of a phenomenon must extend, we cannot know from experience—it is a question which experience cannot answer; it is answered only by the principle of reason which forbids us to consider the empirical regress, in the analysis of extended body, as ever absolutely complete.

Concluding Remark on the Solution of the Transcendental Mathematical Ideas—and Introductory to the Solution of the Dynamical Ideas

We presented the antinomy of pure reason in a tabular form, and we endeavored to show the ground of this self-contradiction on the part of reason, and the only means of bringing it to a conclusion—namely, by declaring both contradictory statements to be false. We represented in these antinomies the conditions of phenomena as belonging to the conditioned according to relations of space and time—which is the usual supposition of the common understanding. In this respect, all dialectical represen-

tations of totality, in the series of conditions to a given conditioned, were perfectly *homogeneous*. The condition was always a member of the series along with the conditioned, and
thus the homogeneity of the whole series was assured. In this
case the regress could never be cogitated as complete; or, if this
was the case, a member really conditioned was falsely regarded
as a primal member, consequently as unconditioned. In such
an antinomy, therefore, we did not consider the object, that is,
the conditioned, but the series of conditions belonging to the
object, and the magnitude of that series. And thus arose the
difficulty—a difficulty not to be settled by any decision regarding
the claims of the two parties, but simply by cutting the knot—
by declaring the series proposed by reason to be either *too long*
or *too short* for the understanding, which could in neither case
make its conceptions adequate with the ideas.

But we have overlooked, up to this point, an essential difference existing between the conceptions of the understanding
which reason endeavors to raise to the rank of ideas—two of
these indicating a *mathematical,* and two a *dynamical* synthesis
of phenomena. Hitherto, it was not necessary to signalize this
distinction; for, just as in our general representation of all
transcendental ideas, we considered them under phenomenal
conditions, so, in the two mathematical ideas, our discussion is
concerned solely with an object in the world of phenomena. But
as we are now about to proceed to the consideration of the *dynamical* conceptions of the understanding, and their adequateness
with ideas, we must not lose sight of this distinction. We shall
find that it opens up to us an entirely new view of the conflict in
which reason is involved. For, while in the first two antinomies,
both parties were *dismissed,* on the ground of having advanced
statements based upon false hypotheses; in the present case the
hope appears of discovering a hypothesis which may be consistent with the demands of reason, and, the judge completing the
statement of the grounds of claim, which both parties had left in
an unsatisfactory state, the question may be settled on its own
merits, not by dismissing the claimants, but by a *comparison* of
the arguments on both sides.—If we consider merely their *extension,* and whether they are adequate with ideas, the series of
conditions may be regarded as all homogeneous. But the conception of the understanding which lies at the basis of these
ideas, contains either a *synthesis of the homogeneous* (presup-

posed in every quantity—in its composition as well as in its division) or of the *heterogeneous,* which is the case in the dynamical synthesis of cause and effect, as well as of the necessary and the contingent.

Thus it happens, that in the mathematical series of phenomena no other than a *sensuous* condition is admissible—a condition which is itself a member of the series; while the dynamical series of sensuous conditions admits a heterogeneous condition, which is not a member of the series, but, as purely *intelligible,* lies out of and beyond it. And thus reason is satisfied, and an unconditioned placed at the head of the series of phenomena, without introducing confusion into or discontinuing it, contrary to the principles of the understanding.

Now, from the fact that the dynamical ideas admit a condition of phenomena which does not form a part of the series of phenomena, arises a result which we should not have expected from an antinomy. In former cases, the result was that both contradictory dialectical statements were declared to be false. In the present case, we find the conditioned in the dynamical series connected with an empirically unconditioned, but *non-sensuous* condition; and thus satisfaction is done to the *understanding* on the one hand and to the *reason* on the other.* While, moreover, the dialectical arguments for unconditioned totality in mere phenomena fall to the ground, *both* propositions of reason·may be shown to be true in their proper signification. This could not happen in the case of the cosmological ideas which demanded a mathematically unconditioned unity; for no condition could be placed at the head of the series of phenomena, except one which was itself a phenomenon, and consequently a member of the series.

III.—SOLUTION OF THE COSMOLOGICAL IDEA OF THE TOTALITY OF THE DEDUCTION OF COSMICAL EVENTS FROM THEIR CAUSES

There are only two modes of causality cogitable—the causality of *nature,* or of *freedom.* The first is the conjunction of a particular state with another preceding it in the world of sense, the former following the latter by virtue of a law. Now, as the causality of phenomena is subject to conditions of time, and the

---

* For the understanding canno⁺ admit among *phenomena* a condition which is itself empirically unconditioned. But if it is possible to cogitate an *intelligible* condition—one which is not a member of the series ot phenomena—for a condi-tioned phenomenon, without breaking the series of empirical conditions, such a condition may be admissible as *empirically unconditioned,* and the empirical regress continue regular, unceasing, and intact.

preceding state, if it had always existed, could not have produced an effect which would make its first appearance at a particular time, the causality of a cause must itself be an effect—must itself have *begun to be,* and therefore, according to the principle of the understanding, itself requires a cause.

We must understand, on the contrary, by the term freedom, in the cosmological sense, a faculty of the *spontaneous* origination of a state; the causality of which, therefore, is not subordinated to another cause determining it in time. Freedom is in this sense a pure transcendental idea, which, in the first place, contains no empirical element; the object of which, in the second place, cannot be given or determined in any experience, because it is a universal law of the very possibility of experience, that everything which happens must have a cause, that consequently the causality of a cause, being itself something that has *happened,* must also have a cause. In this view of the case, the whole field of experience, how far soever it may extend, contains nothing that is not subject to the laws of nature. But, as we cannot by this means attain to an absolute totality of conditions in reference to the series of causes and effects, reason creates the idea of a spontaneity, which can begin to act of itself, and without any external cause determining it to action, according to the natural law of causality.

It is especially remarkable that the practical conception of freedom is based upon the *transcendental idea,* and that the question of the possibility of the former is difficult only as it involves the consideration of the truth of the latter. Freedom, in the *practical sense,* is the independence of the will of *coercion* by sensuous impulses. A will is *sensuous,* in so far as it is *pathologically affected* (by sensuous impulses); it is termed *animal* (*arbitrium brutum*), when it is *pathologically necessitated.* The human will is certainly an *arbitrium sensitivum,* not *brutum,* but *liberum;* because sensuousness does not necessitate its action, a faculty existing in man of self-determination, independently of all sensuous coercion.

It is plain, that, if all causality in the world of sense were natural—and natural only, every event would be determined by another according to necessary laws, and that consequently, phenomena, in so far as they determine the will, must necessitate every action as a natural effect from themselves; and thus all practical freedom would fall to the ground with the transcendental idea. For the latter presupposes that, although a certain thing has not happened, it *ought* to have happened, and that, consequently, its phenomenal cause was not so powerful and determinative as to exclude the causality of our will—a causality capable of producing effects independently of and even in opposition to the power of natural causes, and capable, consequently, of *spontaneously* originating a series of events.

Here, too, we find it to be the case, as we generally found in the self-contradictions and perplexities of a reason which strives to pass the bounds of possible experience, that the problem is properly not *physiological,** but *transcendental.* The question of the possibility of freedom does indeed concern psychology; but, as it rests upon dialectical arguments of pure reason, its solution must engage the attention of transcendental philosophy. Before attempting this solution, a task which transcendental philosophy cannot decline, it will be advisable to make a remark with regard to its procedure in the settlement of the question.

If phenomena were things in themselves, and time and space forms of the existence of things, condition and conditioned would always be members of the same series; and thus would arise in the present case the antinomy common to all transcendental ideas—that their series is either too great or too small for the understanding. The dynamical ideas, which we are about to discuss in this and the following section, possess the peculiarity of relating to an object, not considered as a quantity, but as an *existence;* and thus, in the discussion of the present question, we may make abstraction of the quantity of the series of conditions, and consider merely the dynamical relation of the condition to the conditioned. The question, then, suggests itself, whether freedom is possible; and, if it is, whether it can consist with the universality of the natural law of causality; and, consequently, whether we enounce a proper disjunctive proposition when we say—every effect must have its origin either in nature or in freedom, or whether *both* cannot exist together in the same event in different relations. The principle of an unbroken connection between all events in the phenomenal world, in accordance with the unchangeable laws of nature, is a well-established principle of transcendental analytic which admits of no exception. The question, therefore, is: Whether an effect, determined according to the laws of nature, can at the same time be produced by a free agent, or whether freedom and nature mutually exclude each other? And here, the common, but fallacious hypothesis of the *absolute reality* of phenomena manifests its injurious influence in embarrassing the procedure of reason. For if phenomena are things in themselves, freedom is impossible. In this case, nature is the complete and all-sufficient cause of every event; and condition and conditioned, cause and effect, are contained in the same series, and necessitated by the same law. If, on the contrary, phenomena are held to be, as they are in fact, nothing more than mere representations, connected with each other in accordance with empirical laws, they must have a ground which is *not* phenomena! But the causality of such an intelligible cause is not determined or determinable by phenomena; although its effects, as phenomena, must be determined by other phenomenal existences. This cause and its causality exist therefore out of and apart from the series of phenomena; while its effects do exist and are discoverable in the series of empirical conditions. Such an effect may therefore be considered to be free in relation to its intelligible cause, and necessary in relation to the phenomena from which it is a necessary consequence—a distinction which, stated in this perfectly general and abstract manner, must appear in the highest degree subtle and obscure. The sequel will explain. It is sufficient, at present, to remark that, as the complete and unbroken connection of phenomena is an unalterable law of nature, freedom is impossible—on the supposition that phenomena are absolutely real. Hence those philosophers who adhere to the common opinion on this subject can never succeed in reconciling the ideas of nature and freedom.

Possibility of Freedom in harmony with the Universal Law of Natural Necessity

That element in a sensuous object which is not itself sensuous, I may be allowed to term *intelligible*. If, accordingly, an object which must be regarded as a sensuous phenomenon possesses a faculty which is not an object of sensuous intuition, but by means of which it is capable of being the cause of phenomena, the *causality* of an object or existence of this kind may be regarded from two different points of view. It may be considered to be *intelligible*, as regards its *action*—the action of a thing which is a thing in itself, and *sensuous*, as regards its *effects*—

the effects of a phenomenon belonging to the sensuous world. We should, accordingly, have to form both an empirical and an intellectual conception of the causality of such a faculty or power—both, however, having reference to the same effect. This two-fold manner of cogitating a power residing in a sensuous object does not run counter to any of the conceptions, which we ought to form of the world of phenomena or of a possible experience. Phenomena—not being things in themselves— must have a transcendental object as a foundation, which determines them as mere representations; and there seems to be no reason why we should not ascribe to this transcendental object, in addition to the property of self-phenomenization, a *causality* whose effects are to be met with in the world of phenomena, although it is not itself a phenomenon. But every effective cause must possess a *character*, that is to say, a law of its causality, without which it would cease to be a cause. In the above case, then, every sensuous object would possess an *empirical* character, which guaranteed that its actions, as phenomena, stand in complete and harmonious connection, conformably to unvarying natural laws, with all other phenomena, and can be deduced from these, as conditions, and that they do thus, in connection with these, constitutes a series in the order of nature. This sensuous object must, in the second place, possess an *intelligible character*, which guarantees it to be the cause of those actions, as phenomena, although it is not itself a phenomenon nor subordinate to the conditions of the world of sense. The former may be termed the character of the thing as a phenomenon, the latter the character of the thing as a thing in itself.

Now this active subject would, in its character of intelligible subject, be subordinate to no conditions of time, for time is only a condition of phenomena, and not of things in themselves. No *action* would *begin* or *cease* to be in this subject; it would consequently be free from the law of all determination of time—the law of change, namely, that everything *which happens* must have a cause in the phenomena of a preceding state. In one word, the causality of the subject, in so far as it is intelligible, would not form part of the series of empirical conditions which determine and necessitate an event in the world of sense. Again this intelligible character of a thing cannot be immediately cognized, because we can perceive nothing but phenomena, but it must be capable of being cogitated in harmony with the empirical character; for we always find ourselves compelled to place, in thought, a transcendental object at the basis of phenomena, although we can never know what this object is in itself.

In virtue of its empirical character, this subject would at the same time be subordinate to all the empirical laws of causality, and, as a phenomenon and member of the sensuous world, its effects would have to be accounted for by a reference to preceding phenomena. External phenomena must be capable of influencing it; and its actions, in accordance with natural laws, must explain to us how its empirical character, that is, the law of its causality, is to be cognized in and by means of experience. In a word, all requisites for a complete and necessary determination of these actions must be presented to us by experience.

In virtue of its intelligible character, on the other hand, (although we possess only a general conception of this character), the subject must be regarded as free from all sensuous influences, and from all phenomenal determination. Moreover, as nothing *happens* in this subject—for it is a *noumenon,* and there does not consequently exist in it any change, demanding the dynamical determination of time, and for the same reason no connection with phenomena as causes—this active existence must in its actions be free from and independent of natural necessity, for this necessity exists only in the world of phenomena. It would be quite correct to say, that it originates or begins its effects in the world of sense *from itself,* although the action productive of these effects does not begin *in itself.* We should not be in this case affirming that these sensuous effects began to exist of themselves, because they are always determined by prior empirical conditions—by virtue of the empirical character, which is the phenomenon of the intelligible character—and are possible only as constituting a continuation of the series of natural causes. And thus nature and freedom, each in the complete and absolute signification of these terms, can exist, without contradiction or disagreement, in the same action.

Exposition of the Cosmological Idea of Freedom in harmony with the Law of Natural Necessity

I have thought it advisable to lay before the reader at first merely a sketch of the solution of this transcendental problem, in order to enable him to form with greater ease a clear conception of the course which reason must adopt in the solution. I shall now proceed to exhibit the several momenta of this solution, and to consider them in their order.

The natural law, that everything which happens must have a cause, that the causality of this cause, that is, the action of the cause, (which cannot always have existed, but must be itself an *event,* for it precedes in time some effect which it has originated), must have itself a phenomenal cause, by which it is determined, and, consequently, that all events are empirically determined in an order of nature—this law, I say, which lies at the foundation of the possibility of experience, and of a connected system of phenomena or *nature,* is a law of the understanding, from which no departure, and to which no exception, can be admitted. For to except even a single phenomenon from its operation, is to exclude it from the sphere of possible experience, and thus to admit it to be a mere fiction of thought or phantom of the brain.

Thus we are obliged to acknowledge the existence of a chain of causes, in which, however, *absolute totality* cannot be found. But we need not detain ourselves with this question, for it has already been sufficiently answered in our discussion of the antinomies into which reason falls, when it attempts to reach the unconditioned in the series of phenomena. If we permit ourselves to be deceived by the illusion of transcendental idealism, we shall find that neither nature nor freedom exists. Now the question is: Whether, admitting the existence of natural necessity in the world of phenomena, it is possible to consider an effect as at the same time an effect of nature and an effect of freedom—or, whether these two modes of causality are contradictory and incompatible?

No phenomenal cause can absolutely and of itself begin a series. Every action, in so far as it is productive of an event, is itself an event or occurrence, and presupposes another preceding state, in which its cause existed. Thus everything that happens is but a continuation of a series, and an absolute beginning is impossible in the sensuous world. The actions of natural causes are, accordingly, themselves effects, and presuppose causes preceding them in time. A *primal* action—an action which forms an absolute beginning, is beyond the causal power of phenomena.

Now, is it absolutely necessary that, granting that all effects are phenomena, the causality of the cause of these effects must also be a phenomenon, and belong to the empirical world? Is it not rather possible that, although every effect in the phenomenal world must be connected with an empirical cause, according to the universal law of nature, this empirical causality may be itself the effect of a non-empirical and intelligible causality—its connection with natural causes remaining nevertheless intact? Such a causality would be considered, in reference to phenomena, as the primal action of a cause, which is in so far, therefore, not phenomenal, but, by reason of this faculty or power, intelligible; although it must, at the same time, as a link in the chain of nature, be regarded as belonging to the sensuous world.

A belief in the reciprocal causality of phenomena is necessary, if we are required to look for and to present the natural conditions of natural events, that is to say, their causes. This being admitted as unexceptionably valid, the requirements of the understanding, which recognizes nothing but nature in the region of phenomena, are satisfied, and our physical explanations of physical phenomena may proceed in their regular course, without hindrance and without opposition. But it is no stumbling-block in the way, even assuming the idea to be a pure fiction, to admit that there are some natural causes in the possession of a faculty which is not empirical, but intelligible, inasmuch as it is not determined to action by empirical conditions, but purely and solely upon grounds brought forward by the understanding—this action being still, when the cause is phenomenized, in perfect accordance with the laws of empirical causality. Thus the acting subject, as a *causal phenomenon,* would continue to preserve a complete connection with nature and natural conditions; and the *phenomenon* only of the subject (with all its phenomenal causality) would contain certain conditions, which, if we ascend from the empirical to the transcendental object, must necessarily be regarded as intelligible. For, if we attend, in our inquiries with regard to causes in the world of phenomena, to the directions of nature alone, we need not trouble ourselves about the relation in which the transcendental subject, which is completely unknown to us, stands to these phenomena and their connection in nature. The intelligible ground of phenomena in this subject does not concern empirical questions. It has to do only with pure thought; and, although the effects of this thought and action of the pure understanding are discoverable in phenomena, these phenomena must nevertheless be capable of a full and complete explanation, upon purely physical grounds, and in accordance with natural laws. And in this case we attend solely to their empirical, and omit all consideration of their intelligible character, (which is the transcendental cause of the former,) as completely unknown, except in so far as it is exhibited by the latter as its empirical symbol. Now let us apply this to experience. Man is a phenomenon of the sensuous world, and at the same time, therefore, a natural cause, the causality of which must be regulated by empirical laws. As such, he must possess an empirical character, like all other natural phenomena. We remark this empirical character in his actions, which reveal the presence of certain powers and faculties. If we consider inanimate, or merely animal nature, we can discover no reason for ascribing to ourselves any other than a faculty which is determined in a purely sensuous manner. But man, to whom nature reveals herself only through sense, cognizes himself not only by his senses, but also through pure apperception; and this in actions and internal determinations which he cannot regard as sensuous impressions. He is thus to himself, on the one hand, a phenomenon, but on the other hand in respect of certain faculties, a purely intelligible object—intelligible, because its action cannot be ascribed to sensuous receptivity. These faculties are understanding and reason. The latter, especially, is in a peculiar manner distinct from all empirically-conditioned faculties, for it employs ideas alone in the consideration of its objects, and by means of these determines the understanding, which then proceeds to make an empirical use of its own conceptions, which, like the ideas of reason, are pure and non-empirical.

That reason possesses the faculty of causality, or that at least we are compelled so to represent it, is evident from the *imperatives*, which in the sphere of the practical we impose on many of our executive powers. The words *I ought* express a species of necessity, and imply a connection with grounds which nature does not and cannot present to the mind of man. Understanding knows nothing in nature but that *which is*, or has been, or will be. It would be absurd to say that anything in nature *ought* to be other than it is in the relations of time in which it stands; indeed, the *ought*, when we consider merely the course of nature,

has neither application nor meaning. The question, what ought
to happen in the sphere of nature, is just as absurd as the question, what ought to be the properties of a circle? All that we
are entitled to ask is, what takes place in nature, or, in the latter
case, what *are* the properties of a circle?

But the idea of an *ought* or of duty indicates a possible action, the ground of which is a pure conception; while the ground
of a merely natural action is, on the contrary, always a phenomenon. This action must certainly be possible under physical
conditions, if it is prescribed by the moral imperative *ought;*
but these physical or natural conditions do not concern the determination of the will itself, they relate to its effect alone, and the
consequences of the effect in the world of phenomena. Whatever number of motives nature may present to my will, whatever sensuous impulses—the moral *ought* it is beyond their
power to produce. They may produce a volition, which, so far
from being necessary, is always conditioned—a volition to
which the *ought* enunciated by reason, sets an aim and a standard, gives permission or prohibition. Be the object what it
may, purely sensuous—as pleasure, or presented by pure reason—as good, reason will not yield to grounds which have an
empirical origin. Reason will not follow the order of things
presented by experience, but, with perfect spontaneity, rear-
ranges them according to ideas, with which it compels empirical
conditions to agree. It declares, in the name of these ideas,
certain actions to be necessary which nevertheless *have not taken
place,* and which perhaps never will take place; and yet presupposes that it possesses the faculty of causality in relation to these
actions. For, in the absence of this supposition, it could not
expect its ideas to produce certain effects in the world of experience.

Now, let us stop here, and admit it to be at least possible, that
reason does stand in a really causal relation to phenomena. In
this case it must—pure reason as it is—exhibit an empirical
character. For every cause supposes a rule, according to which
certain phenomena follow as effects from the cause, and every
rule requires uniformity in these effects; and this is the proper
ground of the conception of a cause—as a faculty or power.
Now this conception (of a cause) may be termed the empirical
character of reason; and this character is a permanent one,
while the effects produced appear, in conformity with the vari-

ous conditions which accompany and partly limit them, in various forms.

Thus the volition of every man has an empirical character, which is nothing more than the causality of his reason, in so far as its effects in the phenomenal world manifest the presence of a rule, according to which we are enabled to examine, in their several kinds and degrees, the actions of this causality and the rational grounds for these actions, and in this way to decide upon the subjective principles of the volition. Now we learn what this empirical character is only from phenomenal effects and from the rule of these which is presented by experience; and for this reason all the actions of man in the world of phenomena are determined by his empirical character, and the co-operative causes of nature. If, then, we could investigate all the phenomena of human volition to their lowest foundation in the mind, there would be no action which we could not anticipate with certainty, and recognize to be absolutely necessary from its preceding conditions. So far as relates to this empirical character, therefore, there can be no freedom; and it is only in the light of this character that we can consider the human will, when we confine ourselves to simple *observation*, and, as is the case in anthropology, institute a physiological investigation of the motive causes of human actions.

But when we consider the same actions in relation to reason —not for the purpose of *explaining* their origin, that is, in relation to speculative reason—but to practical reason, as the producing cause of these actions, we shall discover a rule and an order very different from those of nature and experience. For the declaration of this mental faculty may be, that what *has* and could not but *take place* in the course of nature, *ought not* to have taken place. Sometimes, too, we discover, or believe that we discover, that the ideas of reason did actually stand in a causal relation to certain actions of man; and that these actions have taken place because they were determined, not by empirical causes, but by the act of the will upon grounds of reason.

Now, granting that reason stands in a causal relation to phenomena; can an action of reason be called free, when we know that, sensuously—in its empirical character, it is completely determined and absolutely necessary? But this empirical character is itself determined by the intelligible character. The latter we cannot cognize; we can only indicate it by means of phenomena, which enable us to have an immediate cognition only of the empirical character.* An action, then, in so far as it is to be ascribed to an intelligible cause, does not result from it in accordance with empirical laws. That is to say, not the conditions of pure reason, but only their effects in the internal sense, precede the act. Pure reason, as a purely intelligible faculty, is not subject to the conditions of time. The causality of reason in its intelligible character *does not begin to be;* it does not make its appearance at a certain time, for the purpose of producing an effect. If this were not the case, the causality of reason would be subservient to the natural law of phenomena, which determines them according to time, and as a series of causes and effects in time; it would consequently cease to be freedom, and become a part of nature. We are therefore justified in saying—If reason stands in a causal relation to phenomena, it is a faculty which originates the sensuous condition of an empirical series of effects. For the condition, which resides in the reason, is non-sensuous, and therefore cannot be originated, or begin to be. And thus we find—what we could not discover in any empirical series—a *condition* of a successive series of events itself empirically unconditioned. For, in the present case, the condition stands *out of* and beyond the series of phenomena—it is intelligible, and it consequently cannot be subject to any sensuous condition, or to any time-determination by a preceding cause.

But, in another respect, the same cause belongs also to the series of phenomena. Man is himself a phenomenon. His will has an empirical character, which is the empirical cause of all his actions. There is no condition—determining man and his volition in conformity with this character—which does not itself form part of the series of effects in nature, and is subject to their law—the law according to which an empirically undetermined cause of an event in time cannot exist. For this reason no given action can have an absolute and spontaneous origination, all actions being phenomena, and belonging to the world of experience. But it cannot be said of reason, that the state in which it determines the will is always preceded by some other

* The real morality of actions—their merit or demerit, and even that of our own conduct, is completely unknown to us. Our estimates can relate only to their empirical character. How much is the result of the action of free-will, how much is to be ascribed to nature and to blameless error, or to a happy constitution of temperament (*merito fortunæ*), no one can discover, nor, for this reason, determine with perfect justice.

state determining it. For reason is not a phenomenon, and therefore not subject to sensuous conditions; and, consequently, even in relation to its causality, the sequence or conditions of time do not influence reason, nor can the dynamical law of nature, which determines the sequence of time according to certain rules, be applied to it.

Reason is consequently the permanent condition of all actions of the human will. Each of these is determined in the empirical character of the man, even before it has taken place. The intelligible character, of which the former is but the sensuous schema, knows no *before* or *after;* and every action, irrespective of the time-relation in which it stands with other phenomena, is the immediate effect of the intelligible character of pure reason, which, consequently, enjoys freedom of action, and is not dynamically determined either by internal or external preceding conditions. This freedom must not be described, in a merely negative manner, as independence of empirical conditions, for in this case the faculty of reason would cease to be a cause of phenomena; but it must be regarded, positively, as a faculty which can spontaneously originate a series of events. At the same time, it must not be supposed that any beginning can take place in reason; on the contrary, reason as the unconditioned condition of all action of the will, admits of no time-conditions, although its effect does really begin in a series of phenomena—a beginning which is not, however, absolutely primal.

I shall illustrate this regulative principle of reason by an example, from its employment in the world of experience; proved it cannot be by any amount of experience, or by any number of facts, for such arguments cannot establish the truth of transcendental propositions. Let us take a voluntary action—for example, a falsehood—by means of which a man has introduced a certain degree of confusion into the social life of humanity, which is judged according to the motives from which it originated, and the blame of which and of the evil consequences arising from it, is imputed to the offender. We at first proceed to examine the empirical character of the offence, and for this purpose we endeavor to penetrate to the sources of that character, such as a defective education, bad company, a shameless and wicked disposition, frivolity, and want of reflection—not forgetting also the occasioning causes which prevailed at the mo-

ment of the transgression. In this the procedure is exactly the
same as that pursued in the investigation of the series of causes
which determine a given physical effect. Now, although we
believe the action to have been determined by all these circumstances, we do not the less blame the offender. We do not
blame him for his unhappy disposition, nor for the circumstances which influenced him, nay, not even for his former
course of life; for we presuppose that all these considerations
may be set aside, that the series of preceding conditions may be
regarded as having never existed, and that the action may be
considered as completely unconditioned in relation to any state
preceding, just as if the agent commenced with it an entirely
new series of effects. Our blame of the offender is grounded
upon a law of reason, which requires us to regard this faculty
as a cause, which could have and ought to have otherwise determined the behavior of the culprit, independently of all empirical
conditions. This causality of reason we do not regard as a co-
operating agency, but as complete in itself. It matters not
whether the sensuous impulses favored or opposed the action
of this causality, the offence is estimated according to its intelligible character—the offender is decidedly worthy of blame, the
moment he utters a falsehood. It follows that we regard reason, in spite of the empirical conditions of the act, as completely
free, and therefore, as in the present case, culpable.

The above judgment is complete evidence that we are accustomed to think that reason is not affected by sensuous conditions, that in it no change takes place—although its phenomena,
in other words, the mode in which it appears in its effects, are
subject to change—that in it no preceding state determines the
following, and, consequently, that it does not form a member
of the series of sensuous conditions which necessitate phenomena according to natural laws. Reason is present and the same
in all human actions, and at all times; but it does not itself exist
in time, and therefore does not enter upon any state in which
it did not formerly exist. It is, relatively to new states or conditions, *determining*, but not *determinable*. Hence we cannot
ask: Why did not reason determine itself in a different manner? The question ought to be thus stated: Why did not reason
employ its power of causality to determine certain *phenomena*
in a different manner? But this is a question which admits of
no answer. For a different intelligible character would have

exhibited a different empirical character; and, when we say that, in spite of the course which his whole former life has taken, the offender could have refrained from uttering the falsehood, this means merely that the act was subject to the power and authority—permissive or prohibitive—of reason. Now, reason is not subject in its causality to any conditions of phenomena or of time; and a difference in time may produce a difference in the relation of phenomena to each other—for these are not things, and therefore not causes in themselves—but it cannot produce any difference in the relation in which the action stands to the faculty of reason.

Thus, then, in our investigation into free actions and the causal power which produced them, we arrive at an intelligible cause, beyond which, however, we cannot go; although we can recognize that it is free, that is, independent of all sensuous conditions, and that, in this way, it may be the sensuously unconditioned condition of phenomena. But for what reason the intelligible character generates such and such phenomena, and exhibits such and such an empirical character under certain circumstances, it is beyond the power of our reason to decide. The question is as much above the power and the sphere of reason as the following would be: Why does the transcendental object of our external sensuous intuition allow of no other form than that of intuition *in space?* But the problem, which we were called upon to solve, does not require us to entertain any such questions. The problem was merely this—whether freedom and natural necessity can exist without opposition in the same action. To this question we have given a sufficient answer; for we have shown that, as the former stands in a relation to a different kind of conditions from those of the latter, the law of the one does not affect the law of the other, and that, consequently, both can exist together in independence of and without interference with each other.

The reader must be careful to remark that my intention in the above remarks has not been to prove the *actual existence* of freedom, as a faculty in which resides the cause of certain sensuous phenomena. For, not to mention that such an argument would not have a transcendental character, nor have been limited to the discussion of pure conceptions—all attempts at inferring from experience what cannot be cogitated in accordance with its laws, must ever be unsuccessful. Nay, more,

I have not even aimed at demonstrating the *possibility* of freedom; for this too would have been a vain endeavor, inasmuch
as it is beyond the power of the mind to cognize the possibility
of a reality or of a causal power, by the aid of mere *à priori* conceptions. Freedom has been considered in the foregoing remarks only as a transcendental idea, by means of which reason
aims at originating a series of conditions in the world of phenomena with the help of that which is sensuously unconditioned,
involving itself, however, in an antinomy with the laws which
itself prescribes for the conduct of the understanding. That
this antinomy is based upon a mere illusion, and that nature and
freedom are at least *not opposed*—this was the only thing in our
power to prove, and the question which it was our task to solve.

IV.—SOLUTION OF THE COSMOLOGICAL IDEA OF THE TOTALITY
OF THE DEPENDENCE OF PHENOMENAL EXISTENCES

In the preceding remarks, we considered the changes in the
world of sense as constituting a dynamical series, in which each
member is subordinated to another—as its cause. Our present
purpose is to avail ourselves of this series of states or conditions
as a guide to an existence which may be the highest condition
of all changeable phenomena, that is, to a *necessary being*. Our
endeavor is to reach, not the unconditioned causality, but the
unconditioned existence, of substance. The series before us is
therefore a series of conceptions, and not of intuitions, (in which
the one intuition is the condition of the other).

But it is evident that, as all phenomena are subject to change,
and conditioned in their existence, the series of dependent existences cannot embrace an unconditioned member, the existence of which would be absolutely necessary. It follows that,
if phenomena were things in themselves, and—as an immediate
consequence from this supposition—condition and conditioned
belonged to the same series of phenomena, the existence of a
necessary being, as the condition of the existence of sensuous
phenomena, would be perfectly impossible.

An important distinction, however, exists between the dynamical and the mathematical regress. The latter is engaged
solely with the combination of parts into a whole, or with the
division of a whole into its parts; and therefore are the conditions of its series parts of the series, and to be consequently
regarded as homogeneous, and for this reason, as consisting,

without exception, of phenomena. If the former regress, on the contrary, the aim of which is not to establish the possibility of an unconditioned whole consisting of given parts, or of an unconditioned part of a given whole, but to demonstrate the possibility of the deduction of a certain state from its cause, or of the contingent existence of substance from that which exists necessarily, it is not requisite that the condition should form part of an empirical series along with the conditioned.

In the case of the apparent antinomy with which we are at present dealing, there exists a way of escape from the difficulty; for it is not impossible that both of the contradictory statements may be true in different relations. All sensuous phenomena may be contingent, and consequently possess only an empirically conditioned existence, and yet there may also exist a non-empirical condition of the whole series, or, in other words, a necessary being. For this necessary being, as an intelligible condition, would not form a member—not even the highest member—of the series; the whole world of sense would be left in its empirically determined existence uninterfered with and uninfluenced. This would also form a ground of distinction between the modes of solution employed for the third and fourth antinomies. For, while in the consideration of freedom in the former antinomy, the thing itself—the cause (*substantia phœnomenon*) was regarded as belonging to the series of conditions, and only its *causality* to the intelligible world—we are obliged in the present case to cogitate this necessary being as purely intelligible and as existing entirely apart from the world of sense (as an *ens extramundanum*); for otherwise it would be subject to the phenomenal law of contingency and dependence.

In relation to the present problem, therefore, the *regulative principle* of reason is that everything in the sensuous world possesses an empirically conditioned existence—that no property of the sensuous world possesses unconditioned necessity—that we are bound to expect, and, so far as is possible, to seek for the empirical condition of every member in the series of conditions —and that there is no sufficient reason to justify us in deducing any existence from a condition which lies out of and beyond the empirical series, or in regarding any existence as independent and self-subsistent; although this should not prevent us from recognizing the possibility of the whole series being based upon a being which is intelligible, and for this reason free from all empirical conditions.

But it has been far from my intention, in these remarks, to prove the existence of this unconditioned and necessary being, or even to evidence the possibility of a purely intelligible condition of the existence of all sensuous phenomena. As bounds were set to reason, to prevent it from leaving the guiding thread of empirical conditions, and losing itself in *transcendent* theories which are incapable of *concrete* presentation; so, it was my purpose, on the other hand, to set bounds to the law of the purely empirical understanding, and to protest against any attempts on its part at deciding on the possibility of things, or declaring the existence of the intelligible to be *impossible*, merely on the ground that it is not available for the explanation and exposition of phenomena. It has been shown, at the same time, that the contingency of all the phenomena of nature and their empirical conditions is quite consistent with the arbitrary hypothesis of a necessary, although purely intelligible condition, that no real contradiction exists between them, and that, consequently, *both may be true.* The existence of such an absolutely necessary being may be impossible; but this can never be demonstrated from the universal contingency and dependence of sensuous phenomena, nor from the principle which forbids us to discontinue the series at some member of it, or to seek for its cause in some sphere of existence beyond the world of nature. Reason goes its way in the empirical world, and follows, too, its peculiar path in the sphere of the transcendental.

The sensuous world contains nothing but phenomena, which are mere representations, and always sensuously conditioned; things in themselves are not, and cannot be, objects to us. It is not to be wondered at, therefore, that we are not justified in leaping from some member of an empirical series beyond the world of sense, as if empirical representations were things in themselves, existing apart from their transcendental ground in the human mind, and the cause of whose existence may be sought out of the empirical series. This would certainly be the case with contingent *things;* but it cannot be with mere *representations* of things, the contingency of which is itself merely a phenomenon, and can relate to no other regress than that which determines phenomena, that is, the empirical. But to cogitate an intelligible ground of phenomena, as free, moreover, from the contingency of the latter, conflicts neither with the unlimited nature of the empirical regress, nor with the complete contingency of phenomena. And the demonstration of this was the only thing necessary for the solution of this apparent antinomy. For if the condition of every conditioned—as regards its existence—is sensuous, and for this reason a part of the same series, it must be itself conditioned, as was shown in the Antithesis of the fourth Antinomy. The embarrassments into which a reason, which postulates the unconditioned, necessarily falls, must, therefore, continue to exist; or the unconditioned must be placed in the sphere of the intelligible. In this way, its necessity does not require, nor does it even permit, the presence of an empirical condition: and it is, consequently, unconditionally necessary.

The empirical employment of reason is not affected by the assumption of a purely intelligible being; it continues its operations on the principle of the contingency of all phenomena, proceeding from empirical conditions to still higher and higher conditions, themselves empirical. Just as little does this regulative principle exclude the assumption of an intelligible cause, when the question regards merely the pure employment of reason—in relation to ends or aims. For, in this case, an intelligible cause signifies merely the transcendental and to us unknown ground of the possibility of sensuous phenomena, and its existence necessary and independent of all sensuous conditions, is not inconsistent with the contingency of phenomena, or with the unlimited possibility of regress which exists in the series of empirical conditions.

Concluding Remarks on the Antinomy of Pure Reason

So long as the object of our rational conceptions is the totality of conditions in the world of phenomena, and the satisfaction, from this source, of the requirements of reason, so long are our ideas transcendental and *cosmological*. But when we set the unconditioned—which is the aim of all our inquiries—in a sphere which lies out of the world of sense and possible experience, our ideas become *transcendent*. They are then not merely serviceable towards the completion of the exercise of reason (which remains an idea, never executed, but always to be pursued); they detach themselves completely from experience, and construct for themselves objects, the material of which has

not been presented by experience, and the objective reality of
which is not based upon the completion of the empirical series,
but upon pure *à priori* conceptions. The intelligible object of
these transcendent ideas may be conceded, as a transcendental
object. But we cannot cogitate it as a thing determinable by
certain distinct predicates relating to its internal nature, for it
has no connection with empirical conceptions; nor are we justified in affirming the existence of any such object. It is,
consequently, a mere product of the mind alone. Of all the cosmological ideas, however, it is that occasioning the fourth antinomy which compels us to venture upon this step. For the
existence of phenomena, always conditioned and never self-subsistent, requires us to look for an object different from phenomena—an intelligible object, with which all contingency must
cease. But, as we have allowed ourselves to assume the existence of a self-subsistent reality out of the field of experience,
and are therefore obliged to regard phenomena as merely a
contingent mode of representing intelligible objects employed
by beings which are themselves intelligences—no other course
remains for us than to follow analogy, and employ the same
mode in forming some conception of intelligible things, of which
we have not the least knowledge, which nature taught us to use
in the formation of empirical conceptions. Experience made us
acquainted with the contingent. But we are at present engaged
in the discussion of things which are not objects of experience;
and must, therefore, deduce our knowledge of them from that
which is necessary absolutely and in itself, that is from pure conceptions. Hence the first step which we take out of the world of
sense obliges us to begin our system of new cognition with the
investigation of a necessary being, and to deduce from our conceptions of it, all our conceptions of intelligible things. This we
propose to attempt in the following chapter.

CHAPTER III

The Ideal of Pure Reason

Sec. I.—Of the Ideal in General

We have seen that pure conceptions do not present objects to
the mind, except under sensuous conditions; because the conditions of objective reality do not exist in these conceptions,
which contain, in fact, nothing but the mere form of thought.

They may, however, when applied to phenomena, be presented *in concreto;* for it is phenomena that present to them the materials for the formation of empirical conceptions, which are nothing more than concrete forms of the conceptions of the understanding. But *ideas* are still further removed from objective reality than *categories;* for no phenomenon can ever present them to the human mind *in concreto.* They contain a certain perfection, attainable by no possible empirical cognition; and they give to reason a systematic unity, to which the unity of experience attempts to approximate, but can never completely attain.

But still further removed than the idea from objective reality is the *Ideal,* by which term I understand the idea, not *in concreto,* but *in individuo*—as an individual thing, determinable or determined by the idea alone. The idea of humanity in its complete perfection supposes not only the advancement of all the powers and faculties, which constitute our conception of human nature, to a complete attainment of their final aims, but also everything which is requisite for the complete determination of the idea; for of all contradictory predicates, only one can conform with the idea of the perfect man. What I have termed an ideal, was in Plato's philosophy an *idea of the divine mind*— an individual object present to its pure intuition, the most perfect of every kind of possible beings, and the archetype of all phenomenal existences.

Without rising to these speculative heights, we are bound to confess that human reason contains not only ideas, but ideals, which possess, not, like those of Plato, creative, but certainly *practical* power—as regulative principles, and form the basis of the perfectibility of certain *actions.* Moral conceptions are not perfectly pure conceptions of reason, because an empirical element—of pleasure or pain—lies at the foundation of them. In relation, however, to the principle, whereby reason sets bounds to a freedom which is in itself without law, and consequently when we attend merely to their form, they may be considered as pure conceptions of reason. Virtue and wisdom in their perfect purity, are ideas. But the wise man of the Stoics is an ideal, that is to say, a human being existing only in thought, and in complete conformity with the idea of wisdom. As the idea provides a rule, so the ideal serves as an *archetype* for the perfect and complete determination of the copy. Thus the conduct of this wise and divine man serves us as a standard of action, with which we may compare and judge ourselves, which may help us to reform ourselves, although the perfection it demands can never be attained by us. Although we cannot concede objective reality to these ideals, they are not to be considered as chimeras; on the contrary, they provide reason with a standard, which enables it to estimate, by comparison, the degree of incompleteness in the objects presented to it. But to aim at realizing the ideal in an example in the world of experience—to describe, for instance, the character of the perfectly wise man in a romance is impracticable. Nay more, there is something absurd in the attempt; and the result must be little edifying, as the natural limitations which are continually breaking in upon the perfection and completeness of the idea, destroy the illusion in the story, and throw an air of suspicion even on what is good in the idea, which hence appears fictitious and unreal.

Such is the constitution of the ideal of reason, which is always based upon determinate conceptions, and serves as a rule and a model for imitation or for criticism. Very different is the nature of the ideals of the imagination. Of these it is impossible to present an intelligible conception; they are a kind of *monogram,* drawn according to no determinate rule, and forming rather a vague picture—the production of many diverse experiences—than a determinate image. Such are the ideals which painters and physiognomists profess to have in their minds, and which can serve neither as a model for production nor as a standard for appreciation. They may be termed, though improperly, sensuous ideals, as they are declared to be models of certain possible empirical intuitions. They cannot, however, furnish rules or standards for explanation or examination.

In its ideals, reason aims at complete and perfect determination according to à *priori* rules; and hence it cogitates an object, which must be completely determinable in conformity with principles, although all empirical conditions are absent, and the conception of the object is on this account transcendent.

Sec. II.—Of the Transcendental Ideal—Prototypon Transcendentale

Every conception is, in relation to that which is not contained in it, undetermined and subject to the principle of *determinability.* This principle is, that of *every two* contradictorily opposed predicates, only one can belong to a conception. It is a purely logical principle, itself based upon the principle of contradiction; inasmuch as it makes complete abstraction of the content, and attends merely to the logical form of the cognition.

But again, everything, as regards its possibility, is also subject to the principle * of complete determination, according to which one of *all the possible contradictory predicates* of things must belong to it. This principle is not based merely upon that of contradiction; for, in addition to the relation between two contradictory predicates, it regards everything as standing in a relation to the *sum of possibilities,* as the sum-total of all predicates of things, and, while presupposing this sum as an *à priori* condition, presents to the mind everything as receiving the possibility of its individual existence from the relation it bears to, and the share it possesses in the aforesaid sum of possibilities.† The principle of complete determination relates therefore to the content and not to the logical form. It is the principle of the synthesis of all the predicates which are required to constitute the complete conception of a thing, and not a mere principle of analytical representation, which announces that one of two contradictory predicates must belong to a conception. .It contains, moreover, a transcendental presupposition—that, namely, of the material for *all possibility,* which must contain *à priori* the data for this or that *particular possibility*.

The proposition, *everything which exists is completely determined,* means not only that one of every pair of *given* contradictory attributes, but that one of all *possible* attributes, is always predicable of the thing; in it the predicates are not merely compared logically with each other, but the thing itself is transcendentally compared with the sum-total of all possible predicates. The proposition is equivalent to saying:—to attain to a complete knowledge of a thing, it is necessary to possess a knowledge of everything that is possible, and to determine it thereby, in a positive or negative manner. The conception of complete determination is consequently a conception which cannot be presented in its totality *in concreto,* and is therefore based upon an

---

* *Principium determinationis omnimodæ.* —Tr.

† Thus this principle declares everything to possess a relation to a common correlate—the sum-total of possibility, which, if discovered to exist in the idea of one individual thing, would establish the affinity of all possible things, from the identity of the ground of their complete determination. The *determinability* of every *conception* is subordinate to the *universality* (Allgemeinheit *universalitas*) of the principle of excluded middle; the *determination* of a *thing* to the *totality* (Allheit, *universitas*) of all possible predicates.

idea, which has its seat in the reason—the faculty which prescribes to the understanding the laws of its harmonious and
perfect exercise.

Now, although this idea of the *sum-total of all possibility*, in
so far as it forms the condition of the complete determination
of everything, is itself undetermined in relation to the predicates
which may constitute this sum-total, and we cogitate in it
merely the sum-total of all possible predicates—we nevertheless
find, upon closer examination, that this idea, as a primitive conception of the mind, excludes a large number of predicates—
those deduced and those irreconcilable with others, and that it
is evolved as a conception completely determined *à priori*. Thus
it becomes the conception of an individual object, which is completely determined by and through the mere idea, and must
consequently be termed an ideal of pure reason.

When we consider all possible predicates, not merely logically, but transcendentally, that is to say, with reference to the
content which may be cogitated as existing in them *à priori*,
we shall find that some indicate a being, others merely a non-
being. The logical negation expressed in the word *not*, does
not properly belong to a conception, but only to the relation
of one conception to another in a judgment, and is consequently
quite insufficient to present to the mind the content of a conception. The expression *not moral*, does not indicate that a non-
being is cogitated in the object; it does not concern the content
at all. A transcendental negation, on the contrary, indicates
non-being in itself, and is opposed to transcendental affirmation,
the conception of which of itself expresses a being. Hence this
affirmation indicates a reality, because in and through it objects
are considered to be something—to be things; while the opposite negation, on the other hand, indicates a mere want, or
privation, or absence, and, where such negations alone are attached to a representation, the non-existence of anything corresponding to the representation.

Now a negation cannot be cogitated as determined, without
cogitating at the same time the opposite affirmation. The man
born blind has not the least notion of darkness, because he has
none of light; the vagabond knows nothing of poverty, because
he has never known what it is to be in comfort; * the ignorant

* The investigations and calculations
of astronomers have taught us much
that is wonderful; but the most important lesson we have received from them
is the discovery of the abyss of our
ignorance in relation to the universe—

man has no conception of his ignorance, because he has no conception of knowledge. All conceptions of negatives are accordingly derived or deduced conceptions; and realities contain the *data*, and, so to speak, the material or transcendental content of the possibility and complete determination of all things.

If, therefore, a transcendental substratum lies at the foundation of the complete determination of things—a substratum which is to form the fund from which all possible predicates of things are to be supplied, this substratum cannot be anything else than the idea of a sum-total of reality (*omnitudo realitatis*). In this view, negations are nothing but *limitations*—a term which could not, with propriety, be applied to them, if the unlimited (the all) did not form the true basis of our conception.

This conception of a sum-total of reality is the conception of a *thing in itself*, regarded as completely determined; and the conception of an *ens realissimum* is the conception of an individual being, inasmuch as it is determined by that predicate of all possible contradictory predicates, which indicates and belongs to *being*. It is therefore a transcendental *ideal* which forms the basis of the complete determination of everything that exists, and is the highest material condition of its possibility—a condition on which must rest the cogitation of all objects with respect to their content. Nay, more, this ideal is the only proper ideal of which the human mind is capable; because in this case alone a general conception of a thing is completely determined by and through itself, and cognized as the representation of an individuum.

The logical determination of a conception is based upon a disjunctive syllogism, the major of which contains the logical division of the extent of a general conception, the minor limits this extent to a certain part, while the conclusion determines the conception by this part. The general conception of a reality cannot be divided *à priori*, because, without the aid of experience, we cannot know any determinate kinds of reality, standing under the former as the genus. The transcendental principle of the complete determination of all things is therefore merely the representation of the sum-total of all reality; it is not a conception which is the genus of all predicates *under itself*,

---

an ignorance, the magnitude of which reason, without the information thus derived, could never have conceived.

This discovery of our deficiencies must produce a great change in the determination of the aims of human reason.

but one which comprehends them all *within itself*. The complete determination of a thing is consequently based upon the limitation of this *total* of reality, so much being predicated of the thing, while all that remains over is excluded—a procedure which is in exact agreement with that of the disjunctive syllogism and the determination of the object in the conclusion by one of the members of the division. It follows that reason, in laying the transcendental ideal at the foundation of its determination of all possible things, takes a course in exact analogy with that which it pursues in disjunctive syllogisms—a proposition which formed the basis of the systematic division of all transcendental ideas, according to which they are produced in complete parallelism with the three modes of syllogistic reasoning employed by the human mind.

It is self-evident that reason, in cogitating the necessary complete determination of things, does not presuppose the existence of a being corresponding to its ideal, but merely the idea of the ideal—for the purpose of deducing from the unconditioned totality of complete determination, the conditioned, that is, the totality of limited things. The ideal is therefore the prototype of all things, which, as defective copies (*ectypa*), receive from it the material of their possibility, and approximate to it more or less, though it is impossible that they can ever attain to its perfection.

The possibility of things must therefore be regarded as derived—except that of the thing which contains in itself all reality, which must be considered to be primitive and original. For all negations—and they are the only predicates by means of which all other things can be distinguished from the *ens realissimum*—are mere limitations of a greater and a higher—nay, the highest reality; and they consequently presuppose this reality, and are, as regards their content, derived from it. The manifold nature of things is only an infinitely various mode of limiting the conception of the highest reality, which is their common substratum; just as all figures are possible only as different modes of limiting infinite space. The object of the ideal of reason—an object existing only in reason itself—is also termed the *primal being (ens originarium)*; as having no existence superior to him, the *supreme being (ens summum)*; and as being the condition of all other beings, which rank under it, the *being of all beings (ens entium)*. But none of these terms indicate the objective relation of an actually existing object to other things, but merely that of an *idea to conceptions;* and all our investigations into this subject still leave us in perfect uncertainty with regard to the existence of this being.

A primal being cannot be said to consist of many other beings with an existence which is derivative, for the latter presuppose the former, and therefore cannot be constitutive parts of it. It follows that the ideal of the primal being must be cogitated as simple.

The deduction of the possibility of all other things from this primal being cannot, strictly speaking, be considered as a *limitation,* or as a kind of *division* of its reality; for this would be regarding the primal being as a mere aggregate—which has been shown to be impossible, although it was so represented in our first rough sketch. The highest reality must be regarded rather as the *ground* than as the *sum-total* of the possibility of all things, and the manifold nature of things be based, not upon the limitation of the primal being itself, but upon the complete series of effects which flow from it. And thus all our powers of sense, as well as all phenomenal reality, may be with propriety regarded as belonging to this series of effects, while they could not have formed parts of the idea, considered as an aggregate. Pursuing this track, and hypostatizing this idea, we shall find ourselves authorized to determine our notion of the Supreme Being by means of the mere conception of a highest reality, as one, simple, all-sufficient, eternal, and so on—in one word, to determine it in its unconditioned completeness by the aid of every possible predicate. The conception of such a being is the conception of *God* in its transcendental sense, and thus the ideal of pure reason is the object-matter of a transcendental *Theology.*

But, by such an employment of the transcendental idea, we should be overstepping the limits of its validity and purpose. For reason placed it, as the *conception* of all reality, at the basis of the complete determination of things, without requiring that this conception be regarded as the conception of an objective existence. Such an existence would be purely fictitious, and the hypostatizing of the content of the idea into an ideal, as an individual being, is a step perfectly unauthorized. Nay, more, we are not even called upon to assume the possibility of such an hypothesis, as none of the deductions drawn from such an ideal would affect the complete determination of things in general—for the sake of which alone is the idea necessary.

It is not sufficient to circumscribe the procedure and the dialectic of reason; we must also endeavor to discover the sources of this dialectic, that we may have it in our power to give a rational explanation of this illusion, as a phenomenon of the human mind. For the ideal, of which we are at present speaking, is based, not upon an arbitrary, but upon a natural, idea. The question hence arises: how happens it that reason regards the possibility of all things as deduced from a single possibility, that, to wit, of the highest reality, and presupposes this as existing in an individual and primal being?

The answer is ready; it is at once presented by the procedure of transcendental analytic. The possibility of sensuous objects is a relation of these objects to thought, in which something (the empirical form) may be cogitated *à priori;* while that which constitutes the matter—the reality of the phenomenon (that element which corresponds to sensation)—must be given from without, as otherwise it could not even be cogitated by, nor could its possibility be presentable to the mind. Now, a sensuous object is completely determined, when it has been compared with all phenomenal predicates, and represented by means of these either positively or negatively. But, as that which constitutes the thing itself—the real in a phenomenon, must be given, and that, in which the real of *all phenomena* is given, is experience, one, sole, and all-embracing—the material of the possibility of all sensuous objects must be presupposed as given in a whole, and it is upon the limitation of this whole that the possibility of all empirical objects, their distinction from each other and their complete determination, are based. Now, no other objects are presented to us besides sensuous objects, and these can be given only in connection with a possible experience; it follows that a thing is not an object *to us,* unless it presupposes the whole or sum total of empirical reality as the condition of its possibility. Now, a natural illusion leads us to consider this principle, which is valid only of sensuous objects, as valid with regard to things in general. And thus we are induced to hold the empirical principle of our conceptions of the possibility of things, as phenomena, by leaving out this limitative condition, to be a transcendental principle of the possibility of things in general.

We proceed afterwards to hypostatize this idea of the sum

total of all reality, by changing the *distributive* unity of the empirical exercise of the understanding into the *collective* unity of an empirical whole—a dialectical illusion, and by cogitating this whole or sum of experience as an individual thing, containing in itself all empirical reality. This individual thing or being is then, by means of the above-mentioned transcendental subreption, substituted for our notion of a thing which stands at the head of the possibility of all things, the real conditions of whose complete determination it presents.*

Sec. III.—Of the Arguments employed by Speculative Reason to prove a Supreme Being's Existence

Notwithstanding the pressing necessity which reason feels, to form some presupposition that shall serve the understanding as a proper basis for the complete determination of its conceptions, the idealistic and factitious nature of such a presupposition is too evident to allow reason for a moment to persuade itself into a belief of the objective existence of a mere creation of its own thought. But there are other considerations which compel reason to seek out some resting-place in the regress from the conditioned to the unconditioned, which is not given as an actual existence from the mere conception of it, although it alone can give completeness to the series of conditions. And this is the natural course of every human reason, even of the most uneducated, although the path at first entered it does not always continue to follow. It does not begin from conceptions, but from common experience, and requires a basis in actual existence. But this basis is insecure, unless it rests upon the immovable rock of the absolutely necessary. And this foundation is itself unworthy of trust, if it leave under and above it empty space, if it do not fill all, and leave no room for a *why* or a *wherefore*, if it be not, in one word, infinite in its reality.

If we admit the existence of some one thing, whatever it may be, we must also admit that there is something which exists *necessarily*. For what is contingent exists only under the con-

* This ideal of the *ens realissimum*—although merely a mental representation—is first *objectivized*, that is, has an objective existence attributed to it, then *hypostatized*, and finally, by the natural progress of reason to the completion of unity, *personified*, as we shall show presently. For the regulative unity of experience is not based upon phenomena themselves, but upon the connection of the variety of phenomena by the *understanding* in a *consciousness*, and thus the unity of the supreme reality and the complete determinability of all things, seem to reside in a supreme understanding, and consequently in a conscious intelligence.

dition of some other thing, which is its cause; and from this we must go on to conclude the existence of a cause, which is not contingent, and which consequently exists necessarily and unconditionally. Such is the argument by which reason justifies its advances towards a primal being.

Now reason looks round for the conception of a being that may be admitted, without inconsistency, to be worthy of the attribute of absolute necessity, not for the purpose of inferring *à priori*, from the conception of such a being, its objective existence (for if reason allowed itself to take this course, it would not require a basis in given and actual existence, but merely the support of pure conceptions), but for the purpose of discovering, among all our conceptions of possible things, that conception which possesses no element inconsistent with the idea of absolute necessity. For that there must be some absolutely necessary existence, it regards as a truth already established. Now, if it can remove every existence incapable of supporting the attribute of absolute necessity, excepting one—this must be the absolutely necessary being, whether its necessity is comprehensible by us, that is, deducible from the conception of it alone, or not.

Now that, the conception of which contains a *therefore* to every *wherefore*, which is not defective in any respect whatever, which is all-sufficient as a condition, seems to be the being of which we can justly predicate absolute necessity—for this reason, that, possessing the conditions of all that is possible, it does not and cannot itself require any condition. And thus it satisfies, in one respect at least, the requirements of the conception of absolute necessity. In this view, it is superior to all other conceptions, which, as deficient and incomplete, do not possess the characteristic of independence of all higher conditions. It is true that we cannot infer from this that what does not contain in itself the supreme and complete condition—the condition of all other things, must possess only a conditioned existence; but as little can we assert the contrary, for this supposed being does not possess the only characteristic which can enable reason to cognize by means of an *à priori* conception the unconditioned and necessary nature of its existence.

The conception of an *ens realissimum* is that which best agrees with the conception of an unconditioned and necessary being. The former conception does not satisfy all the requirements of the latter; but we have no choice, we are obliged to adhere to it, for we find that we cannot do without the existence of a necessary being; and even although we admit it, we find it out of our power to discover in the whole sphere of possibility any being that can advance well-grounded claims to such a distinction.

The following is, therefore, the natural course of human reason. It begins by persuading itself of the existence of some necessary being. In this being it recognizes the characteristics of unconditioned existence. It then seeks the conception of that which is independent of all conditions, and finds it in that which is itself the sufficient condition of all other things—in other words, in that which contains all reality. But the unlimited all is an absolute unity, and is conceived by the mind as a being one and supreme; and thus reason concludes that the supreme being, as the primal basis of all things, possesses an existence which is absolutely necessary.

This conception must be regarded as in some degree satisfactory, if we admit the existence of a necessary being, and consider that there exists a necessity for a definite and final answer to these questions. In such a case, we cannot make a better choice, or rather we have no choice at all, but feel ourselves obliged to declare in favor of the absolute unity of complete reality, as the highest source of the possibility of things. But if there exists no motive for coming to a definite conclusion, and we may leave the question unanswered till we have fully weighed both sides—in other words, when we are merely called upon to decide how much we happen to know about the question, and how much we merely flatter ourselves that we know—the above conclusion does not appear to so great advantage, but, on the contrary, seems defective in the grounds upon which it is supported.

For admitting the truth of all that has been said, that namely, the inference from a given existence (my own, for example), to the existence of an unconditioned and necessary being is valid and unassailable; that, in the second place, we must consider a being which contains all reality, and consequently all the conditions of other things, to be absolutely unconditioned; and admitting too, that we have thus discovered the conception of a thing to which may be attributed, without inconsistency, absolute necessity—it does not follow from all this that the conception of a limited being, in which the supreme reality does not reside, is therefore incompatible with the idea of absolute neces-

sity. For, although I do not discover the element of the unconditioned in the conception of such a being—an element which is
manifestly existent in the sum total of all conditions, I am not
entitled to conclude that its existence is therefore conditioned;
just as I am not entitled to affirm, in a hypothetical syllogism,
that where a certain condition does not exist (in the present,
completeness, as far as pure conceptions are concerned), the
conditioned does not exist either. On the contrary, we are free
to consider all limited beings as likewise unconditionally necessary, although we are unable to infer this from the general conception which we have of them. Thus conducted, this argument
is incapable of giving us the least notion of the properties of a
necessary being, and must be in every respect without result.

This argument continues, however, to possess a weight and an
authority, which, in spite of its objective insufficiency, it has
never been divested of. For, granting that certain responsibilities lie upon us, which, as based on the ideas of reason, deserve
to be respected and submitted to, although they are incapable of
a real or practical application to our nature, or, in other words,
would be responsibilities without motives, except upon the supposition of a Supreme Being to give effect and influence to the
practical laws: in such a case we should be bound to obey our
conceptions, which, although objectively insufficient, do, according to the standard of reason, preponderate over and are superior to any claims that may be advanced from any other
quarter. The equilibrium of doubt would in this case be destroyed by a practical addition; indeed, Reason would be compelled to condemn herself, if she refused to comply with the
demands of the judgment, no superior to which we know—however defective her understanding of the grounds of these demands might be.

This argument, although in fact transcendental, inasmuch as
it rests upon the intrinsic insufficiency of the contingent, is so
simple and natural, that the commonest understanding can ap-
preciate its value. We see things around us change, arise, and
pass away; they, or their condition, must therefore have a cause.
The same demand must again be made of the cause itself—as a
datum of experience. Now it is natural that we should place the
highest causality just where we place *supreme* causality, in that
being, which contains the conditions of all possible effects, and
the conception of which is so simple as that of an all-embracing

reality. This highest cause, then, we regard as absolutely necessary, because we find it absolutely necessary to rise to it, and
do not discover any reason for proceeding beyond it. Thus,
among all nations, through the darkest polytheism glimmer
some faint sparks of monotheism, to which these idolaters have
been led, not from reflection and profound thought, but by the
study and natural progress of the common understanding.

There are only three modes of proving the existence of a
Deity, on the grounds of speculative reason.

All the paths conducting to this end, begin either from determinate experience and the peculiar constitution of the world of
sense, and rise, according to the laws of causality, from it to the
highest cause existing apart from the world—or from a purely
indeterminate experience, that is, some empirical existence—or
abstraction is made of all experience, and the existence of a supreme cause is concluded from *à priori* conceptions alone. The
first is the *physico-theological* argument, the second the *cosmological*, the third the *ontological*. More there are not, and more
there cannot be.

I shall show it is as unsuccessful on the one path—the empirical, as on the other—the transcendental, and that it stretches
its wings in vain, to soar beyond the world of sense by the mere
might of speculative thought. As regards the order in which
we must discuss those arguments, it will be exactly the reverse
of that in which reason, in the progress of its development, attains to them—the order in which they are placed above. For it
will be made manifest to the reader, that, although experience
presents the occasion and the starting-point, it is the *transcendental idea* of reason which guides it in its pilgrimage, and is the
goal of all its struggles. I shall therefore begin with an examination of the transcendental argument, and afterwards inquire,
what additional strength has accrued to this mode of proof from
the addition of the empirical element.

Sec. IV.—Of the Impossibility of an Ontological Proof of the Existence of God

It is evident from what has been said, that the conception of
an absolutely necessary being is a mere idea, the objective reality
of which is far from being established by the mere fact that it is
a need of reason. On the contrary, this idea serves merely to indicate a certain unattainable perfection, and rather limits the

operations than, by the presentation of new objects, extends the sphere of the understanding. But a strange anomaly meets us at the very threshold; for the inference from a given existence in general to an absolutely necessary existence, seems to be correct and unavoidable, while the conditions of the *understanding* refuse to aid us in forming any conception of such a being.

Philosophers have always talked of an *absolutely necessary* being, and have nevertheless declined to take the trouble of conceiving, whether—and how—a being of this nature is even cogitable, not to mention that its existence is actually demonstrable. A verbal definition of the conception is certainly easy enough; it is something, the non-existence of which is impossible. But does this definition throw any light upon the conditions which render it impossible to cogitate the non-existence of a thing—conditions which we wish to ascertain, that we may discover whether we think anything in the conception of such a being or not? For the mere fact that I throw away, by means of the word *Unconditioned*, all the conditions which the understanding habitually requires in order to regard anything as necessary, is very far from making clear whether by means of the conception of the unconditionally necessary I think of something, or really of nothing at all.

Nay, more, this chance-conception, now become so current, many have endeavored to explain by examples, which seemed to render any inquiries regarding its intelligibility quite needless. Every geometrical proposition—a triangle has three angles—it was said, is absolutely necessary; and thus people talked of an object which lay out of the sphere of our understanding as if it were perfectly plain what the conception of such a being meant.

All the examples adduced have been drawn, without exception, from *judgments,* and not from *things.* But the unconditioned necessity of a judgment does not form the absolute necessity of a thing. On the contrary, the absolute necessity of a judgment is only a conditioned necessity of a thing, or of the predicate in a judgment. The proposition above-mentioned, does not enounce that three angles necessarily exist, but, upon condition that a triangle exists, three angles must necessarily exist—in it. And thus this logical necessity has been the source of the greatest delusions. Having formed an *à priori* conception of a thing, the content of which was made to embrace existence, we believed ourselves safe in concluding that, because existence belongs necessarily to the object of the conception (that is, under the condition of my positing this thing as given), the existence of the thing is also posited necessarily, and that it is therefore absolutely necessary—merely because its existence has been cogitated in the conception.

If, in an identical judgment, I annihilate the predicate in thought, and retain the subject, a contradiction is the result; and hence I say, the former belongs necessarily to the latter. But if I suppress both subject and predicate in thought, no contradiction arises; for there *is nothing* at all, and therefore no means of forming a contradiction. To suppose the existence of a triangle and not that of its three angles, is self-contradictory; but to suppose the non-existence of both triangle and angles is perfectly admissible. And so is it with the conception of an absolutely necessary being. Annihilate its existence in thought, and you annihilate the thing itself with all its predicates; how then can there be any room for contradiction? Externally, there is nothing to give rise to a contradiction, for a thing cannot be necessary externally; nor internally, for, by the annihilation or suppression of the thing itself, its internal properties are also annihilated. God is omnipotent—that is a necessary judgment. His omnipotence cannot be denied, if the existence of a Deity is posited—the existence, that is, of an infinite being, the two conceptions being identical. But when you say, *God does not exist*, neither omnipotence nor any other predicate is affirmed; they must all disappear with the subject, and in this judgment there cannot exist the least self-contradiction.

You have thus seen, that when the predicate of a judgment is annihilated in thought along with the subject, no internal contradiction can arise, be the predicate what it may. There is no possibility of evading the conclusion—you find yourselves compelled to declare: There are certain subjects which cannot be annihilated in thought. But this is nothing more than saying: There exist subjects which are absolutely necessary—the very hypothesis which you are called upon to establish. For I find myself unable to form the slightest conception of a thing which, when annihilated in thought with all its predicates, leaves behind a contradiction; and contradiction is the only criterion of impossibility, in the sphere of pure *à priori* conceptions.

Against these general considerations, the justice of which no one can dispute, one argument is adduced, which is regarded as furnishing a satisfactory demonstration from the fact. It is affirmed, that there is one and only one conception, in which the non-being or annihilation of the object is self-contradictory, and this is the conception of an *ens realissimum*. It possesses, you say, all reality, and you feel yourselves justified in admitting the possibility of such a being. (This I am willing to grant for the present, although the existence of a conception which is not self-contradictory, is far from being sufficient to prove the possibility of an object.*) Now the notion of all reality embraces in it that of existence; the notion of existence lies, therefore, in the conception of this possible thing. If this thing is annihilated in thought, the internal possibility of the thing is also annihilated, which is self-contradictory.

I answer: It is absurd to introduce—under whatever term disguised—into the conception of a thing, which is to be cogitated solely in reference to its possibility, the conception of its existence. If this is admitted, you will have apparently gained the day, but in reality have enounced nothing but a mere tautology. I ask, is the proposition, *this or that thing* (which I am admitting to be possible) *exists*, an analytical or a synthetical proposition? If the former, there is no addition made to the subject of your thought by the affirmation of its existence; but then the conception in your minds is identical with the thing itself, or you have supposed the existence of a thing to be possible, and then inferred its existence from its internal possibility—which is but a miserable tautology. The word *reality* in the conception of the thing, and the word *existence* in the conception of the predicate, will not help you out of the difficulty. For, supposing you were to term all positing of a thing, reality, you have thereby posited the thing with all its predicates in the conception of the subject and assumed its actual existence, and this you merely repeat in the predicate. But if you confess, as every reasonable person must, that every existential proposition is synthetical, how can it be maintained that the predicate of existence cannot be denied without contradiction—a property which is the characteristic of analytical propositions, alone.

* A conception is always possible, if it is not self-contradictory. This is the logical criterion of possibility, distinguishing the object of such a conception from the *nihil negativum*. But it may be, notwithstanding, an empty conception, unless the objective reality of this synthesis, by which it is generated, is demonstrated; and a proof of this kind must be based upon principles of possible experience, and not upon the principle of analysis or contradiction. This remark may be serviceable as a warning against concluding, from the possibility of a conception—which is logical, the possibility of a thing—which is real.

I should have a reasonable hope of putting an end forever to this sophistical mode of argumentation, by a strict definition of the conception of existence, did not my own experience teach me that the illusion arising from our confounding a logical with a real predicate (a predicate which aids in the determination of a thing) resists almost all the endeavors of explanation and illustration. A *logical predicate* may be what you please, even the subject may be predicated of itself; for logic pays no regard to the content of a judgment. But the determination of a conception is a predicate, which adds to and enlarges the conception. It must not, therefore, be contained in the conception.

Being is evidently not a real predicate, that is, a conception of something which is added to the conception of some other thing. It is merely the positing of a thing, or of certain determinations in it. Logically, it is merely the copula of a judgment. The proposition, *God is omnipotent,* contains two conceptions, which have a certain object or content; the word *is,* is no additional predicate—it merely indicates the relation of the predicate to the subject. Now, if I take the subject (God) with all its predicates (omnipotence being one), and say, *God is,* or, *There is a God,* I add no new predicate to the conception of God, I merely posit or affirm the existence of the subject with all its predicates—I posit the *object* in relation to my *conception.* The content of both is the same; and there is no addition made to the conception, which expresses merely the possibility of the object, by my cogitating the object—in the expression, it *is*—as absolutely given or existing. Thus the real contains no more than the possible. A hundred real dollars contain no more than a hundred possible dollars. For, as the latter indicate the conception, and the former the object, on the supposition that the content of the former was greater than that of the latter, my conception would not be an expression of the whole object, and would consequently be an inadequate conception of it. But in reckoning my wealth there may be said to be more in a hundred real dollars, than in a hundred possible dollars—that is, in the mere conception of them. For the real object—the dollars—is not analytically contained in my conception, but forms a synthetical addition to my conception (which is merely a determination of my mental state), although this objective reality—this existence—apart from my conception, does not in the least degree increase the aforesaid hundred dollars.

By whatever and by whatever number of predicates—even to the complete determination of it—I may cogitate a thing I do not in the least augment the object of my conception by the addition of the statement, this thing exists. Otherwise, not exactly the same, but something more than what was cogitated in my conception, would exist, and I could not affirm that the exact object of my conception had real existence. If I cogitate a thing as containing all modes of reality except one, the mode of reality which is absent is not added to the conception of the thing by the affirmation that the thing exists; on the contrary, the thing exists—if it exist at all—with the same defect as that cogitated in its conception; otherwise not that which was cogitated, but something different, exists. Now, if I cogitate a being as the highest reality, without defect or imperfection, the question still remains—whether this being exists or not? For although no element is wanting in the possible real content of my conception, there is a defect in its relation to my mental state, that is, I am ignorant whether the cognition of the object indicated by the conception is possible *à posteriori*. And here the cause of the present difficulty becomes apparent. If the question regarded an object of sense merely, it would be impossible for me to confound the conception with the existence of a thing. For the conception merely enables me to cogitate an object as according with the general conditions of experience; while the existence of the object permits me to cogitate it as contained in the sphere of actual experience. At the same time, this connection with the world of experience does not in the least augment the conception, although a possible perception has been added to the experience of the mind. But if we cogitate existence by the pure category alone, it is not to be wondered at, that we should find ourselves unable to present any criterion sufficient to distinguish it from mere possibility.

Whatever be the content of our conception of an object, it is necessary to go beyond it, if we wish to predicate existence of the object. In the case of sensuous objects, this is attained by their connection according to empirical laws with some one of my perceptions; but there is no means of cognizing the existence of objects of pure thought, because it must be cognized completely *à priori*. But all our knowledge of existence (be it immediately by perception, or by inferences connecting some object with a perception) belongs entirely to the sphere of experience—which is in perfect unity with itself—and although an existence out of this sphere cannot be absolutely declared to be impossible, it is a hypothesis the truth of which we have no means of ascertaining.

The notion of a supreme being is in many respects a highly useful idea; but for the very reason that it is an idea, it is incapable of enlarging our cognition with regard to the existence of things. It is not even sufficient to instruct us as to the possibility of a being which we do not know to exist. The analytical criterion of possibility, which consists in the absence of contradiction in propositions, cannot be denied it. But the connection of real properties in a thing is a synthesis of the possibility of which an *à priori* judgment cannot be formed, because these realities are not presented to us specifically; and even if this were to happen, a judgment would still be impossible, because the criterion of the possibility of synthetical cognitions must be sought for in the world of experience, to which the object of an idea cannot belong. And thus the celebrated Leibnitz has utterly failed in his attempt to establish upon *à priori* grounds the possibility of this sublime ideal being.

The celebrated ontological or Cartesian argument for the existence of a Supreme Being is therefore insufficient; and we may as well hope to increase our stock of knowledge by the aid of mere ideas, as the merchant to augment his wealth by the addition of noughts to his cash-account.

Sec. V.—Of the Impossibility of a Cosmological Proof of the Existence of God

It was by no means a natural course of proceeding, but, on the contrary, an invention entirely due to the subtlety of the schools, to attempt to draw from a mere idea a proof of the existence of an object corresponding to it. Such a course would never have been pursued, were it not for that need of reason which requires it to suppose the existence of a necessary being as a basis for the empirical regress, and that, as this necessity must be unconditioned and *à priori*, reason is bound to discover a conception which shall satisfy, if possible, this requirement, and enable us to attain to the *à priori* cognition of such a being.

This conception was thought to be found in the idea of an *ens realissimum,* and thus this idea was employed for the attainment of a better defined knowledge of a necessary being, of the existence of which we were convinced, or persuaded, on other grounds. Thus reason was seduced from her natural course; and, instead of concluding with the conception of an *ens realissimum,* an attempt was made to begin with it, for the purpose of inferring from it that idea of a necessary existence, which it was in fact called in to complete. Thus arose that unfortunate ontological argument, which neither satisfies the healthy common sense of humanity, nor sustains the scientific examination of the philosopher.

The *cosmological proof,* which we are about to examine, retains the connection between absolute necessity, and the highest reality; but, instead of reasoning from this highest reality to a necessary existence, like the preceding argument, it concludes from the given unconditioned necessity of some being its unlimited reality. The track it pursues, whether rational or sophistical, is at least natural, and not only goes far to persuade the common understanding, but shows itself deserving of respect from the speculative intellect; while it contains, at the same time, the outlines of all the arguments employed in natural theology—arguments which always have been, and still will be, in use and authority. These, however adorned, and hid under whatever embellishments of rhetoric and sentiment, are at bottom identical with the arguments we are at present to discuss. This proof, termed by Leibnitz the *argumentum a contingentiâ mundi,* I shall now lay before the reader, and subject to a strict examination.

It is framed in the following manner:—If something exists, an absolutely necessary being must likewise exist. Now I, at least, exist. Consequently, there exists an absolutely necessary being. The minor contains an experience, the major reasons from a general experience to the existence of a necessary being.* Thus this argument really begins at experience, and is not completely *à priori,* or ontological. The object of all possible experience being the world, it is called the *cosmological* proof. It contains no reference to any peculiar property of sensuous

* This inference is too well known to require more detailed discussion. It is based upon the spurious transcendental law of causality, that everything which is *contingent* has a cause, which, if itself contingent, must also have a cause; and so on, till the series of subordinated causes must end with an absolutely necessary cause, without which it would not possess completeness.

objects, by which this world of sense might be distinguished from other possible worlds; and in this respect it differs from the physico-theological proof, which is based upon the consideration of the peculiar constitution of our sensuous world.

The proof proceeds thus:—A necessary being can be determined only in one way, that is, it can be determined by only one of all possible opposed predicates; consequently, it must be *completely* determined in and by its conception. But there is only a single conception of a thing possible, which completely determines the thing *à priori:* that is, the conception of the *ens realissimum.* It follows that the conception of the *ens realissimum* is the only conception, by and in which we can cogitate a necessary being. Consequently, a supreme being necessarily exists.

In this cosmological argument are assembled so many sophistical propositions, that speculative reason seems to have exerted in it all her dialectical skill to produce a transcendental illusion of the most extreme character. We shall postpone an investigation of this argument for the present, and confine ourselves to exposing the stratagem by which it imposes upon us an old argument in a new dress, and appeals to the agreement of two witnesses, the one with the credentials of pure reason, and the other with those of empiricism; while, in fact, it is only the former who has changed his dress and voice, for the purpose of passing himself off for an additional witness. That it may possess a secure foundation, it bases its conclusions upon experience, and thus appears to be completely distinct from the ontological argument, which places its confidence entirely in pure *à priori* conceptions. But this experience merely aids reason in making one step—to the existence of a necessary being. What the properties of this being are, cannot be learned from experience; and therefore reason abandons it altogether, and pursues its inquiries in the sphere of pure conceptions, for the purpose of discovering what the properties of an absolutely necessary being ought to be, that is, what among all possible things contain the conditions (*requisita*) of absolute necessity. Reason believes that it has discovered these requisites in the conception of an *ens realissimum*—and in it alone, and hence concludes: The *ens realissimum* is an absolutely necessary being. But it is evident that reason has here presupposed that the conception of an *ens realissimum* is perfectly adequate to the conception of a being of absolute necessity, that is, that we may infer the existence of the latter from that of the former—a proposition, which formed the basis of the ontological argument, and which is now employed in the support of the cosmological argument, contrary to the wish and professions of its inventors. For the existence of an absolutely necessary being is given in conceptions alone. But if I say—the conception of the *ens realissimum* is a conception of this kind, and in fact the only conception which is adequate to our idea of a necessary being, I am obliged to admit, that the latter may be inferred from the former. Thus it is properly the ontological argument which figures in the cosmological, and constitutes the whole strength of the latter; while the spurious basis of experience has been of no further use than to conduct us to the conception of absolute necessity, being utterly insufficient to demonstrate the presence of this attribute in any determinate existence or thing. For when we propose to ourselves an aim of this character, we must abandon the sphere of experience, and rise to that of pure conceptions, which we examine with the purpose of discovering whether any one contains the conditions of the possibility of an absolutely necessary being. But if the possibility of such a being is thus demonstrated, its existence is also proved; for we may then assert that, of all possible beings there is one which possesses the attribute of necessity—in other words, this being possesses an absolutely necessary existence.

All illusions in an argument are more easily detected, when they are presented in the formal manner employed by the schools, which we now proceed to do.

If the proposition, Every absolutely necessary being is likewise an *ens realissimum,* is correct (and it is this which constitutes the *nervus probandi* of the cosmological argument), it must, like all affirmative judgments, be capable of conversion—the *conversio per accidens,* at least. It follows, then, that some *entia realissima* are absolutely necessary beings. But no *ens realissimum* is in any respect different from another, and what is valid of some, is valid of all. In this present case, therefore, I may employ simple conversion, and say, Every *ens realissimum* is a necessary being. But as this proposition is determined à *priori* by the conceptions contained in it, the mere conception of an *ens realissimum* must possess the additional attribute of absolute necessity. But this is exactly what was maintained in the ontological argument, and not recognized by the cosmological, although it formed the real ground of its disguised and illusory reasoning.

Thus the second mode employed by speculative reason of demonstrating the existence of a Supreme Being, is not only, like the first, illusory and inadequate, but possesses the additional blemish of an *ignoratio elenchi*—professing to conduct us by a new road to the desired goal, but bringing us back, after a short circuit, to the old path which we had deserted at its call.

I mentioned above, that this cosmological argument contains a perfect nest of dialectical assumptions, which transcendental criticism does not find it difficult to expose and to dissipate. I shall merely enumerate these, leaving it to the reader, who must by this time be well practised in such matters, to investigate the fallacies residing therein.

The following fallacies, for example, are discoverable in this mode of proof: 1. The transcendental principle, Everything that is contingent must have a cause—a principle without significance, except in the sensuous world. For the purely intellectual conception of the contingent cannot produce any synthetical proposition, like that of causality, which is itself without significance or distinguishing characteristic except in the phenomenal world. But in the present case it is employed to help us beyond the limits of its sphere. 2. From the impossibility of an infinite ascending series of causes in the world of sense a first cause is inferred;—a conclusion which the principles of the employment of reason do not justify even in the sphere of experience, and still less when an attempt is made to pass the limits of this sphere. 3. Reason allows itself to be satisfied upon insufficient grounds, with regard to the completion of this series. It removes all conditions (without which, however, no conception of Necessity can take place); and, as after this it is beyond our power to form any other conception, it accepts this as a completion of the conception it wishes to form of the series. 4. The logical possibility of a conception of the total of reality (the criterion of this possibility being the absence of contradiction) is confounded with the transcendental, which requires a principle of the practicability of such a synthesis—a principle which again refers us to the world of experience. And so on.

The aim of the cosmological argument is to avoid the necessity of proving the existence of a necessary being *à priori* from mere conceptions—a proof which must be ontological, and of which we feel ourselves quite incapable. With this purpose, we reason from an actual existence—an experience in general, to an absolutely necessary condition of that existence. It is in this case unnecessary to demonstrate its possibility. For after having proved that it exists, the question regarding its possibility is superfluous. Now, when we wish to define more strictly the nature of this necessary being, we do not look out for some being the conception of which would enable us to comprehend the necessity of its being—for if we could do this, an empirical presupposition would be unnecessary; no, we try to discover merely the negative condition (*conditio sine quâ non*), without which a being would not be absolutely necessary. Now this would be perfectly admissible in every sort of reasoning, from a consequence to its principle; but in the present case it unfortunately happens that the condition of absolute necessity can be discovered in but a single being, the conception of which must consequently contain all that is requisite for demonstrating the presence of absolute necessity, and thus entitle me to infer this absolute necessity *à priori*. That is, it must be possible to reason conversely, and say—the thing, to which the conception of the highest reality belongs, is absolutely necessary. But if I cannot reason thus—and I cannot, unless I believe in the sufficiency of the ontological argument—I find insurmountable obstacles in my new path, and am really no further than the point from which I set out. The conception of a Supreme Being satisfies all questions *à priori* regarding the internal determinations of a thing, and is for this reason an ideal without equal or parallel, the general conception of it indicating it as at the same time an *ens individuum* among all possible things. But the conception does not satisfy the question regarding its existence—which was the purpose of all our inquiries; and, although the existence of a necessary being were admitted, we should find it impossible to answer the question—What of all things in the world must be regarded as such?

It is certainly allowable to *admit* the existence of an all-sufficient being—a cause of all possible effects, for the purpose of enabling reason to introduce unity into its mode and grounds of explanation with regard to phenomena. But to assert that such a being *necessarily exists*, is no longer the modest enunciation of an admissible hypothesis, but the boldest declaration of an apodictic certainty; for the cognition of that which is absolutely necessary, must itself possess that character.

The aim of the transcendental ideal formed by the mind is, either to discover a conception which shall harmonize with the idea of absolute necessity, or a conception which shall contain that idea. If the one is possible, so is the other; for reason recognizes that alone as absolutely necessary, which is necessary from its conception. But both attempts are equally beyond our power—we find it impossible to *satisfy* the understanding upon this point, and as impossible to induce it to remain at rest in relation to this incapacity.

Unconditioned necessity, which, as the ultimate support and stay of all existing things, is an indispensable requirement of the mind, is an abyss on the verge of which human reason trembles in dismay. Even the idea of eternity, terrible and sublime as it is, as depicted by Haller, does not produce upon the mental vision such a feeling of awe and terror; for, although it *measures* the duration of things, it does not *support* them. We cannot bear, nor can we rid ourselves of the thought, that a being, which we regard as the greatest of all possible existences, should *say to himself:* I am from eternity to eternity; beside me there is nothing, except that which exists by my will; *but whence then am I?* Here all sinks away from under us; and the greatest, as the smallest, perfection, hovers without stay or footing in presence of the speculative reason, which finds it as easy to part with the one as with the other.

Many physical powers, which evidence their existence by their effects, are perfectly inscrutable in their nature; they elude all our powers of observation. The transcendental object which forms the basis of phenomena, and, in connection with it, the reason why our sensibility possesses this rather than that particular kind of conditions, are and must ever remain hidden from our mental vision; the fact is there, the reason of the fact we cannot see. But an ideal of pure reason cannot be termed mysterious or *inscrutable*, because the only credential of its reality is the need of it felt by reason, for the purpose of giving completeness to the world of synthetical unity. An ideal is not even given as a cogitable *object*, and therefore cannot be inscrutable; on the contrary, it must, as a mere idea, be based on the constitution of reason itself, and on this account must be capable of explanation and solution. For the very essence of reason consists in its ability to give an account of all our conceptions, opinions, and assertions—upon objective, or, when they happen to be illusory and fallacious, upon subjective grounds.

Detection and Explanation of the Dialectical Illusion in all Transcendental Arguments for the Existence of a Necessary Being

Both of the above arguments are transcendental; in other words, they do not proceed upon empirical principles. For, although the cosmological argument professed to lay a basis of experience for its edifice of reasoning, it did not ground its procedure upon the peculiar constitution of experience, but upon pure principles of reason—in relation to an existence given by empirical consciousness; utterly abandoning its guidance, however, for the purpose of supporting its assertions entirely upon pure conceptions. Now what is the cause, in these transcendental arguments, of the dialectical, but natural, illusion, which connects the conceptions of necessity and supreme reality, and hypostatizes that which cannot be anything but an idea? What is the cause of this unavoidable step on the part of reason, of admitting that someone among all existing things must be necessary, while it falls back from the assertion of the existence of such a being as from an abyss? And how does reason proceed to explain this anomaly to itself, and from the wavering condition of a timid and reluctant approbation—always again withdrawn, arrive at a calm and settled insight into its cause?

It is something very remarkable that, on the supposition that something exists, I cannot avoid the inference, that something exists necessarily. Upon this perfectly natural—but not on that account reliable—inference does the cosmological argument rest. But, let me form any conception whatever of a thing, I find that I cannot cogitate the existence of the thing as absolutely necessary, and that nothing prevents me—be the thing or being what it may—from cogitating its non-existence. I may thus be obliged to admit that all existing things have a necessary basis, while I cannot cogitate any single or individual thing as necessary. In other words, I can never *complete* the regress through the conditions of existence, without admitting the existence of a necessary being; but, on the other hand, I cannot make a *commencement* from this beginning.

If I must cogitate something as existing necessarily as the basis of existing things, and yet am not permitted to cogitate any individual thing as in itself necessary, the inevitable inference is, that necessity and contingency are not properties of things themselves—otherwise an internal contradiction would result; that consequently neither of these principles are objective, but merely subjective principles of reason—the one requiring us to seek for a necessary ground for everything that exists, that is, to be satisfied with no other explanation than that which is complete à priori, the other forbidding us ever to hope for the attainment of this completeness, that is, to regard no member of the empirical world as unconditioned. In this mode of viewing them, both principles, in their purely heuristic and regulative character, and as concerning merely the formal interest of reason, are quite consistent with each other. The one says—you must philosophize upon nature, as if there existed a necessary primal basis of all existing things, solely for the purpose of introducing systematic unity into your knowledge, by pursuing an idea of this character—a foundation which is arbitrarily admitted to be ultimate; while the other warns you to consider no individual determination, concerning the existence of things, as such an ultimate foundation, that is, as absolutely necessary, but to keep the way always open for further progress in the deduction, and to treat every determination as determined by some other. But if all that we perceive must be regarded as conditionally necessary, it is impossible that anything which is empirically given should be absolutely necessary.

It follows from this, that you must accept the absolutely necessary as *out of* and beyond the world, inasmuch as it is useful only as a principle of the highest possible unity in experience, and you cannot discover any such necessary existence in the *world*, the second rule requiring you to regard all empirical causes of unity as themselves deduced.

The philosophers of antiquity regarded all the forms of nature as contingent; while matter was considered by them, in accordance with the judgment of the common reason of mankind, as primal and necessary. But if they had regarded matter, not relatively—as the substratum of phenomena, but absolutely and *in itself*—as an independent existence, this idea of absolute necessity would have immediately disappeared. For there is nothing absolutely connecting reason with such an existence; on the contrary, it can annihilate it in thought, always and without self-contradiction. But in thought alone lay the idea of absolute necessity. A regulative principle must, therefore, have been at the foundation of this opinion. In fact, extension and impenetrability—which together constitute our conception of matter—form the supreme empirical principle of the unity of phenomena, and this principle, in so far as it is empirically unconditioned, possesses the property of a regulative principle. But, as every determination of matter which constitutes what is real in it—and consequently impenetrability—is an effect, which must have a cause, and is for this reason always derived, the notion of matter cannot harmonize with the idea of a necessary being, in its character of the principle of all derived unity. For every one of its real properties, being derived, must be only conditionally necessary, and can therefore be annihilated in thought; and thus the whole existence of matter can be so annihilated or suppressed. If this were not the case, we should have found in the world of phenomena the highest ground or condition of unity—which is impossible, according to the second regulative principle. It follows, that matter, and, in general, all that forms part of the world of sense, cannot be a necessary primal being, nor even a principle of empirical unity, but that this being or principle must have its place assigned without the world. And, in this way, we can proceed in perfect confidence to deduce the phenomena of the world and their existence from other phenomena, just as if there existed no necessary being; and we can at the same time, strive without ceasing towards the attainment of completeness for our deduction, just as if such a being—the supreme condition of all existences—were presupposed by the mind.

These remarks will have made it evident to the reader that the ideal of the Supreme Being, far from being an enouncement of the existence of a being in itself necessary, is nothing more than a *regulative principle* of reason, requiring us to regard all connection existing between phenomena as if it had its origin from an all-sufficient necessary cause, and basing upon this the rule of a systematic and necessary unity in the explanation of phenomena. We cannot, at the same time, avoid regarding, by a transcendental *subreptio*, this formal principle as constitutive, and hypostatizing this unity. Precisely similar is the case with our notion of space. Space is the primal condition of all forms, which are properly just so many different limitations of it; and thus, although it is merely a principle of sensibility, we cannot help regarding it as an absolutely necessary and self-subsistent thing—as an object given *à priori* in itself. In the same way, it is quite natural that, as the systematic unity of nature cannot be established as a principle for the empirical employment of reason, unless it is based upon the idea of an *ens realissimum*, as the supreme cause, we should regard this idea as a real object, and this object, in its character of supreme condition, as absolutely necessary, and that in this way a *regulative* should be transformed into a *constitutive* principle. This interchange becomes evident when I regard this supreme being, which, relatively to the world, was absolutely (unconditionally) necessary, as a thing *per se*. In this case, I find it impossible to represent this necessity in or by any conception, and it exists merely in my own mind, as the formal condition of thought, but not as a material and hypostatic condition of existence.

Sec. VI.—Of the Impossibility of a Physico-Theological Proof

If, then, neither a pure conception nor the general experience of an existing being can provide a sufficient basis for the proof of the existence of the Deity, we can make the attempt by the only other mode—that of grounding our argument upon a *determinate experience* of the phenomena of the present world, their constitution and disposition, and discover whether we can thus attain to a sound conviction of the existence of a Supreme Being. This argument we shall term the *physico-theological* argument. If it is shown to be insufficient, speculative reason cannot present us with any satisfactory proof of the existence of a being corresponding to our transcendental idea.

It is evident from the remarks that have been made in the preceding sections, that an answer to this question will be far from being difficult or unconvincing. For how can any experience be adequate with an idea? The very essence of an idea consists in the fact that no experience can ever be discovered congruent or adequate with it. The transcendental idea of a necessary and all-sufficient being is so immeasurably great, so high above all that is empirical, which is always conditioned, that we hope in vain to find materials in the sphere of experience sufficiently ample for our conception, and in vain seek the unconditioned among things that are conditioned, while examples, nay, even guidance, is denied us by the laws of empirical synthesis.

If the Supreme Being forms a link in the chain of empirical conditions, it must be a member of the empirical series, and, like the lower members which it precedes, have its origin in some higher member of the series. If, on the other hand, we disengage it from the chain, and cogitate it as an intelligible being, apart from the series of natural causes—how shall reason bridge the abyss that separates the latter from the former? All laws respecting the regress from effects to causes, all synthetical additions to our knowledge relate solely to possible experience and the objects of the sensuous world, and, apart from them, are without significance.

The world around us opens before our view so magnificent a spectacle of order, variety, beauty, and conformity to ends, that whether we pursue our observations into the infinity of space in the one direction, or into its illimitable divisions on the other, whether we regard the world in its greatest or its least manifestations—even after we have attained to the highest summit of knowledge which our weak minds can reach, we find that language in the presence of wonders so inconceivable has lost its force, and number its power to reckon, nay, even thought fails to conceive adequately, and our conception of the whole dissolves into an astonishment without the power of expression— all the more eloquent that it is dumb. Everywhere around us we observe a chain of causes and effects, of means and ends, of death and birth; and, as nothing has entered of itself into the condition in which we find it, we are constantly referred to some other thing, which itself suggests the same inquiry regarding its cause, and thus the universe must sink into the abyss of nothingness, unless we admit that, besides this infinite chain of contingencies, there exists something that is primal and self-subsistent—something which, as the cause of this phenomenal world, secures its continuance and preservation.

This highest cause—what magnitude shall we attribute to it? Of the content of the world we are ignorant; still less can we estimate its magnitude by comparison with the sphere of the possible. But this supreme cause being a necessity of the human mind, what is there to prevent us from attributing to it such a degree of perfection as to place it above the sphere of *all that* is possible? This we can easily do, although only by the aid of the faint outline of an abstract conception, by representing this being to ourselves as containing in itself, as an individual substance, all possible perfection—a conception which satisfies that requirement of reason which demands parsimony in principles, which is free from self-contradiction, which even contributes to the extension of the employment of reason in experience, by means of the guidance afforded by this idea to order and system, and which in no respect conflicts with any law of experience.

This argument always deserves to be mentioned with respect. It is the oldest, the clearest, and that most in conformity with the common reason of humanity. It animates the study of nature, as it itself derives its existence and draws ever new strength from that source. It introduces aims and ends into a sphere in which our observation could not of itself have discovered them, and extends our knowledge of nature, by directing our attention to a unity, the principle of which lies beyond nature. This knowledge of nature again re-acts upon this idea —its cause; and thus our belief in a divine author of the universe rises to the power of an irresistible conviction.

For these reasons it would be utterly hopeless to attempt to rob this argument of the authority it has always enjoyed. The mind, unceasingly elevated by these considerations, which, although empirical, are so remarkably powerful, and continually adding to their force, will not suffer itself to be depressed by the doubts suggested by subtle speculation; it tears itself out of this state of uncertainty, the moment it casts a look upon the wondrous forms of nature and the majesty of the universe, and rises from height to height, from condition to condition, till it has elevated itself to the supreme and unconditioned author of all.

But although we have nothing to object to the reasonableness and utility of this procedure, but have rather to commend and encourage it, we cannot approve of the claims which this argument advances to demonstrative certainty and to a reception upon its own merits, apart from favor or support by other arguments. Nor can it injure the cause of morality to endeavor to lower the tone of the arrogant sophist, and to teach him that modesty and moderation which are the properties of a belief that brings calm and content into the mind, without prescribing to it an unworthy subjection. I maintain, then, that the physico-theological argument is insufficient of itself to prove the existence of a Supreme Being, that it must entrust this to the ontological argument—to which it serves merely as an introduction, and that, consequently, this argument contains the *only possible ground of proof* (possessed by speculative reason) for the existence of this being.

The chief momenta in the physico-theological argument are as follows: 1. We observe in the world manifest signs of an arrangement full of purpose, executed with great wisdom, and existing in a whole of a content indescribably various, and of an extent without limits. 2. This arrangement of means and ends is entirely foreign to the things existing in the world—it belongs to them merely as a contingent attribute; in other words, the nature of different things could not of itself, whatever means were employed, harmoniously tend towards certain purposes, were they not chosen and directed for these purposes by a rational and disposing principle, in accordance with certain fundamental ideas. 3. There exists, therefore, a sublime and wise cause (or several), which is not merely a blind, all-powerful nature, producing the beings and events which fill the world in unconscious *fecundity*, but a *free* and intelligent cause of the world. 4. The unity of this cause may be inferred from the unity of the reciprocal relation existing between the parts of the world, as portions of an artistic edifice—an inference which all our observation favors, and all principles of analogy support.

In the above argument, it is inferred from the analogy of certain products of nature with those of human art, when it compels Nature to bend herself to its purposes, as in the case of a house, a ship, or a watch, that the same kind of causality—namely, understanding and will—resides in nature. It is also declared that the internal possibility of this freely acting nature (which is the source of all art, and perhaps also of human reason) is derivable from another and superhuman art—a conclusion which would perhaps be found incapable of standing the test of subtle transcendental criticism. But to neither of these opinions shall we at present object. We shall only remark that it must be confessed that, if we are to discuss the subject of cause at all, we cannot proceed more securely than with the guidance of the analogy subsisting between nature and such products of design—these being the only products whose causes and modes of origination are completely known to us. Reason would be unable to satisfy her own requirements, if she passed from a causality which she does know, to obscure and indemonstrable principles of explanation which she does not know.

According to the physico-theological argument, the connection and harmony existing in the world evidence the contingency of the form merely, but not of the matter, that is, of the substance of the world. To establish the truth of the latter opinion, it would be necessary to prove that all things would be in themselves incapable of this harmony and order, unless they were, even as regards their *substance,* the product of a supreme wisdom. But this would require very different grounds of proof from those presented by the analogy with human art. This proof can at most, therefore, demonstrate the existence of an *architect of the world,* whose efforts are limited by the capabilities of the material with which he works, but not of a *creator of the world,* to whom all things are subject. Thus this argument is utterly insufficient for the task before us—a demonstration of the existence of an all-sufficient being. If we wish to prove the contingency of matter, we must have recourse to a transcendental argument, which the physico-theological was constructed expressly to avoid.

We infer, from the order and design visible in the universe, as a disposition of a thoroughly contingent character, the existence of a cause *proportionate thereto.* The conception of this cause must contain certain *determinate* qualities, and it must therefore be regarded as the conception of a being which possesses all power, wisdom, and so on, in one word, all perfection—the conception, that is, of an all-sufficient being. For the predicates of *very great,* astonishing, or immeasurable power and excellence, give us no determinate conception of the thing, nor do they inform us what the thing may be in itself. They merely indicate the relation existing between the magnitude of the object and the observer, who compares it with himself and with his own power of comprehension, and are mere expressions of praise and reverence, by which the object is either magnified, or the observing subject depreciated in relation to the object. Where we have to do with the magnitude (of the perfection) of a thing, we can discover no determinate conception, except that which comprehends all possible perfection or completeness, and it is only the total (*omnitudo*) of reality which is completely determined in and through its conception alone.

Now it cannot be expected that anyone will be bold enough to declare that he has a perfect insight into the relation which the magnitude of the world he contemplates, bears (in its extent as well as in its content) to omnipotence, into that of the order and design in the world to the highest wisdom, and that of the unity of the world to the absolute unity of a Supreme Being. Physico-theology is therefore incapable of presenting a determinate conception of a supreme cause of the world, and is therefore insufficient as a principle of theology—a theology which is itself to be the basis of religion.

The attainment of absolute totality is completely impossible on the path of empiricism. And yet this is the path pursued in the physico-theological argument. What means shall we employ to bridge the abyss?

After elevating ourselves to admiration of the magnitude of the power, wisdom, and other attributes of the author of the world, and finding we can advance no further, we leave the argument on empirical grounds, and proceed to infer the contingency of the world from the order and conformity to aims that are observable in it. From this contingency we infer, by the help of transcendental conceptions alone, the existence of something absolutely necessary; and, still advancing, proceed from the conception of the absolute necessity of the first cause to the completely determined or determining conception thereof—the conception of an 'all-embracing reality. Thus the physico-theological, failing in its undertaking, recurs in its embarrassment to the cosmological argument; and, as this is merely the ontological argument in disguise, it executes its design solely by the aid of pure reason, although it at first professed to have no connection with this faculty, and to base its entire procedure upon experience alone.

The physico-theologians have therefore no reason to regard with such contempt the transcendental mode of argument, and to look down upon it, with the conceit of clear-sighted observers of nature, as the brain-cobweb of obscure speculatists. For if they reflect upon and examine their own arguments, they will find that, after following for some time the path of nature and experience, and discovering themselves no nearer their object, they suddenly leave this path and pass into the region of pure possibility, where they hope to reach upon the wings of ideas, what had eluded all their empirical investigations. Gain-ing, as they think, a firm footing after this immense leap, they extend their determinate conception—into the possession of which they have come, they know not how—over the whole sphere of creation, and explain their ideal, which is entirely a product of pure reason, by illustrations drawn from experience —though in a degree miserably unworthy of the grandeur of the object, while they refuse to acknowledge that they have arrived at this cognition or hypothesis by a very different road from that of experience.

Thus the physico-theological is based upon the cosmological, and this upon the ontological proof of the existence of a Supreme Being; and as besides these three there is no other path open to speculative reason, the ontological proof, on the ground of pure conceptions of reason, is the only possible one, if any proof of a proposition so far transcending the empirical exercise of the understanding is possible at all.

Sec. VII.—Critique of all Theology based upon Speculative Principles of Reason

If by the term *Theology* I understand the cognition of a primal being, that cognition is based either upon reason alone (*theologia rationalis*) or upon revelation (*theologia revelata*). The former cogitates its object either by means of pure transcendental conceptions, as an *ens originarium, realissimum, ens entium,* and is termed *transcendental theology;* or, by means of a conception derived from the nature of our own mind, as a supreme intelligence, and must then be entitled *natural* theology. The person who believes in a transcendental theology alone, is termed a *Deist;* he who acknowledges the possibility of a *natural* theology also, a *Theist.* The former admits that we can cognize by pure reason alone the existence of a supreme being, but at the same time maintains that our conception of this being is purely transcendental, and that all we can say of it is, that it possesses all reality, without being able to define it more closely. The second asserts that reason is capable of presenting us, from the analogy with nature, with a more definite conception of this being, and that its operations, as the cause of all things, are the results of intelligence and free will. The former regards the Supreme Being as the *cause of the world*—whether by the necessity of his nature, or as a free agent, is left undetermined; the latter considers this being as the *author of the world.*

Transcendental theology aims either at inferring the existence of a Supreme Being from a general experience—without any closer reference to the world to which this experience belongs, and in this case it is called *Cosmotheology;* or it endeavors to cognize the existence of such a being, through mere conceptions, without the aid of experience, and is then termed *Ontotheology.*

Natural theology infers the attributes and the existence of an author of the world, from the constitution of, the order and unity observable in, the world, in which two modes of causality must be admitted to exist—those of nature and freedom. Thus it rises from this world to a supreme intelligence, either as the principle of all natural, or of all moral order and perfection. In the former case it is termed Physico-theology, in the latter Ethical or Moral-theology.*

As we are wont to understand by the term *God* not merely an eternal nature, the operations of which are insensate and blind, but a Supreme Being, who is the free and intelligent author of all things, and as it is this latter view alone that can be of interest to humanity, we might, in strict rigor, deny to the *Deist* any belief in God at all, and regard him merely as a maintainer of the existence of a primal being or thing—the supreme cause of all other things. But, as no one ought to be blamed, merely because he does not feel himself justified in maintaining a certain opinion, as if he altogether denied its truth and asserted the opposite, it is more correct—as it is less harsh—to say, the Deist believes in a God, the Theist in a *living God* (*summa intelligentia*). We shall now proceed to investigate the sources of all these attempts of reason to establish the existence of a Supreme Being.

It may be sufficient in this place to define theoretical knowledge or cognition as knowledge of that which *is,* and practical knowledge as knowledge of that which *ought to be.* In this view, the theoretical employment of reason is that by which I cognize *à priori* (as necessary) that something is, while the practical is that by which I cognize *à priori* what ought to happen. Now, if it is an indubitably certain, though at the same time an entirely conditioned truth, that something is, or ought to happen, either a certain determinate condition of this truth is

---

* Not theological ethics; for this science contains ethical laws, which *presuppose* the existence of a Supreme Governor of the world; while Moral-theology, on the contrary, is the expression of a conviction of the existence of a Supreme Being, founded upon ethical laws.

absolutely necessary, or such a condition may be arbitrarily pre-supposed. In the former case the condition is postulated (*per thesin*), in the latter supposed (*per hypothesin*). There are certain practical laws—those of morality—which are absolutely necessary. Now, if these laws necessarily presuppose the exist-ence of some being, as the condition of the possibility of their *obligatory* power, this being must be *postulated,* because the conditioned, from which we reason to this determinate condi-tion, is itself cognized *à priori* as absolutely necessary. We shall at some future time show that the moral laws not merely pre-suppose the existence of a Supreme Being, but also, as them-selves absolutely necessary in a different relation, demand or postulate it—although only from a practical point of view. The discussion of this argument we postpone for the present.

When the question relates merely to that which is, not to that which ought to be, the conditioned which is presented in experi-ence, is always cogitated as contingent. For this reason its con-dition cannot be regarded as absolutely necessary, but merely as relatively necessary, or rather as *needful;* the condition is in itself and *à priori* a mere arbitrary presupposition in aid of the cognition, by reason, of the conditioned. If, then, we are to possess a theoretical cognition of the absolute necessity of a thing, we cannot attain to this cognition otherwise than *à priori* by means of *conceptions;* while it is impossible in this way to cognize the existence of a cause which bears any relation to an existence given in experience.

Theoretical cognition is *speculative* when it relates to an ob-ject or certain conceptions of an object which is not given and cannot be discovered by means of experience. It is opposed to the *cognition of nature,* which concerns only those objects or predicates which can be presented in a possible experience.

The principle that everything which happens (the *empirically* contingent) must have a cause, is a principle of the cognition of nature, but not of speculative cognition. For, if we change it into an abstract principle, and deprive it of its reference to experience and the empirical, we shall find that it cannot with justice be regarded any longer as a synthetical proposition, and that it is impossible to discover any mode of transition from that which exists to something entirely different—termed cause. Nay, more, the conception of a cause—as likewise that of the contingent—loses, in this speculative mode of employing it, all significance, for its objective reality and meaning are comprehensible from experience alone.

When from the existence of the universe and the things in it the existence of a cause of the universe is inferred, reason is proceeding not in the *natural,* but in the *speculative* method. For the principle of the former announces, not that things themselves or substances, but only that which *happens* or their *states*—as empirically contingent, have a cause: the assertion that the existence of substance itself is contingent is not justified by experience, it is the assertion of a reason employing its principles in a speculative manner. If, again, I infer from the form of the universe, from the way in which all things are connected and act and react upon each other, the existence of a cause entirely distinct from the universe—this would again be a judgment of purely speculative reason; because the object in this case—the cause—can never be an object of possible experience. In both these cases the principle of causality, which is valid only in the field of experience—useless and even meaningless beyond this region, would be diverted from its proper destination.

Now I maintain that all attempts of reason to establish a theology by the aid of speculation alone are fruitless, that the principles of reason as applied to nature do not conduct us to any theological truths, and, consequently, that a rational theology can have no existence, unless it is founded upon the laws of morality. For all synthetical principles of the understanding are valid only as *immanent* in experience; while the cognition of a Supreme Being necessitates their being employed transcendentally, and of this the understanding is quite incapable. If the empirical law of causality is to conduct us to a Supreme Being, this being must belong to the chain of empirical objects—in which case it would be, like all phenomena, itself conditioned. If the possibility of passing the limits of experience be admitted, by means of the dynamical law of the relation of an effect to its cause, what kind of conception shall we obtain by this procedure? Certainly not the conception of a Supreme Being, because experience never presents us with the greatest of all possible effects, and it is only an effect of this character that could witness to the existence of a corresponding cause. If, for the purpose of fully satisfying the requirements of Reason, we recognize her right to assert the existence of a perfect and absolutely necessary being, this can be admitted only from favor, and cannot be regarded as the result of irresistible demonstration. The physico-theological proof may add weight to others —if other proofs there are—by connecting speculation with experience; but in itself it rather prepares the mind for theological cognition, and gives it a right and natural direction, than establishes a sure foundation for theology.

It is now perfectly evident that transcendental questions admit only of transcendental answers—those presented *à priori* by pure conceptions without the least empirical admixture. But the question in the present case is evidently synthetical—it aims at the extension of our cognition beyond the bounds of experience—it requires an assurance respecting the existence of a being corresponding with the idea in our minds, to which no experience can ever be adequate. Now it has been abundantly proved that all *à priori* synthetical cognition is possible only as the expression of the formal conditions of a possible experience; and that the validity of all principles depends upon their immanence in the field of experience, that is, their relation to objects of empirical cognition, or phenomena. Thus all transcendental procedure in reference to speculative theology is without result.

If any one prefers doubting the conclusiveness of the proofs of our Analytic to losing the persuasion of the validity of these old and time-honored arguments, he at least cannot decline answering the question—how he can pass the limits of all possible experience by the help of mere ideas. If he talks of new arguments, or of improvements upon old arguments—I request him to spare me. There is certainly no great choice in this sphere of discussion, as all speculative arguments must at last look for support to the ontological, and I have, therefore, very little to fear from the argumentative fecundity of the dogmatical defenders of a non-sensuous reason. Without looking upon myself as a remarkably combative person, I shall not decline the challenge to detect the fallacy and destroy the pretensions of every attempt of speculative theology. And yet the hope of better fortune never deserts those who are accustomed to the dogmatical mode of procedure. I shall, therefore, restrict myself to the simple and equitable demand that such reasoners will demonstrate, from the nature of the human mind as well as from that of the other sources of knowledge, how we are to proceed to extend our cognition completely *à priori*, and to carry it to that point where experience abandons us, and no means exist of guaranteeing the objective reality of our conceptions. In whatever way the understanding may have attained to a conception, the existence of the object of the conception cannot be discovered in it by analysis, because the cognition of the *existence* of the object depends upon the object's being posited and given in itself *apart from the conception*. But it is utterly impossible to go beyond our conception, without the aid of experience—which presents to the mind nothing but phenomena, or to attain by the help of mere conceptions to a conviction of the existence of new kinds of objects or supernatural beings.

But although pure speculative reason is far from sufficient to demonstrate the existence of a Supreme Being, it is of the highest utility in *correcting* our conception of this being—on the supposition that we can attain to the cognition of it by some other means—in making it consistent with itself and with all other conceptions of intelligible objects, clearing it from all that is incompatible with the conception of an *ens summum,* and eliminating from it all limitations or admixture of empirical elements.

Transcendental theology is still therefore, notwithstanding its objective insufficiency, of importance in a negative respect; it is useful as a test of the procedure of reason when engaged with pure ideas, no other than a transcendental standard being in this case admissible. For if, from a practical point of view, the hypothesis of a Supreme and All-sufficient Being is to maintain its validity without opposition, it must be of the highest importance to define this conception in a correct and rigorous manner—as the transcendental conception of a necessary being, to eliminate all phenomenal elements (anthropomorphism in its most extended signification), and at the same time to overthrow all contradictory assertions—be they *atheistic, deistic,* or *anthropomorphic.* This is of course very easy; as the same arguments which demonstrated the inability of human reason to *affirm* the existence of a Supreme Being, must be alike sufficient to prove the invalidity of its denial. For it is impossible to gain from the pure speculation of reason demonstration that there exists no Supreme Being, as the ground of all that exists, or that this being possesses none of those properties which we regard as analogical with the dynamical qualities of a thinking being, or that, as the anthropomorphists would have us believe, it is subject to all the limitations which sensibility imposes upon those intelligences which exist in the world of experience.

A Supreme Being is, therefore, for the speculative reason, a mere ideal, though a *faultless* one—a conception which perfects and crowns the system of human cognition, but the objective reality of which can neither be proved nor disproved by pure reason. If this defect is ever supplied by a Moral Theology, the problematic Transcendental Theology which has preceded, will have been at least serviceable as demonstrating the mental necessity existing for the conception, by the complete determination of it which it has furnished, and the ceaseless testing of the conclusions of a reason often deceived by sense, and not always in harmony with its own ideas. The attributes of necessity, infinitude, unity, existence apart from the world (and not as a world-soul), eternity—free from conditions of time, omnipresence—free from the conditions of space, omnipotence and others, are pure transcendental predicates; and thus the accurate conception of a Supreme Being, which every theology requires, is furnished by transcendental theology alone.

APPENDIX

The Transcendental Dialectic

Of the Regulative Employment of the Ideas of Pure Reason

The result of all the dialectical attempts of pure reason not only confirms the truth of what we have already proved in our Transcendental Analytic, namely, that all inferences which would lead us beyond the limits of experience are fallacious and groundless, but it at the same time teaches us this important lesson, that human reason has a natural inclination to overstep these limits, and that transcendental ideas are as much the natural property of the reason as categories are of the understanding. There exists this difference, however, that while the categories never mislead us, outward objects being always in perfect harmony therewith, ideas are the parents of irresistible illusions, the severest and most subtle criticism being required to save us from the fallacies which they induce.

Whatever is grounded in the nature of our powers, will be found to be in harmony with the final purpose and proper employment of these powers, when once we have discovered their true direction and aim. We are entitled to suppose, there-fore, that there exists a mode of employing transcendental ideas which is proper and *immanent;* although, when we mis-take their meaning, and regard them as conceptions of actual things, their mode of application is *transcendent* and delusive. For it is not the idea itself, but only the employment of the idea in relation to possible experience, that is transcendent or immanent. An idea is employed transcendently, when it is applied to an object falsely believed to be adequate with and to correspond to it; immanently, when it is applied solely to the employment of the *understanding* in the sphere of expe-rience. Thus all errors of *subreptio*—of misapplication, are to be ascribed to defects of judgment, and not to understand-ing or reason.

Reason never has an immediate relation to an object; it relates immediately to the understanding alone. It is only through the understanding that it can be employed in the field of experience. It does not *form* conceptions of objects, it mere-ly *arranges them* and gives to them that unity which they are capable of possessing when the sphere of their application has been extended as widely as possible. Reason avails itself of the conceptions of the understanding for the sole purpose of producing totality in the different series. This totality the understanding does not concern itself with; its only occupation is the connection of experiences, by which *series* of conditions in accordance with conceptions are established. The object of reason is therefore the understanding and its proper destina-tion. As the latter brings unity into the diversity of objects by means of its conceptions, so the former brings unity into the diversity of conceptions by means of ideas; as it sets the final aim of a collective unity to the operations of the understanding, which without this occupies itself with a distributive unity alone.

I accordingly maintain, that transcendental ideas can never be employed as constitutive ideas, that they cannot be con-ceptions of objects, and that, when thus considered, they as-sume a fallacious and dialectical character. But, on the other hand, they are capable of an admirable and indispensably neces-sary application to objects—as regulative ideas, directing the understanding to a certain aim, the guiding lines towards which all its laws follow, and in which they all meet in one point.

This point—though a mere idea (*focus imaginarius*), that is, not a point from which the conceptions of the understanding do really proceed, for it lies beyond the sphere of possible experience—serves notwithstanding to give to these conceptions the greatest possible unity combined with the greatest possible extension. Hence arises the natural illusion which induces us to believe that these lines proceed from an object which lies out of the sphere of empirical cognition, just as objects reflected in a mirror appear to be behind it. But this illusion—which we may hinder from imposing upon us—is necessary and unavoidable, if we desire to see, not only those objects which lie before us, but those which are at a great distance behind us; that is to say, when, in the present case, we direct the aims of the understanding, beyond every given experience, towards an extension as great as can possibly be attained.

If we review our cognitions in their entire extent, we shall find that the peculiar business of reason is to arrange them into a *system*, that is to say, to give them connection according to a principle. This unity presupposes an idea—the idea of the form of a whole (of cognition), preceding the determinate cognition of the parts, and containing the conditions which determine *à priori* to every part its place and relation to the other parts of the whole system. This idea accordingly demands complete unity in the cognition of the understanding—not the unity of a contingent aggregate, but that of a system connected according to necessary laws. It cannot be affirmed with propriety that this idea is a conception of an object; it is merely a conception of the complete unity of the conceptions of objects, in so far as this unity is available to the understanding as a rule. Such conceptions of reason are not derived from nature; on the contrary, we employ them for the interrogation and investigation of nature, and regard our cognition as defective so long as it is not adequate to them. We admit that such a thing as *pure earth*, *pure water* or *pure air*, is not to be discovered. And yet we require these conceptions (which have their origin in the reason, so far as regards their absolute purity and completeness) for the purpose of determining the share which each of these natural causes has in every phenomenon. Thus the different kinds of matter are all referred to earths —as mere weight, to salts and inflammable bodies—as pure force, and finally, to water and air—as the *vehicula* of the former, or the machines employed by them in their operations—for the purpose of explaining the chemical action and reaction of bodies in accordance with the idea of a mechanism. For, although not actually so expressed, the influence of such ideas of reason is very observable in the procedure of natural philosophers.

If reason is the faculty of deducing the particular from the general, and if the general be certain *in se* and given, it is only necessary that the *judgment* should subsume the particular under the general, the particular being thus necessarily determined. I shall term this the demonstrative or apodictic employment of reason. If, however, the general is admitted as *problematical* only, and is a mere idea, the particular case is certain, but the universality of the rule which applies to this particular case remains a problem. Several particular cases, the certainty of which is beyond doubt, are then taken and examined, for the purpose of discovering whether the rule is applicable to them; and if it appears that all the particular cases which can be collected follow from the rule, its universality is inferred, and at the same time, all the causes which have not, or cannot be presented to our observations, are concluded to be of the same character with those which we have observed. This I shall term the hypothetical employment of the reason.

The hypothetical exercise of reason by the aid of ideas employed as problematical conceptions is properly not *constitutive*. That is to say, if we consider the subject strictly, the truth of the rule, which has been employed as an hypothesis, does not follow from the use that is made of it by reason. For how can we know all the possible cases that may arise?—some of which may, however, prove exceptions to the universality of the rule. This employment of reason is merely regulative, and its sole aim is the introduction of unity into the aggregate of our particular cognitions, and thereby the *approximating* of the rule to universality.

The object of the hypothetical employment of reason is therefore the systematic unity of cognitions; and this unity is the *criterion* of the *truth* of a rule. On the other hand, this systematic unity—as a mere idea—is in fact merely a unity *projected*, not to be regarded as given, but only in the light of a problem— a problem which serves, however, as a principle for the various and particular exercise of the understanding in experience, directs it with regard to those cases which are not presented to our observation, and introduces harmony and consistency into all its operations.

All that we can be certain of from the above considerations is, that this systematic unity is a logical principle, whose aim is to assist the understanding, where it cannot of itself attain to rules, by means of ideas, to bring all these various rules under one principle, and thus to insure the most complete consistency and connection that can be attained. But the assertion that objects and the understanding by which they are cognized are so constituted as to be determined to systematic unity, that this may be postulated *à priori*, without any reference to the interest of reason, and that we are justified in declaring all possible cognitions—empirical and others—to possess systematic unity, and to be subject to general principles from which, notwithstanding their various character, they are all derivable—such an assertion can be founded only upon a *transcendental* principle of reason, which would render this systematic unity not subjectively and logically—in its character of a method, but objectively necessary.

We shall illustrate this by an example. The conceptions of the understanding make us acquainted, among many other kinds of unity, with that of the causality of a substance, which is termed *power*. The different phenomenal manifestations of the same substance appear at first view to be so very dissimilar, that we are inclined to assume the existence of just as many different powers as there are different effects—as, in the case of the human mind, we have feeling, consciousness, imagination, memory, wit, analysis, pleasure, desire, and so on. Now we are required by a logical maxim to reduce these differences to as small a number as possible, by comparing them and discovering the hidden identity which exists. We must inquire, for example, whether or not imagination (connected with consciousness), memory, wit, and analysis are not merely different forms of understanding and reason. The idea of a *fundamental power*, the existence of which no effort of logic can assure us of, is the problem to be solved, for the systematic representation of the existing variety of powers. The logical principle of reason requires us to produce as great a unity as is possible in the system of our cognitions; and the more the phenomena of this and the other power are found to be identical, the more probable does it become, that they are nothing but different manifestations of one and the same power, which may be called, relatively speaking, a *fundamental power*. And so with other cases.

These relatively fundamental powers must again be compared with each other, to discover, if possible, the one radical and *absolutely* fundamental power of which they are but the manifestations. But this unity is purely hypothetical. It is not maintained, that this unity does really exist, but that we must, in the interest of reason, that is, for the establishment of principles for the various rules presented by experience, try to discover and introduce it, so far as is practicable, into the sphere of our cognitions.

But the transcendental employment of the understanding would lead us to believe that this idea of a fundamental power is not problematical, but that it possesses objective reality, and thus the systematic unity of the various powers or forces in a substance is demanded by the understanding and erected into an apodictic or necessary principle. For, without having attempted to discover the unity of the various powers existing in nature, nay, even after all our attempts have failed, we notwithstanding presuppose that it does exist, and may be, sooner or later, discovered. And this reason does, not only, as in the case above adduced, with regard to the unity of substance, but where many substances, although all to a certain extent homogeneous, are discoverable, as in the case of matter in general. Here also does reason presuppose the existence of the systematic unity of various powers—inasmuch as particular laws of nature are subordinate to general laws; and parsimony in principles is not merely an economical principle of reason, but an essential law of nature.

We cannot understand, in fact, how a logical principle of unity can of right exist, unless we presuppose a transcendental principle, by which such a systematic unity—as a property of objects themselves—is regarded as necessary *à priori*. For with what right can reason, in its logical exercise, require us to regard the variety of forces which nature displays, as in effect a disguised unity, and to deduce them from one fundamental force or power, when she is free to admit that it is just as possible that all forces should be different in kind, and that a systematic unity is not comformable to the design of nature? In this view of the case, reason would be proceeding in direct opposition to her own destination, by setting as an aim an idea which entirely conflicts with the procedure and arrangement of nature. Neither can we assert that reason has previously inferred this unity from the contingent nature of phenomena. For the law of reason which requires us to seek for this unity is a necessary law, inasmuch as without it we should not possess a faculty of reason, not without reason a consistent and self-accordant mode of employing the understanding, nor, in the absence of this, any proper and sufficient criterion of empirical truth. In relation to this criterion, therefore, we must suppose the idea of the systematic unity of nature to possess objective validity and necessity.

We find this transcendental presupposition lurking in different forms in the principles of philosophers, although they have neither recognized it nor confessed to themselves its presence. That the diversities of individual things do not exclude identity of species, that the various species must be considered as merely different determinations of a few *genera,* and these again as divisions of still higher *races,* and so on—that, accordingly, a certain systematic unity of all possible empirical conceptions, in so far as they can be deduced from higher and more general conceptions, must be sought for, is a scholastic maxim or logical principle, without which reason could not be employed by us. For we can infer the particular from the general, only in so far as general properties of things constitute the foundation upon which the particular rest.

That the same unity exists in nature is presupposed by philosophers in the well-known scholastic maxim, which forbids us unnecessarily to augment the number of entities or principles (*entia præter necessitatem non esse multiplicanda*). This maxim asserts that nature herself assists in the establishment of this unity of reason, and that the seemingly infinite diversity of phenomena should not deter us from the expectation of discovering beneath this diversity a unity of fundamental properties, of which the aforesaid variety is but a more or less determined form. This unity, although a mere idea, has been always pursued with so much zeal, that thinkers have found it necessary rather to moderate the desire than encourage it. It was considered a great step when chemists were able to reduce all salts to two main genera—acids and alkalis; and they regard this difference as itself a mere variety, or different manifestation of one and the same fundamental material. The different kinds of earths (stones and even metals) chemists have endeavored to reduce to three, and afterwards to two; but still, not content with this advance, they cannot but think that behind these diversities there lurks but one genus—nay, that even salts and earths have a common principle. It might be conjectured that this is merely an economical plan of reason, for the purpose of sparing itself trouble, and an attempt of a purely hypothetical character, which, when successful, gives an appearance of probability to the principle of explanation employed by the reason. But a selfish purpose of this kind is easily to be distinguished from the idea, according to which every one presupposes that this unity is in accordance with the laws of nature, and that reason does not in this case *request*, but *requires*, although we are quite unable to determine the proper limits of this unity.

If the diversity existing in phenomena—a diversity not of form (for in this they may be similar) but of content—were so great that the subtlest human reason could never by comparison discover in them the least similarity (which is not impossible), in this case the logical law of genera would be without foundation, the conception of a genus, nay, all general conceptions would be impossible, and the faculty of the understanding, the exercise of which is restricted to the world of conceptions, could not exist. The logical principle of genera, accordingly, if it is to be applied to nature (by which I mean objects presented to our senses), presupposes a transcendental principle. In accordance with this principle, homogeneity is necessarily presupposed in the variety of phenomena (although we are unable to determine à *priori* the degree of this homogeneity), because without it no empirical conceptions, and consequently no experience, would be possible.

The logical principle of genera, which demands identity in phenomena, is balanced by another principle—that of *species*, which requires variety and diversity in things, notwithstanding their accordance in the same genus, and directs the understanding to attend to the one no less than to the other. This principle (of the faculty of distinction) acts as a check upon the levity of the former (the faculty of wit); and reason exhibits in this respect a double and conflicting interest—on the one hand the interest in the *extent* (the interest of generality) in relation to genera, on the other that of the *content* (the interest of individuality) in relation to the variety of species. In the former case, the understanding cogitates more *under* its conceptions, in the latter it cogitates more *in* them. This distinction manifests itself likewise in the habits of thought peculiar to natural philosophers, some of whom—the remarkably speculative heads—may be said to be hostile to heterogeneity in phenomena, and have their eyes always fixed on the unity of genera, while others —with a strong empirical tendency—aim unceasingly at the analysis of phenomena, and almost destroy in us the hope of ever being able to estimate the character of these according to general principles.

The latter mode of thought is evidently based upon a logical principle, the aim of which is the systematic completeness of all cognitions. This principle authorizes me, beginning at the genus, to descend to the various and diverse contained under it; and in this way extension, as in the former case unity, is assured to the system. For if we merely examine the sphere of the conception which indicates a genus, we cannot discover how far it is possible to proceed in the division of that sphere; just as it is impossible, from the consideration of the space occupied by matter, to determine how far we can proceed in the division of it. Hence every *genus* must contain different *species,* and these again different *sub-species;* and as each of the latter must itself contain a sphere (must be of a certain extent, as a *conceptus communis*), reason demands that no species or sub-species is to be considered as the lowest possible. For a species or sub-species, being always a conception, which contains only what is common to a number of different things, does not completely determine any individual thing, or relate immediately to it, and must consequently contain other conceptions, that is, other sub-species under it. This law of specification may be thus expressed:—*Entium varietates non temere sunt minuendæ.*

But it is easy to see that this logical law would likewise be without sense or application, were it not based upon a transcendental *law of specification,* which certainly does not require that the differences existing in phenomena should be *infinite* in number, for the logical principle, which merely maintains the *indeterminateness* of the logical sphere of a conception, in relation to its possible division, does not authorize this statement; while it does impose upon the understanding the duty of searching for sub-species to every species, and minor differences in every difference. For, were there no lower conceptions, neither could there be any higher. Now the understanding cognizes only by means of conceptions; consequently, how far soever it may proceed in division, never by mere intuition, but always by lower and lower conceptions. The cognition of phenomena in their complete determination (which is possible only by means of the understanding) requires an unceasingly continued specification of conceptions, and a progression to ever smaller differences, of which abstraction had been made in the conception of the species, and still more in that of the genus.

This law of specification cannot be deduced from experience; it can never present us with a principle of so universal an application. Empirical specification very soon stops in its distinction of diversities, and requires the guidance of the transcendéntal law, as a principle of the reason—a law which imposes on us the necessity of never ceasing in our search for differences, even although these may not present themselves to the senses. That absorbent earths are of different kinds, could only be discovered by obeying the anticipatory law of reason, which imposes upon the understanding the task of discovering the differences existing between these earths, and supposes that nature is richer in substances than our senses would indicate. The faculty of the understanding belongs to us just as much under the presupposition of differences in the objects of nature, as under the condition that these objects are homogeneous, because we could not possess conceptions, nor make any use of our understanding, were not the phenomena included under these conceptions in some respects dissimilar, as well as similar, in their character.

Reason thus prepares the sphere of the understanding for the operations of this faculty, 1, by the principle of the *homogeneity* of the diverse in higher genera; 2, by the principle of the *variety* of the homogeneous in lower species; and, to complete the systematic unity, it adds, 3, a law of the *affinity* of all conceptions, which prescribes a continuous transition from one species to every other by the gradual increase of diversity. We may term these the principles of the *homogeneity* the *specification,* and the *continuity* of forms. The latter results from the union of the two former, inasmuch as we regard the systematic connection as complete in thought, in the ascent to higher genera, as well as in the descent to lower species. For all diversities must be related to each other, as they all spring from one highest genus, descending through the different gradations of a more and more extended determination.

We may illustrate the systematic unity produced by the three logical principles in the following manner. Every conception may be regarded as a point, which, as the stand-point of a spectator, has a certain horizon, which may be said to enclose a number of things that may be viewed, so to speak, from that centre. Within this horizon there must be an infinite number of other points, each of which has its own horizon, smaller and more circumscribed; in other words, every species contains sub-species, according to the principle of specification, and the logical horizon consists of smaller horizons (sub-species), but not of points (individuals), which possess no extent. But different horizons or genera, which include under them so many conceptions, may have one common horizon, from which, as from a mid-point, they may be surveyed; and we may proceed thus till we arrive at the highest genus, or universal and true horizon, which is determined by the highest conception, and which contains under itself all differences and varieties, as genera, species, and sub-species.

To this highest stand-point I am conducted by the law of homogeneity, as to all lower and more variously-determined conceptions by the law of specification. Now as in this way there exists no void in the whole extent of all possible conceptions, and as out of the sphere of these the mind can discover nothing, there arises from the presupposition of the universal horizon above mentioned, and its complete division, the principle: *Non datur vacuum formarum.* This principle asserts that there are not different primitive and highest genera, which stand isolated, so to speak, from each other, but all the various genera are mere divisions and limitations of one highest and universal genus; and hence follows immediately the principle: *Datur continuum formarum.* This principle indicates that all differences of species limit each other, and do not admit of transition from one to another by a *saltus,* but only through smaller degrees of the difference between the one species and the other. In one word, there are no species or sub-species which (in the view of reason) are the nearest possible to each other; intermediate species or sub-species being always possible, the difference of which from each of the former is always smaller than the difference existing between these.

The first law, therefore, directs us to avoid the notion that there exist different primal genera, and enounces the fact of perfect homogeneity; the second imposes a check upon this tendency to unity and prescribes the distinction of sub-species, before proceeding to apply our general conceptions to individuals. The third unites both the former, by enouncing the fact of homogeneity as existing even in the most various diversity, by means of the gradual transition from one species to another. Thus it indicates a relationship between the different branches or species, in so far as they all spring from the same stem.

But this logical law of the *continuum specierum* (*formarum logicarum*) presupposes a transcendental principle (*lex continui in natura*), without which the understanding might be led into error, by following the guidance of the former, and thus perhaps pursuing a path contrary to that prescribed by nature. This law must consequently be based upon pure transcendental, and not upon empirical considerations. For, in the latter case, it would come later than the system; whereas it is really itself the parent of all that is systematic in our cognition of nature. These principles are not mere hypotheses employed for the purpose of experimenting upon nature; although when any such connection is discovered, it forms a solid ground for regarding the hypothetical unity as valid in the sphere of nature—and thus they are in this respect not without their use. But we go farther, and maintain that it is manifest that these principles of parsimony in fundamental causes, variety in effects, and affinity in phenomena, are in accordance both with reason and nature, and that they are not mere methods or plans devised for the purpose of assisting us in our observation of the external world.

But it is plain that this continuity of forms is a mere idea, to which no adequate object can be discovered in experience. And this for two reasons. First, because the species in nature are really divided, and hence form *quanta discreta;** and, if the gradual progression through their affinity were continuous, the intermediate members lying between two given species must be infinite in number, which is impossible. Secondly, because we cannot make any determinate empirical use of this law, ina-

* Not *quanta continua*, like space or a line.

much as it does not present us with any criterion of affinity which could aid us in determining how far we ought to pursue the graduation of differences; it merely contains a general indication that it is our duty to seek for and, if possible, to discover them.

When we arrange these principles of systematic unity in the order comformable to their employment in experience, they will stand thus: *Variety, Affinity, Unity,* each of them, as ideas, being taken in the highest degree of their completeness. Reason presupposes the existence of cognitions of the understanding, which have a direct relation to experience, and aims at the ideal unity of these cognitions—a unity which far transcends all experience or empirical notions. The affinity of the diverse, notwithstanding the differences existing between its parts, has a relation to things, but a still closer one to the mere properties and powers of things. For example, imperfect experience may represent the orbits of the planets as circular. But we discover variations from this course, and we proceed to suppose that the planets revolve in a path which, if not a circle, is of a character very similar to it. That is to say, the movements of those planets which do not form a circle, will approximate more or less to the properties of a circle, and probably form an ellipse. The paths of comets exhibit still greater variations, for, so far as our observation extends, they do not return upon their own course in a circle or ellipse. But we proceed to the conjecture that comets describe a parabola, a figure which is closely allied to the ellipse. In fact, a parabola is merely an ellipse, with its longer axis produced to an indefinite extent. Thus these principles conduct us to a unity in the genera of the forms of these orbits, and, proceeding further, to a unity as regards the cause of the motions of the heavenly bodies—that is, gravitation. But we go on extending our conquests over nature, and endeavor to explain all seeming deviations from these rules, and even make additions to our system which no experience can ever substantiate—for example, the theory, in affinity with that of ellipses, of hyperbolic paths of comets, pursuing which, these bodies leave our solar system, and, passing from sun to sun, unite the most distant parts of the infinite universe, which is held together by the same moving power.

The most remarkable circumstance connected with these principles is, that they seem to be transcendental, and, although only containing ideas for the guidance of the empirical exercise of reason, and although this empirical employment stands to these ideas in an asymptotic relation alone (to use a mathematical term), that is, continually approximate, without ever being able to attain to them, they possess, notwithstanding, as *à priori* synthetical propositions, objective though undetermined validity, and are available as rules for possible experience. In the elaboration of our experience, they may also be employed with great advantage, as heuristic * principles. A transcendental deduction of them cannot be made; such a deduction being always impossible in the case of ideas, as has been already shown.

We distinguished, in the Transcendental Analytic, the *dynamical* principles of the understanding, which are regulative principles of *intuition*, from the mathematical, which are constitutive principles of intuition. These dynamical laws are, however, constitutive in relation to *experience*, inasmuch as they render the conceptions without which experience could not exist, possible *à priori*. But the principles of pure reason cannot be constitutive even in regard to empirical *conceptions*, because no sensuous schema corresponding to them can be discovered, and they cannot therefore have an object *in concreto*. Now, if I grant that they cannot be employed in the sphere of experience, as constitutive principles, how shall I secure for them employment and objective validity as regulative principles, and in what way can they be so employed?

The understanding is the object of reason, as sensibility is the object of the understanding. The production of systematic unity in all the empirical operations of the understanding is the proper occupation of reason; just as it is the business of the understanding to connect the various content of phenomena by means of conceptions, and subject them to empirical laws. But the operations of the understanding are, without the schemata of sensibility, *undetermined;* and, in the same manner, the unity of reason is perfectly *undetermined* as regards the conditions under which, and the extent to which, the understanding ought to carry the systematic connection of its conceptions. But, although it is impossible to discover in *intuition* a schema for the complete systematic unity of all the conceptions of the understanding, there must be some *analogon* of this schema. This analogon is the idea of the *maximum* of the division and

* From the Greek αἴσκα.

the connection of our cognition in one principle. For we may have a determinate notion of a *maximum* and an absolutely perfect, all the restrictive conditions which are connected with an indeterminate and various content, having been abstracted. Thus the idea of reason is analogous with a sensuous schema, with this difference, that the application of the categories to the schema of reason does not present a cognition of any object (as is the case with the application of the categories to sensuous schemata), but merely provides us with a rule or principle for the systematic unity of the exercise of the understanding. Now, as every principle which imposes upon the exercise of the understanding *à priori* compliance with the rule of systematic unity, also relates, although only in an indirect manner, to an object of experience, the principles of pure reason will also possess objective reality and validity in relation to experience. But they will not aim at *determining* our knowledge in regard to any empirical object; they will merely indicate the procedure following which the empirical and determinate exercise of the understanding may be in complete harmony and connection with itself —a result which is produced by its being brought into harmony with the principle of systematic unity, so far as that is possible, and deduced from it.

I term all subjective principles which are not derived from observation of the constitution of an object, but from the interest which Reason has in producing a certain completeness in her cognition of that object, *maxims* of reason. Thus there are maxims of speculative reason, which are based solely upon its speculative interest, although they appear to be objective principles.

When principles which are really regulative are regarded as constitutive, and employed as objective principles, contradictions must arise; but if they are considered as mere maxims, there is no room for contradictions of any kind, as they then merely indicate the different interests of reason, which occasion differences in the mode of thought. In effect, Reason has only one single interest, and the seeming contradiction existing between her maxims merely indicates a difference in, and a reciprocal limitation of, the methods by which this interest is satisfied.

This reasoner has at heart the interest of *diversity*—in accordance with the principle of specification; another, the interest of *unity*—in accordance with the principle of aggregation. Each believes that his judgment rests upon a thorough insight into the subject he is examining, and yet it has been influenced solely by a greater or less degree of adherence to some one of the two principles, neither of which are objective, but originate solely from the interest of reason, and on this account to be termed maxims rather than principles. When I observe intelligent men disputing about the distinctive characteristics of men, animals, or plants, and even of minerals, those on the one side assuming the existence of certain national characteristics, certain well-defined and hereditary distinctions of family, race, and so on, while the other side maintain that nature has endowed all races of men with the same faculties and dispositions, and that all differences are but the result of external and accidental circumstances—I have only to consider for a moment the real nature of the subject of discussion, to arrive at the conclusion that it is a subject far too deep for us to judge of, and that there is little probability of either party being able to speak from a perfect insight into and understanding of the nature of the subject itself. Both have, in reality, been struggling for the two-fold interest of reason; the one maintaining the one interest, the other the other. But this difference between the maxims of diversity and unity may easily be reconciled and adjusted; although, so long as they are regarded as objective principles, they must occasion not only contradictions and polemic, but place hindrances in the way of the advancement of truth, until some means is discovered of reconciling these conflicting interests, and bringing reason into union and harmony with itself.

The same is the case with the so-called law discovered by Leibnitz,* and supported with remarkable ability by Bonnet †—the law of the *continuous gradation* of created beings, which is nothing more than an inference from the principle of affinity; for observation and study of the order of nature could never present it to the mind as an objective truth. The steps of this ladder, as they appear in experience, are too far apart from each other, and the so-called petty differences between different kinds of animals are in nature commonly so wide separations, that no confidence can be placed in such views (particularly when we reflect on the great variety of things, and the ease with which we can discover resemblances), and no faith in the laws which

* Leibnitz, " Nouveaux Essais," Liv. iii. ch. 6.   † Bonnet, "Betrachtungen über die Natur," pp. 29—85.

are said to express the aims and purposes of nature. On the other hand, the method of investigating the order of nature in the light of this principle, and the maxim which requires us to regard this order—it being still undetermined how far it extends—as really existing in nature, is beyond doubt a legitimate and excellent principle of reason—a principle which extends further than any experience or observation of ours, and which, without giving us any positive knowledge of anything in the region of experience, guides us to the goal of systematic unity.

Of the Ultimate End of the Natural Dialectic of Human Reason.

The ideas of pure reason cannot be, of themselves and in their own nature, dialectical; it is from their misemployment alone that fallacies and illusions arise. For they originate in the nature of reason itself, and it is impossible that this supreme tribunal for all the rights and claims of speculation should be itself undeserving of confidence and promotive of error. It is to be expected, therefore, that these ideas have a genuine and legitimate aim. It is true, the mob of sophists raise against reason the cry of inconsistency and contradiction, and affect to despise the government of that faculty, because they cannot understand its constitution, while it is to its beneficial influences alone that they owe the position and the intelligence which enable them to criticise and to blame its procedure.

We cannot employ an *à priori* conception with certainty, until we have made a transcendental deduction thereof. The ideas of pure reason do not admit of the same kind of deduction as the categories. But if they are to possess the least objective validity, and to represent anything but mere creations of thought (*entia rationis ratiocinantis*), a deduction of them must be possible. This deduction will complete the critical task imposed upon pure reason; and it is to this part of our labors that we now proceed.

There is a great difference between a thing's being presented to the mind as an *object in an absolute sense,* or merely as an *ideal object.* In the former case I employ my conceptions to determine the object; in the latter case nothing is present to the mind but a mere schema, which does not relate directly to an object, not even in a hypothetical sense, but which is useful only for the purpose of representing other objects to the mind, in a mediate and indirect manner, by means of their relation to the idea in the intellect. Thus I say, the conception of a supreme intelligence is a mere idea; that is to say, its objective reality does not consist in the fact that it has an immediate relation to an object (for in this sense we have no means of establishing its objective validity), it is merely a schema constructed according to the necessary conditions of the unity of reason—the schema of a thing in general, which is useful towards the production of the highest degree of systematic unity in the empirical exercise of reason, in which we deduce this or that object of experience from the imaginary object of this idea, as the ground or cause of the said object of experience. In this way, the idea is properly a heuristic, and not an ostensive conception; it does not give us any information respecting the constitution of an object, it merely indicates how, under the guidance of the idea, we ought to *investigate* the constitution and the relations of objects in the world of experience. Now, if it can be shown that the three kinds of transcendental ideas (psychological, cosmological, and theological), although not relating directly to any object nor determining it, do nevertheless, on the supposition of the existence of an *ideal object,* produce systematic unity in the laws of the empirical employment of the reason, and extend our empirical cognition, without ever being inconsistent or in opposition with it—it must be a necessary *maxim* of reason to regulate its procedure according to these ideas. And this forms the transcendental deduction of all speculative ideas, not as *constitutive* principles of the extension of our cognition beyond the limits of our experience, but as *regulative* principles of the systematic unity of empirical cognition, which is by the aid of these ideas arranged and emended within its own proper limits, to an extent unattainable by the operation of the principles of the understanding alone.

I shall make this plainer. Guided by the principles involved in these ideas, we must, in the *first* place, so connect all the phenomena, actions and feelings of the mind, as if it were a simple substance, which, endowed with personal identity, possesses a permanent existence (in this life at least), while its states, among which those of the body are to be included as external conditions, are in continual change. *Secondly,* in cosmology, we must investigate the conditions of all natural phenomena, internal as well as external, as if they belonged to a chain infinite and without any prime or supreme member, while we do not, on this account, deny the existence of intelligible grounds of these phenomena, although we never employ them to explain phenomena, for the simple reason that they are not objects of our cognition. *Thirdly,* in the sphere of theology, we must regard the whole system of possible experience as forming an absolute, but dependent and sensuously-conditioned unity, and at the same time as based upon a sole, supreme, and all-sufficient ground existing apart from the world itself—a ground which is a self-subsistent, primeval and creative reason, in relation to which we so employ our reason in the field of experience, as if all objects drew their origin from that archetype of all reason. In other words, we ought not to deduce the internal phenomena of the mind from a simple thinking substance, but deduce them from each other under the guidance of the regulative idea of a simple being; we ought not to deduce the phenomena, order, and unity of the universe from a supreme intelligence, but merely draw from this idea of a supremely wise cause the rules which must guide reason in its connection of causes and effects.

Now there is nothing to hinder us from *admitting* these ideas to possess an objective and hyperbolic existence, except the cosmological ideas, which lead reason into an antinomy: the psychological and theological ideas are not antinomial. They contain no contradiction; and how then can any one dispute their objective reality, since he who denies it knows as little about their possibility, as we who affirm? And yet, when we wish to admit the existence of a thing, it is not sufficient to convince ourselves that there is no positive obstacle in the way; for it cannot be allowable to regard mere creations of thought, which transcend, though they do not contradict, all our conceptions, as real and determinate objects, solely upon the authority of a speculative reason striving to compass its own aims. They cannot, therefore, be admitted to be real in themselves; they can only possess a comparative reality—that of a schema of the regulative principle of the systematic unity of all cognition. They are to be regarded not as actual things, but as in some measure analogous to them. We abstract from the object of the idea all the conditions which limit the exercise of our understanding, but which, on the other hand, are the sole conditions of our possessing a determinate conception of any given thing. And thus we cogitate a something, of the real nature of which we have not the least conception, but which we represent

to ourselves as standing in a relation to the whole system of phenomena, analogous to that in which phenomena stand to each
other.

By admitting these ideal beings, we do not really extend our
cognitions beyond the objects of possible experience; we extend
merely the empirical unity of our experience, by the aid of
systematic unity, the schema of which is furnished by the idea,
which is therefore valid—not as a constitutive, but as a regulative principle. For although we posit a thing corresponding to
the idea—a something, an actual existence, we do not on that
account aim at the extension of our cognition by means of transcendent conceptions. This existence is purely ideal, and not
objective; it is the mere expression of the systematic unity
which is to be the guide of reason in the field of experience.
There are no attempts made at deciding what the ground
of this unity may be, or what the real nature of this imaginary
being.

Thus the transcendental and only determinate conception of
God, which is presented to us by speculative reason, is in the
strictest sense *deistic.* In other words, reason does not assure
us of the objective validity of the conception; it merely gives us
the idea of something, on which the supreme and necessary unity
of all experience is based. This something we cannot, following
the analogy of a real substance, cogitate otherwise than as the
cause of all things operating in accordance with rational laws,
if we regard it as an individual object; although we should rest
contented with the idea alone as a regulative principle of reason,
and make no attempt at completing the sum of the conditions
imposed by thought. This attempt is, indeed, inconsistent with
the grand aim of complete systematic unity in the sphere of
cognition—a unity to which no bounds are set by reason.

Hence it happens that, admitting a divine being, I can have
no conception of the internal possibility of its perfection, or of
the necessity of its existence. The only advantage of this admission is, that it enables me to answer all other questions relating to the contingent, and to give reason the most complete
satisfaction as regards the unity which it aims at attaining in
the world of experience. But I cannot satisfy reason with regard to this hypothesis itself; and this proves that it is not its
intelligence and insight into the subject, but its speculative interest alone which induces it to proceed from a point lying far

beyond the sphere of our cognition, for the purpose of being able to consider all objects as parts of a systematic whole.

Here a distinction presents itself, in regard to the way in which we may cogitate a presupposition—a distinction which is somewhat subtle, but of great importance in transcendental philosophy. I may have sufficient grounds to admit something, or the existence of something, in a relative point of view (*suppositio relativa*), without being justified in admitting it in an absolute sense (*suppositio absoluta*). This distinction is undoubtedly requisite, in the case of a regulative principle, the necessity of which we recognize, though we are ignorant of the source and cause of that necessity, and which we assume to be based upon some ultimate ground, for the purpose of being able to cogitate the universality of the principle in a more determinate way. For example, I cogitate the existence of a being corresponding to a pure transcendental idea. But I cannot admit that this being exists absolutely and in itself, because all of the conceptions, by which I can cogitate an object in a determinate manner, fall short of assuring me of its existence; nay, the conditions of the objective validity of my conceptions are excluded by the idea—by the very fact of its being an idea. The conceptions of reality, substance, causality, nay, even that of necessity in existence, have no significance out of the sphere of empirical cognition, and cannot, beyond that sphere, determine any object. They may, accordingly, be employed to explain the possibility of things in the world of sense, but they are utterly inadequate to explain the possibility of the *universe itself* considered as a whole; because in this case the ground of explanation must lie out of and beyond the world, and cannot, therefore, be an object of possible experience. Now, I may admit the existence of an incomprehensible being of this nature —the object of a mere idea, relatively to the world of sense; although I have no ground to admit its existence absolutely and in itself. For if an idea (that of a systematic and complete unity, of which I shall presently speak more particularly) lies at the foundation of the most extended empirical employment of reason, and if this idea cannot be adequately represented *in concreto*, although it is indispensably necessary for the approximation of empirical unity to the highest possible degree—I am not only authorized, but compelled to realize this idea, that is, to posit a real object corresponding thereto. But I cannot profess to know this object; it is to me merely a something, to which, as the ground of systematic unity in cognition, I attribute such properties as are analogous to the conceptions employed by the understanding in the sphere of experience. Following the analogy of the notions of reality, substance, causality, and necessity, I cogitate a being which possesses all these attributes in the highest degree; and, as this idea is the offspring of my reason alone, I cogitate this being as *self-subsistent reason*, and as the cause of the universe operating by means of ideas of the greatest possible harmony and unity. Thus I abstract all conditions that would limit my idea, solely for the purpose of rendering systematic unity possible in the world of empirical diversity, and thus securing the widest possible extension for the exercise of reason in that sphere. This I am enabled to do, by regarding all connections and relations in the world of sense, *as if* they were the dispositions of a supreme reason, of which our reason is but a faint image. I then proceed to cogitate this Supreme Being by conceptions which have, properly, no meaning or application, except in the world of sense. But as I am authorized to employ the transcendental hypothesis of such a being in a relative respect alone, that is, as the substratum of the greatest possible unity in experience—I may attribute to a being which I regard as distinct from the world, such properties as belong solely to the sphere of sense and experience. For I do not desire, and am not justified in desiring, to cognize this object of my idea, as it exists in itself; for I possess no conceptions sufficient for this task, those of reality, substance, causality, nay, even that of necessity in existence, losing all significance, and becoming merely the signs of conceptions, without content and without applicability, when I attempt to carry them beyond the limits of the world of sense. I cogitate merely the relation of a perfectly unknown being to the greatest possible systematic unity of experience, solely for the purpose of employing it as the schema of the regulative principle which directs reason in its empirical exercise.

It is evident, at the first view, that we cannot presuppose the reality of this transcendental object, by means of the conceptions of reality, substance, causality, and so on; because these conceptions cannot be applied to anything that is distinct from the world of sense. Thus the supposition of a Supreme Being or cause is purely relative; it is cogitated only in behalf of the systematic unity of experience; such a being is but a something, of whose existence in itself we have not the least conception. Thus, too, it becomes sufficiently manifest, why we required the idea of a necessary being in relation to objects given by sense, although we can never have the least conception of this being, or of its absolute necessity.

And now we can clearly perceive the result of our transcendental dialectic, and the proper aim of the ideas of pure reason —which become dialectical solely from misunderstanding and inconsiderateness. Pure reason is, in fact, occupied with itself, and not with any object. Objects are not presented to it to be embraced in the unity of an empirical conception; it is only the cognitions of the understanding that are presented to it, for the purpose of receiving the unity of a rational conception, that is, of being connected according to a principle. The unity of reason is the unity of system; and this systematic unity is not an objective principle, extending its dominion over objects, but a subjective maxim, extending its authority over the empirical cognition of objects. The systematic connection which reason gives to the empirical employment of the understanding, not only advances the extension of that employment, but ensures its correctness, and thus the principle of a systematic unity of this nature is also objective, although only in an indefinite respect (*principium vagum*). It is not, however, a constitutive principle, determining an object to which it directly relates; it is merely a regulative principle or maxim, advancing and strengthening the empirical exercise of reason, by the opening up of new paths of which the understanding is ignorant, while it never conflicts with the laws of its exercise in the sphere of experience.

But reason cannot cogitate this systematic unity, without at the same time cogitating an object of the idea—an object that cannot be presented in any experience, which contains no concrete example of a complete systematic unity. This being (*ens rationis ratiocinatæ*) is therefore a mere idea, and is not assumed to be a thing which is real absolutely and in itself. On the contrary, it forms merely the problematical foundation of the connection which the mind introduces among the phenomena of the sensuous world. We look upon this connection, in the light of the above-mentioned idea, as if it drew its origin from the supposed being which corresponds to the idea. And yet all we aim

at is the possession of this idea as a secure foundation for the
systematic unity of experience—a unity indispensable to reason,
advantageous to the understanding, and promotive of the interests of empirical cognition.

We mistake the true meaning of this idea, when we regard
it as an announcement, or even as a hypothetical declaration of
the existence of a real thing, which we are to regard as the origin
or ground of a systematic constitution of the universe. On the
contrary, it is left completely undetermined what the nature or
properties of this so-called ground may be. The idea is merely
to be adopted as a point of view, from which this unity, so essential to reason and so beneficial to the understanding, may be
regarded as radiating. In one word, this transcendental thing
is merely the schema of a regulative principle, by means of
which Reason, so far as in her lies, extends the dominion of systematic unity over the whole sphere of experience.

The first object of an idea of this kind is the Ego, considered
merely as a thinking nature or soul. If I wish to investigate
the properties of a thinking being, I must interrogate experience. But I find that I can apply none of the categories to this
object, the schema of these categories, which is the condition of
their application, being given only in sensuous intuition. But I
cannot thus attain to the cognition of a systematic unity of all
the phenomena of the internal sense. Instead, therefore of an
empirical conception of what the soul really is, reason takes the
conception of the empirical unity of all thought, and, by cogitating this unity as unconditioned and primitive, constructs the
rational conception or idea of a simple substance which is in
itself unchangeable, possessing personal identity, and in connection with other real things external to it; in one word, it
constructs the idea of a simple self-subsistent intelligence. But
the real aim of reason in this procedure is the attainment of
principles of systematic unity for the explanation of the phenomena of the soul. That is, reason desires to be able to represent all the determinations of the internal sense, as existing in
one subject, all powers as deduced from one fundamental power,
all changes as mere varieties in the condition of a being which is
permanent and always the same, and all *phenomena* in space as
entirely different in their nature from the procedure of thought.
Essential simplicity (with the other attributes predicated of the
Ego) is regarded as the mere schema of this regulative prin-

ciple; it is not assumed that it is the actual ground of the properties of the soul. For these properties may rest upon quite different grounds, of which we are completely ignorant; just as the above predicates could not give us any knowledge of the soul as it is in itself, even if we regarded them as valid in respect of it, inasmuch as they constitute a mere idea, which cannot be represented *in concreto*. Nothing but good can result from a psychological idea of this kind, if we only take proper care not to consider it as more than an idea; that is, if we regard it as valid merely in relation to the employment of reason, in the sphere of the phenomena of the soul. Under the guidance of this idea, or principle, no empirical laws of corporeal phenomena are called in to explain that which is a phenomenon of the *internal sense* alone; no windy hypotheses of the generation, annihilation, and palingenesis of souls are admitted. Thus the consideration of this object of the internal sense is kept pure, and unmixed with heterogeneous elements; while the investigation of reason aims at reducing all the grounds of explanation employed in this sphere of knowledge to a single principle. All this is best effected, nay, cannot be effected otherwise than by means of such a schema, which requires us to regard this ideal thing as an actual existence. The psychological idea is therefore meaningless and inapplicable, except as the schema of a regulative conception. For, if I ask whether the soul is not really of a spiritual nature,—it is a question which has no meaning. From such a conception has been abstracted, not merely all corporeal nature, but all nature, that is, all the predicates of a possible experience; and consequently, all the conditions which enable us to cogitate an object to this conception have disappeared. But, if these conditions are absent, it is evident that the conception is meaningless.

The second regulative idea of speculative reason is the conception of the universe. For nature is properly the only object presented to us, in regard to which reason requires regulative principles. Nature is two-fold—thinking and corporeal nature. To cogitate the latter in regard to its internal possibility, that is, to determine the application of the categories to it, no idea is required—no representation which transcends experience. In this sphere, therefore, an idea is impossible, sensuous intuition being our only guide; while, in the sphere of psychology, we require the fundamental idea (I), which contains *à priori* a certain form of thought, namely, the unity of the Ego. Pure reason has therefore nothing left but nature in general, and the completeness of conditions in nature in accordance with some principle. The absolute totality of the series of these conditions is an idea, which can never be fully realized in the empirical exercise of reason, while it is serviceable as a rule for the procedure of reason in relation to that totality. It requires us, in the explanation of given phenomena (in the regress or ascent in the series), to proceed, as if the series were infinite in itself, that is, were prolonged *in indefinitum;* while, on the other hand, where reason is regarded as itself the determining cause (in the region of freedom), we are required to proceed as if we had not before us an object of sense, but of the pure understanding. In this latter case, the conditions do not exist in the series of phenomena, but may be placed quite out of and beyond it, and the series of conditions may be regarded as if it had an absolute beginning from an intelligible cause. All this proves that the cosmological ideas are nothing but regulative principles, and not constitutive; and that their aim is not to realize an actual totality in such series. The full discussion of this subject will be found in its proper place in the chapter on the antinomy of pure reason.

The third idea of pure reason, containing the hypothesis of a being which is valid merely as a relative hypothesis, is that of the one and all-sufficient cause of all cosmological series, in other words, the idea of God. We have not the slightest ground absolutely to admit the existence of an object corresponding to this idea; for what can empower or authorize us to affirm the existence of a being of the highest perfection—a being whose existence is absolutely necessary, merely because we possess the conception of such a being? The answer is,—it is the existence of the world which renders this hypothesis necessary. But this answer makes it perfectly evident, that the idea of this being, like all other speculative ideas, is essentially nothing more than a demand upon reason that it shall regulate the connection which it and its subordinate faculties introduce into the phenomena of the world by principles of systematic unity, and consequently, that it shall regard all phenomena as originating from one all-embracing being, as the supreme and all-sufficient cause. From this it is plain that the only aim of reason in this procedure is the establishment of its own formal rule for the extension of its dominion in the world of experience; that it does not aim at an extension of its cognition *beyond the limits of experience;* and that, consequently, this idea does not contain any constitutive principle.

The highest formal unity, which is based upon ideas alone, is the unity of all things—a unity in accordance with an aim or purpose; and the speculative interest of reason renders it necessary to regard all order in the world, as if it originated from the intention and design of a supreme reason. This principle unfolds to the view of reason in the sphere of experience new and enlarged prospects, and invites it to connect the phenomena of the world according to teleological laws, and in this way to attain to the highest possible degree of systematic unity. The hypothesis of a supreme intelligence, as the sole cause of the universe—an intelligence which has for us no more than an ideal existence, is accordingly always of the greatest service to reason. Thus, if we presuppose, in relation to the figure of the earth (which is round, but somewhat flattened at the poles),* or that of mountains or seas, wise designs on the part of an author of the universe, we cannot fail to make, by the light of this supposition, a great number of interesting discoveries. If we keep to this hypothesis, as a principle which is purely regulative, even error cannot be very detrimental. For, in this case, error can have no more serious consequences than that, where we expected to discover a teleological connection (*nexus finalis*), only a mechanical or physical connection appears. In such a case, we merely fail to find the additional form of unity we expected, but we do not lose the rational unity which the mind requires in its procedure in experience. But even a miscarriage of this sort cannot affect the law in its general and teleological relations. For although we may convict an anatomist of an error, when he connects the limb of some animal with a certain purpose; it is quite impossible to *prove* in a single case, that any arrangement of nature, be it what it may, is entirely without aim or design. And thus medical physiology, by the aid

* The advantages which a circular form, in the case of the earth, has over every other, are well known. But few are aware that the slight flattening at the poles, which gives it the figure of a spheroid, is the only cause which prevents the elevations of continents or even of mountains, perhaps thrown up by some internal convulsion, from continually altering the position of the axis of the earth—and that to some considerable degree in a short time. The great protuberance of the earth under the equator serves to overbalance the impetus of all other masses of earth, and thus to preserve the axis of the earth, so far as we can observe, in its present position. And yet this wise arrangement has been unthinkingly explained from the equilibrium of the formerly fluid mass.

of a principle presented to it by pure reason, extends its very
limited empirical knowledge of the purposes of the different
parts of an organized body so far, that it my be asserted with
the utmost confidence, and with the approbation of all reflecting
men, that every organ or bodily part of an animal has its use and
answers a certain design. Now, this is a supposition, which, if
regarded as of a constitutive character, goes much farther than
any experience or observation of ours can justify. Hence it is
evident that it is nothing more than a regulative principle of
reason, which aims at the highest degree of systematic unity, by
the aid of the idea of a causality according to design in a supreme cause—a cause which it regards as the highest intelligence.

If, however, we neglect this restriction of the idea to a purely
regulative influence, reason is betrayed into numerous errors.
For it has then left the ground of experience, in which alone are
to be found the criteria of truth, and has ventured into the
region of the incomprehensible and unsearchable, on the heights
of which it loses its power and collectedness, because it has completely severed its connection with experience.

The first error which arises from our employing the idea of a
Supreme Being as a constitutive (in repugnance to the very
nature of an idea) and not as a regulative principle is the error
of inactive reason (*ignava ratio* *). We may so term every
principle which requires us to regard our investigations of nature as absolutely complete, and allows reason to cease its
inquiries, as if it had fully executed its task. Thus the psychological idea of the Ego, when employed as a constitutive principle for the explanation of the phenomena of the soul, and for
the extension of our knowledge regarding this subject beyond
the limits of experience—even to the condition of the soul after
death, is convenient enough for the purposes of pure reason,
but detrimental and even ruinous to its interests in the sphere
of nature and experience. The dogmatizing spiritualist explains
the unchanging unity of our personality through all changes of
condition from the unity of a thinking substance, the interest
which we take in things and events that can happen only after
our death, from a consciousness of the immaterial nature of our

* This was the term applied by the
old dialecticians to a sophistical argument, which ran thus: If it is your
fate to die of this disease, you will die,
whether you employ a physician or not.
Cicero says that this mode of reasoning
has received this appellation, because, if
followed, it puts an end to the employment of reason in the affairs of life.
For a similar reason I have applied this
designation to the sophistical argument
of pure reason.

thinking subject, and so on. Thus he dispenses with all empirical investigations into the cause of these internal phenomena, and with all possible explanations of them upon purely natural grounds; while, at the dictation of a transcendent reason, he passes by the immanent sources of cognition in experience, greatly to his own ease and convenience, but to the sacrifice of all genuine insight and intelligence. These prejudicial consequences become still more evident, in the case of the dogmatical treatment of our idea of a Supreme Intelligence, and the theological system of nature (physico-theology) which is falsely based upon it. For, in this case, the aims which we observe in nature, and often those which we merely fancy to exist, make the investigation of causes a very easy task, by directing us to refer such and such phenomena immediately to the unsearchable will and counsel of the Supreme Wisdom, while we ought to investigate their causes in the general laws of the mechanism of matter. We are thus recommended to consider the labor of reason as ended, when we have merely dispensed with its employment, which is guided surely and safely, only by the order of nature and the series of changes in the world—which are arranged according to immanent and general laws. This error may be avoided, if we do not merely consider from the viewpoint of final aims certain parts of nature, such as the division and structure of a continent, the constitution and direction of certain mountain-chains, or even the organization existing in the vegetable and animal kingdoms, but look upon this systematic unity of nature in a perfectly *general* way, in relation to the idea of a Supreme Intelligence. If we pursue this advice, we lay as a foundation for all investigation the conformity to aims of all phenomena of nature in accordance with universal laws, for which no particular arrangement of nature is exempt, but only cognized by us with more or less difficulty; and we possess a regulative principle of the systematic unity of a teleological connection, which we do not attempt to anticipate or predetermine. All that we do, and ought to do, is to follow out the physico-mechanical connection in nature according to general laws, with the hope of discovering, sooner or later, the teleological connection also. Thus, and thus only, can the principle of final unity aid in the extension of the employment of reason in the sphere of experience, without being in any case detrimental to its interests.

The second error which arises from the misconception of the principle of systematic unity is that of perverted reason (*perversa ratio, ὕστερον πρότερον rationis*). The idea of systematic unity is available as a regulative principle in the connection of phenomena according to general natural laws; and, how far soever we have to travel upon the path of experience to discover some fact or event, this idea requires us to believe that we have approached all the more nearly to the completion of its use in the sphere of nature, although that completion can never be attained. But this error reverses the procedure of reason. We begin by hypostatizing the principle of systematic unity, and by giving an anthropomorphic determination to the conception of a Supreme Intelligence, and then proceed forcibly to impose aims upon nature. Thus not only does teleology, which ought to aid in the completion of unity in accordance with general laws, operate to the destruction of its influence, but it hinders reason from attaining its proper aim, that is, the proof, upon natural grounds, of the existence of a supreme intelligent cause. For, if we cannot presuppose supreme finality in nature *à priori*, that is, as essentially belonging to nature, how can we be directed to endeavor to discover this unity, and, rising gradually through its different degrees, to approach the supreme perfection of an author of all—a perfection which is absolutely necessary, and therefore cognizable *à priori?* The regulative principle directs us to presuppose systematic unity absolutely, and, consequently, as following from the essential nature of things—but only as a *unity of nature,* not merely cognized empirically, but presupposed *à priori,* although only in an indeterminate manner. But if I insist on basing nature upon the foundation of a supreme ordaining Being, the unity of nature is in effect lost. For, in this case, it is quite foreign and unessential to the nature of things, and cannot be cognized from the general laws of nature. And thus arises a vicious circular argument, what ought to have been proved having been presupposed.

To take the regulative principle of systematic unity in nature for a constitutive principle, and to hypostatize and make a cause out of that which is properly the ideal ground of the consistent and harmonious exercise of reason, involves reason in inextricable embarrassments. The investigation of nature pursues its own path under the guidance of the chain of natural causes, in accordance with the general laws of nature, and ever follows the light of the idea of an author of the universe—not for the purpose of deducing the finality, which it constantly pursues, from this Supreme Being, but to attain to the cognition of his existence from the finality which it seeks in the existence of the phenomena of nature, and, if possible, in that of all things—to cognize this being, consequently, as absolutely necessary. Whether this latter purpose succeed or not, the idea is and must always be a true one, and its employment, when merely regulative, must always be accompanied by truthful and beneficial results.

Complete unity, in conformity with aims, constitutes absolute perfection. But if we do not find this unity in the nature of the things which go to constitute the world of experience, that is, of objective cognition, consequently in the universal and necessary laws of nature, how can we infer from this unity the idea of the supreme and absolutely necessary perfection of a primal being, which is the origin of all causality? The greatest systematic unity, and consequently teleological unity, constitutes the very foundation of the possibility of the most extended employment of human reason. The idea of unity is therefore essentially and indissolubly connected with the nature of our reason. This idea is a legislative one; and hence it is very natural that we should assume the existence of a legislative reason corresponding to it, from which the systematic unity of nature—the object of the operations of reason—must be derived.

In the course of our discussion of the antinomies, we stated that it is always possible to answer all the questions which pure reason may raise; and that the plea of the limited nature of our cognition, which is unavoidable and proper in many questions regarding natural phenomena, cannot in this case be admitted, because the questions raised do not relate to the nature of things, but are necessarily originated by the nature of reason itself, and relate to its own internal constitution. We can now establish this assertion, which at first sight appeared so rash, in relation to the two questions in which reason takes the greatest interest, and thus complete our discussion of the dialectic of pure reason.

If, then, the question is asked, in relation to transcendental theology;* *first,* whether there is anything distinct from the world, which contains the ground of cosmical order and connection according to general laws? The answer is, *Certainly.* For the world is a sum of phenomena; there must therefore be some transcendental basis of these phenomena, that is, a basis cogitable by the pure understanding alone. If, *secondly,* the question is asked, whether this being is substance, whether it is of the greatest reality, whether it is necessary, and so forth? I answer that *this question is utterly without meaning.* For all the categories which aid me in forming a conception of an object, cannot be employed except in the world of sense, and are without meaning, when not applied to objects of actual or possible experience. Out of this sphere, they are not properly conceptions, but the mere marks or indices of conceptions, which we may admit, although they cannot, without the help of experience, help us to understand any subject or thing. If, *thirdly,* the question is, whether we may not cogitate this being, which is distinct from the world, in analogy with the objects of experience? The answer is, *undoubtedly,* but only as an ideal, and not as a real object. That is, we must cogitate it only as an unknown substratum of the systematic unity, order, and finality of the world—a unity which reason must employ as the regulative principle of its investigation of nature. Nay, more, we may admit into the idea certain anthropomorphic elements, which are promotive of the interests of this regulative principle. For it is no more than an idea, which does not relate directly to a being distinct from the world, but to the regulative principle of the systematic unity of the world, by means, however, of a schema of this unity—the schema of a Supreme Intelligence, who is the wisely designing author of the universe. What this basis of cosmical unity may be in itself, we know not—we cannot discover from the idea; we merely know how we ought to employ the idea of this unity, in relation to the systematic operation of reason in the sphere of experience.

But, it will be asked again, *can* we on these grounds, admit the existence of a wise and omnipotent author of the world? *Without doubt;* and not only so, but we *must* assume the ex-

---

* After what has been said of the psychological idea of the Ego and its proper employment as a regulative principle of the operations of reason, I need not enter into details regarding the transcendental illusion by which the systematic unity of all the various phenomena of the internal sense is hypostatised. The procedure is in this case very similar to that which has been discussed in our remarks on the theological ideal.

istence of such a being. But do we thus extend the limits of our knowledge beyond the field of possible experience? *By no means.* For we have merely presupposed a something, of which we have no conception, which we do not know as it is in itself; but, in relation to the systematic disposition of the universe, which we must presuppose in all our observation of nature, we have cogitated this unknown being *in analogy* with an intelligent existence (an empirical conception), that is to say, we have endowed it with those attributes, which, judging from the nature of our own reason, may contain the ground of such a systematic unity. This idea is therefore valid only relatively to the employment in experience of our reason. But if we attribute to it absolute and objective validity, we overlook the fact that it is merely an ideal being that we cogitate; and, by setting out from a basis which is not determinable by considerations drawn from experience, we place ourselves in a position which incapacitates us from applying this principle to the empirical employment of reason.

But, it will be asked further, can I make any use of this conception and hypothesis in my investigations into the world and nature? *Yes,* for this very purpose was the idea established by reason as a fundamental basis. But may I regard certain arrangements, which seemed to have been made in conformity with some fixed aim, as the arrangements of design, and look upon them as proceeding from the divine will, with the intervention, however, of certain other particular arrangements disposed to that end? Yes, you may do so; but at the same time you must regard it as indifferent, whether it is asserted that divine wisdom has disposed all things in conformity with his highest aims, or that the idea of supreme wisdom is a regulative principle in the investigation of nature, and at the same time a principle of the systematic unity of nature according to general laws, even in those cases where we are unable to discover that unity. In other words, it must be perfectly indifferent to you, whether you say, when you have discovered this unity—God has wisely willed it so, or, nature has wisely arranged this. For it was nothing but the systematic unity, which reason requires as a basis for the investigation of nature, that justified you in accepting the idea of a supreme intelligence as a schema for a regulative principle; and, the further you advance in the discovery of design and finality, the more certain the validity of your idea. But, as the whole aim of this regulative principle was the discovery of a necessary and systematic unity in nature, we have, in so far as we attain this, to attribute our success to the idea of a Supreme Being; while, at the same time, we cannot, without involving ourselves in contradictions, overlook the general laws of nature, as it was in reference to them alone that this idea was employed. We cannot, I say, overlook the general laws of nature, and regard this conformity to aims observable in nature as contingent or hyperphysical in its origin; inasmuch as there is no ground which can justify us in the admission of a being with such properties distinct from and above nature. All that we are authorized to assert is, that this idea may be employed as a principle, and that the properties of the being which is assumed to correspond to it may be regarded as systematically connected in analogy with the causal determination of phenomena.

For the same reasons we are justified in introducing into the idea of the supreme cause other anthropomorphic elements (for without these we could not predicate anything of it) ; we may regard it as allowable to cogitate this cause as a being with understanding, the feelings of pleasure and displeasure, and faculties of desire and will corresponding to these. At the same time, we may attribute to this being infinite perfection—a perfection which necessarily transcends that which our knowledge of the order and design in the world would authorize us to predicate of it. For the regulative law of systematic unity requires us to study nature on the supposition that systematic and final unity *in infinitum* is everywhere discoverable, even in the highest diversity. For, although we may discover little of this cosmical perfection, it belongs to the legislative prerogative of reason, to require us always to seek for and to expect it; while it must always be beneficial to institute all inquiries into nature in accordance with this principle. But it is evident that, by this idea of a supreme author of all, which I place as the foundation of all inquiries into nature, I do not mean to assert the existence of such a being, or that I have any knowledge of its existence; and, consequently, I do not really deduce anything from the existence of this being, but merely from its idea, that is to say, from the nature of things in this world, in accordance with this idea. A certain dim consciousness of the true use of this idea seems to have dictated to the philosophers of all times the moderate language used by them regarding the cause of the world. We find them employing the expressions, wisdom and care of nature, and divine wisdom, as synonymous—nay, in purely speculative discussions, preferring the former, because it does not carry the appearance of greater pretensions than such as we are entitled to make, and at the same time directs reason to its proper field of action—nature and her phenomena.

Thus, pure reason, which at first seemed to promise us nothing less than the extension of our cognition beyond the limits of experience, is found, when thoroughly examined, to contain nothing but regulative principles, the virtue and function of which is to introduce into our cognition a higher degree of unity than the understanding could of itself. These principles, by placing the goal of all our struggles at so great a distance, realize for us the most thorough connection between the different parts of our cognition, and the highest degree of systematic unity. But, on the other hand, if misunderstood and employed as constitutive principles of transcendent cognition, they become the parents of illusions and contradictions, while pretending to introduce us to new regions of knowledge.

Thus all human cognition begins with intuitions, proceeds from thence to conceptions, and ends with ideas. Although it possesses in relation to all three elements, à priori sources of cognition, which seemed to transcend the limits of all experience, a thorough-going criticism demonstrates, that speculative reason can never, by the aid of these elements, pass the bounds of possible experience, and that the proper destination of this highest faculty of cognition, is to employ all methods, and all the principles of these methods, for the purpose of penetrating into the innermost secrets of nature, by the aid of the principles of unity (among all kinds of which teleological unity is the highest), while it ought not to attempt to soar above the sphere of experience, beyond which there lies nought for us but the void inane. The critical examination, in our Transcendental Analytic, of all the propositions which professed to extend cognition beyond the sphere of experience, completely demonstrated that they can only conduct us to a possible experience. If we were not distrustful even of the clearest abstract theorems, if we were not allured by specious and inviting prospects to escape from the constraining power of their evidence, we might spare ourselves the laborious examination of all the dialectical arguments which a transcendent reason adduces in support of its pretensions; for we should know with the most complete certainty that, however honest such professions might be, they are null and valueless, because they relate to a kind of knowledge to which no man can by any possibility attain. But, as there is no end to discussion, if we cannot discover the true cause of the illusions by which even the wisest are deceived, and as the analysis of all our transcendent cognition into its elements is of itself of no slight value as a psychological study, while it is a duty incumbent on every philosopher—it was found necessary to investigate the dialectical procedure of reason in its primary sources. And as the inferences of which this dialectic is the parent, are not only deceitful, but naturally possess a profound interest for humanity, it was advisable at the same time, to give a full account of the momenta of this dialectical procedure, and to deposit it in the archives of human reason, as a warning to all future metaphysicians to avoid these causes of speculative error.

TRANSCENDENTAL DOCTRINE

OF

METHOD

INTRODUCTION

IF we regard the sum of the cognition of pure speculative reason as an edifice, the idea of which, at least, exists in the human mind, it may be said that we have in the Transcendental Doctrine of Elements examined the materials and determined to what edifice these belong, and what its height and stability. We have found, indeed, that, although we had purposed to build for ourselves a tower which should reach to Heaven, the supply of materials sufficed merely for a habitation, which was spacious enough for all terrestrial purposes, and high enough to enable us to survey the level plain of experience, but that the bold undertaking designed necessarily failed for want of materials—not to mention the confusion of tongues, which gave rise to endless disputes among the laborers on the plan of the edifice, and at last scattered them over all the world, each to erect a separate building for himself, according to his own plans and his own inclinations. Our present task relates not to the materials, but to the plan of an edifice; and, as we have had sufficient warning not to venture blindly upon a design which may be found to transcend our natural powers, while, at the same time, we cannot give up the intention of erecting a secure abode for the mind, we must proportion our design to the material which is presented to us, and which is, at the same time, sufficient for all our wants.

I understand, then, by the transcendental doctrine of method, the determination of the formal conditions of a complete system of pure reason. We shall accordingly have to treat of the *Discipline*, the *Canon*, the *Architectonic*, and, finally, the *History* of pure reason. This part of our Critique will accomplish, from the transcendental point of view, what has been usually attempted, but miserably executed, under the name of *practical logic*. It has been badly executed, I say, because general logic, not being limited to any particular kind of cognition (not even to the pure cognition of the understanding) or to any particular objects, cannot, without borrowing from other sciences, do more than present merely the titles or signs of *possible methods* and the technical expressions, which are employed in the systematic parts of all sciences; and thus the pupil is made acquainted with names, the meaning and application of which he is to learn only at some future time.

CHAPTER I

The Discipline of Pure Reason

Negative judgments—those which are so not merely as regards their logical form, but in respect of their content—are not commonly held in especial respect. They are, on the contrary, regarded as jealous enemies of our insatiable desire for knowledge; and it almost requires an apology to induce us to tolerate, much less to prize and to respect them.

All propositions, indeed, may be *logically* expressed in a negative form; but, in relation to the content of our cognition, the peculiar province of negative judgments is solely to *prevent error*. For this reason, too, negative propositions, which are framed for the purpose of correcting false cognitions where error is absolutely impossible, are undoubtedly true, but inane and senseless; that is, they are in reality purposeless, and for this reason often very ridiculous. Such is the proposition of the schoolman, that Alexander could not have subdued any countries without an army.

But where the limits of our possible cognition are very much contracted, the attraction to new fields of knowledge great, the illusions to which the mind is subject of the most deceptive character, and the evil consequences of error of no inconsiderable magnitude—the *negative* element in knowledge, which is useful only to guard us against error, is of far more importance than much of that positive instruction which makes additions to the sum of our knowledge. The *restraint* which is employed to repress, and finally to extirpate the constant inclination to depart from certain rules, is termed *Discipline*. It is distinguished from *culture*, which aims at the formation of a certain degree of skill, without attempting to repress or to destroy any other mental power, already existing. In the cultivation of a talent which has given evidence of an impulse towards self-development, discipline takes a negative,* culture and doctrine, a positive part.

That natural dispositions and talents (such as imagination and wit), which ask a free and unlimited development, require in many respects the corrective influence of discipline, every one will readily grant. But it may well appear strange, that reason, whose proper duty it is to prescribe rules of discipline to all the other powers of the mind, should itself require this corrective. It has, in fact, hitherto escaped this humiliation, only because, in presence of its magnificent pretensions and high position, no one could readily suspect it to be capable of substituting fancies for conceptions, and words for things.

Reason, when employed in the field of experience, does not stand in need of criticism, because its principles are subjected to the continual test of empirical observations. Nor is criticism requisite in the sphere of mathematics, where the conceptions of reason must always be presented *in concreto* in pure intuition, and baseless or arbitrary assertions are discovered without difficulty. But where reason is not held in a plain track by the influence of empirical or of pure intuition, that is, when it is employed in the transcendental sphere of pure conceptions, it stands in great need of discipline, to restrain its propensity to overstep the limits of possible experience, and to keep it from wandering into error. In fact, the utility of the philosophy of pure reason is entirely of this negative character. Particular errors may be corrected by particular animadversions, and the causes of these errors may be eradicated by criticism. But where we find, as in the case of pure reason, a complete system of illusions and fallacies, closely connected with each other and depending upon grand general principles, there seems to be required a peculiar and negative code of mental legislation, which, under the denomination of a *discipline*, and founded upon the nature of reason and the objects of its exercise, shall constitute a system of thorough examination and testing, which no fallacy will be able to withstand or escape from, under whatever disguise or concealment it may lurk.

* I am well aware that, in the language of the schools, the term *discipline* is usually employed as synonymous with *instruction*. But there are so many cases in which it is necessary to distinguish the notion of the former, as a course of corrective training, from that of the latter, as the communication of knowledge, and as the nature of things itself demands the appropriation of the most suitable expressions for this distinction, it is my desire that the former term should never be employed in any other than a negative signification.

But the reader must remark that, in this the second division of our Transcendental Critique, the discipline of pure reason is not directed to the content, but to the method of the cognition of pure reason. The former task has been completed in the Doctrine of Elements. But there is so much similarity in the mode of employing the faculty of reason, whatever be the object to which it is applied, while, at the same time, its employment in the transcendental sphere is so essentially different in kind from every other, that, without the warning negative influence of a discipline specially directed to that end, the errors are unavoidable which spring from the unskilful employment of the methods which are originated by reason but which are out of place in this sphere.

Section I.—The Discipline of Pure Reason in the Sphere of Dogmatism

The science of Mathematics presents the most brilliant example of the extension of the sphere of pure reason without the aid of experience. Examples are always contagious; and they exert an especial influence on the same faculty, which naturally flatters itself that it will have the same good fortune in other cases as fell to its lot in one fortunate instance. Hence pure reason hopes to be able to extend its empire in the transcendental sphere with equal success and security, especially when it applies the same method which was attended with such brilliant results in the science of Mathematics. It is, therefore, of the highest importance for us to know, whether the method of arriving at demonstrative certainty, which is termed *mathematical*, be identical with that by which we endeavor to attain the same degree of certainty in philosophy, and which is termed in that science *dogmatical*.

Philosophical cognition is the *cognition* of *reason* by *means* of *conceptions;* mathematical cognition is *cognition* by means of the *construction* of *conceptions*. The *construction* of a conception is the presentation à *priori* of the intuition which corresponds to the conception. For this purpose a *non-empirical* intuition is requisite, which, as an intuition, is an *individual* object; while, as the construction of a conception (a general representation), it must be seen to be universally valid for all the possible intuitions which rank under that conception. Thus I construct a triangle, by the presentation of the object which corresponds to this conception, either by mere imagination—in pure intuition, or upon paper—in empirical intuition, in both cases completely *à priori*, without borrowing the type of that figure from any experience. The individual figure drawn upon paper is empirical; but it serves, notwithstanding, to indicate the conception, even in its universality, because in this empirical intuition we keep our eye merely on the act of the construction of the conception, and pay no attention to the various modes of determining it, for example, its size, the length of its sides, the size of its angles, these not in the least affecting the essential character of the conception.

Philosophical cognition, accordingly, regards the particular only in the general; mathematical the general in the particular, nay, in the individual. This is done, however, entirely *à priori* and by means of pure reason, so that, as this individual figure is determined under certain universal conditions of construction, the object of the conception, to which this individual figure corresponds as its schema, must be cogitated as universally determined.

The essential difference of these two modes of cognition consists, therefore, in this formal quality; it does not regard the difference of the matter or objects of both. Those thinkers who aim at distinguishing philosophy from mathematics by asserting that the former has to do with *quality* merely, and the latter with *quantity*, have mistaken the effect for the cause. The reason why mathematical cognition can relate only to quantity, is to be found in its form alone. For it is the conception of quantities only that is capable of being constructed, that is, presented *à priori* in intuition; while quantities cannot be given in any other than an empirical intuition. Hence the cognition of qualities by reason is possible only through conceptions. No one can find an intuition which shall correspond to the conception of reality, except in experience; it cannot be presented to the mind *à priori*, and antecedently to the empirical consciousness of reality. We can form an intuition, by means of the mere conception of it, of a cone without the aid of experience; but the color of the cone we cannot know except from experience. I cannot present an intuition of a cause, except in an example which experience offers to me. Besides, philosophy, as well as mathematics, treats of quantities; as, for example, of totality, infinity, and so on. Mathematics, too, treats of the difference of lines and surfaces—as spaces of different quality, of the continuity of extension—as a quality thereof. But, although in such cases they have a common object, the mode in which reason considers that object is very different in philosophy from what it is in mathematics. The former confines itself to the general conceptions; the latter can do nothing with a mere conception; it hastens to intuition. In this intuition it regards the conception *in concreto,* not empirically, but in an *à priori* intuition which it has constructed; and in which all the results which follow from the general conditions of the construction of the conception are in all cases valid for the object of the constructed conception.

Suppose that the conception of a triangle is given to a philosopher, and that he is required to discover, by the philosophical method, what relation the sum of its angles bears to a right angle. He has nothing before him but the conception of a figure enclosed within three right lines, and, consequently, with the same number of angles. He may analyze the conception of a right line, of an angle, or of the number three as long as he pleases, but he will not discover any properties not contained in these conceptions. But if this question is proposed to a geometrician, he at once begins by constructing a triangle. He knows that two right angles are equal to the sum of all the contiguous angles which proceed from one point in a straight line; and he goes on to produce one side of his triangle, thus forming two adjacent angles which are together equal to two right angles. He then divides the exteriors of these angles by drawing a line parallel with the opposite side of the triangle, and immediately perceives that he has thus got an exterior adjacent angle which is equal to the interior. Proceeding in this way, through a chain of inferences, and always on the ground of intuition, he arrives at a clear and universally valid solution of the question.

But mathematics does not confine itself to the construction of quantities (*quanta*), as in the case of geometry; it occupies itself with pure quantity also (*quantitas*), as in the case of algebra, where complete abstraction is made of the properties of the object indicated by the conception of quantity. In algebra a certain method of notation by signs is adopted, and these indicate the difference possible constructions of quantities, the extraction of roots, and so on. After having thus denoted the general conception of quantities, according to their different relations, the different operations by which quantity or number is increased or diminished are presented in intuition in accordance with general rules. Thus, when one quantity is to be divided by another, the signs which denote both are placed in the form peculiar to the operation of division; and thus algebra, by means of a symbolical construction of quantity, just as geometry, with its ostensible or geometrical construction (a construction of the objects themselves), arrives at results which discursive cognition cannot hope to reach by the aid of mere conceptions.

Now, what is the cause of this difference in the fortune of the philosopher and the mathematician, the former of whom follows the path of conceptions, while the latter pursues that of intuitions, which he represents, à priori, in correspondence with his conceptions. The cause is evident, from what has been already demonstrated in the introduction to this Critique. We do not, in the present case, want to discover analytical propositions, which may be produced merely by analyzing our conceptions—for in this the philosopher would have the advantage over his rival; we aim at the discovery of synthetical propositions—such synthetical propositions, moreover, as can be cognized à priori. I must not confine myself to that which I actually cogitate in my conception of a triangle, for this is nothing more than the mere definition; I must try to go beyond that, and to arrive at properties which are not contained in, although they belong to, the conception. Now, this is impossible unless I determine the object present to my mind according to the conditions either of empirical or of pure intuition. In the former case, I should have an empirical proposition (arrived at by actual measurement of the angles of the triangle) which would possess neither universality nor necessity; but that would be of no value. In the latter, I proceed by geometrical construction, by means of which I collect, in a pure intuition, just as I would in an empirical intuition, all the various properties which belong to the schema of a triangle in general, and consequently to its conception, and thus construct synthetical propositions which possess the attribute of universality.

It would be vain to philosophize upon the triangle, that is, to reflect on it discursively; I should get no further than the definition with which I had been obliged to set out. There are certainly transcendental synthetical propositions which are framed by means of pure conceptions, and which form the peculiar distinction of philosophy; but these do not relate to any particular thing, but to a thing in general, and enounce the conditions under which the perception of it may become a part of possible experience. But the science of mathematics has nothing to do with such questions, nor with the question of existence in any fashion; it is concerned merely with the properties of objects in themselves, only in so far as these are connected with the conception of the objects.

In the above example, we have merely attempted to show the great difference which exists between the discursive employment of reason in the sphere of conceptions and its intuitive exercise by means of the construction of conceptions. The question naturally arises—What is the cause which necessitates this twofold exercise of reason, and how are we to discover whether it is the philosophical or the mathematical method which reason is pursuing in an argument?

All our knowledge relates, finally, to possible intuitions, for it is these alone that present objects to the mind. An *à priori* or non-empirical conception contains either a pure intuition— and in this case it can be constructed; or it contains nothing but the synthesis of possible intuitions, which are not given *à priori*. In this latter case, it may help us to form synthetical *à priori* judgments, but only in the discursive method, by conceptions, not in the intuitive, by means of the construction of conceptions.

The only *à priori* intuition is that of the pure form of phenomena—space and time. A conception of space and time as *quanta* may be presented *à priori* in intuition, that is, constructed, either along with their quality (figure), or as pure quantity (the mere synthesis of the homogeneous), by means of number. But the matter of phenomena, by which *things* are given in space and time, can be presented only in perception, *à posteriori*. The only conception which represents *à priori* this empirical content of phenomena is the conception of a *thing* in general; and the *à priori* synthetical cognition of this conception can give us nothing more than the rule for the synthesis of that which may be contained in the corresponding *à posteriori* perception; it is utterly inadequate to present an *à priori* intuition of the real object, which must necessarily be empirical.

Synthetical propositions, which relate to *things* in general, an *à priori* intuition of which is impossible, are transcendental. For this reason transcendental propositions cannot be framed by means of the construction of conceptions; they are *à priori*, and based entirely on conceptions themselves. They contain merely the rule, by which we are to seek in the world of perception or experience the synthetical unity of that which cannot be intuited *à priori*. But they are incompetent to present any of the conceptions which appear in them in an *à priori* intuition; these can be given only *à posteriori*, in experience, which, however, is itself possible only through these synthetical principles.

If we are to form a synthetical judgment regarding a conception, we must go beyond it, to the intuition in which it is given. If we keep to what is contained in the conception, the judgment is merely analytical—it is merely an explanation of what we have cogitated in the conception. But I can pass from the conception to the pure or empirical intuition which corresponds to it. I can proceed to examine my conception *in concreto*, and to cognize, either *à priori* or *à posteriori*, what I find in the object of the conception. The former—*à priori* cognition—is rational-mathematical cognition by means of the construction of the conception; the latter—*à posteriori* cognition—is purely empirical cognition, which does not possess the attributes of necessity and universality. Thus I may analyze the conception I have of gold; but I gain no new information from this analysis; I merely enumerate the different properties which I had connected with the notion indicated by the word. My knowledge has gained in logical clearness and arrangement, but no addition has been made to it. But if I take the matter which is indicated by this name, and submit it to the examination of my senses, I am enabled to form several synthetical—although still empirical—propositions. The mathematical conception of a triangle I should construct, that is, present *à priori* in intuition, and in this way attain to rational-synthetical cognition. But when the transcendental conception of reality, or substance, or power is presented to my mind, I find that it does not relate to or indicate either an empirical or pure intuition, but that it indicates merely the synthesis of empirical intuitions, which cannot of course be given *à priori*. The synthesis in such a conception cannot proceed *à priori*—without the aid of experience—to the intuition which corresponds to the conception; and, for this reason, none of these conceptions can produce a determinative synthetical proposition, they can never present more than a principle of the synthesis* of possible empirical intuitions. A transcendental proposition is, therefore, a synthetical cognition of reason by means of pure conceptions and the discursive method, and it renders possible all synthetical unity in empirical cognition, though it cannot present us with any intuition *à priori*.

There is thus a twofold exercise of reason. Both modes have the properties of universality and an *à priori* origin in common, but are, in their procedure, of widely different character. The reason of this is, that in the world of phenomena, in which alone objects are presented to our minds, there are two main elements—the form of intuition (space and time), which can be cognized and determined completely *à priori*, and the matter or content—that which is presented in space and time, and which, consequently, contains a something—an existence corresponding to our powers of sensation. As regards the latter, which can never be given in a determinate mode except by experience, there are no *à priori* notions which relate to it, except the undetermined conceptions of the synthesis of possible sensations, in so far as these belong (in a possible experience) to the unity of consciousness. As regards the former, we can determine our conceptions *à priori* in intuition, inasmuch as we are ourselves the creators of the objects of the conceptions in space and time—these objects being regarded simply as *quanta*. In the one case, reason proceeds according to conceptions, and can do nothing more than subject phenomena to these—which can only be determined empirically, that is *à posteriori*—in conformity, however, with those conceptions as the rules of all empirical synthesis. In the other case, reason proceeds by the construction of conceptions; and, as these conceptions relate to an *à priori* intuition, they may be given and determined in pure intuition *à priori*, and without the aid of empirical data.

* In the case of the conception of cause, I do really go beyond the empirical conception of an event—but not to the intuition which presents this conception *in concreto*, but only to the time-conditions, which may be found in experience to correspond to the conception. My procedure is, therefore, strictly according to conceptions; I cannot in a case of this kind employ the construction of conceptions, because the conception is merely a rule for the synthesis of perceptions, which are not pure intuitions, and which, therefore, cannot be given *à priori*.

The examination and consideration of everything that exists in space or time—whether it is a quantum or not, in how far the particular something (which fills space or time) is a primary substratum, or a mere determination of some other existence, whether it relates to anything else—either as cause or effect, whether its existence is isolated or in reciprocal connection with and dependence upon others, the possibility of this existence, its reality and necessity or their opposites—all these form part of the *cognition of reason* on the ground of conceptions, and this cognition is termed *philosophical*. But to determine *à priori* an intuition in space (its figure), to divide time into periods, or merely to cognize the quantity of an intuition in space and time, and to determine it by number—all this is an *operation of reason* by means of the construction of conceptions, and is called *mathematical*.

The success which attends the efforts of reason in the sphere of mathematics naturally fosters the expectation that the same good fortune will be its lot, if it applies the mathematical method in other regions of mental endeavor besides that of quantities. Its success is thus great, because it can support all its conceptions by *à priori* intuitions, and in this way make itself a master, as it were, over nature; while pure philosophy, with its *à priori* discursive conceptions, bungles about in the world of nature, and cannot accredit or show any *à priori* evidence of the reality of these conceptions. Masters in the science of mathematics are confident of the success of this method; indeed, it is a common persuasion, that it is capable of being applied to any subject of human thought. They have hardly ever reflected or philosophized on their favorite science—a task of great difficulty; and the specific difference between the two modes of employing the faculty of reason has never entered their thoughts. Rules current in the field of common experience, and which common sense stamps everywhere with its approval, are regarded by them as axiomatic. From what source the conceptions of space and time, with which (as the only primitive quanta) they have to deal, enter their minds, is a question which they do not trouble themselves to answer; and they think it just as unnecessary to examine into the origin of the pure conceptions of the understanding and the extent of their validity. All they have to do with them is to employ them. In all this they are perfectly right, if they do not overstep the limits of the sphere of *nature.* But they pass, unconsciously, from the world of sense to the insecure ground of pure transcendental conceptions (*instabilis tellus, innabilis unda*), where they can neither stand nor swim, and where the tracks of their footsteps are obliterated by time; while the march of mathematics is pursued on a broad and magnificent highway, which the latest posterity shall frequent without fear of danger or impediment.

As we have taken upon us the task of determining, clearly and certainly, the limits of pure reason in the sphere of transcendentalism, and as the efforts of reason in this direction are persisted in, even after the plainest and most expressive warnings, hope still beckoning us past the limits of experience into the splendors of the intellectual world—it becomes necessary to cut away the last anchor of this fallacious and fantastic hope. We shall accordingly show that the mathematical method is unattended in the sphere of philosophy by the least advantage —except, perhaps, that it more plainly exhibits its own inadequacy—that geometry and philosophy are two quite different things, although they go hand in hand in the field of natural science, and, consequently, that the procedure of the one can never be imitated by the other.

The evidence of mathematics rests upon definitions, axioms, and demonstrations. I shall be satisfied with showing that none of these forms can be employed or imitated in philosophy in the sense in which they are understood by mathematicians; and that the geometrician, if he employs his method in philosophy, will succeed only in building card-castles, while the employment of the philosophical method in mathematics, can result in nothing but mere verbiage. The essential business of philosophy, indeed, is to mark out the limits of the science; and even the mathematician, unless his talent is naturally circumscribed and limited to this particular department of knowledge, cannot turn a deaf ear to the warnings of philosophy, or set himself above its direction.

1. *Of Definitions.*—A *definition* is, as the term itself indicates, the representation, upon primary grounds, of the complete conception of a thing within its own limits.* Accord-

---

* The definition must describe the conception *completely*, that is, omit none of the marks or signs of which it is composed; *within its own limits*, that is, it must be precise, and enumerate no more signs than belong to the conception; and *on primary grounds*, that is to say, the limitation of the bounds of the conception must not be deduced from other conceptions, as in this case a proof would be necessary, and the so-called definition would be incapable of taking its place at the head of all the judgments we have to form regarding an object.

ingly, an *empirical* conception cannot be defined, it can only be *explained*. For, as there are in such a conception only a certain number of marks or signs, which denote a certain class of sensuous objects, we can never be sure that we do not cogitate under the word which indicates the same object, at one time a greater, at another a smaller number of signs. Thus, one person may cogitate in his conception of gold, in addition to its properties of weight, color, malleability, that of resisting rust, while another person may be ignorant of this quality. We employ certain signs only so long as we require them for the sake of distinction; new observations abstract some and add new ones, so that an empirical conception never remains within permanent limits. It is, in fact, useless to define a conception of this kind. If, for example, we are speaking of water and its properties, we do not stop at what we actually think by the word *water*, but proceed to observation and experiment; and the word, with the few signs attached to it, is more properly a *designation* than a conception of the thing. A definition in this case, would evidently be nothing more than a determination of the word. In the second place, no *à priori* conception, such as those of substance, cause, right, fitness, and so on, can be defined. For I can never be sure, that the clear representation of a given conception (which is given in a confused state) has been fully developed, until I know that the representation is adequate with its object. But, inasmuch as the conception, as it is presented to the mind, may contain a number of obscure representations, which we do not observe in our analysis, although we employ them in our application of the conception, I can never be sure that my analysis is complete, while examples may make this probable, although they can never demonstrate the fact. Instead of the word *definition*, I should rather employ the term exposition—a more modest expression, which the critic may accept without surrendering his doubts as to the completeness of the analysis of any such conception. As, therefore, neither empirical nor *à priori* conceptions are capable of definition, we have to see whether the only other kind of conceptions—arbitrary conceptions—can be subjected to this mental operation. Such a conception can always be defined; for I must know thoroughly what I wished to cogitate in it, as it was I who created it, and it was not given to my mind either by the nature of my understanding or by experience. At the same time, I cannot say that, by such a definition, I have defined a real object. If the conception is based upon empirical conditions, if, for example, I have a conception of a clock for a ship, this arbitrary conception does not assure me of the existence or even of the possibility of the object. My definition of such a conception would with more propriety be termed a declaration of a project than a definition of an object. There are no other conceptions which can bear definition, except those which contain an arbitrary synthesis, which can be constructed à *priori*. Consequently, the science of mathematics alone possesses definitions. For the object here thought is presented à *priori* in intuition; and thus it can never contain more or less than the conception, because the conception of the object has been given by the definition—and primarily, that is, without deriving the definition from any other source. Philosophical definitions are, therefore, merely expositions of given conceptions, while mathematical definitions are constructions of conceptions originally formed by the mind itself; the former are produced by analysis, the completeness of which is never demonstratively certain, the latter by a synthesis. In a mathematical definition the conception is *formed*, in a philosophical definition it is only *explained*. From this it follows:

a. That we must not imitate, in philosophy, the mathematical usage of commencing with definitions—except by way of hypothesis or experiment. For, as all so-called philosophical definitions are merely analyses of given conceptions, these conceptions, although only in a confused form, must precede the analysis; and the incomplete exposition must precede the complete, so that we may be able to draw certain inferences from the characteristics which an incomplete analysis has enabled us to discover, before we attain to the complete exposition or definition of the conception. In one word, a full and clear definition ought, in philosophy, rather to form the conclusion than the commencement of our labors.* In mathematics, on the contrary, we cannot have a conception prior to the definition; it is

---

* Philosophy abounds in faulty definitions, especially such as contain some of the elements requisite to form a complete definition. If a conception could not be employed in reasoning before it had been defined, it would fare ill with all philosophical thought. But, as incompletely defined conceptions may always be employed without detriment to truth, so far as our analysis of the elements contained in them proceeds, imperfect definitions, that is, propositions which are properly not definitions, but merely approximations thereto, may be used with great advantage. In mathematics, definition belongs *ad esse*, in philosophy *ad melius esse*. It is a difficult task to construct a proper definition. Jurists are still without a complete definition of the idea of right.

the definition which gives us the conception, and it must for this reason form the commencement of every chain of mathematical reasoning.

b. Mathematical definitions cannot be erroneous. For the conception is given only in and through the definition, and thus it contains only what has been cogitated in the definition. But although a definition cannot be incorrect, as regards its content, an error may sometimes, although seldom, creep into the form. This error consists in a want of precision. Thus the common definition of a circle—that it is a curved line, every point in which is equally distant from another point called the centre— is faulty, from the fact that the determination indicated by the word *curved* is superfluous. For there ought to be a particular theorem, which may be easily proved from the definition, to the effect that every line, which has all its points at equal distances from another point, must be a curved line—that is, that not even the smallest part of it can be straight. Analytical definitions, on the other hand, may be erroneous in many respects, either by the introduction of signs which do not actually exist in the conception, or by wanting in that completeness which forms the essential of a definition. In the latter case, the definition is necessarily defective, because we can never be fully certain of the completeness of our analysis. For these reasons, the method of definition employed in mathematics cannot be imitated in philosophy.

2. *Of Axioms.* These, in so far as they are immediately certain, are *à priori* synthetical principles. Now, one conception cannot be connected synthetically and yet immediately with another; because, if we wish to proceed out of and beyond a conception, a third mediating cognition is necessary. And, as philosophy is a cognition of reason by the aid of conceptions alone, there is to be found in it no principle which deserves to be called an axiom. Mathematics, on the other hand, may possess axioms, because it can always connect the predicates of an object *à priori*, and without any mediating term, by means of the construction of conceptions in intuition. Such is the case with the proposition, Three points can always lie in a plane. On the other hand, no synthetical principle which is based upon conceptions can ever be immediately certain (for example, the proposition, Everything that happens has a cause), because I require a mediating term to connect the two conceptions of event

and cause—namely, the condition of time-determination in an experience, and I cannot cognize any such principle immediately and from conceptions alone. Discursive principles are, accordingly, very different from intuitive principles or axioms. The former always require deduction, which in the case of the latter may be altogether dispensed with. Axioms are, for this reason, always self-evident, while philosophical principles, whatever may be the degree of certainty they possess, cannot lay any claim to such a distinction. No synthetical proposition of pure transcendental reason can be so evident, as is often rashly enough declared, as the statement, *Twice two are four.* It is true that in the Analytic I introduced into the list of principles of the pure understanding certain axioms of intuition; but the principle there discussed was not itself an axiom, but served merely to present the principle of the possibility of axioms in general, while it was really nothing more than a principle based upon conceptions. For it is one part of the duty of transcendental philosophy to establish the possibility of mathematics itself. Philosophy possesses, then, no axioms, and has no right to impose its *à priori* principles upon thought, until it has established their authority and validity by a thorough-going deduction.

3. *Of Demonstrations.* Only an apodictic proof, based upon intuition, can be termed a demonstration. Experience teaches us what is, but it cannot convince us that it might have been otherwise. Hence a proof upon empirical grounds cannot be apodictic. *A priori* conceptions, in discursive cognition, can never produce intuitive certainty or evidence, however certain the judgment they present may be. Mathematics alone, therefore, contains demonstrations, because it does not deduce its cognition from conceptions, but from the construction of conceptions, that is, from intuition, which can be given *à priori* in accordance with conceptions. The method of algebra, in equations, from which the correct answer is deduced by reduction, is a kind of construction—not geometrical, but by symbols—in which all conceptions, especially those of the relations of quantities, are represented in intuition by signs; and thus the conclusions in that science are secured from errors by the fact that every proof is submitted to ocular evidence. Philosophical cognition does not possess this advantage, it being required to consider the general always *in abstracto* (by means of conceptions), while mathematics can always consider it *in concreto*

(in an individual intuition), and at the same time by means of *à priori* representation, whereby all errors are rendered manifest to the senses. The former—discursive proofs—ought to be termed *acroamatic proofs*, rather than *demonstrations*, as only words are employed in them, while demonstrations proper, as the term itself indicates, always require a reference to the intuition of the object.

It follows from all these considerations, that it is not consonant with the nature of philosophy, especially in the sphere of pure reason, to employ the dogmatical method, and to adorn itself with the titles and insignia of mathematical science. It does not belong to that order, and can only hope for a fraternal union with that science. Its attempts at mathematical evidence are vain pretensions, which can only keep it back from its true aim, which is to detect the illusory procedure of reason when transgressing its proper limits, and by fully explaining and analyzing our conceptions, to conduct us from the dim regions of speculation, to the clear region of modest self-knowledge. Reason must not, therefore, in its transcendental endeavors, look forward with such confidence, as if the path it is pursuing led straight to its aim, nor reckon with such security upon its premises, as to consider it unnecessary to take a step back, or to keep a strict watch for errors, which, overlooked in the principles, may be detected in the arguments themselves—in which case it may be requisite either to determine these principles with greater strictness, or to change them entirely.

I divide all apodictic propositions, whether demonstrable or immediately certain, into *dogmata* and *mathemata*. A direct synthetical proposition, based on conceptions, is a *dogma; a* proposition of the same kind, based on the construction of conceptions, is a *mathema*. Analytical judgments do not teach us any more about an object, than what was contained in the conception we had of it; because they do not extend our cognition beyond our conception of an object, they merely elucidate the conception. They cannot therefore be with propriety termed dogmas. Of the two kinds of *à priori* synthetical propositions above-mentioned, only those which are employed in philosophy can, according to the general mode of speech, bear this name; those of arithmetic or geometry would not be rightly so denominated. Thus the customary mode of speaking confirms the explanation given above, and the conclusion arrived at, that only those judgments which are based upon conceptions, not on the construction of conceptions, can be termed dogmatical.

Thus, pure reason, in the sphere of speculation, does not contain a single direct synthetical judgment based upon conceptions. By means of ideas, it is, as we have shown, incapable of producing synthetical judgments, which are objectively valid; by means of the conceptions of the understanding, it establishes certain indubitable principles, not, however, directly on the basis of conceptions, but only indirectly by means of the relation of these conceptions to something of a purely contingent nature, namely, possible experience. When experience is presupposed, these principles are apodictically certain, but in themselves, and directly, they cannot even be cognized à *priori*. Thus the given conceptions of *cause* and *event* will not be sufficient for the demonstration of the proposition, every event has a cause. For this reason, it is not a dogma; although from another point of view—that of experience, it is capable of being proved to demonstration. The proper term for such a proposition is *principle*, and not *theorem* (although it does require to be proved), because it possesses the remarkable peculiarity of being the condition of the possibility of its own ground of proof, that is, experience, and of forming a necessary presupposition in all empirical observation.

If then, in the speculative sphere of pure reason, no dogmata are to be found; all *dogmatical* methods, whether borrowed from mathematics, or invented by philosophical thinkers, are alike inappropriate and inefficient. They only serve to conceal errors and fallacies, and to deceive philosophy, whose duty it is to see that reason pursues a safe and straight path. A philosophical method may, however, be *systematical*. For our reason is, subjectively considered, itself a system, and, in the sphere of mere conceptions, a system of investigation according to principles of unity, the material being supplied by experience alone. But this is not the proper place for discussing the peculiar method of transcendental philosophy, as our present task is simply to examine whether our faculties are capable of erecting an edifice on the basis of pure reason, and how far they may proceed with the materials at their command.

Section II.—The Discipline of Pure Reason in Polemics

Reason must be subject, in all its operations, to criticism, which must always be permitted to exercise its functions without restraint; otherwise its interests are imperilled, and its influence obnoxious to suspicion. There is nothing, however useful, however sacred it may be, that can claim exemption from the searching examination of this supreme tribunal, which has no respect of persons. The very existence of reason depends upon this freedom; for the voice of reason is not that of a dictatorial and despotic power, it is rather like the vote of the citizen of a free state, every member of which must have the privilege of giving free expression to his doubts, and possess even the right of *veto.*

But while reason can never decline to submit itself to the tribunal of criticism, it has not always cause to *dread* the judgment of this court. Pure reason, however, when engaged in the sphere of dogmatism is not so thoroughly conscious of a strict observance of its highest laws, as to appear before a higher judicial reason with perfect confidence. On the contrary, it must renounce its magnificent dogmatical pretensions in philosophy.

Very different is the case, when it has to defend itself, not before a judge, but against an equal. If dogmatical assertions are advanced on the negative side, in opposition to those made by reason on the positive side, its justification κατ’ ἄνθρωπον is complete, although the proof of its propositions is κατ’ ἀλή-θειαν unsatisfactory.

By the polemic of pure reason I mean the defence of its propositions made by reason, in opposition to the dogmatical counter-propositions advanced by other parties. The question here is not whether its own statements may not also be false; it merely regards the fact that reason proves that the opposite cannot be established with demonstrative certainty, nor even asserted with a higher degree of probability. Reason does not hold her possessions upon sufferance; for, although she cannot show a perfectly satisfactory title to them, no one can prove that she is *not* the rightful possessor.

It is a melancholy reflection that reason, in its highest exercise, falls into an antithetic; and that the supreme tribunal for the settlement of differences should not be at union with itself. It is true that we had to discuss the question of an apparent antithetic, but we found that it was based upon a misconception. In conformity with the common prejudice, phenomena were regarded as things in themselves, and thus an absolute completeness in their synthesis was required in the one mode or in the other (it was shown to be impossible in both); a demand entirely out of place in regard to phenomena. There was, then, no real self-contradiction of reason in the propositions—the series of phenomena *given in themselves* has an absolutely first beginning, and, this series is absolutely and *in itself* without beginning. The two propositions are perfectly consistent with each other, because phenomena as phenomena, are *in themselves* nothing, and consequently the hypothesis that they are things in themselves, must lead to self-contradictory inferences.

But there are cases in which a similar misunderstanding cannot be provided against, and the dispute must remain unsettled. Take, for example, the theistic proposition: There is a Supreme Being; and on the other hand, the atheistic counter-statement: There exists no Supreme Being; or, in psychology: Everything that thinks possesses the attribute of absolute and permanent unity, which is utterly different from the transitory unity of material phenomena; and the counter proposition: The soul is not an immaterial unity, and its nature is transitory, like that of phenomena. The objects of these questions contain no heterogeneous or contradictory elements, for they relate to *things in themselves,* and not to phenomena. There would arise indeed, a real contradiction if reason came forward with a statement on the negative side of these questions alone. As regards the criticism to which the grounds of proof on the affirmative side must be subjected, it may be freely admitted, without necessitating the surrender of the affirmative propositions, which have, at least, the interest of reason in their favor— an advantage which the opposite party cannot lay claim to.

I cannot **agree** with the opinion of several admirable thinkers —Sulzer among the rest—that in spite of the weakness of the arguments hitherto in use, we may hope, one day, to see sufficient demonstrations of the two cardinal propositions of pure reason—the existence of a Supreme Being, and the immortality of the soul. I am certain, on the contrary, that this will never be the case. For on what ground can reason base such synthetical propositions, which do not relate to the objects of experience and their internal possibility?—But it is also demonstratively certain that no one will ever be able to maintain the contrary with the least show of probability. For, as he can attempt such a proof solely upon the basis of pure reason, he is bound to prove that a Supreme Being, and a thinking subject in the character of a pure intelligence, are *impossible*. But where will he find the knowledge which can enable him to enounce synthetical judgments in regard to things which transcend the region of experience? We may, therefore, rest assured that the opposite never will be demonstrated. We need not, then, have recourse to scholastic arguments; we may always admit the truth of those propositions which are consistent with the speculative interests of reason in the sphere of experience, and form, moreover, the only means of uniting the speculative with the practical interest. Our opponent, who must not be considered here as a critic solely, we can be ready to meet with a *non liquet* which cannot fail to disconcert him; while we cannot deny his right to a similar retort, as we have on our side the advantage of the support of the subjective maxim of reason, and can therefore look upon all his sophistical arguments with calm indifference.

From this point of view, there is properly no antithetic of pure reason. For the only arena for such a struggle would be upon the field of pure theology and psychology; but on this ground there can appear no combatant whom we need to fear. Ridicule and boasting can be his only weapons; and these may be laughed at, as mere child's play. This consideration restores to reason her courage; for what source of confidence could be found, if she, whose vocation it is to destroy error, were at variance with herself and without any reasonable hope of ever reaching a state of permanent repose?

Everything in nature is good for some purpose. Even poisons are serviceable; they destroy the evil effects of other poisons generated in our system, and must always find a place in every complete pharmacopœia. The objections raised against the fallacies and sophistries of speculative reason, are objections given by the nature of this reason itself, and must therefore have a destination and purpose which can only be for the good of humanity. For what purpose has Providence raised many objects, in which we have the deepest interest, so far above us, that we vainly try to cognize them with certainty, and our powers of mental vision are rather excited than satisfied by the glimpses we may chance to seize? It is very doubtful whether it is for our benefit to advance bold affirmations regarding subjects involved in such obscurity; perhaps it would even be detrimental to our best interests. But it is undoubtedly always beneficial to leave the investigating, as well as the critical reason, in perfect freedom, and permit it to take charge of its own interests, which are advanced as much by its limitation, as by its extension of its views, and which always suffer by the interference of foreign powers forcing it, against its natural tendencies, to bend to certain preconceived designs.

Allow your opponent to say what he thinks reasonable, and combat him only with the weapons of reason. Have no anxiety for the practical interests of humanity—these are never imperilled in a purely speculative dispute. Such a dispute serves merely to disclose the antinomy of reason, which, as it has its source in the nature of reason, ought to be thoroughly investigated. Reason is benefited by the examination of a subject on both sides, and its judgments are corrected by being limited. It is not the *matter* that may give occasion to dispute, but the *manner*. For it is perfectly permissible to employ, in the presence of reason, the language of a firmly rooted *faith*, even after we have been obliged to renounce all pretensions to *knowledge*.

If we were to ask the dispassionate David Hume—a philosopher endowed, in a degree that few are, with a well-balanced judgment: What motive induced you to spend so much labor and thought in undermining the consoling and beneficial persuasion that reason is capable of assuring us of the existence, and presenting us with a determinate conception of a Supreme Being?—His answer would be: Nothing but the desire of teaching reason to know its own powers better, and, at the same time, a dislike of the procedure by which that faculty was compelled to support foregone conclusions, and prevented from confessing the internal weaknesses which it cannot but feel when it enters upon a rigid self-examination. If, on the other hand, we were to ask Priestley—a philosopher who had no taste for transcendental speculation, but was entirely devoted to the principles of *empiricism*—what his motives were for overturning those two main pillars of religion—the doctrines of the freedom of the will and the immortality of the soul (in his view the hope of a future life is but the expectation of the miracle of resurrection)—this philosopher, himself a zealous and pious teacher of religion, could give no other answer than this: I acted in the interest of reason, which always suffers, when certain objects are explained and judged by a reference to other supposed laws than those of material nature—the only laws which we know in a determinate manner. It would be unfair to decry the latter philosopher, who endeavored to harmonize his paradoxical opinions with the interests of religion, and to undervalue an honest and reflecting man, because he finds himself at a loss the moment he has left the field of natural science. The same grace must be accorded to Hume, a man not less well-disposed, and quite as blameless in his moral character, and who pushed his abstract speculations to an extreme length, because, as he rightly believed, the object of them lies entirely beyond the bounds of natural science, and within the sphere of pure ideas.

What is to be done to provide against the danger which seems in the present case to menace the best interests of humanity? The course to be pursued in reference to this subject is a perfectly plain and natural one. Let each thinker pursue his own path; if he shows talent, if he gives evidence of profound thought, in one word, if he shows that he possesses the power of reasoning—reason is always the gainer. If you have recourse to other means, if you attempt to coerce reason, if you raise the cry of treason to humanity, if you excite the feelings of the crowd, which can neither understand nor sympathize with such subtle speculations—you will only make yourselves ridiculous. For the question does not concern the advantage or disadvantage which we are expected to reap from such inquiries; the question is merely, how far reason can advance in the field of speculation, apart from all kinds of interest, and whether we may depend upon the exertions of speculative reason, or must renounce all reliance on it. Instead of joining the combatants, it is your part to be a tranquil spectator of the struggle—a laborious struggle for the parties engaged, but attended, in its progress as well as in its results, with the most advantageous consequences for the interests of thought and knowledge. It is absurd to expect to be enlightened by reason, and at the same time to prescribe to her what side of the question she must adopt. Moreover, reason is sufficiently held in check by its own power, the limits imposed on it by its own nature are sufficient; it is unnecessary for you to place over it additional guards, as if its power were dangerous to the constitution of the intellectual state. In the dialectic of reason there is no victory gained, which needs in the least disturb your tranquillity.

The strife of dialectic is a necessity of reason, and we cannot but wish that it had been conducted long ere this with that perfect freedom which ought to be its essential condition. In this case, we should have had at an earlier period a matured and profound criticism, which must have put an end to all dialectical disputes, by exposing the illusions and prejudices in which they originated.

There is in human nature an unworthy propensity—a propensity which, like everything that springs from nature, must in its final purpose be conducive to the good of humanity— to conceal our real sentiments, and to give expression only to certain received opinions, which are regarded as at once safe and promotive of the common good. It is true, this tendency, not only to conceal our real sentiments, but to profess those which may gain us favor in the eyes of society, has not only *civilized*, but, in a certain measure, *moralized* us; as no one can break through the outward covering of respectability, honor, and morality, and thus the seemingly good examples which we see around us, form an excellent school for moral improvement, so long as our belief in their genuineness remains unshaken. But this disposition to represent ourselves as better than we are, and to utter opinions which are not our own, can be nothing more than a kind of *provisionary* arrangement of nature to lead us from the rudeness of an uncivilized state, and to teach us how to assume at least the appearance and *manner* of the good we see. But when true principles have been developed, and have obtained a sure foundation in our habit of thought, this conventionalism must be attacked with earnest vigor, otherwise it corrupts the heart, and checks the growth of good dispositions with the mischievous weed of fair appearances.

I am sorry to remark the same tendency to misrepresentation and hypocrisy in the sphere of speculative discussion, where there is less temptation to restrain the free expression of thought. For what can be more prejudicial to the interests of intelligence, than to falsify our real sentiments, to conceal the doubts which we feel in regard to our statements, or to maintain the validity of grounds of proof which we well know to be insufficient? So long as mere personal vanity is the source of these unworthy artifices—and this is generally the case in speculative discussions, which are mostly destitute of practical interest, and are incapable of complete demonstration—the vanity of the opposite party exaggerates as much on the other side; and thus the result is the same, although it is not brought about so soon as if the dispute had been conducted in a sincere and upright spirit. But where the mass entertains the notion that the aim of certain subtle speculators is nothing less than to shake the very foundations of public welfare and morality—it seems not only prudent, but even praiseworthy, to maintain the good cause by illusory arguments, rather than to give to our supposed opponents the advantage of lowering our declarations to the moderate tone of a merely practical conviction, and of compelling us to confess our inability to attain to apodictic certainty in speculative subjects. But we ought to reflect that there is nothing in the world more fatal to the maintenance of a good cause than deceit, misrepresentation, and falsehood. That the strictest laws of honesty should be observed in the discussion of a purely speculative subject, is the least requirement that can be made. If we could reckon with security even upon so little, the conflict of speculative reason regarding the important questions of God, immortality, and freedom, would have been either decided long ago, or would very soon be brought to a conclusion. But, in general, the uprightness of the defense stands in an inverse ratio to the goodness of the cause; and perhaps more honesty and fairness are shown by those who deny, than by those who uphold these doctrines.

I shall persuade myself, then, that I have readers who do not wish to see a righteous cause defended by unfair arguments. Such will now recognize the fact that, according to the principles of this Critique, if we consider not what is, but what ought to be the case, there can be really no polemic of pure reason. For how can two persons dispute about a thing, the reality of which neither can present in actual or even in possible experience? Each adopts the plan of meditating on his idea for the purpose of drawing from the idea, if he can, what is *more than the idea,* that is, the reality of the object which it indicates. How shall they settle the dispute, since neither is able to make his assertions directly comprehensible and certain, but must restrict himself to attacking and confuting those of his opponent? All statements enounced by pure reason transcend the conditions of possible experience, beyond the sphere of which we can discover no criterion of truth, while they are at the same time framed in accordance with the laws of the understanding, which are applicable only to experience; and thus it is the fate of all such speculative discussions, that while the one party attacks the weaker side of his opponent, he infallibly lays open his own weaknesses.

The critique of pure reason may be regarded as the highest tribunal for all speculative disputes; for it is not involved in these disputes, which have an immediate relation to certain objects and not to the laws of the mind, but is instituted for the purpose of determining the rights and limits of reason.

Without the control of criticism reason is, as it were, in a state of nature, and can only establish its claims and assertions by *war.* Criticism, on the contrary, deciding all questions according to the fundamental laws of its own institution, secures to us the peace of law and order, and enables us to discuss all differences in the more tranquil manner of a legal *process.* In the former case, disputes are ended by *victory,* which both sides may claim, and which is followed by a hollow armistice; in the latter, by a *sentence,* which, as it strikes at the root of all speculative differences, insures to all concerned a lasting peace. The endless disputes of a dogmatizing reason compel us to look for some mode of arriving at a settled decision by a critical investigation of reason itself; just as Hobbes maintains that the state of nature is a state of injustice and violence, and that we must leave it and submit ourselves to the constraint of law, which indeed limits individual freedom, but only that it may consist with the freedom of others and with the common good of all.

This freedom will, among other things, permit of our openly stating the difficulties and doubts which we are ourselves unable to solve, without being decried on that account as turbulent and dangerous citizens. This privilege forms part of the native rights of human reason, which recognizes no other judge than the universal reason of humanity; and as this reason is the source of all progress and improvement, such a privilege is to be held sacred and inviolable. It is unwise, moreover, to denounce as dangerous, any bold assertions against, or rash attacks upon, an opinion which is held by the largest and most moral class of the community; for that would be giving them an importance which they do not deserve. When I hear that the freedom of the will, the hope of a future life, and the existence of God have been overthrown by the arguments of some able writer, I feel a strong desire to read his book; for I expect that he will add to my knowledge, and impart greater clearness and distinctness to my views by the argumentative power shown in his writings. But I am perfectly certain, even before I have opened the book, that he has not succeeded in a single point, not because I believe I am in possession of irrefutable demonstrations of these important propositions, but because this transcendental critique, which has disclosed to me the power and the limits of pure reason, has fully convinced me that, as it is insufficient to establish the affirmative, it is as powerless, and even more so, to assure us of the truth of the negative answer to these questions. From what source does this free-thinker derive his knowledge that there is, for example, no Supreme Being? This proposition lies out of the field of possible experience, and, therefore, beyond the limits of human cognition. But I would not read at all the answer which the dogmatical maintainer of the good cause makes to his opponent, because I know well beforehand, that he will merely attack the fallacious grounds of his adversary, without being able to establish his own assertions. Besides, a new illusory argument, in the construction of which talent and acuteness are shown, is suggestive of new ideas and new trains of reasoning, and in this respect the old and everyday sophistries are quite useless. Again, the dogmatical opponent of religion gives employment to criticism, and enables us to test and correct its principles, while there is no occasion for anxiety in regard to the influence and results of his reasoning.

But, it will be said, must we not warn the youth intrusted to academical care against such writings, must we not preserve them from the knowledge of these dangerous assertions, until their judgment is ripened, or rather until the doctrines which we wish to inculcate are so firmly rooted in their minds as to withstand all attempts at instilling the contrary dogmas, from whatever quarter they may come?

If we are to confine ourselves to the dogmatical procedure in the sphere of pure reason, and find ourselves unable to settle such disputes otherwise than by becoming a party in them, and setting counter-assertions against the statements advanced by our opponents, there is certainly no plan more advisable *for the*

moment, but, at the same time, none more absurd and inefficient
for the future, than this retaining of the youthful mind under
guardianship for a time, and thus preserving it—for so long at
least—from seduction into error. But when, at a later period,
either curiosity, or the prevalent fashion of thought, places such
writings in their hands, will the so-called convictions of their
youth stand firm? The young thinker, who has in his armory
none but dogmatical weapons with which to resist the attacks of
his opponent, and who cannot detect the latent dialectic which
lies in his own opinions as well as in those of the opposite party,
sees the advance of illusory arguments and grounds of proof
which have the advantage of novelty, against as illusory
grounds of proof destitute of this advantage and which, perhaps, excite the suspicion that the natural credulity of his youth
has been abused by his instructors. He thinks he can find no
better means of showing that he has outgrown the discipline
of his minority, than by despising those well-meant warnings,
and, knowing no system of thought but that of dogmatism, he
drinks deep draughts of the poison that is to sap the principles
in which his early years were trained.

Exactly the opposite of the system here recommended ought
to be pursued in academical instruction. This can only be effected, however, by a thorough training in the critical investigation of pure reason. For, in order to bring the principles
of this critique into exercise as soon as possible, and to demonstrate their perfect sufficiency, even in the presence of the highest degree of dialectical illusion, the student ought to examine
the assertions made on both sides of speculative questions step
by step, and to test them by these principles. It cannot be a
difficult task for him to show the fallacies inherent in these
propositions, and thus he begins early to feel his own power of
securing himself against the influence of such sophistical arguments, which must finally lose, for him, all their illusory
power. And, although the same blows which overturn the edifice of his opponent are as fatal to his own speculative struct-
ures, if such he has wished to rear; he need not feel any sorrow
in regard to this seeming misfortune, as he has now before him
a fair prospect into the practical region, in which he may reasonably hope to find a more secure foundation for a rational system.

There is, accordingly, no proper polemic in the sphere of
pure reason. Both parties beat the air and fight with their

own shadows, as they pass beyond the limits of nature, and can find no tangible point of attack—no firm footing for their dogmatical conflict. Fight as vigorously as they may, the shadows which they hew down, immediately start up again, like the heroes in Walhalla, and renew the bloodless and unceasing contest.

But neither can we admit that there is any proper sceptical employment of pure reason, such as might be based upon the principle of *neutrality* in all speculative disputes. To excite reason against itself, to place weapons in the hands of the party on the one side as well as in those of the other, and to remain an undisturbed and sarcastic spectator of the fierce struggle that ensues, seems, from the dogmatical point of view, to be a part fitting only a malevolent disposition. But, when the sophist evidences an invincible obstinacy and blindness, and a pride which no criticism can moderate, there is no other practicable course than to oppose to this pride and obstinacy similar feelings and pretensions on the other side, equally well or ill founded, so that reason, staggered by the reflections thus forced upon it, finds it necessary to moderate its confidence in such pretensions, and to listen to the advices of criticism. But we cannot stop at these doubts, much less regard the conviction of our ignorance, not only as a cure for the conceit natural to dogmatism, but as the settlement of the disputes in which reason is involved with itself. On the contrary, scepticism is merely a means of awakening reason from its dogmatic dreams, and exciting it to a more careful investigation into its own powers and pretensions. But, as scepticism appears to be the shortest road to a permanent peace in the domain of philosophy, and as it is the track pursued by the many who aim at giving a philosophical coloring to their contemptuous dislike of all inquiries of this kind, I think it necessary to present to my readers this mode of thought in its true light.

Scepticism not a Permanent State for Human Reason

The consciousness of ignorance—unless this ignorance is recognized to be absolutely necessary—ought, instead of forming the conclusion of my inquiries, to be the strongest motive to the pursuit of them. All ignorance is either ignorance of things, or of the limits of knowledge. If my ignorance is accidental and not necessary, it must incite me, in the first case, to a *dogmatical* inquiry regarding the objects of which I am ignorant; in the second, to a *critical* investigation into the bounds of all possible knowledge. But that my ignorance is absolutely necessary and unavoidable, and that it consequently absolves from the duty of all further investigation, is a fact which cannot be made out upon empirical grounds—from *observation*, but upon critical grounds alone, that is, by a thorough-going *investigation* into the primary sources of cognition. It follows that the determination of the bounds of reason can be made only on *à priori* grounds; while the empirical limitation of reason, which is merely an indeterminate cognition of an ignorance that can never be completely removed, can take place only *à posteriori*. In other words, our empirical knowledge is limited by that which yet remains for us to know. The former cognition of our ignorance, which is possible only on a rational basis, is a *science;* the latter is merely a *perception*, and we cannot say how far the inferences drawn from it may extend. If I regard the earth, as it really appears to my senses, as a flat surface, I am ignorant how far this surface extends. But experience teaches me that, how far soever I go, I always see before me a space in which I can proceed further; and thus I know the limits—merely visual—of my actual knowledge of the earth, although I am ignorant of the limits of the earth itself. But if I have got so far as to know that the earth is a sphere, and that its surface is spherical I can cognize *à priori* and determine upon principles, from my knowledge of a small part of this surface—say to the extent of a degree of the diameter and circumference of the earth; and although I am ignorant of the objects which this surface contains I have a perfect knowledge of its limits and extent.

The sum of all the possible objects of our cognition seems to us to be a level surface, with an apparent horizon—that which forms the limit of its extent, and which has been termed by us the idea of unconditioned totality. To reach this limit by empirical means is impossible, and all attempts to determine it *à priori* according to a principle, are alike in vain. But all the questions raised by pure reason relate to that which lies beyond this horizon, or, at least, in its boundary line.

The celebrated David Hume was one of those geographers of human reason who believe that they have given a sufficient answer to all such questions, by declaring them to lie beyond the horizon of our knowledge—a horizon which, however, Hume was unable to determine. His attention especially was directed to the principle of causality; and he remarked with perfect justice, that the truth of this principle, and even the objective validity of the conception of a cause, was not commonly based upon clear insight, that is, upon à *priori* cognition. Hence he concluded that this law does not derive its authority from its universality and necessity, but merely from its general applicability in the course of experience, and a kind of subjective necessity thence arising, which he termed *habit*. From the inability of reason to establish this principle as a necessary law for the acquisition of all experience, he inferred the nullity of all the attempts of reason to pass the region of the empirical.

This procedure, of subjecting the *facta* of reason to examination, and, if necessary, to disapproval, may be termed the *censura* of reason. This *censura* must inevitably lead us to *doubts* regarding *all* transcendent employment of principles. But this is only the second step in our inquiry. The first step in regard to the subjects of pure reason, and which marks the infancy of that faculty, is that of *dogmatism*. The second, which we have just mentioned, is that of *scepticism,* and it gives evidence that our judgment has been improved by experience. But a third step is necessary—indicative of the maturity and manhood of the judgment, which now lays a firm foundation upon universal and necessary principles. This is the period of *criticism,* in which we do not examine the *facta* of reason, but reason itself, in the whole extent of its powers, and in regard to its capability of à *priori* cognition; and thus we determine not merely the empirical and ever-shifting bounds of our knowledge, but its necessary and eternal limits. We demonstrate from indubitable principles, not merely our ignorance in respect to this or that subject, but in regard to all possible questions of a certain class. Thus scepticism is a resting-place for reason, in which it may reflect on its dogmatical wanderings, and gain some knowledge of the region in which it happens to be, that it may pursue its way with greater certainty; but it cannot be its permanent dwelling-place. It must take up its abode only in the region of complete certitude, whether this relates to the cognition of objects themselves, or to the limits which bound all our cognition.

Reason is not to be considered as an indefinitely extended

plane, of the bounds of which we have only a general knowledge; it ought rather to be compared to a sphere, the radius of which may be found from the curvature of its surface—that is, the nature of *à priori* synthetical propositions—and, consequently, its circumference and extent. Beyond the sphere of experience there are no objects which it can cognize; nay, even questions regarding such supposititious objects relate only to the subjective principles of a complete determination of the relations which exist between the understanding-conceptions which lie within this sphere.

We are actually in possession of *à priori* synthetical cognitions, as is proved by the existence of the principles of the understanding, which anticipate experience. If anyone cannot comprehend the possibility of these principles, he may have some reason to doubt whether they are really *à priori;* but he cannot on this account declare them to be impossible, and affirm the nullity of the steps which reason may have taken under their guidance. He can only say: If we perceived their origin and their authenticity, we should be able to determine the extent and limits of reason; but, till we can do this, all propositions regarding the latter are mere random assertions. In this view, the doubt respecting all dogmatical philosophy, which proceeds without the guidance of criticism, is well grounded; but we cannot therefore deny to reason the ability to construct a sound philosophy, when the way has been prepared by a thorough critical investigation. All the conceptions produced, and all the questions raised, by pure reason, do not lie in the sphere of experience, but in that of reason itself, and hence they must be solved, and shown to be either valid or inadmissible, by that faculty. We have no right to decline the solution of such problems, on the ground that the solution can be discovered only from the nature of things, and under pretense of the limitation of human faculties, for reason is the sole creator of all these ideas, and is therefore bound either to establish their validity or to expose their illusory nature.

The polemic of scepticism is properly directed against the dogmatist, who erects a system of philosophy without having examined the fundamental objective principles on which it is based, for the purpose of evidencing the futility of his designs, and thus bringing him to a knowledge of his own powers. But, in itself, scepticism does not give us any certain information in

regard to the bounds of our knowledge. All unsuccessful dogmatical attempts of reason are *facta* which it is always useful
to submit to the censure of the sceptic. But this cannot help
us to any decision regarding the expectations which reason
cherishes of better success in future endeavors; the investigations of scepticism cannot, therefore, settle the dispute regarding the rights and powers of human reason.

Hume is perhaps the ablest and most ingenious of all sceptical
philosophers, and his writings have, undoubtedly, exerted the
most powerful influence in awakening reason to a thorough investigation into its own powers. It will, therefore, well repay
our labors to consider for a little the course of reasoning which
he followed, and the errors into which he strayed, although setting out on the path of truth and certitude.

Hume was probably aware, although he never clearly developed the notion, that we proceed in judgments of a certain class
beyond our conception of the object. I have termed this kind
of judgments synthetical. As regards the manner in which I
pass beyond my conception by the aid of experience, no doubts
can be entertained. Experience is itself a synthesis of perceptions; and it employs perceptions to increment the conception,
which I obtain by means of another perception. But we feel
persuaded that we are able to proceed beyond a conception, and
to extend our cognition *à priori*. We attempt this in two ways
—either, through the pure understanding, in relation to that
which may become an *object of experience,* or, through pure
reason, in relation to such properties of things, or of the existence of things, as can never be presented in any experience.
This sceptical philosopher did not distinguish these two kinds
of judgments, as he ought to have done, but regarded this aug-
mentation of conceptions, and, if we may so express ourselves,
the spontaneous generation of understanding and reason, independently of the impregnation of experience, as altogether impossible. The so-called *à priori* principles of these faculties he
consequently held to be invalid and imaginary, and regarded
them as nothing but subjective habits of thought originating in
experience, and therefore purely empirical and contingent rules,
to which we attribute a spurious necessity and universality.
In support of this strange assertion, he referred us to the generally acknowledged principle of the relation between cause
and effect. No faculty of the mind can conduct us from the

conception of a thing to the existence of something else; and hence he believed he could infer that, without experience, we possess no source from which we can augment a conception, and no ground sufficient to justify us in framing a judgment that is to extend our cognition *à priori.* That the light of the sun, which shines upon a piece of wax, at the same time melts it, while it hardens clay, no power of the understanding could infer from the conceptions which we previously possessed of these substances; much less is there any *à priori* law that could conduct us to such a conclusion, which experience alone can certify. On the other hand, we have seen in our discussion of Transcendental Logic, that, although we can never proceed *immediately* beyond the content of the conception which is given us, we can always cognize completely *à priori*—in relation, however, to a third term, namely, *possible* experience— the law of its connection with other things. For example, if I observe that a piece of wax melts, I can cognize *à priori* that there must have been something (the sun's heat) preceding, which this effect follows according to a fixed law; although, without the aid of experience, I could not cognize *à priori* and in a *determinate* manner, either the cause from the effect, or the effect from the cause. Hume was therefore wrong in inferring, from the contingency of the determination *according to law,* the contingency of *the law* itself; and the passing beyond the conception of a thing to possible experience (which is an *à priori* proceeding, constituting the objective reality of the conception), he confounded with our synthesis of objects in actual experience, which is always, of course, empirical. Thus, too, he regarded the principle of affinity, which, has its seat in the understanding and indicates a necessary connection, as a mere rule of association, lying in the imitative faculty of imagination, which can present only contingent, and not objective connections.

The sceptical errors of this remarkably acute thinker arose principally from a defect, which was common to him with the dogmatists, namely, that he had never made a systematic review of all the different kinds of *à priori* synthesis performed by the understanding. Had he done so, he would have found, to take one example among many, that the *principle of permanence* was of this character, and that it, as well as the principle of causality, anticipates experience. In this way he might have been able to describe the determinate limits of the *à priori* operations of understanding and reason. But he merely declared the understanding to be limited, instead of showing what its limits were; he created a general mistrust in the power of our faculties, without giving us any determinate knowledge of the bounds of our necessary and unavoidable ignorance; he examined and condemned some of the principles of the understanding, without investigating all its powers with the completeness necessary to criticism. He denies, with truth, certain powers to the understanding, but he goes further, and declares it to be utterly inadequate to the *à priori* extension of knowledge, although he has not fully examined all the powers which reside in the faculty; and thus the fate which always overtakes scepticism meets him too. That is to say, his own declarations are doubted, for his objections were based upon *facta*, which are contingent, and not upon principles, which can alone demonstrate the necessary invalidity of all dogmatical assertions.

As Hume makes no distinction between the well-grounded claims of the understanding and the dialectical pretensions of reason, against which, however, his attacks are mainly directed, reason does not feel itself shut out from all attempts at the extension of *à priori* cognition, and hence it refuses, in spite of a few checks in this or that quarter, to relinquish such efforts. For one naturally arms one's self to resist an attack, and becomes more obstinate in the resolve to establish the claims he has advanced. But a complete review of the powers of reason, and the conviction thence arising that we are in possession of a limited field of action, while we must admit the vanity of higher claims, puts an end to all doubt and dispute, and induces reason to rest satisfied with the undisturbed possession of its limited domain.

To the uncritical dogmatist, who has not surveyed the sphere of his understanding, nor determined, in accordance with principles, the limits of possible cognition, who, consequently, is ignorant of his own powers, and believes he will discover them by the attempts he makes in the field of cognition, these attacks of scepticism are not only dangerous, but destructive. For if there is one proposition in his chain of reasoning which he cannot prove, or the fallacy in which he cannot evolve in accordance with a principle, suspicion falls on all his statements, however plausible they may appear.

And thus scepticism, the bane of dogmatical philosophy, conducts us to a sound investigation into the understanding and the reason. When we are thus far advanced, we need fear no further attacks; for the limits of our domain are clearly marked out, and we can make no claims nor become involved in any disputes regarding the region that lies beyond these limits. Thus the sceptical procedure in philosophy does not present any *solution* of the problems of reason, but it forms an excellent *exercise* for its powers, awakening its circumspection, and indicating the means whereby it may most fully establish its claims to its legitimate possessions.

Section III.—The Discipline of Pure Reason in Hypothesis

This critique of reason has now taught us that all its efforts to extend the bounds of knowledge, by means of pure speculation, are utterly fruitless. So much the wider field, it may appear, lies open to hypothesis; as, where we cannot know with certainty, we are at liberty to make guesses, and to form suppositions.

Imagination may be allowed, under the strict surveillance of reason, to invent suppositions; but, these must be based on something that is perfectly certain—and that is the *possibility* of the object. If we are well assured upon this point, it is allowable to have recourse to supposition in regard to the reality of the object; but this supposition must, unless it is utterly groundless, be connected, as its ground of explanation, with that which is really given and absolutely certain. Such a supposition is termed a *hypothesis.*

It is beyond our power to form the least conception *à priori* of the possibility of dynamical connection in phenomena; and the category of the pure understanding will not enable us to excogitate any such connection, but merely helps us to understand it, when we meet with it in experience. For this reason we cannot, in accordance with the categories, imagine or invent any object or any property of an object not given, or that may not be given in experience, and employ it in a hypothesis; otherwise, we should be basing our chain of reasoning upon mere chimerical fancies, and not upon conceptions of things. Thus, we have no right to assume the existence of new powers, not existing in nature—for example, an understanding with a non-sensuous intuition, a force of attraction without contact, or some new kind of substances occupying space, and yet without the property of impenetrability; and, consequently, we cannot assume that there is any other kind of community among substances than that observable in experience, any kind of presence than that in space, or any kind of duration than that in time. In one word, the conditions of possible experience are for reason the only conditions of the possibility of things; reason cannot venture to form, independently of these conditions, any conceptions of things, because such conceptions, although not self-contradictory, are without object and without application.

The conceptions of reason are, as we have already shown, mere ideas, and do not relate to any object in any kind of experience. At the same time, they do not indicate imaginary or possible objects. They are purely problematical in their nature, and, as aids to the heuristic exercise of the faculties, form the basis of the regulative principles for the systematic employment of the understanding in the field of experience. If we leave this ground of experience, they become mere fictions of thought, and possibility of which is quite indemonstrable; and they cannot consequently be employed, as hypotheses, in the explanation of real phenomena. It is quite admissible to *cogitate* the soul as simple, for the purpose of enabling ourselves to employ the idea of a perfect and necessary unity of all the faculties of the mind as the principle of all our inquiries into its internal phenomena, although we cannot cognize this unity *in concreto*. But to *assume* that the soul is a simple substance (a transcendental conception) would be enouncing a proposition which is not only indemonstrable—as many physical hypotheses are, but a proposition which is purely arbitrary, and in the highest degree rash. The simple is never presented in experience; and, if by substance is here meant the permanent object of sensuous intuition, the possibility of a *simple phenomenon* is perfectly inconceivable. Reason affords no good grounds for admitting the existence of intelligible beings, or of intelligible properties of sensuous things, although—as we have no conception either of their possibility or of their impossibility—it will always be out of our power to affirm dogmatically that they do not exist.

In the explanation of given phenomena, no other things and no other grounds of explanation can be employed, than those which stand in connection with the given phenomena according to the known laws of experience. A *transcendental hypothesis,* in which a mere idea of reason is employed to explain the phenomena of nature, would not give us any better insight into a phenomenon, as we should be trying to explain what we do not sufficiently understand from known empirical principles, by what we do not understand at all. The principle of such a hypothesis might conduce to the satisfaction of reason, but it would not assist the understanding in its application to objects. Order and conformity to aims in the sphere of nature must be themselves explained upon natural grounds and according to natural laws; and the wildest hypotheses, if they are only physical, are here more admissible than a hyperphysical hypothesis, such as that of a divine author. For such a hypothesis would introduce the principle of *ignava ratio,* which requires us to give up the search for causes that might be discovered in the course of experience, and to rest satisfied with a mere idea. As regards the absolute totality of the grounds of explanation in the series of these causes, this can be no hindrance to the understanding in the case of phenomena; because, as they are to us nothing more than phenomena, we have no right to look for anything like completeness in the synthesis of the series of their conditions.

Transcendental hypotheses are therefore inadmissible; and we cannot use the liberty of employing, in the absence of physical, hyperphysical grounds of explanation. And this for two reasons; first, because such hypotheses do not advance reason, but rather stop it in its progress; secondly, because this license would render fruitless all its exertions in its own proper sphere, which is that of experience. For, when the explanation of natural phenomena happens to be difficult, we have constantly at hand a transcendental ground of explanation, which lifts us above the necessity of investigating nature; and our inquiries are brought to a close, not because we have obtained all the requisite knowledge, but because we abut upon a principle which is incomprehensible, and which, indeed, is so far back in the track of thought, as to contain the conception of the absolutely primal being.

The next requisite for the admissibility of a hypothesis is its sufficiency. That is, it must determine *à priori* the consequences which are given in experience, and which are supposed to follow from the hypothesis itself. If we require to employ, auxiliary hypotheses, the suspicion naturally arises that they are mere fictions; because the necessity for each of them requires the same justification as in the case of the original hypothesis, and thus their testimony is invalid. If we suppose the existence of an infinitely perfect cause, we possess sufficient grounds for the explanation of the conformity to aims, the order and the greatness which we observe in the universe; but we find ourselves obliged, when we observe the evil in the world and the exceptions to these laws, to employ new hypotheses in support of the original one. We employ the idea of the simple nature of the human soul as the foundation of all the theories we may form of its phenomena; but when we meet with difficulties in our way, when we observe in the soul phenomena similar to the changes which take place in matter, we require to call in new auxiliary hypotheses. These may, indeed, not be false, but we do not know them to be true, because the only witness to their certitude is the hypothesis which they themselves have been called in to explain.

We are not discussing the above-mentioned assertions regarding the immaterial unity of the soul and the existence of a Supreme Being as dogmata, which certain philosophers profess to demonstrate *à priori*, but purely as hypotheses. In the former case, the dogmatist must take care that his arguments possess the apodictic certainty of a demonstration. For the assertion that the reality of such ideas is *probable*, is as absurd as a proof of the probability of a proposition in geometry. Pure abstract reason, apart from all experience, can either cognize a proposition entirely *à priori*, and as necessary, or it can cognize nothing at all; and hence the judgments it enounces are never mere opinions, they are either apodictic certainties, or declarations that nothing can be known on the subject. Opinions and probable judgments on the nature of things can only be employed to explain given phenomena, or they may relate to the effect, in accordance with empirical laws, of an actually existing cause. In other words, we must restrict the sphere of opinion to the world of experience and nature. Beyond this region *opinion* is mere invention; unless we are groping about for the truth on a path not yet fully known, and have some hopes of stumbling upon it by chance.

But, although hypotheses are inadmissible in answers to the questions of pure speculative reason, they may be employed in the defense of these answers. That is to say, hypotheses are admissible in polemic, but not in the sphere of dogmatism. By the defense of statements of this character, I do not mean an attempt at discovering new grounds for their support, but merely the refutation of the arguments of opponents. All *à priori* synthetical propositions possess the peculiarity, that, although the philosopher who maintains the reality of the ideas contained in the proposition, is not in possession of sufficient knowledge to establish the certainty of his statements, his opponent is as little able to prove the truth of the opposite. This equality of fortune does not allow the one party to be superior to the other in the sphere of speculative cognition; and it is this sphere accordingly that is the proper arena of these endless speculative conflicts. But we shall afterwards show that, in relation to its *practical exercise,* reason has the right of admitting what, in the field of pure speculation, she would not be justified in supposing, except upon perfectly sufficient grounds; because all such suppositions destroy the necessary completeness of speculation—a condition which the practical reason, however, does not consider to be requisite. In this sphere, therefore, reason is mistress of a possession, her title to which she does not require to prove—which, in fact, she could not do. The burden of proof accordingly rests upon the opponent. But as he has just as little knowledge regarding the subject discussed, and is as little able to prove the non-existence of the object of an idea, as the philosopher on the other side is to demonstrate its reality, it is evident that there is an advantage on the side of the philosopher who maintains his proposition as a practically necessary supposition (*melior est conditio possidentis*). For he is at liberty to employ, in self-defense, the same weapons as his opponent makes use of in attacking him; that is, he has a right to use hypotheses not for the purpose of supporting the arguments in favor of his own propositions, but to show that his opponent knows no more than himself regarding the subject under discussion, and cannot boast of any speculative advantage.

Hypotheses are, therefore, admissible in the sphere of pure reason, only as weapons for self-defense, and not as supports to dogmatical assertions. But the opposing party we must always seek for in ourselves. For speculative reason is, in the sphere of transcendentalism, dialectical *in its own nature.* The difficulties and objections we have to fear lie in ourselves. They are like old but never superannuated claims; and we must seek them out, and settle them once and forever, if we are to expect a permanent peace. External tranquillity is hollow and unreal. The root of these contradictions, which lies in the nature of human reason, must be destroyed; and this can only be done, by giving it, in the first instance, freedom to grow, nay, by nourishing it, that it may send out shoots, and thus betray its own existence. It is our duty, therefore, to try to discover new objections, to put weapons in the hands of our opponent, and to grant him the most favorable position in the arena that he can wish. We have nothing to fear from these concessions; on the contrary, we may rather hope that we shall thus make ourselves master of a possession which no one will ever venture to dispute.

The thinker requires, to be fully equipped, the hypotheses of pure reason, which, although but leaden weapons (for they have not been steeled in the armory of experience), are as useful as any that can be employed by his opponents. If, accordingly, we have assumed, from a non-speculative point of view, the immaterial nature of the soul, and are met by the objection that experience seems to prove that the growth and decay of our mental faculties are mere modifications of the sensuous organism—we can weaken the force of this objection, by the assumption that the body is nothing but the fundamental phenomenon, to which, as a necessary condition, all sensibility and consequently all thought relate in the present state of our existence; and that the separation of soul and body forms the conclusion of the sensuous exercise of our power of cognition and the beginning of the intellectual. The body would, in this view of the question, be regarded, not as the cause of thought, but merely as its restrictive condition, as promotive of the sensuous and animal, and as a hindrance to the pure and spiritual life; and the dependence of the animal life on the constitution of the body would not prove that the *whole* life of man was also dependent on the state of the organism. We might go still further, and discover new objections, or carry out to their extreme consequences those which have already been adduced.

Generation, in the human race as well as among the irrational animals, depends on so many accidents—of occasion, of proper sustenance, of the laws enacted by the government of a country, of vice even—that it is difficult to believe in the eternal existence of a being whose life has begun under circumstances so mean and trivial, and so entirely dependent upon our own control. As regards the continuance of the existence of the whole race, we need have no difficulties, for accident in single cases is subject to general laws; but, in the case of each individual, it would seem as if we could hardly expect so wonderful an effect from causes so insignificant. But, in answer to these objections, we may adduce the transcendental hypothesis, that all life is properly intelligible, and not subject to changes of time, and that it neither began in birth, nor will end in death. We may assume that this life is nothing more than a sensuous representation of pure spiritual life; that the whole world of sense is but an image, hovering before the faculty of cognition which we exercise in this sphere, and with no more objective reality than a dream; and that if we could intuit ourselves and other things as they really are, we should see ourselves in a world of spiritual natures, our connection with which did not begin at our birth, and will not cease with the destruction of the body. And so on.

We cannot be said to know what has been above asserted, nor do we seriously maintain the truth of these assertions; and the notions therein indicated are not even ideas of reason, they are purely *fictitious* conceptions. But this hypothetical procedure is in perfect conformity with the laws of reason. Our opponent mistakes the absence of empirical conditions for a proof of the complete impossibility of all that we have asserted; and we have to show him that he has not exhausted the whole sphere of possibility, and that he can as little compass that sphere by the laws of experience and nature, as we can lay a secure foundation for the operations of reason beyond the region of experience. Such hypothetical defences against the pretensions of an opponent must not be regarded as declarations of opinion. The philosopher abandons them, so soon as the opposite party renounces its dogmatical conceit. To maintain a simply negative position in relation to propositions which rest on an insecure foundation well befits the moderation of a true philosopher; but to uphold the objections urged against an opponent as proofs of the opposite statement, is a proceeding just as unwarrantable and arrogant as it is to attack the position of a philosopher who advances affirmative propositions regarding such a subject.

It is evident, therefore, that hypotheses, in the speculative sphere, are valid, not as independent propositions, but only relatively to opposite transcendent assumptions. For, to make the principles of possible experience conditions of the possibility of things in general is just as transcendent a procedure as to maintain the objective reality of ideas which can be applied to no objects except such as lie without the limits of possible experience. The judgments enounced by pure reason must be necessary, or they must not be enounced at all. Reason cannot trouble herself with opinions. But the hypotheses we have been discussing are merely problematical judgments, which can neither be confuted nor proved; while, therefore, they are not personal opinions, they are indispensable as answers to objections which are liable to be raised. But we must take care to confine them to this function, and guard against any assumption on their part of absolute validity, a proceeding which would involve reason in inextricable difficulties and contradictions.

Section IV. — The Discipline of Pure Reason in relation to Proofs

It is a peculiarity which distinguishes the proofs of transcendental synthetical propositions from those of all other *à priori* synthetical cognitions, that reason, in the case of the former, does not apply its conceptions directly to an object, but is first obliged to prove, *à priori*, the objective validity of these conceptions and the possibility of their syntheses. This is not merely a prudential rule; it is essential to the very possibility of the proof of a transcendental proposition. If I am required to pass, *à priori*, beyond the conception of an object, I find that it is utterly impossible without the guidance of something which is not contained in the conception. In mathematics, it is *à priori* intuition that guides my synthesis; and, in this case, all our conclusions may be drawn immediately from pure intuition. In transcendental cognition, so long as we are dealing only with conceptions of the understanding, we are guided by possible experience. That is to say, a proof in the sphere of transcendental cognition does not show that the given conception (that of an event, for example) leads directly to another conception (that of a cause)—for this would be a *saltus* which nothing can justify; but it shows that experience itself, and consequently the object of experience, is impossible without the connection indicated by these conceptions. It follows that such a proof must demonstrate the possibility of arriving, synthetically and *à priori*, at a certain knowledge of things, which was not contained in our conceptions of these things. Unless we pay particular attention to this requirement, our proofs, instead of pursuing the straight path indicated by reason, follow the tortuous road of mere subjective association. The illusory conviction, which rests upon subjective causes of association, and which is considered as resulting from the perception of a real and objective natural affinity, is always open to doubt and suspicion. For this reason, all the attempts which have been made to prove the principle of sufficient reason have, according to the universal admission of philosophers, been quite unsuccessful; and, before the appearance of transcendental criticism, it was considered better, as this principle could not be abandoned, to appeal boldly to the common sense of mankind (a proceeding which always proves that the problem, which reason ought to solve, is one in which philosophers find great difficulties), rather than attempt to discover new dogmatical proofs.

But, if the proposition to be proved is a proposition of pure reason, and if I aim at passing beyond my empirical conceptions by the aid of mere ideas, it is necessary that the proof should first show that such a step in synthesis is possible (which it is not), before it proceeds to prove the truth of the proposition itself. The so-called proof of the simple nature of the soul from the unity of apperception, is a very plausible one. But it contains no answer to the objection that, as the notion of absolute simplicity is not a conception which is directly applicable to a perception, but is an idea which must be inferred—if at all —from observation, it is by no means evident how the mere fact of consciousness, which is contained *in all thought,* although in so far a simple representation, can conduct me to the consciousness and cognition of a thing which is purely a thinking substance. When I represent to my mind the power of my body as in motion, my body in this thought is so far absolute unity, and my representation of it is a simple one; and hence I can indicate this representation by the motion of a point, because I have made abstraction of the size or volume of the body. But I cannot hence infer that, given merely the moving power of a body, the body may be cogitated as simple substance, merely because the representation in my mind takes no account of its content in space, and is consequently simple. The simple, in abstraction, is very different from the objectively simple; and hence the Ego, which is simple in the first sense, may, in the second sense, as indicating the soul itself, be a very complex conception, with a very various content. Thus it is evident, that in all such arguments, there lurks a paralogism. We guess (for without some such surmise our suspicion would not be excited in reference to a proof of this character) at the presence of the paralogism, by keeping ever before us a criterion of the possibility of those synthetical propositions which aim at proving more than experience can teach us. This criterion is obtained from the observation that such proofs do not lead us directly from the subject of the proposition to be proved to the required predicate, but find it necessary to presuppose the possibility of extending our cognition à *priori* by means of ideas. We must, accordingly, always use the greatest caution; we require, before attempting any proof, to consider how it is possible to extend the sphere of cognition by the operations of pure reason, and from what source we are to derive knowledge, which is neither obtained from the analysis of conceptions, nor relates, by anticipation, to possible experience. We shall thus spare ourselves much severe and fruitless labor, by not expecting from reason what is beyond its power, or rather by subjecting it to discipline, and teaching it to moderate its vehement desires for the extension of the sphere of cognition.

The first rule for our guidance is, therefore, not to attempt a transcendental proof, before we have considered from what source we are to derive the principles upon which the proof is to be based, and what right we have to expect that our conclusions from these principles will be veracious. If they are principles of the understanding, it is vain to expect that we should attain by their means to ideas of pure reason; for these principles are valid only in regard to objects of possible experience. If they are principles of pure reason, our labor is alike in vain. For the principles of reason, if employed as objective, are without exception dialectical, and possess no validity or truth, except as regulative principles of the systematic employment of reason in experience. But when such delusive proofs are presented to us, it is our duty to meet them with the *non liquet* of a matured judgment; and, although we are unable to expose the particular sophism upon which the proof is based, we have a right to demand a deduction of the principles employed in it; and, if these principles have their origin in pure reason alone, such a deduction is absolutely impossible. And thus it is unnecessary that we should trouble ourselves with the exposure and confutation of every sophistical illusion; we may, at once, bring all dialectic, which is inexhaustible in the production of fallacies, before the bar of critical reason, which tests the principles upon which all dialectical procedure is based. The second peculiarity of transcendental proof is, that a transcendental proposition cannot rest upon more than *a single* proof. If I am drawing conclusions, not from conceptions, but from intuition corresponding to a conception, be it pure intuition, as in mathematics, or empirical, as in natural science, the intuition which forms the basis of my inferences, presents me with materials for many synthetical propositions, which I can connect in various modes, while, as it is allowable to proceed from different points in the intention, I can arrive by different paths at the same proposition.

But every transcendental proposition sets out from a conception, and posits the synthetical condition of the possibility of an object according to this conception. There must, therefore, be but one ground of proof, because it is the conception alone which determines the object; and thus the proof cannot contain anything more than the determination of the object according to the conception. In our Transcendental Analytic, for example, we inferred the principle, Every event has a cause, from the only condition of the objective possibility of our conception of an event. This is that an event cannot be determined in time, and consequently cannot form a part of experience, unless it stands under this dynamical law. This is the only possible ground for proof; for our conception of an event possesses objective validity, that is, is a true conception, only because the law of causality determines an object to which it can refer. Other arguments in support of this principle have been attempted—such as that from the contingent nature of a phenomenon; but when this argument is considered, we can discover no criterion of contingency, except the fact of an event—of something *happening*, that is to say, the existence which is preceded by the non-existence of an object, and thus we fall back on the

very thing to be proved. If the proposition, Every thinking being is simple, is to be proved, we keep to the conception of the
Ego, which is simple, and to which all thought has a relation.
The same is the case with the transcendental proof of the existence of a Deity, which is based solely upon the harmony and
reciprocal fitness of the conceptions of an *ens realissimum* and
a necessary being, and cannot be attempted in any other manner.

This caution serves to simplify very much the criticism of all
propositions of reason. When reason employs conceptions
alone, only one proof of its thesis is possible, if any. When,
therefore, the dogmatist advances with ten arguments in favor
of a proposition, we may be sure that not one of them is conclusive. For if he possessed one which proved the proposition
he brings forward to demonstration—as must always be the
case with the propositions of pure reason—what need is there
for any more? His intention can only be similar to that of the
advocate, who had different arguments for different judges;
thus availing himself of the weakness of those who examine his
arguments, who, without going into any profound investigation, adopt the view of the case which seems most probable at
first sight, and decide according to it.

The third rule for the guidance of pure reason in the conduct
of a proof is, that all transcendental proofs must never be *apagogic* or indirect, but always ostensive or direct. The direct
or ostensible proof not only establishes the truth of the proposition to be proved, but exposes the grounds of its truth; the
apagogic, on the other hand, may assure us of the truth of the
proposition, but it cannot enable us to comprehend the grounds
of its possibility. The latter is, accordingly, rather an auxiliary
to an argument, than a strictly philosophical and rational mode
of procedure. In one respect, however, they have an advantage
over direct proofs, from the fact that the mode of arguing by
contradiction, which they employ, renders our understanding of
the question more clear, and approximates the proof to the certainty of an intuitional demonstration.

The true reason why indirect proofs are employed in different sciences is this. When the grounds upon which we seek to
base a cognition are too various or too profound, we try whether
or not we may not discover the truth of our cognition from its
consequences. The *modus ponens* of reasoning from the truth

of its inferences to the truth of a proposition, would be admissible if all the inferences that can be drawn from it are known to be true; for in this case there can be only one possible ground for these inferences, and that is the true one. But this is a quite impracticable procedure, as it surpasses all our powers to discover all the possible inferences that can be drawn from a proposition. But this mode of reasoning is employed, under favor, when we wish to prove the truth of a hypothesis; in which case we admit the truth of the conclusion—which is supported by, analogy—that, if all the inferences we have drawn and examined agree with the proposition assumed, all other possible inferences will also agree with it. But, in this way, an hypothesis can never be established as a demonstrated truth. The *modus tollens* of reasoning from known inferences to the unknown proposition is not only a rigorous but a very easy mode of proof. For if it can be shown that but one inference from a proposition is false, then the proposition must itself be false. Instead, then, of examining, in an ostensible argument, the whole series of the grounds on which the truth of a proposition rests, we need only take the opposite of this proposition, and if one inference from it be false, then must the opposite be itself false; and, consequently, the proposition which we wished to prove must be true.

The apagogic method of proof is admissible only in those sciences where it is impossible to mistake a subjective representation for an objective cognition. Where this is possible, it is plain that the opposite of a given proposition may contradict merely the subjective conditions of thought, and not the objective cognition; or it may happen that both propositions contradict each other only under a subjective condition, which is incorrectly considered to be objective, and, as the condition is itself false, both propositions may be false, and it will, consequently, be impossible to conclude the truth of the one from the falseness of the other.

In mathematics such subreptions are impossible; and it is in this science, accordingly, that the indirect mode of proof has its true place. In the science of nature, where all assertion is based upon empirical intuition, such subreptions may be guarded against by the repeated comparison of observations; but this mode of proof is of little value in this sphere of knowledge. But the transcendental efforts of pure reason are all made in the

sphere of the subjective, which is the real medium of all dialectical illusion; and thus reason endeavors, in its premises, to impose upon us subjective representations for objective cognitions.
In the transcendental sphere of pure reason, then, and in the
case of synthetical propositions, it is inadmissible to support a
statement by disproving the counter-statement. For only two
cases are possible; either, the counter-statement is nothing but
the announcement of the inconsistency of the opposite opinion
with the subjective conditions of reason, which does not affect
the real case (for example, we cannot comprehend the unconditioned necessity of the existence of a being, and hence every
speculative proof of the existence of such a being must be opposed on *subjective* grounds, while the possibility of this being
in itself cannot with justice be denied); or, both propositions,
being dialectical in their nature, are based upon an impossible
conception. In this latter case the rule applies—*non entis nulla
sunt predicata;* that is to say, what we affirm and what we
deny, respecting such an object, are equally untrue, and the
apagogic mode of arriving at the truth is in this case impossible.
If, for example, we presuppose that the world of sense is given
in itself in its totality, it is false, *either* that is infinite, *or* that it
is finite and limited in space. Both are false, because the hypothesis is false. For the notion of phenomena (as mere representations) which are given *in themselves* (as objects) is self-
contradictory; and the infinitude of this imaginary whole would,
indeed, be unconditioned, but would be inconsistent (as everything in the phenomenal world is conditioned) with the unconditioned determination and finitude of quantities which is presupposed in our conception.

The apagogic mode of proof is the true source of those illusions which have always had so strong an attraction for the
admirers of dogmatical philosophy. It may be compared to
a champion who maintains the honor and claims of the party he
has adopted, by offering battle to all who doubt the validity of
these claims and the purity of that honor; while nothing can be
proved in this way, except the respective strength of the combatants, and the advantage, in this respect, is always on the side
of the attacking party. Spectators, observing that each party is
alternately conqueror and conquered, are led to regard the subject of dispute as beyond the power of man to decide upon. But

such an opinion cannot be justified; and it is sufficient to apply
to these reasoners the remark:—

> " Non defensoribus istis
> Tempus eget."

Each must try to establish his assertions by a transcendental
deduction of the grounds of proof employed in his argument,
and thus enable us to see in what way the claims of reason may
be supported. If an opponent bases his assertions upon subjective grounds, he may be refuted with ease; not, however to
the advantage of the dogmatist, who likewise depends upon subjective sources of cognition, and is in like manner driven into a
corner by his opponent. But, if parties employ the direct
method of procedure, they will soon discover the difficulty, nay,
the impossibility of proving their assertions, and will be forced
to appeal to prescription and precedence; or they will, by the
help of criticism, discover with ease the dogmatical illusions by
which they had been mocked, and compel reason to renounce
its exaggerated pretensions to speculative insight, and to confine itself within the limits of its proper sphere—that of practical principles.

CHAPTER II

The Canon of Pure Reason

It is a humiliating consideration for human reason, that it is
incompetent to discover truth by means of pure speculation, but,
on the contrary, stands in need of discipline to check its deviations from the straight path, and to expose the illusions which
it originates. But, on the other hand, this consideration ought
to elevate and to give it confidence, for this discipline is exercised by itself alone, and it is subject to the censure of no other
power. The bounds, moreover, which it is forced to set to its
speculative exercise, form likewise a check upon the fallacious
pretensions of opponents; and thus what remains of its possessions, after these exaggerated claims have been disallowed,
is secure from attack or usurpation. The greatest, and perhaps
the only, use of all philosophy of pure reason is, accordingly,
of a purely negative character. It is not an organon for the extension, but a discipline for the determination of the limits of

its exercise; and without laying claim to the discovery of new truth, it has the modest merit of guarding against error.

At the same time, there must be some source of positive cognitions which belong to the domain of pure reason, and which become the causes of error only, from our mistaking their true character, while they form the goal towards which reason continually strives. How else can we account for the inextinguishable desire in the human mind to find a firm footing in some region beyond the limits of the world of experience?—It hopes to attain to the possession of a knowledge in which it has the deepest interest. It enters upon the path of pure speculation; but in vain. We have some reason, however, to expect that, in the only other way that lies open to it—the path of *practical* reason—it may meet with better success.

I understand by a canon a list of the *à priori* principles of the proper employment of certain faculties of cognition. Thus general logic, in its analytical department, is a formal canon for the faculties of understanding and reason. In the same way, Transcendental Analytic was seen to be a canon of the pure *understanding;* for it alone is competent to announce true *à priori* synthetical cognitions. But, when no proper employment of a faculty of cognition is possible, no canon can exist. But the synthetical cognition of pure speculative *reason* is, as has been shown, completely impossible. There cannot, therefore, exist any canon for the speculative exercise of this faculty—for its speculative exercise is entirely dialectical; and consequently, transcendental logic, in this respect, is merely a discipline, and not a canon. If, then, there is any proper mode of employing the faculty of pure reason,—in which case there must be a canon for this faculty,—this canon will relate, not to the speculative, but to the *practical use of reason.* This canon we now proceed to investigate.

Section I.—Of the Ultimate End of the Pure Use of Reason

There exists in the faculty of reason a natural desire to venture beyond the field of experience, to attempt to reach the utmost bounds of all cognition by the help of ideas alone, and not to rest satisfied, until it has fulfilled its course and raised the sum of its cognitions into a self-subsistent systematic whole. Is the motive for this endeavor to be found in its speculative, or in its practical interests alone?

Setting aside, at present, the results of the labors of pure reason in its speculative exercise, I shall merely inquire regarding the problems, the solution of which forms its ultimate aim—whether reached or not, and in relation to which all other aims are but partial and intermediate. These highest aims must, from the nature of reason, possess complete unity; otherwise the highest interest of humanity could not be successfully promoted.

The transcendental speculation of reason relates to three things: the freedom of the will, the immortality of the soul, and the existence of God. The speculative interest which reason has in those questions is very small; and, for its sake alone, we should not undertake the labor of transcendental investigation —a labor full of toil and ceaseless struggle. We should be loth to undertake this labor, because the discoveries we might make would not be of the smallest use in the sphere of concrete or physical investigation. We may find out that the will is free, but this knowledge only relates to the intelligible cause of our volition. As regards the phenomena or expressions of this will, that is, our actions, we are bound, in obedience to an inviolable maxim, without which reason cannot be employed in the sphere of experience, to explain these in the same way as we explain all the other phenomena of nature, that is to say, according to its unchangeable laws. We may have discovered the spirituality and immortality of the soul, but we cannot employ this knowledge to explain the phenomena of this life, nor the peculiar nature of the future; because our conception of an incorporeal nature is purely negative and does not add anything to our knowledge, and the only inferences to be drawn from it are purely fictitious. If, again, we prove the existence of a supreme intelligence, we should be able from it to make the conformity to aims existing in the arrangement of the world comprehensible; but we should not be justified in deducing from it any particular arrangement or disposition, or, inferring any, where it is not perceived. For it is a necessary rule of the speculative use of reason, that we must not overlook natural causes, or refuse to listen to the teaching of experience, for the sake of deducing what we know and perceive from something that transcends all our knowledge. In one word, these three propositions are, for the speculative reason, always transcendent, and cannot be employed as immanent principles in relation to the objects of experience; they are, consequently, of no use to us in this sphere, being but the valueless results of the severe but unprofitable efforts of reason.

If, then, the actual *cognition* of these three cardinal propositions is perfectly useless, while reason uses her utmost endeavors to induce us to admit them, it is plain that their real value and importance relate to our *practical,* and not to our speculative interest.

I term all that is possible through free-will, practical. But if the conditions of the exercise of free volition are empirical, reason can have only a regulative, and not a constitutive, influence upon it, and is serviceable merely for the introduction of unity into its empirical laws. In the moral philosophy of prudence, for example, the sole business of reason is to bring about a union of all the ends, which are aimed at by our inclinations, into one ultimate end—that of *happiness,* and to show the agreement which should exist among the means of attaining that end. In this sphere, accordingly, reason cannot present to us any other than *pragmatical* laws of free action, for our guidance towards the aims set up by the senses, and is incompetent to give us laws which are pure and determined completely *à priori.* On the other hand, pure practical laws, the ends of which have been given by reason entirely *à priori,* and which are not empirically conditioned, but are, on the contrary, absolutely imperative in their nature, would be products of pure reason. Such are the *moral* laws; and these alone belong to the sphere of the practical exercise of reason, and admit of a canon.

All the powers of reason, in the sphere of what may be termed pure philosophy, are, in fact, directed to the three above-mentioned problems alone. These again have a still higher end—the answer to the question, *what we ought to do,* if the will is free, if there is a God, and a future world. Now, as this problem relates to our conduct, in reference to the highest aim of humanity, it is evident that the ultimate intention of nature, in the constitution of our reason, has been directed to the *moral* alone.

We must take care, however, in turning our attention to an object which is foreign * to the sphere of transcendental philoso-

---

* All practical conceptions relate to objects of pleasure and pain, and consequently—in an indirect manner, at least—to objects of feeling. But as feeling is not a faculty of representation, but lies out of the sphere of our powers of cognition, the elements of our judgments, in so far as they relate to pleasure or pain, that is, the elements of our practical judgments, do not belong to transcendental philosophy, which has to do with *à priori* cognitions alone.

phy, not to injure the unity of our system by digressions, nor, on the other hand, to fail in clearness, by saying too little on the new subject of discussion. I hope to avoid both extremes, by keeping as close as possible to the transcendental, and excluding all psychological, that is, empirical elements.

I have to remark, in the first place, that at present I treat of the conception of freedom in the practical sense only, and set aside the corresponding transcendental conception, which cannot be employed as a ground of explanation in the phenomena' world, but is itself a problem for pure reason. A will is purely *animal* (*arbitrium brutum*), when it is determined by sensuous impulses or instincts only, that is, when it is determined in a *pathological* manner. A will, which can be determined independently of sensuous impulses, consequently by motives presented by reason alone, is called a *free will* (*arbitrium liberum*); and everything which is connected with this free will, either as principle or consequence, is termed *practical*. The existence of practical freedom can be proved from experience alone. For the human will is not determined by that alone which immediately affects the senses; on the contrary, we have the power, by calling up the notion of what is useful or hurtful in a more distant relation, of overcoming the immediate impressions on our sensuous faculty of desire. But these considerations of what is desirable in relation to our whole state, that is, is in the end good and useful, are based entirely upon reason. This faculty, accordingly, announces laws, which are imperative or objective *laws of freedom,* and which tell us what *ought to take place,* thus distinguishing themselves from the *laws of nature,* which relate to that which *does take place.* The laws of freedom or of free will are hence termed practical laws.

Whether reason is not itself, in the actual delivery of these laws, determined in its turn by other influences, and whether the action which, in relation to sensuous impulses, we call free, may not, in relation to higher and more remote operative causes, really form a part of *nature,*—these are questions which do not here concern us. They are purely speculative questions; and all we have to do, in the practical sphere, is to inquire into the *rule* of conduct which reason has to present. Experience demonstrates to us the existence of practical freedom as one of the causes which exist in nature, that is, it shows the causal power of reason in the determination of the will. The idea of tranᵥcendental freedom, on the contrary, requires that reason—in relation to its causal power of commencing a series of phenomena—should be independent of all sensuous determining causes; and thus it seems to be in opposition to the law of nature and to all possible experience. It therefore remains a problem for the human mind. But this problem does not concern reason in its practical use; and we have, therefore, in a canon of pure reason, to do with only two questions, which relate to the practical interest of pure reason—Is there a God? and, Is there a future life? The question of transcendental freedom is purely speculative, and we may therefore set it entirely aside when we come to treat of practical reason. Besides, we have already fully discussed this subject in the antinomy of pure reason.

Section II.—Of the Ideal of the Summum Bonum as a Determining Ground of the Ultimate End of Pure Reason

Reason conducted us, in its speculative use, through the field of experience, and, as it can never find complete satisfaction in that sphere, from thence to speculative ideas,—which, however, in the end brought us back again to experience, and thus fulfilled the purpose of reason, in a manner which, though useful, was not at all in accordance with our expectations. It now remains for us to consider whether pure reason can be employed in a practical sphere, and whether it will here conduct us to those ideas which attain the highest ends of pure reason, as we have just stated them. We shall thus ascertain whether, from the point of view of its practical interest, reason may not be able to supply us with that which, on the speculative side, it wholly denies us.

The whole interest of reason, speculative as well as practical, is centred in the three following questions:

1. *What can I know?*
2. *What ought I to do?*
3. *What may I hope?*

The first question is purely speculative. We have, as I flatter myself, exhausted all the replies of which it is susceptible, and have at last found the reply with which reason must content itself, and with which it ought to be content, so long as it pays no regard to the practical. But from the two great ends to the attainment of which all these efforts of pure reason were in fact directed, we remain just as far removed as if we had consulted our ease, and declined the task at the outset. So far, then, as *knowledge* is concerned, thus much, at least, is established, that, in regard to those two problems, it lies beyond our reach.

The second question is purely practical. As such it may indeed fall within the province of pure reason, but still it is not transcendental, but moral, and consequently cannot in itself form the subject of our criticism.

The third question, If I act as I ought to do, what may I then hope?—is at once practical and theoretical. The practical forms a clue to the answer of the theoretical, and—in its highest form —speculative question. For all *hoping* has happiness for its object, and stands in precisely the same relation to the practical and the law of morality, as *knowing* to the theoretical cognition of things and the law of nature. The former arrives finally at the conclusion that *something is* (which determines the ultimate end), because *something ought to take place;* the latter, that *something is* (which operates as the highest cause), because *something does take place.*

Happiness is the satisfaction of all our desires; *extensive* in regard to their multiplicity; *intensive,* in regard to their degree; and *protensive,* in regard to their duration. The practical law based on the motive of *happiness,* I term a pragmatical law (or prudential rule); but that law, assuming such to exist, which has no other motive than the *worthiness of being happy,* I term a moral or ethical law. The first tells us what we have to do, if we wish to become possessed of happiness; the second dictates how we ought to act, in order to deserve happiness. The first is based upon empirical principles; for it is only by experience that I can learn either what inclinations exist which desire satisfaction, or what are the natural means of satisfying them. The second takes no account of our desires or the means of satisfying them, and regards only the freedom of a rational being, and the necessary conditions under which alone this freedom can harmonize with the distribution of happiness according to principles. This second law may therefore rest upon mere ideas of pure reason, and may be cognized *à priori.*

I assume that there are pure moral laws which determine, entirely *à priori* (without regard to empirical motives, that is, to happiness), the conduct of a rational being, or in other words, the use which it makes of its freedom, and that these laws are *absolutely* imperative (not merely hypothetically, on the supposition of other empirical ends), and therefore in all respects necessary. I am warranted in assuming this, not only by the arguments of the most enlightened moralists, but by the moral judgment of every man who will make the attempt to form a distinct conception of such a law.

Pure reason, then, contains, not indeed in its speculative, but in its practical, or, more strictly, its moral use, principles of the *possibility* of *experience,* of such actions, namely, as, in accordance with ethical precepts, *might* be met with in the *history* of man. For since reason commands that such actions should take place, it must be possible for them to take place; and hence a particular kind of systematic unity—the moral, must be possible. We have found, it is true, that the systematic unity of nature could not be established according to speculative principles of reason, because, while reason possesses a causal power in relation to freedom, it has none in relation to the whole sphere of nature; and, while moral principles of reason can produce free actions, they cannot produce natural laws. It is, then, in its practical, but especially in its moral use, that the principles of pure reason possess objective reality.

I call the world *a moral world,* in so far as it may be in accordance with all the ethical laws—which, by virtue of the *freedom* of reasonable beings it *can* be, and according to the necessary laws of *morality* i. *ought to be.* But this world must be conceived only as an intelligible world, inasmuch as abstraction is therein made of all conditions (ends), and even of all impediments to morality (the weakness or pravity of human nature). So far, then, it is a mere idea—though still a practical idea—which may have, and ought to have, an influence on the world of sense, so as to bring it as far as possible into conformity with itself. The idea of a moral world has, therefore, objective reality, not as referring to an object of intelligible intuition—for of such an object we can form no conception whatever—but to the world of sense—conceived, however, as an object of pure reason in its practical use—and to a *corpus mysticum* of rational beings in it, in so far as the *liberum arbitrium* of the individual is placed, under and by virtue of moral laws, in complete systematic unity both with itself, and with the freedom of all others.

That **is** the answer to the first of the two questions of pure reason which relate to its practical interest:—*Do that which will render thee worthy of happiness.* The second question is this: If I conduct myself so as not to be unworthy of happiness, may I hope thereby to obtain happiness? In order to arrive at the solution of this question, we must inquire whether the principles of pure reason, which prescribe *à priori* the law, necessarily also connect this hope with it.

I say, then, that just as the moral principles are necessary according to reason in its *practical* use, so it is equally necessary according to reason in its *theoretical* use, to assume that every one has ground to hope for happiness in the measure in which he has made himself worthy of it in his conduct, and that therefore the system of morality is inseparably (though only in the idea of pure reason) connected with that of happiness.

Now in an intelligible, that is, in the moral world, in the conception of which we make abstraction of all the impediments to morality (sensuous desires), such a system of happiness, connected with and proportioned to morality, may be conceived as necessary, because freedom of volition—partly incited, and partly restrained by moral laws—would be itself the cause of general happiness; and thus rational beings, under the guidance of such principles, would be themselves the authors both of their own enduring welfare and that of others. But such a system of self-rewarding morality is only an idea, the carrying out of which depends upon the condition that every one acts as he ought; in other words, that all actions of reasonable beings be such as they would be if they sprung from a Supreme Will, comprehending in, or under, itself all particular wills. But since the moral law is binding on each individual in the use of his freedom of volition, even if others should not act in conformity with this law, neither the nature of things, nor the causality of actions and their relation to morality, determine how the consequences of these actions will be related to happiness; and the necessary connection of the hope of happiness with the unceasing endeavor to become worthy of happiness, cannot be cognized by reason, if we take nature alone for our guide. This connection can be hoped for only on the assumption that the cause of nature is a supreme reason, which governs according to moral laws.

I term the idea of an intelligence in which the morally most perfect will, united with supreme blessedness, is the cause of all

happiness in the world, so far as happiness stands in strict relation to morality (as the worthiness of being happy), *the Ideal
of the Supreme Good.* It is only, then, in the ideal of the supreme *original* good, that pure reason can find the ground of the
practically necessary connection of both elements of the highest
derivative good, and accordingly of an intelligible, that is, *moral*
world. Now since we are necessitated by reason to conceive ourselves as belonging to such a world, while the senses present to
us nothing but a world of phenomena, we must assume the
former as a consequence of our conduct in the world of sense
(since the world of sense gives us no hint of it), and therefore
as future in relation to us. Thus God and a future life are two
hypotheses which, according to the principles of pure reason, are
inseparable from the obligation which this reason imposes upon
us.

Morality *per se* constitutes a system. But we can form no
system of happiness, except in so far as it is dispensed in strict
proportion to morality. But this is only possible in the intelligible world, under a wise author and ruler. Such a ruler, together with life in such a world, which we must look upon as
future, reason finds itself compelled to assume; or it must regard the moral laws as idle dreams, since the necessary consequence which this same reason connects with them, must,
without this hypothesis, fall to the ground. Hence also the
moral laws are universally regarded as *commands,* which they
could not be, did they not connect *à priori* adequate consequences with their dictates, and thus carry with them *promises*
and *threats.* But this, again, they could not do, did they not
reside in a necessary being, as the Supreme Good, which alone
can render such a teleological unity possible.

Leibnitz termed the world, when viewed in relation to the
rational beings which it contains, and the moral relations in
which they stand to each other, under the government of the
Supreme Good, *the kingdom of Grace,* and distinguished it from
the *kingdom of Nature,* in which these rational beings live, under moral laws, indeed, but expect no other consequences from
their actions than such as follow according to the course of
nature in the world of sense. To view ourselves, therefore, as in
the kingdom of grace, in which all happiness awaits us, except
in so far as we ourselves limit our participation in it by actions
which render us unworthy of happiness, is a practically necessary idea of reason.

Practical laws, in so far as they are subjective grounds of actions, that is, subjective principles, are termed *maxims*. The *judgments* of morality, in its purity and ultimate results, are framed according to *ideas;* the *observance* of its laws, according to *maxims*.

The whole course of our life must be subject to moral maxims; but this is impossible, unless with the moral law, which is a mere idea, reason connects an efficient cause which ordains to all conduct which is in conformity with the moral law an issue either in this or in another life, which is in exact conformity with our highest aims. Thus, without a God and without a world, invisible to us now, but hoped for, the glorious ideas of morality are, indeed, objects of approbation and of admiration, but cannot be the springs of purpose and action. For they do not satisfy all the aims which are natural to every rational being, and which are determined *à priori* by pure reason itself, and necessary.

Happiness alone is, in the view of reason, far from being the complete good. Reason does not approve of it (however much inclination may desire it), except as united with desert. On the other hand, morality alone, and with it, mere *desert*, is likewise far from being the complete good. To make it complete, he who conducts himself in a manner not unworthy of happiness, must be able to hope for the possession of happiness. Even reason, unbiassed by private ends, or interested considerations, cannot judge otherwise, if it puts itself in the place of a being whose business it is to dispense all happiness to others. For in the practical idea both points are essentially combined, though in such a way that participation in happiness is rendered possible by the moral disposition, as its condition, and not conversely, the moral disposition by the prospect of happiness. For a disposition which should require the prospect of happiness as its necessary condition, would not be moral, and hence also would not be worthy of complete happiness—a happiness which, in the view of reason, recognizes no limitation but such as arises from our own immoral conduct.

Happiness, therefore, in exact proportion with the morality of rational beings (whereby they are made worthy of happiness), constitutes alone the supreme good of a world into which we absolutely must transport ourselves according to the commands of pure but practical reason. This world is, it is true, only an intelligible world; for of such a systematic unity of ends as it requires, the world of sense gives us no hint. Its reality can be based on nothing else but the hypothesis of a supreme original good. In it independent reason, equipped with all the sufficiency of a supreme cause, founds, maintains, and fulfils the universal order of things, with the most perfect teleological harmony, however much this order may be hidden from us in the world of sense.

This moral theology has the peculiar advantage, in contrast with speculative theology, of leading inevitably to the conception of a *sole, perfect,* and *rational* First Cause, whereof speculative theology does not give us any *indication* on objective grounds, far less any convincing *evidence.* For we find neither in transcendental nor in natural theology, however far reason may lead us in these, any ground to warrant us in assuming the existence of *one only* Being, which stands at the head of all natural causes, and on which these are entirely dependent. On the other hand, if we take our stand on moral unity as a necessary law of the universe, and from this point of view consider what is necessary to give this law adequate efficiency and, for us, obligatory force, we must come to the conclusion that there is one only supreme will, which comprehends all these laws in itself. For how, under different wills, should we find complete unity of ends? This will must be omnipotent, that all nature and its relation to morality in the world may be subject to it; omniscient, that it may have knowledge of the most secret feelings and their moral worth; omnipresent, that it may be at hand to supply every necessity to which the highest weal of the world may give rise; eternal, that this harmony of nature and liberty may never fail; and so on.

But this systematic unity of ends in this world of intelligences —which, as mere nature, is only a world of sense, but as a system of freedom of volition, may be termed an intelligible, that is, moral world (*regnum gratiæ*)—leads inevitably also to the teleological unity of all things which constitute this great whole, according to universal natural laws—just as the unity of the former is according to universal and necessary moral laws— and unites the practical with the speculative reason. The world must be represented as having originated from an idea, if it is to harmonize with that use of reason without which we cannot even consider ourselves as worthy of reason—namely, the moral

use, which rests entirely on the idea of the supreme good.
Hence the investigation of nature receives a teleological direction, and becomes, in its widest extension, physico-theology.
But this, taking its rise in moral order as a unity founded on the
essence of freedom, and not accidentally instituted by external
commands, establishes the teleological view of nature on
grounds which must be inseparably connected with the internal
possibility of things. This gives rise to a *transcendental theology*, which takes the ideal of the highest ontological perfection
as a principle of systematic unity; and this principle connects
all things according to universal and necessary natural laws,
because all things have their origin in the absolute necessity of
the one only Primal Being.

What *use* can we make of our understanding, even in respect
of experience, if we do not propose ends to ourselves? But
the highest ends are those of morality, and it is only pure reason
that can give us the knowledge of these. Though supplied with
these, and putting ourselves under their guidance, we can make
no teleological use of the knowledge of nature, as regards *cognition*, unless nature itself has established teleological unity.
For without this unity we should not even possess reason, because we should have no school for reason, and no cultivation
through objects which afford the materials for its conceptions.
But teleological unity is a necessary unity, and founded on the
essence of the individual will itself. Hence this will, which is
the condition of the application of this unity *in concreto*, must
be so likewise. In this way the transcendental enlargement of
our rational cognition would be, not the cause, but merely the
effect of the practical teleology, which pure reason imposes
upon us.

Hence, also, we find in the history of human reason that,
before the moral conceptions were sufficiently purified and determined, and before men had attained to a perception of the
systematic unity of ends according to these conceptions and
from necessary principles, the knowledge of nature, and even
a considerable amount of intellectual culture in many other
sciences, could produce only rude and vague conceptions of the
Deity, sometimes even admitting of an astonishing indifference
with regard to this question altogether. But the more enlarged
treatment of moral ideas, which was rendered necessary by the
extremely pure moral law of our religion, awakened the interest,

and thereby quickened the perceptions of reason in relation to this object. In this way, and without the help either of an extended acquaintance with nature, or of a reliable transcendental insight (for these have been wanting in all ages), a conception of the Divine Being was arrived at, which we now hold to be the correct one, not because speculative reason convinces us of its correctness, but because it accords with the moral principles of reason. Thus it is to pure reason, but only in its practical use, that we must ascribe the merit of having connected with our highest interest a cognition, of which mere speculation was able only to form a conjecture, but the validity of which it was unable to establish—and of having thereby rendered it, not indeed a demonstrated dogma, but a hypothesis absolutely necessary to the essential ends of reason.

But if practical reason has reached this elevation, and has attained to the conception of a sole Primal Being, as the supreme good, it must not, therefore, imagine that it has transcended the empirical conditions of its application, and risen to the immediate cognition of new objects; it must not presume to start from the conception which it has gained, and to deduce from it the moral laws themselves. For it was these very laws, the *internal* practical necessity of which led us to the hypothesis of an independent cause, or of a wise ruler of the universe, who should give them effect. Hence we are not entitled to regard them as accidental and derived from the mere will of the ruler, especially as we have no conception of such a will, except as formed in accordance with these laws. So far, then, as practical reason has the right to conduct us, we shall not look upon actions as binding on us, because they are the commands of God, but we shall regard them as divine commands, because we are internally bound by them. We shall study freedom under the teleological unity which accords with principles of reason; we shall look upon ourselves as acting in conformity with the divine will only in so far as we hold sacred the moral law which reason teaches us from the nature of actions themselves, and we shall believe that we can obey that will only by promoting the weal of the universe in ourselves and in others. Moral theology is, therefore, only of immanent use. It teaches us to fulfil our destiny here in the world, by placing ourselves in harmony with the general system of ends, and warns us against the fanaticism, nay, the crime of depriving reason of its legislative authority

in the moral conduct of life, for the purpose of directly connecting this authority with the idea of the Supreme Being. For
this would be, not an immanent, but a transcendent use of moral
theology, and, like the transcendent use of mere speculation,
would inevitably pervert and frustrate the ultimate ends of
reason.

Section III.—Of Opinion, Knowledge, and Belief

The holding of a thing to be true, is a phenomenon in our
understanding which may rest on objective grounds, but requires, also, subjective causes in the mind of the person judging.
If a judgment is valid for every rational being, then its ground
is objectively sufficient, and it is termed a *conviction*. If, on the
other hand, it has its ground in the particular character of the
subject, it is termed a *persuasion*.

Persuasion is a mere illusion, the ground of the judgment,
which lies solely in the subject, being regarded as objective.
Hence a judgment of this kind has only private validity—is
only valid for the individual who judges, and the holding of
a thing to be true in this way cannot be communicated. But
truth depends upon agreement with the object, and consequently
the judgments of all understandings, if true, must be in agreement with each other (*consentientia uni tertio consentiunt inter
se*). Conviction may, therefore, be distinguished, from an external point of view, from persuasion, by the possibility of
communicating it, and by showing its validity for the reason
of every man; for in this case the presumption, at least, arises,
that the agreement of all judgments with each other, in spite
of the different characters of individuals, rests upon the common ground of the agreement of each with the object, and thus
the correctness of the judgment is established.

Persuasion, accordingly, cannot be *subjectively* distinguished
from conviction, that is, so long as the subject views its judgment simply as a phenomenon of its own mind. But if we
inquire whether the grounds of our judgment, which are valid
for us, produce the same effect on the reason of others as on
our own, we have then the means, though only subjective means,
not, indeed, of producing conviction, but of detecting the merely
private validity of the judgment; in other words, of discovering that there is in it the element of mere persuasion.

If we can, in addition to this, develop the *subjective causes* of the judgment, which we have taken for its *objective grounds,* and thus explain the deceptive judgment as a phenomenon in our mind, apart altogether from the objective character of the object, we can then expose the illusion and need be no longer deceived by it, although, if its subjective cause lies in our nature, we cannot hope altogether to escape its influence.

I can only *maintain,* that is, affirm as necessarily valid for everyone, that which produces conviction. Persuasion I may keep for myself, if it is agreeable to me; but I cannot, and ought not, to attempt to impose it as binding upon others.

Holding for true, or the subjective validity of a judgment in relation to conviction (which is, at the same time, objectively valid), has the three following degrees: *Opinion, Belief,* and *Knowledge.* Opinion is a consciously insufficient judgment, subjectively as well as objectively. Belief is subjectively sufficient, but is recognized as being objectively insufficient. Knowledge is both subjectively and objectively sufficient. Subjective sufficiency is termed *conviction* (for myself); objective sufficiency is termed *certainty* (for all). I need not dwell longer on the explanation of such simple conceptions.

I must never venture to *be of opinion,* without *knowing* something, at least, by which my judgment, in itself merely problematical, is brought into connection with the truth—which connection, although not perfect, is still something more, than an arbitrary fiction. Moreover, the law of such a connection must be certain. For if, in relation to this law; I have nothing more than opinion, my judgment is but a play of the imagination, without the least relation to truth.—In the judgments of pure reason, opinion has no place. For as they do not rest on empirical grounds, and as the sphere of pure reason is that of necessary truth and *à priori* cognition, the principle of connection in it requires universality and necessity, and consequently perfect certainty—otherwise we should have no guide to the truth at all. Hence it is absurd to have an opinion in pure mathematics; we must know, or abstain from forming a judgment altogether. The case is the same with the maxims of morality. For we must not hazard an action on the mere opinion that it is allowed, but we must know it to be so.

In the transcendental sphere of reason, on the other hand, the term opinion is too weak, while the word knowledge is too strong. From the merely speculative point of view, therefore, we cannot form a judgment at all. For the subjective grounds of a judgment, such as produce belief, cannot be admitted in speculative inquiries, inasmuch as they cannot stand without empirical support, and are incapable of being communicated to others in equal measure.

But it is only from the *practical* point of view that a *theoretically* insufficient judgment can be termed belief. Now the practical reference is either to *skill* or to *morality;* to the former, when the end proposed is arbitrary and accidental, to the latter, when it is absolutely necessary.

If we propose to ourselves any end whatever, the conditions of its attainment are hypothetically necessary. The necessity is subjectively, but still only comparatively, sufficient, if I am acquainted with no other conditions under which the end can be attained. On the other hand, it is sufficient, absolutely, and for everyone, if I know for certain that no one can be acquainted with any other conditions, under which the attainment of the proposed end would be possible. In the former case my supposition—my judgment with regard to certain conditions, is a merely accidental belief; in the latter it is a necessary belief. The physician must pursue some course in the case of a patient who is in danger, but is ignorant of the nature of the disease. He observes the symptoms, and concludes, according to the best of his judgment, that it is a case of phthisis. His belief is, even in his own judgment, only contingent: another man might, perhaps, come nearer the truth. Such a belief, contingent indeed, but still forming the ground of the actual use of means for the attainment of certain ends, I term *pragmatical belief.*

The usual test, whether that which anyone maintains is merely his persuasion, or his subjective conviction at least, that is, his firm belief, is a *bet.* It frequently happens that a man delivers his opinions with so much boldness and assurance, that he appears to be under no apprehension as to the possibility of his being in error. The offer of a bet startles him, and makes him pause. Sometimes it turns out that his persuasion may be valued at a ducat, but not at ten. For he does not hesitate, perhaps, to venture a ducat, but if it is proposed to stake ten, he immediately becomes aware of the possibility of his being mistaken—a possibility which has hitherto escaped his observation. If we imagine to ourselves that we have to stake the happiness of our whole life on the truth of any proposition, our judgment drops its air of triumph, we take the alarm, and discover the actual strength of our belief. Thus pragmatical belief has degrees, varying in proportion to the interests at stake.

Now, in cases where we cannot enter upon any course of action in reference to some object, and where, accordingly, our judgment is purely theoretical, we can still represent to ourselves, in thought, the possibility of a course of action, for which we suppose that we have sufficient grounds, if any means existed of ascertaining the truth of the matter. Thus we find in purely theoretical judgments an *analogon* of practical judgments, to which the word *belief* may properly be applied, and which we may term *doctrinal belief*. I should not hesitate to stake my all on the truth of the proposition—if there were any possibility of bringing it to the test of experience—that, at least, some one of the planets, which we see, is inhabited. Hence I say that I have not merely the opinion, but the strong belief, on the correctness of which I would stake even many of the advantages of life, that there are inhabitants in other worlds.

Now we must admit that the doctrine of the existence of God belongs to doctrinal belief. For, although in respect to the theoretical cognition of the universe I do not require to form any theory which necessarily involves this idea, as the condition of my explanation of the phenomena which the universe presents, but, on the contrary, am rather bound so to use my reason as if everything were mere nature, still teleological unity is so important a condition of the application of my reason to nature, that it is impossible for me to ignore it—especially since, in addition to these considerations, abundant examples of it are supplied by experience. But the sole condition, so far as my knowledge extends, under which this unity can be my guide in the investigation of nature, is the assumption that a supreme intelligence has ordered all things according to the wisest ends. Consequently the hypothesis of a wise author of the universe is necessary for my guidance in the investigation of nature—is the condition under which alone I can fulfil an end which is contingent indeed, but by no means unimportant. Moreover, since the result of my attempts so frequently confirms the utility of this assumption, and since nothing decisive can be adduced against it, it follows that it would be saying far too little to term my judgment, in this case, a mere opinion, and that, even in this theoretical connection, I may assert that I firmly believe in God. Still, if we use words strictly, this must not be called a practical, but a doctrinal belief, which the theology of nature (physico-theology) must also produce in my mind. In the wisdom of a Supreme Being, and in the shortness of life, so inadequate to the development of the glorious powers of human nature, we may find equally sufficient grounds for a doctrinal belief in the future life of the human soul.

The expression of belief is, in such cases, an expression of modesty from the *objective* point of view, but, at the same time, of firm confidence, from the *subjective*. If I should venture to term this merely theoretical judgment even so much as a hypothesis which I am entitled to assume; a more complete conception, with regard to another world and to the cause of the world, might then be justly required of me than I am, in reality, able to give. For, if I assume anything, even as a mere hypothesis, I must, at least, know so much of the properties of *such* a being as will enable me, not to form the *conception*, but to imagine the *existence* of it. But the word *belief* refers only to the guidance which an idea gives me, and to its subjective influence on the conduct of my reason, which forces me to hold it fast, though I may not be in a position to give a speculative account of it.

But mere doctrinal belief is, to some extent, wanting in stability. We often quit our hold of it, in consequence of the difficulties which occur in speculation, though in the end we inevitably return to it again.

It is quite otherwise with *moral belief*. For in this sphere action is absolutely necessary, that is, I must act in obedience to the moral law in all points. The end is here incontrovertibly established, and there is only one condition possible, according to the best of my perception, under which this end can harmonize with all other ends, and so have practical validity—namely, the existence of a God and of a future world. I know also, to a certainty, that no one can be acquainted with any other conditions which conduct to the same unity of ends under the moral law. But since the moral precept is, at the same time, my maxim (as reason requires that it should be), I am irresistibly constrained to believe in the existence of God and in a future life; and I am sure that nothing can make me waver in this belief, since I should thereby overthrow my moral maxims, the renunciation of which would render me hateful in my own eyes.

Thus, while all the ambitious attempts of reason to penetrate beyond the limits of experience end in disappointment, there is still enough left to satisfy us in a practical point of view. No one, it is true, will be able to boast that he knows that there is a God and a future life; for, if he knows this, he is just the man whom I have long wished to find. All knowledge, regarding an object of mere reason, can be communicated; and I should thus be enabled to hope that my own knowledge would receive this wonderful extension, through the instrumentality of his instruction. No, my conviction is not *logical*, but *moral* certainty; and since it rests on subjective grounds (of the moral sentiment), I must not even say: *It is* morally certain that there is a God, etc., but: *I am* morally certain, that is, my belief in God and in another world is so interwoven with my moral nature, that I am under as little apprehension of having the former torn from me as of losing the latter.

The only point in this argument that may appear open to suspicion, is that this rational belief presupposes the existence of moral sentiments. If we give up this assumption, and take a man who is entirely indifferent with regard to moral laws, the question which reason proposes, becomes then merely a problem for speculation, and may, indeed, be supported by strong grounds from analogy, but not by such as will compel the most obstinate scepticism to give way.* But in these questions no man is free from all interest. For though the want of good sentiments may place him beyond the influence of moral interests, still even in this case enough may be left to make him *fear* the existence of God and a future life. For he cannot pretend to any *certainty* of the non-existence of God and of a future life, unless—since it could only be proved by mere reason, and therefore apodictically—he is prepared to establish the *impossibility* of both, which certainly no reasonable man would undertake to do. This would be a *negative* belief, which

* The human mind (as, I believe, every rational being must of necessity do) takes a natural interest in morality, although this interest is not undivided, and may not be practically in preponderance. If you strengthen and increase it, you will find the reason become docile, more enlightened, and more capable of uniting the speculative interest with the practical. But if you do not take care at the outset, or at least mid-way, to make men good, you will never force them into an honest belief.

could not, indeed, produce morality and good sentiments, but still could produce an analogon of these, by operating as a powerful restraint on the outbreak of evil dispositions.

But, it will be said, is this all that pure reason can effect, in opening up prospects beyond the limits of experience? Nothing more than two articles cf belief? Common sense could have done as much as this, without taking the philosophers to counsel in the matter.

I shall not here eulogize philosophy for the benefits which the laborious efforts of its criticism have conferred on human reason—even granting that its merit should turn out in the end to be only negative—for on this point something more will be said in the next section. But I ask, do you require that that knowledge which concerns all men, should transcend the common understanding, and should only be revealed to you by philosophers? The very circumstance which has called forth your censure is the best confirmation of the correctness of our previous assertions, since it discloses, what could not have been foreseen, that Nature is not chargeable with any partial distribution of her gifts in those matters which concern all men without distinction, and that in respect to the essential ends of human nature, we cannot advance further with the help of the highest philosophy, than under the guidance which nature has vouchsafed to the meanest understanding.

Chapter III

The Architectonic of Pure Reason

By the term *Architectonic* I mean the art of constructing a system. Without systematic unity, our knowledge cannot become science; it will be an aggregate, and not a system. Thus Architectonic is the doctrine of the scientific in cognition, and therefore necessarily forms part of our Methodology.

Reason cannot permit our knowledge to remain in an unconnected and rhapsodistic state, but requires that the sum of our cognitions should constitute a system. It is thus alone that they can advance the ends of reason. By a system I mean the unity of various cognitions under one idea. This idea is the conception—given by reason—of the form of a whole, in so far as the conception determines à *priori* not only the limits of its content, but the place which each of its parts is to occupy. The scientific idea contains, therefore, the end, and the form of the whole which is in accordance with that end. The unity of the end, to which all the parts of the system relate, and through which all have a relation to each other, communicates unity to the whole system, so that the absence of any part can be immediately detected from our knowledge of the rest; and it determines à *priori* the limits of the system, thus excluding all contingent or arbitrary additions. The whole is thus an organism (*articulatio*), and not an aggregate (*coacervatio*); it may grow from within (*per intussusceptionem*), but it cannot increase by external additions (*per appositionem*). It is thus like an animal body, the growth of which does not add any limb, but, without changing their proportions, makes each in its sphere stronger and more active.

We require, for the execution of the idea of a system, a *schema*, that is, a content and an arrangement of parts determined à *priori* by the principle which the aim of the system prescribes. A schema which is not projected in accordance with an idea, that is, from the standpoint of the highest aim of reason, but merely empirically, in accordance with accidental aims and purposes (the number of which cannot be predetermined), can give us nothing more than *technical* unity. But the schema which is originated from an idea (in which case reason presents us with aims à *priori*, and does not look for them to experience) forms the basis of *architectonical* unity. A science, in the proper acceptation of that term, cannot be formed *technically*, that is, from observation of the similarity existing between different objects, and the purely contingent use we make of our knowledge *in concreto* with reference to all kinds of arbitrary external aims; its constitution must be framed on architectonical principles, that is, its parts must be shown to possess an essential affinity, and be capable of being deduced from one supreme and internal aim or end, which forms the condition of the possibility of the scientific whole. The schema of a science must give à *priori* the plan of it (*monogramma*), and the division of the whole into parts, in conformity with the idea of the science; and it must also distinguish this whole from all others, according to certain understood principles.

No one will attempt to construct a science, unless he have

some idea to rest on as a proper basis. But, in the elaboration of the science he finds that the schema, nay, even the definition which he at first gave of the science, rarely corresponds with his idea; for this idea lies, like a germ, in our reason, its parts undeveloped and hid even from microscopical observation. For this reason, we ought to explain and define sciences, not according to the description which the originator gives of them, but according to the idea which we find based in reason itself, and which is suggested by the natural unity of the parts of the science already accumulated. For it will often be found, that the originator of a science, and even his latest successors, remain attached to an erroneous idea, which they cannot render clear to themselves, and that they thus fail in determining the true content, the articulation or systematic unity, and the limits of their science.

It is unfortunate that, only after having occupied ourselves for a long time in the collection of materials, under the guidance of an idea which lies undeveloped in the mind, but not according to any definite plan of arrangement—nay, only after we have spent much time and labor in the technical disposition of our materials, does it become possible to view the idea of a science in a clear light, and to project, according to architectonical principles, a plan of the whole, in accordance with the aims of reason. Systems seem, like certain worms, to be formed by a kind of *generatio æquivoca*—by the mere confluence of conceptions, and to gain completeness only with the progress of time. But the schema or germ of all lies in reason; and thus is not only every system organized according to its own idea, but all are united into one grand system of human knowledge, of which they form members. For this reason, it is possible to frame an architectonic of all human cognition, the formation of which, at the present time, considering the immense materials collected or to be found in the ruins of old systems, would not indeed be very difficult. Our purpose at present is merely to sketch the plan of the *Architectonic* of all cognition given by *pure reason;* and we begin from the point where the main root of human knowledge divides into two, one of which is *reason* By reason I understand here the whole higher faculty of cognition, the *rational* being placed in contradistinction to the *empirical.*

If I make complete abstraction of the content of cognition,

objectively considered, all cognition is, from a subjective point of view, either historical or rational. Historical cognition is *cognitio ex datis*, rational, *cognitio ex principiis*. Whatever may be the original source of a cognition, it is, in relation to the person who possesses it, merely historical, if he knows only what has been given him from another quarter, whether that knowledge was communicated by direct experience or by instruction. Thus the person who has *learned* a system of philosophy—say the Wolfian—although he has a perfect knowledge of all the principles, definitions and arguments in that philosophy, as well as of the divisions that have been made of the system, he possesses really no more than a *historical* knowledge of the Wolfian system; he knows only what has been told him, his judgments are only those which he has received from his teachers. Dispute the validity of a definition, and he is at completely a loss to find another. He has formed his mind on another's; but the imitative faculty is not the productive. His knowledge has not been drawn from reason; and, although, objectively considered, it is rational knowledge, subjectively, it is merely historical. He has learned this or that philosophy, and is merely a plaster-cast of a living man. Rational cognitions which are objective, that is, which have their source in reason, can be so termed from a subjective point of view only when they have been drawn by the individual himself from the sources of reason, that is, from principles; and it is in this way alone that criticism, or even the rejection of what has been already learned, can spring up in the mind.

All rational cognition is, again, based either on conceptions or on the construction of conceptions. The former is termed philosophical, the latter mathematical. I have already shown the essential difference of these two methods of cognition in the first chapter. A cognition may be objectively philosophical and subjectively historical—as is the case with the majority of scholars and those who cannot look beyond the limits of their system, and who remain in a state of pupilage all their lives. But it is remarkable that mathematical knowledge, when committed to memory, is valid from the subjective point of view as rational knowledge also, and that the same distinction cannot be drawn here as in the case of philosophical cognition. The reason is that the only way of arriving at this knowledge is through the essential principles of reason, and thus it is always certain and indisputable; because reason is employed *in con-creto*—but at the same time *à priori*—that is, in pure, and therefore, infallible intuition; and thus all causes of illusion and error are excluded. Of all the *à priori* sciences of reason, therefore, mathematics alone can be learned. Philosophy—unless it be in an historical manner—cannot be learned; we can at most learn to *philosophize*.

Philosophy is the system of all philosophical cognition. We must use this term in an objective sense, if we understand by it the archetype of all attempts at philosophizing, and the standard by which all subjective philosophies are to be judged. In this sense, philosophy is merely the idea of a possible science, which does not exist *in concreto*, but to which we endeavor in various ways to approximate, until we have discovered the right path to pursue—a path overgrown by the errors and illusions of sense—and the image we have hitherto tried to shape in vain, has become a perfect copy of the great prototype. Until that time we cannot learn philosophy—it does not exist; if it does, where is it, who possesses it, and how shall we know it? We can only learn to philosophize; in other words, we can only exercise our powers of reasoning in accordance with general principles, retaining at the same time, the right of investigating the sources of these principles, of testing, and even of rejecting them.

Until then, our conception of philosophy is only a *scholastic conception*—a conception, that is, of a system of cognition which we are trying to elaborate into a science; all that we at present know being the systematic unity of this cognition, and consequently the *logical* completeness of the cognition for the desired end. But there is also a *cosmical conception (conceptus cosmicus)* of philosophy, which has always formed the true basis of this term, especially when philosophy was personified and presented to us in the ideal of a *philosopher*. In this view philosophy is the science of the relation of all cognition to the ultimate and essential aims of human reason (*teleologia rationis humanæ*), and the philosopher is not merely an artist who occupies himself with conceptions, but a law-giver legislating for human reason. In this sense of the word, it would be in the highest degree arrogant to assume the title of philosopher, and to pretend that we had reached the perfection of the prototype which lies in the idea alone.

The mathematician, the natural philosopher, and the logician —how far soever the first may have advanced in rational, and the two latter in philosophical knowledge—are merely artists, engaged in the arrangement and formation of conceptions; they cannot be termed philosophers. Above them all, there is the ideal teacher, who employs them as instruments for the advancement of the essential aims of human reason. Him alone can we call philosopher; but he nowhere exists. But the idea of his legislative power resides in the mind of every man, and it alone teaches us what kind of systematic unity philosophy demands in view of the ultimate aims of reason. This idea is, therefore, a cosmical conception.*

In view of the complete systematic unity of reason, there can only be one ultimate end of all the operations of the mind. To this all other aims are subordinate, and nothing more than means for its attainment. This ultimate end is the destination of man, and the philosophy which relates to it is termed Moral Philosophy. The superior position occupied by moral philosophy, above all other spheres for the operations of reason, sufficiently indicates the reason why the ancients always included the idea—and in an especial manner—of Moralist in that of Philosopher. Even at the present day, we call a man who appears to have the power of self-government, even although his knowledge may be very limited, by the name of philosopher.

The legislation of human reason, or philosophy, has two objects—Nature and Freedom, and thus contains not only the laws of nature, but also those of ethics, at first in two separate systems, which, finally, merge into one grand philosophical system of cognition. The philosophy of Nature relates to that *which is,* that of Ethics to that which *ought to be.*

But all philosophy is either cognition on the basis of pure reason, or the cognition of reason on the basis of empirical principles. The former is termed pure, the latter empirical, philosophy.

The philosophy of pure reason is either *propædeutic,* that is, an inquiry into the powers of reason in regard to pure *à priori* cognition, and is termed Critical Philosophy; or it is, secondly, the system of pure reason—a science containing the systematic

* By a *cosmical conception,* I mean one in which all men necessarily take an interest; the *aim* of a science must accordingly be determined according to scholastic [or partial] *conceptions,* if it is regarded merely as a means to certain arbitrarily proposed ends.

presentation of the whole body of philosophical knowledge, true as well as illusory, given by pure reason, and is called Metaphysic. This name may, however, be also given to the whole system of pure philosophy, critical philosophy included, and may designate the investigation into the sources or possibility of *à priori* cognition, as well as the presentation of the *à priori* cognitions which form a system of pure philosophy—excluding, at the same time, all empirical and mathematical elements.

Metaphysic is divided into that of the *speculative* and that of the *practical* use of pure reason, and is, accordingly, either the *Metaphysic of Nature,* or the *Metaphysic of Ethics.* The former contains all the pure rational principles—based upon conceptions alone (and thus excluding mathematics)—of all *theoretical* cognition; the latter, the principles which determine and necessitate *à priori* all *action.* Now moral philosophy alone contains a code of laws—for the regulation of our actions— which are deduced from principles entirely *à priori.* Hence the Metaphysic of Ethics is the only pure and moral philosophy, as it is not based upon anthropological or other empirical considerations. The metaphysic of speculative reason is what is commonly called Metaphysic in the more limited sense. But as pure Moral Philosophy properly forms a part of this system of cognition, we must allow it to retain the name of Metaphysic, although it is not requisite that we should insist on so terming it in our present discussion.

It is of the highest importance to separate those cognitions which differ from others both in kind and in origin, and to take great care that they are not confounded with those with which they are generally found connected. What the chemist does in the analysis of substances, what the mathematician in pure mathematics, is, in a still higher degree, the duty of the philosopher, that the value of each different kind of cognition, and the part it takes in the operations of the mind, may be clearly defined. Human reason has never wanted a Metaphysic of some kind, since it attained the power of thought, or rather of reflection; but it has never been able to keep this sphere of thought and cognition pure from all admixture of foreign elements. The idea of a science of this kind is as old as speculation itself; and what mind does not speculate—either in the scholastic or in the popular fashion? At the same time, it must be admitted that even thinkers by profession have been unable clearly to explain the distinction between the two elements of our cognition—the one completely à *priori*, the other à *posteriori;* and hence the proper definition of a peculiar kind of cognition, and with it the just idea of a science which has so long and so deeply engaged the attention of the human mind, has never been established. When it was said—Metaphysic is the science of the first principles of human cognition, this definition did not signalize a peculiarity in kind, but only a difference in degree; these first principles were thus declared to be more general than others, but no criterion of distinction from empirical principles was given. Of these some are more general, and therefore higher, than others; and—as we cannot distinguish what is completely à *priori*, from that which is known to be à *posteriori*—where shall we draw the line which is to separate the higher and so-called first principles, from the lower and subordinate principles of cognition? What would be said if we were asked to be satisfied with a division of the epochs of the world into the earlier centuries and those following them? Does the fifth or the tenth century belong to the earlier centuries? it would be asked. In the same way I ask: Does the conception of extension belong to metaphysics? You answer, Yes. Well, that of body too? Yes. And that of a fluid body? You stop, you are unprepared to admit this; for if you do, everything will belong to metaphysics. From this it is evident that the mere degree of subordination—of the particular to the general—cannot determine the limits of a science; and that, in the present case, we must expect to find a difference in the conceptions of metaphysics both in kind and in origin. The fundamental idea of metaphysic was obscured on another side, by the fact that this kind of à *priori* cognition showed a certain similarity in character with the science of mathematics. Both have the property in common of possessing an à *priori* origin; but, in the one, our knowledge is based upon conceptions, in the other, on the construction of conceptions. Thus a decided dissimilarity between philosophical and mathematical cognition comes out—a dissimilarity which was always felt, but which could not be made distinct for want of an insight into the criteria of the difference. And thus it happened that, as philosophers themselves failed in the proper development of the idea of their science, the elaboration of the science could not proceed with a definite aim, or under trustworthy guidance. Thus, too, philosophers, ignorant of the path they ought to pursue, and always disputing with each other regarding the discoveries which each asserted he had made, brought their science in disrepute with the rest of the world, and finally, even among themselves.

All pure *à priori* cognition forms, therefore, in view of the peculiar faculty which originates it, a peculiar and distinct unity; and metaphysic is the term applied to the philosophy which attempts to represent that cognition in this systematic unity. The speculative part of metaphysic, which has especially appropriated this appellation—that, which we have called the *Metaphysic* of *Nature*—and which considers everything, as it is (not as it ought to be), by means of *à priori* conceptions, is divided in the following manner.

Metaphysic, in the more limited acceptation of the term, consists of two parts—*Transcendental Philosophy* and the *Physiology* of pure reason. The former presents the system of all the conceptions and principles belonging to the understanding and the reason, and which relate to objects in general, but not to any particular given objects (*Ontologia*); the latter has *nature* for its subject-matter, that is, the sum of given objects—whether given to the senses, or, if we will, to some other kind of intuition—and is accordingly *Physiology*, although only *rationalis*. But the use of the faculty of reason in this rational mode of regarding nature is either physical or hyperphysical, or, more properly speaking, *immanent* or *transcendent*. The former relates to nature, in so far as our knowledge regarding it may be applied in experience (*in concreto*); the latter to that connection of the objects of experience, which transcends all experience. *Transcendent Physiology* has, again, an *internal* and an *external* connection with its object, both, however, transcending possible experience; the former is the Physiology of nature as a whole, or *transcendental cognition of the world,* the latter of the connection of the whole of nature with a being above nature, or transcendental *cognition of God.*

Immanent physiology, on the contrary, considers nature as the sum of all sensuous objects, consequently, as it is presented to us—but still according to *à priori* conditions, for it is under these alone that nature can be presented to our minds at all. The objects of immanent physiology are of two kinds: 1. those of the external senses, or *corporeal nature;* 2. the object of the internal sense, the soul, or, in accordance with our fundamental conceptions of it, *thinking nature*. The metaphysic of corporeal nature is called *Physics*, but, as it must contain only the principles of an *à priori* cognition of nature, we must term it *rational physics*. The metaphysic of thinking nature is called *Psychology*, and for the same reason is to be regarded as merely the *rational cognition* of the soul.

Thus the whole system of metaphysic consists of four principal parts: 1. *Ontology;* 2. *Rational Physiology;* 3. *Rational Cosmology;* and 4. *Rational Theology.* The second part—that of the rational doctrine of nature—may be subdivided into two, *physica rationalis* * and *psychologia rationalis.*

The fundamental idea of a philosophy of pure reason of necessity dictates this division; it is, therefore, *architectonical*—in accordance with the highest aims of reason, and not merely *technical*, or according to certain accidentally observed similarities existing between the different parts of the whole science. For this reason, also, is the division immutable and of legislative authority. But the reader may observe in it a few points to which he ought to demur, and which may weaken his conviction of its truth and legitimacy.

In the first place, how can I desire an *à priori* cognition or metaphysic of objects, in so far as they are given *à posteriori?* and how is it possible to cognize the nature of things according to *à priori* principles, and to attain to a *rational* physiology? The answer is this. We take from experience nothing more than is requisite to present us with an object (in general) of the external, or of the internal sense; in the former case, by the mere conception of matter (impenetrable and inanimate extension), in the latter, by the conception of a thinking being—given in the internal empirical representation, *I think*. As to the rest, we must not employ in our metaphysic of these objects any empirical principles (which add to the content of our conceptions by means of experience), for the purpose of forming by their help any judgments respecting these objects.

Secondly, what place shall we assign to *empirical psychology*,

---

* It must not be supposed that I mean by this appellation what is generally called *physica generalis*, and which is rather mathematics than a philosophy of nature. For the metaphysic of nature is completely different from mathematics, nor is it so rich in results, although it is of great importance as a critical test of the application of pure understanding-cognition to nature. For want of its guidance, even mathematicians, adopting certain common notions—which are, in fact, metaphysical—have unconsciously crowded their theories of nature with hypotheses, the fallacy of which becomes evident upon the application of the principles of this metaphysic, without detriment, however, to the employment of mathematics in this sphere of cognition.

which has always been considered a part of Metaphysic, and from which in our time such important philosophical results have been expected, after the hope of constructing an *à priori* system of knowledge had been abandoned? I answer: It must be placed by the side of empirical physics or physics proper; that it, must be regarded as forming a part of *applied* philosophy, the *à priori* principles of which are contained in pure philosophy, which is therefore connected, although it must not be confounded, with psychology. Empirical psychology must therefore be banished from the sphere of Metaphysic, and is indeed excluded by the very idea of that science. In conformity, however, with scholastic usage, we must permit it to occupy a place in metaphysic—but only as an appendix to it. We adopt this course from motives of economy; as psychology is not as yet full enough to occupy our attention as an independent study, while it is, at the same time, of too great importance, to be entirely excluded or placed where it has still less affinity than it has with the subject of metaphysic. It is a stranger who has been long a guest; and we make it welcome to stay, until it can take up a more suitable abode in a complete system of Anthropology — the pendant to empirical physics.

The above is the general idea of Metaphysic, which, as more was expected from it than could be looked for with justice, and as these pleasant expectations were unfortunately never realized, fell into general disrepute. Our Critique must have fully convinced the reader, that, although metaphysic cannot form the foundation of religion, it must always be one of its most important bulwarks, and that human reason, which naturally pursues a dialectical course, cannot do without this science, which checks its tendencies towards dialectic, and, by elevating reason to a scientific and clear self-knowledge, prevents the ravages which a lawless speculative reason would infallibly commit in the sphere of morals as well as in that of religion. We may be sure, therefore, whatever contempt may be thrown upon metaphysics by those who judge a science not by its own nature, but according to the accidental effects it may have produced, that it can never be completely abandoned, that we must always return to it as to a beloved one who has been for a time estranged, because the questions with which it is engaged relate to the highest aims of humanity, and reason must always labor either to attain to settled views in regard to these, or to destroy those which others have already established.

Metaphysic, therefore—that of nature, as well as that of ethics, but in an especial manner the criticism which forms the propædeutic to all the operations of reason—forms properly that department of knowledge which may be termed, in the truest sense of the word, philosophy. The path which it pursues is that of science, which, when it has once been discovered, is never lost, and never misleads. Mathematics, natural science, and the common experience of men, have a high value as means, for the most part, to accidental ends—but at last also, to those which are necessary and essential to the existence of humanity. But to guide them to this high goal, they require the aid of rational cognition on the basis of pure conceptions, which, be it termed as it may, is properly nothing but metaphysics.

For the same reason, metaphysic forms likewise the completion of the *culture* of human reason. In this respect it is indispensable, setting aside altogether the influence which it exerts as a science. For its subject-matter are the elements and highest maxims of reason, which form the basis of the *possibility* of some sciences and of the *use* of all. That, as a purely speculative science, it is more useful in preventing error, than in the extension of knowledge, does not detract from its value; on the contrary, the supreme office of censor which it occupies, assures to it the highest authority and importance. This office it administers for the purpose of securing order, harmony, and well-being to science, and of directing its noble and fruitful labors to the highest possible aim—the happiness of all mankind.

Chapter IV

The History of Pure Reason

This title is placed here merely for the purpose of designating a division of the system of pure reason, of which I do not intend to treat at present. I shall content myself with casting a cursory glance, from a purely transcendental point of view—that of the nature of pure reason, on the labors of philosophers up to the present time. They have aimed at erecting an edifice of philosophy; but to my eye this edifice appears to be in a very ruinous condition.

It is very remarkable, although naturally it could not have been otherwise, that, in the infancy of philosophy, the study of the nature of God, and the constitution of a future world, formed the commencement, rather than the conclusion, as we should have it, of the speculative efforts of the human mind. However rude the religious conceptions generated by the remains of the old manners and customs of a less cultivated time, the intelligent classes were not thereby prevented from devoting themselves to free inquiry into the existence and nature of God; and they easily saw that there could be no surer way of pleasing the invisible ruler of the world, and of attaining to happiness in another world at least, than a good and honest course of life in this. Thus theology and morals formed the two chief motives, or rather the points of attraction in all abstract inquiries. But it was the former that especially occupied the attention of speculative reason, and which afterwards became so celebrated under the name of metaphysics.

I shall not at present indicate the periods of time at which the greatest changes in metaphysics took place, but shall merely give a hasty sketch of the different ideas which occasioned the most important revolutions in this sphere of thought. There are three different ends, in relation to which these revolutions have taken place.

1. *In relation to the object* of the cognition of reason, philosophers may be divided into *Sensualists* and *Intellectualists*. *Epicurus* may be regarded as the head of the former, *Plato* of the latter. The distinction here signalized, subtle as it is, dates from the earliest times, and was long maintained. The former asserted, that reality resides in sensuous objects alone, and that everything else is merely imaginary; the latter, that the senses are the parents of illusion, and that truth is to be found in the understanding alone. The former did not deny to the conceptions of the understanding a certain kind of reality; but with them it was merely *logical*, with the others it was *mystical*. The former admitted *intellectual* conceptions, but declared that sensuous objects alone possessed real existence. The latter maintained that all real objects were *intelligible*, and believed that the pure understanding possessed a faculty of *intuition* apart form sense, which, in their opinion, served only to confuse the ideas of the understanding.

2. *In relation to the origin* of the pure cognitions of reason,

we find one school maintaining that they are derived entirely from experience, and another, that they have their origin in reason alone. *Aristotle* may be regarded as the head of the *Empiricists,* and *Plato,* of the *Noologists.* *Locke,* the follower of Aristotle in modern times, and *Leibnitz* of Plato (although he cannot be said to have imitated him in his mysticism), have not been able to bring this question to a settled conclusion. The procedure of Epicurus in his sensual system, in which he always restricted his conclusions to the sphere of experience, was much more consequent than that of Aristotle and Locke. The latter especially, after having derived all the conceptions and principles of the mind from experience, goes so far, in the employment of these conceptions and principles, as to maintain that we can prove the existence of God and the immortality of the soul—both of them objects lying beyond the limits of possible experience—with the same force of demonstration, as any mathematical proposition.

3. *In relation to method.* Method is procedure *according to principles.* We may divide the methods at present employed in the field of inquiry into the *naturalistic* and the *scientific.* The *naturalist* of pure reason lays it down as his principles, that common reason, without the aid of science—which he calls sound reason, or common sense—can give a more satisfactory answer to the most important questions of metaphysics than speculation is able to do. He must maintain, therefore, that we can determine the content and circumference of the moon more certainly by the naked eye, than by the aid of mathematical reasoning. But this system is mere misology reduced to principles; and, what is the most absurd thing in this doctrine, the neglect of all scientific means is paraded as a *peculiar method* of extending our cognition. As regards those who are *naturalists* because they know no better, they are certainly not to be blamed. They follow common sense, without parading their ignorance as a method which is to teach us the wonderful secret, how we are to find the truth which lies at the bottom of the well of Democritus.

" Quod sapio satis est mihi, non ego curo
Esse quod Arcesilas ærumnosique Solones."—Persius.

is their motto, under which they may lead a pleasant and praiseworthy life, without troubling themselves with science, or troubling science with them.

As regards those who wish to pursue a *scientific* method, they have now the choice of following either the *dogmatical* or the *sceptical*, while they are bound never to desert the *systematic* mode of procedure. When I mention, in relation to the former, the celebrated *Wolf*, and as regards the latter, *David Hume*, I may leave, in accordance with my present intention, all others unnamed. The *critical* path alone is still open. If my reader has been kind and patient enough to accompany me on this hitherto untravelled route, he can now judge whether, if he and others will contribute their exertions towards making this narrow foot-path a high-road of thought, that, which many centuries have failed to accomplish, may not be executed before the close of the present—namely, to bring Reason to perfect contentment in regard to that which has always, but without permanent results, occupied her powers and engaged her ardent desire for knowledge.

GREAT BOOKS IN PHILOSOPHY PAPERBACK SERIES

ESTHETICS

❏ Aristotle—*The Poetics*
❏ Aristotle—*Treatise on Rhetoric*

ETHICS

❏ Aristotle—*The Nicomachean Ethics*
❏ Marcus Aurelius—*Meditations*
❏ Jeremy Bentham—*The Principles of Morals and Legislation*
❏ John Dewey—*The Moral Writings of John Dewey, Revised Edition*
   (edited by James Gouinlock)
❏ Epictetus—*Enchiridion*
❏ Immanuel Kant—*Fundamental Principles of the Metaphysic of Morals*
❏ John Stuart Mill—*Utilitarianism*
❏ George Edward Moore—*Principia Ethica*
❏ Friedrich Nietzsche—*Beyond Good and Evil*
❏ Plato—*Protagoras, Philebus,* and *Gorgias*
❏ Bertrand Russell—*Bertrand Russell On Ethics, Sex, and Marriage*
   (edited by Al Seckel)
❏ Arthur Schopenhauer—*The Wisdom of Life* and *Counsels and Maxims*
❏ Adam Smith—*The Theory of Moral Sentiments*
❏ Benedict de Spinoza—*Ethics* and *The Improvement of the Understanding*

METAPHYSICS/EPISTEMOLOGY

❏ Aristotle—*De Anima*
❏ Aristotle—*The Metaphysics*
❏ Francis Bacon—*Essays*
❏ George Berkeley—*Three Dialogues Between Hylas and Philonous*
❏ W. K. Clifford—*The Ethics of Belief and Other Essays*
   (introduction by Timothy J. Madigan)
❏ René Descartes—*Discourse on Method* and *The Meditations*
❏ John Dewey—*How We Think*
❏ John Dewey—*The Influence of Darwin on Philosophy and Other Essays*
❏ Epicurus—*The Essential Epicurus: Letters, Principal Doctrines, Vatican Sayings,*
   and Fragments (translated, and with an introduction, by Eugene O'Connor)
❏ Sidney Hook—*The Quest for Being*
❏ David Hume—*An Enquiry Concerning Human Understanding*
❏ David Hume—*Treatise of Human Nature*
❏ William James—*The Meaning of Truth*
❏ William James—*Pragmatism*
❏ Immanuel Kant—*Critique of Practical Reason*
❏ Immanuel Kant—*Critique of Pure Reason*
❏ Gottfried Wilhelm Leibniz—*Discourse on Metaphysics* and the *Monadology*
❏ John Locke—*An Essay Concerning Human Understanding*
❏ Charles S. Peirce—*The Essential Writings*
   (edited by Edward C. Moore, preface by Richard Robin)
❏ Plato—*The Euthyphro, Apology, Crito,* and *Phaedo*
❏ Plato—*Lysis, Phaedrus,* and *Symposium*
❏ Bertrand Russell—*The Problems of Philosophy*
❏ George Santayana—*The Life of Reason*
❏ Sextus Empiricus—*Outlines of Pyrrhonism*

PHILOSOPHY OF RELIGION

- ❑ Marcus Tullius Cicero—*The Nature of the Gods* and *On Divination*
- ❑ Ludwig Feuerbach—*The Essence of Christianity*
- ❑ David Hume—*Dialogues Concerning Natural Religion*
- ❑ John Locke—*A Letter Concerning Toleration*
- ❑ Lucretius—*On the Nature of Things*
- ❑ John Stuart Mill—*Three Essays on Religion*
- ❑ Thomas Paine—*The Age of Reason*
- ❑ Bertrand Russell—*Bertrand Russell On God and Religion* (edited by Al Seckel)

SOCIAL AND POLITICAL PHILOSOPHY

- ❑ Aristotle—*The Politics*
- ❑ Mikhail Bakunin—*The Basic Bakunin: Writings, 1869–1871* (translated and edited by Robert M. Cutler)
- ❑ Edmund Burke—*Reflections on the Revolution in France*
- ❑ John Dewey—*Freedom and Culture*
- ❑ John Dewey—*Individualism Old and New*
- ❑ John Dewey—*Liberalism and Social Action*
- ❑ G. W. F. Hegel—*The Philosophy of History*
- ❑ G. W. F. Hegel—*Philosophy of Right*
- ❑ Thomas Hobbes—*The Leviathan*
- ❑ Sidney Hook—*Paradoxes of Freedom*
- ❑ Sidney Hook—*Reason, Social Myths, and Democracy*
- ❑ John Locke—*Second Treatise on Civil Government*
- ❑ Niccolo Machiavelli—*The Prince*
- ❑ Karl Marx (with Friedrich Engels)—*The German Ideology*, including *Theses on Feuerbach and Introduction to the Critique of Political Economy*
- ❑ Karl Marx—*The Poverty of Philosophy*
- ❑ Karl Marx/Friedrich Engels—*The Economic and Philosophic Manuscripts of 1844* and *The Communist Manifesto*
- ❑ John Stuart Mill—*Considerations on Representative Government*
- ❑ John Stuart Mill—*On Liberty*
- ❑ John Stuart Mill—*On Socialism*
- ❑ John Stuart Mill—*The Subjection of Women*
- ❑ Friedrich Nietzsche—*Thus Spake Zarathustra*
- ❑ Thomas Paine—*Common Sense*
- ❑ Thomas Paine—*Rights of Man*
- ❑ Plato—*Laws*
- ❑ Plato—*The Republic*
- ❑ Jean-Jacques Rousseau—*The Social Contract*
- ❑ Mary Wollstonecraft—*A Vindication of the Rights of Men*
- ❑ Mary Wollstonecraft—*A Vindication of the Rights of Women*

GREAT MINDS PAPERBACK SERIES

CRITICAL ESSAYS

- ❑ Desiderius Erasmus—*The Praise of Folly*
- ❑ Jonathan Swift—*A Modest Proposal and Other Satires* (with an introduction by George R. Levine)
- ❑ H. G. Wells—*The Conquest of Time* (with an introduction by Martin Gardner)

ECONOMICS

- ❏ Charlotte Perkins Gilman—*Women and Economics: A Study of the Economic Relation between Women and Men*
- ❏ John Maynard Keynes—*The General Theory of Employment, Interest, and Money*
- ❏ John Maynard Keynes—*A Tract on Monetary Reform*
- ❏ Thomas R. Malthus—*An Essay on the Principle of Population*
- ❏ Alfred Marshall—*Principles of Economics*
- ❏ Karl Marx—*Theories of Surplus Value*
- ❏ David Ricardo—*Principles of Political Economy and Taxation*
- ❏ Adam Smith—*Wealth of Nations*
- ❏ Thorstein Veblen—*Theory of the Leisure Class*

HISTORY

- ❏ Edward Gibbon—*On Christianity*
- ❏ Alexander Hamilton, John Jay, and James Madison—*The Federalist*
- ❏ Herodotus—*The History*
- ❏ Thucydides—*History of the Peloponnesian War*
- ❏ Andrew D. White—*A History of the Warfare of Science with Theology in Christendom*

PSYCHOLOGY

- ❏ Sigmund Freud—*Totem and Taboo*

RELIGION

- ❏ Thomas Henry Huxley—*Agnosticism and Christianity and Other Essays*
- ❏ Ernest Renan—*The Life of Jesus*
- ❏ Elizabeth Cady Stanton—*The Woman's Bible*
- ❏ Voltaire—*A Treatise on Toleration and Other Essays*

SCIENCE

- ❏ Nicolaus Copernicus—*On the Revolutions of Heavenly Spheres*
- ❏ Charles Darwin—*The Descent of Man*
- ❏ Charles Darwin—*The Origin of Species*
- ❏ Charles Darwin—*The Voyage of the Beagle*
- ❏ Albert Einstein—*Relativity*
- ❏ Michael Faraday—*The Forces of Matter*
- ❏ Galileo Galilei—*Dialogues Concerning Two New Sciences*
- ❏ Ernst Haeckel—*The Riddle of the Universe*
- ❏ William Harvey—*On the Motion of the Heart and Blood in Animals*
- ❏ Werner Heisenberg—*Physics and Philosophy: The Revolution in Modern Science* (introduction by F. S. C. Northrop)
- ❏ Julian Huxley—*Evolutionary Humanism*
- ❏ Edward Jenner—*Vaccination against Smallpox*
- ❏ Johannes Kepler—*Epitome of Copernican Astronomy and Harmonies of the World*
- ❏ Isaac Newton—*The Principia*
- ❏ Louis Pasteur and Joseph Lister—*Germ Theory and Its Application to Medicine and On the Antiseptic Principle of the Practice of Surgery*
- ❏ Alfred Russel Wallace—*Island Life*

SOCIOLOGY

- ❏ Emile Durkheim—*Ethics and the Sociology of Morals* (translated with an introduction by Robert T. Hall)